U.S. National Security Law
An International Perspective

★ ★ ★

H. L. Pohlman
Dickinson College

ROWMAN & LITTLEFIELD
Lanham • Boulder • New York • London

Executive Editor: Traci Crowell
Assistant Editor: Mary Malley
Senior Marketing Manager: Amy Whitaker
Interior Designer: Roseanne Schloss

Published by Rowman & Littlefield
An imprint of The Rowman & Littlefield Publishing Group, Inc.
4501 Forbes Boulevard, Suite 200, Lanham, Maryland 20706
www.rowman.com

Unit A, Whitacre Mews, 26-34 Stannary Street, London SE11 4AB, United Kingdom

British Library Cataloguing in Publication Information Available

Library of Congress Cataloging-in-Publication Data
Names: Pohlman, H. L., 1952– author.
Title: U.S. national security law : an international perspective / H.L. Pohlman, Dickinson College.
Description: First edition. | Lanham : Rowman & Littlefield, 2019. | Includes index.
Identifiers: LCCN 2018010586 (print) | LCCN 2018011363 (ebook) | ISBN 9781538104040 (ebook) | ISBN 9781538104026 (cloth : alk. paper) | ISBN 9781538104033 (pbk. : alk. paper)
Subjects: LCSH: Military law—United States. | War (International law) | International and municipal law—United States.
Classification: LCC KF7209 (ebook) | LCC KF7209 .P64 2018 (print) | DDC 343.73/01—dc23
LC record available at https://lccn.loc.gov/2018010586

∞™ The paper used in this publication meets the minimum requirements of American National Standard for Information Sciences—Permanence of Paper for Printed Library Materials, ANSI/NISO Z39.48-1992.

Printed in the United States of America

To
Katrina and Nathan

Contents

★ ★ ★

Preface

★ ★ ★

The importance of U.S. national security law as a dimension of political science emanates largely from the many and diverse threats that the United States confronts in today's world. While adversarial nation-states, such as Russia, Iran, North Korea, and China, continue to be a major concern, nonstate Islamic groups, such as al-Qaeda, the Taliban, ISIS (or ISIL), Al-Shabaab, and Boko Haram, have directed or inspired a wave of attacks against Western targets, killing thousands of innocent civilians. Failed or failing states throughout the Middle East, such as Syria, Libya, Yemen, Somalia, and Afghanistan, magnify the problem because they provide these nonstate groups with safe haven in the midst of civil wars and insurgencies. In this context, the proliferation of weapons of mass destruction (nuclear, radiological, biological, or chemical) is an alarming possibility. While these weapons are becoming more lethal, it is unfortunate that the knowledge and the technical capacity needed to produce them have become more generally available, leading to a reasonable fear that terrorist groups might acquire them. Last, international arms dealers market weapons around the world, indirectly promoting violence and crime of all sorts, while drug cartels engage in turf battles that often encourage political corruption and undermine political stability.

Confronted with these threats, the tendency of the federal government has been to do whatever it takes to protect the American people; this tendency has led to actions and policies that have strained and stretched U.S. national security law in a number of different directions. These stretches and strains are problematic because the legitimacy of the federal government rests on the assumption that it is a government of limited powers defined by law. There are at least three layers of law that relate to what the federal government can legally do to counter current threats. First and foremost, any national security policy must not only be within one of the powers granted to the federal government by the Constitution but also not violate any individual's constitutional right. A second layer of law is statutory law enacted by Congress: does the policy fall within the scope of a statutory grant of authority to the executive branch? If it does, the presumption is that the policy is legal, unless it can be shown that the statute is itself unconstitutional.

The third type of law that is arguably relevant to how the United States can and should react to national security threats is international law. However, while constitutional and statutory law are clearly binding on U.S. policymakers, the legal status of international law is more debatable. It may be "law," but U.S. national security policymakers may at times choose to ignore it or, if possible, to figure out some way to pay it lip service while circumventing its spirit if not its substance. Despite these shortcomings of international law, its status is becoming an ever more pressing issue for a number of reasons.

First, the world is becoming increasingly more integrated and globalized with an ever-expanding internet, new forms of mass media technology, sophisticated international communications systems, and sharp increases in international trade and travel. All of these developments of globalization highlight the salience and status of international law, yet there is the growing transnational perception that the United States does not play by international rules; that the United States somehow thinks it has an "exceptional" character or role that permits it to engage in conduct that it condemns or criticizes when done by other countries; and that its role as the world's sole superpower purportedly gives it a license that no other country enjoys. This tension between an increasingly globalized and integrated world and the role that the United States plays in that world is one that will not be resolved anytime soon. This context is one rationale for a textbook on U.S. national security law to be organized around issues of international law. It gives students an opportunity to consider the degree to which international law is or should be binding on the United States in the field of national security law, considering the role it plays in an increasingly globalized world.

Second, a related development is the growth of international judicial institutions since the end of World War II. Apart from the infamous Nuremberg trials of Nazi war criminals by the International Military Tribunal (IMT) and the comparable Tokyo trials of Japanese war criminals by the International Military Tribunal for the Far East (IMTFE), a number of post–World War II treaties created international courts or tribunals, including the United Nations International Court of Justice (1945), the European Court of Justice (1952), the European Court of Human Rights (1959), the International Criminal Tribunal for the former Yugoslavia (1993), the International Tribunal for Rwanda (1994), and the International Criminal Court (2002).

This trend of expanding the role of international courts has sharply increased since the end of the Cold War and the disintegration of the Soviet Union. In a recent study, Karen J. Alter notes that there are currently twenty-four permanent international courts, with 80 percent having broad compulsory jurisdiction and 84 percent authorizing nonstate actors to initiate litigation. In addition, Alter finds that these courts have issued "over 37,000 binding rulings in individual cases, 91 percent of which were issued since the fall of the Berlin Wall."[1] According to Alter, this large increase in litigation at international courts is rooted in a "largely unquestioned presumption that legal obligations should be meaningful, that they should give rise to rights, that the legal bodies tasked with interpreting and applying applicable laws should be prioritizing the law over the wishes of governments, and that legitimate governments should display a fundamental respect for the rule of law, including international law."[2] Although Alter perhaps overstates her case by overestimating the binding character of international law and underestimating the degree to which national sovereignty is still the reigning principle of international relations, it is indisputable that international courts play an unprecedented role today, one that will have a broad and pervasive impact on the evolving status of international law in the years to come.

A third reason the interplay between U.S. national security law and international law is a topic worth considering is that lawyers are increasingly involved in the national security policymaking process, at least in the United States. Perhaps it is partly because, in the post-9/11 world, national policymakers have widely accepted the view of Michael Hayden, former director of the National Security Agency and the Central Intelligence Agency, who said he intended to fight the war against radical Islamic groups "with chalk on his cleats"[3]—meaning he wanted to fight the war up to the limits of the law. Such an approach obviously requires a close alignment of national security policy with law, insofar as the former cannot really be implemented without deeply analyzing the latter. More recently, Charlie Savage, a *New York Times* reporter and author of a recent book on national security policy during the Obama administration, argued that the Obama administration was much more "legalistic" than the Bush administration in terms of "personnel, mindset, and deliberative approach."[4] Accordingly, even if international law is not considered as "binding" as constitutional or statutory law, a textbook that examines U.S. national security law from the perspective of international law will contribute significantly to an understanding of the U.S. national security–making process.

Last, from a historical point of view, the status of international law has always been an important question for Americans. For example, the Supremacy Clause of Article VI of the Constitution proclaimed that "all Treaties made, or which shall be made, under the Authority of the United States shall be the supreme Law of the Land . . ." Moreover, in 1793, Chief Justice John Jay claimed that the laws of the United States could be classified under three heads: "1st. All treaties made under the authority of the United States. 2d. The laws of nations. 3dly. The constitution and statutes of the United States."[5] The fact that Jay listed treaties and "the law of nations" prior to the Constitution and statutes is noteworthy. The "laws of nations" was the eighteenth-century term for what is now commonly called "customary international law." This type of international law is based not on formal ratification by states, as treaties are, but rather on "a general and consistent practice of states followed by them from a sense of legal obligation."[6] An early Supreme Court case—*Murray v. The Schooner Charming Betsy I*—held that "an act of Congress ought never to be construed to violate the law of nations if any other possible construction remains."[7] This rule—often referred to as the Charming Betsy canon—held sway throughout much of the nineteenth century.

The current formulation of the Charming Betsy canon contained in *Restatement (Third) of the Foreign Relations Law of the United States* is arguably somewhat weaker: "Where fairly possible, a United States statute is to be construed so as not to conflict with international law or with an international agreement of the United States,"[8] but it too presumes that the United States will respect customary international law. This general attitude toward customary international law and treaties has been, and continues to be, a part of the legal identity of this country. The attitude has certainly evolved, but it has not died away. Accordingly, it is worthwhile to look backward for help answering the tough questions regarding national security law that we are currently confronting. For this reason, each chapter of this text has, to the extent appropriate, a historical dimension, which will give the reader an opportunity to consider today's challenges with the benefit of insights inherited from earlier generations.

At the same time, questions regarding national security law require us to examine the challenges of the present and the future. The 2016 election of Donald Trump may mark a milestone in the relationship of national security law to international law. Trump sums up much of his political ideology with the slogan "America First." His antiglobalization policies of trade protectionism and his bellicose rhetoric regarding ISIS, Iran, and North Korea strongly suggest that he is a leader who has less than a serious commitment to international law. In fact, Jack Goldsmith has written that the Trump administration has initiated "the greatest presidential onslaught on international law and international institutions in American history." Only time will tell whether Goldsmith is correct. At a minimum, as Goldsmith recounts, Trump has "gutted" State Department capacity; eliminated domestic agencies linked to international relations; halted or withdrawn from or threatened to "unwind" international agreements, such as the Trans-Pacific Partnership, the Iran Deal, the Paris Agreement, and NAFTA; reduced funding for international organizations; distanced the administration from international courts; and downplayed the significance of human rights in U.S. foreign policy.[9] The political coalition that put Trump in the White House shares his skeptical, if not hostile, attitude toward international law and institutions. For this reason, it is more imperative than ever for undergraduate students to consider the relationship of U.S. national security law to international law, a question that will likely surface and resurface for the foreseeable future.

This textbook is divided into ten chapters. The first is an introduction that examines in more detail the impact that international law has on the domestic law of the United States and the principles of U.S. constitutional law that are at the core of U.S. national security law. The second chapter considers how the right to wage war has evolved over time in terms of both international law and U.S. constitutional law. The third chapter explores how international and U.S. domestic law limits or regulates the ways in which the United States can engage in armed conflict. The fourth and fifth chapters, respectively, discuss who can legitimately be subject to military detention during an armed conflict and what techniques of interrogation of detainees are permitted. The sixth chapter unpacks the law of military commissions, a type of military tribunal that has been used in U.S. history to try enemy war criminals. The seventh chapter explores the law governing the murky subject of covert action—that is, actions by the U.S. government, primarily by the Central Intelligence Agency, that are intended to influence events in foreign countries without disclosing who is sponsoring them. The eighth chapter takes up the difficult subject of targeted killing during armed conflicts, including whether the U.S. government could ever target a citizen without violating due process of law. The ninth chapter tries to unravel the law bearing on the foggy world of U.S. electronic foreign intelligence gathering, which is conducted primarily by the National Security Agency. The last chapter sketches the legal parameters of cyber war, a new form of warfare that raises puzzling questions regarding the law of armed conflict.

Each chapter is organized in similar fashion, with key readings from treaties, international court decisions, legal documents or memoranda, and U.S. judicial opinions that constitute the "backbone" of each chapter. A boldface number (such as **5.2**, meaning the second reading in chapter 5) and a boldfaced title identify each reading. The readings of each chapter are arranged in chronological order, which underscores how the international, constitutional, and statutory laws governing the chapter topic have evolved over time. Each chapter begins with a brief introduction to the topic, and the readings within each chapter are linked by editorial commentary between the excerpts. This editorial commentary does not summarize the excerpts but instead leads the student from the specific issue discussed in one excerpt to the specific issue of the next. Provocative questions are added after each excerpt. These questions encourage students to read the excerpts closely and to promote discussion and debate. The structured format of each chapter is useful because U.S. national security law is a complex and difficult subject. Students will be better able to explore this subject with a textbook that has a clear predictable structure and that will give them an appreciation of the nuanced relationships that exist between U.S. national security law and international law. The readings that are excerpts from judicial opinions do not always include excerpts from every judicial opinion issued in the case. Parenthetical material and footnotes in judicial opinions are not included in the excerpts. Spelling, capitalization, and italicization have at times been changed to ensure consistency and to avoid confusion. Brackets in the readings were in the original document or they have been added.

NOTES

1. Karen J. Alter, *The New Terrain of International Law: Courts, Politics, Rights* (Princeton, NJ: Princeton University Press, 2014), 4.
2. Alter, *New Terrain of International Law*, xvi.
3. See, generally, Michael V. Hayden, *Playing to the Edge: American Intelligence in the Age of Terror* (New York: Penguin, 2016).
4. See Charlie Savage, *Power Wars: Inside Obama's Post-9/11 Presidency* (New York: Little, Brown, 2015); and "Eight Things the Obama Administration Did Not Do Because of Legal Concerns (at Least in Part)," *Power Wars Blog by Charlie Savage*, January 13, 2016, http://www.charliesavage.com.
5. Quoted in Stephen Dycus et al., *National Security Law*, 6th ed. (New York: Wolters Kluwer, 2016), 177.

6. *Restatement (Third) of the Foreign Relations Law of the United States* (1987), §102(2).
7. *Murray v. The Schooner Charming Betsy I*, 6 U.S. 64, 118 (1804).
8. *Restatement (Third) of the Foreign Relations Law of the United States* (1987), §114.
9. Jack Goldsmith, "The Trump Onslaught on International Law and Institutions," *Lawfare* (blog), March 17, 2017, https://www.lawfareblog.com.

Acknowledgments

★ ★ ★

I would like to take this opportunity to thank the Dickinson students who have taken my national security law seminar and my constitutional law classes in the past as well as those who will venture into these courses in the future. All of you, both individually and collectively, have helped me immeasurably in probing the nuances and the dilemmas of this difficult and opaque subject, and I am confident that you will continue to do so for years to come. Your chief contribution is that you come at the legal topics with energy, fresh eyes, and sincere commitments and, at the same time, with a readiness to consider the political realities, both in terms of domestic politics and international relations. I also commend you for the perseverance you exhibit overcoming the challenging readings and negotiating the unyielding tradeoffs. All of you have given me much over the years.

I also want to express my appreciation for all the support I have received from Dickinson College, my professional home since 1983, especially from Neil Weissman, the provost and dean of the college, who has been unwavering in his commitment to the completion of this project on U.S. national security law. He understands why it is so important for undergraduate students to have access to materials that will enable them to evaluate future national-security controversies in an intelligent and thoughtful manner.

I am also indebted to my colleagues in the political science department at Dickinson, a group of independent-minded thinkers who nonetheless respect each other's point of view and work with each other in a professional, collegial manner. It is a great privilege to work with all of you.

A former colleague, Andrew Rudalevige, now at Bowdoin, has been a source of inspiration as well as constructive criticism. Andy has the knack of getting at the nub of a matter and articulating it with clarity and precision, which is why I always listen to what he has to say with due diligence.

I think it is also important to acknowledge the contributions the founders of lawfareblog.com (Robert Chesney, Jack Goldsmith, and Benjamin Wittes) and justsecurity.org (Ryan Goodman and Steve Vladeck) have made to the study of U.S. national security law. It is hard to believe that ten years ago, these two invaluable websites did not exist. Today I do not see how I could live—

professionally, that is—without them. A hearty thanks to the founders of these websites and the knowledgeable and thoughtful people who post on them.

A tip of the hat must also go to my editors at Rowman & Littlefield: Dhara Snowden, Traci Crowell, Mary Malley, and Janice Braunstein—all of you have been terrific. Thank you for putting up with my revisions, quibbles, and suggestions.

Lastly, I am very grateful to my wife, Patricia, who proofed the manuscript of this text a couple of times, finding many typos, grammatical blunders, and stylistic embarrassments. I doubt very much whether I would have ever finished this project without her help, assistance, and support.

Abbreviations

★ ★ ★

ACLU	American Civil Liberties Union
AECA	Arms Export Control Act
AP I	Additional Protocol I (Geneva Conventions)
AP II	Additional Protocol II (Geneva Conventions)
AQ	al-Qaeda
AQAP	al-Qaeda in the Arabian Peninsula
AQI	al-Qaeda in Iraq
AUMF	Authorization for Use of Military Force
BIA	Bilateral Immunity Agreement
CAATSA	Countering America's Adversaries Through Sanctions Act
CAT	Convention against Torture and Other Cruel, Inhuman or Degrading Treatment or Punishment
CCDCOE	NATO Cooperative Cyber Defence Centre of Excellence
CCF	continuous combat function
CIA	Central Intelligence Agency
CIG	Central Intelligence Group
CJEU	Court of Justice of the European Union
CRS	Congressional Research Service
DDOS	distributed denial-of-service
DNC	Democratic National Committee
DOD	Department of Defense
DOJ	Department of Justice
DPH	directly participate in hostilities
DTA	Detainee Treatment Act
ECHR	European Court of Human Rights
EIT	enhanced interrogation technique
FAA	FISA Amendments Act
FAA	Foreign Assistance Act
FBI	Federal Bureau of Investigation
FISA	Foreign Intelligence Surveillance Act
FISC	Foreign Intelligence Surveillance Court

FISCR	Foreign Intelligence Surveillance Court of Review
FLN	National Liberation Front
GBNB	Guantanamo Bay Naval Base
GGE	UN Group of Governmental Experts
GSS	General Security Services, Israel
HRC	United Nations Human Rights Committee
HRL	human rights law
ICC	International Criminal Court
ICCPR	International Covenant on Civil and Political Rights
ICJ	United Nations International Court of Justice
ICRC	International Committee of the Red Cross
ICT	Information and Communications Technology
ICTY	International Criminal Tribunal for the former Yugoslavia
IEEPA	International Emergency Economic Powers Act
IHL	international humanitarian law
IMT	International Military Tribunal
IMTFE	International Military Tribunal for the Far East
IRA	Irish Republican Army
IRS	Internal Revenue Service
ISIL	Islamic State of Iraq and Levant
ISIS	Islamic State of Iraq and Syria
KSM	Khalid Sheikh Mohammad
MCA	Military Commissions Act
MCT	multiple communication transaction
MLA	Mutual Legal Assistance
M.O.	morale operations (propaganda)
NAFTA	North American Free Trade Agreement
NATO	North Atlantic Treaty Organization
NDAA	National Defense Authorization Act
NGO	nongovernmental organization
NSA	National Security Agency
NSC	National Security Council
OLC	Department of Justice, Office of Legal Counsel
OSP	Central Intelligence Agency, Office of Special Projects
OSS	Office of Strategic Services
PKK	Kurdistan Workers' Party
POW	prisoner of war
PPD-28	Presidential Policy Directive—Signal Intelligence Activities
PPG	Presidential Policy Guidance (Obama administration)
PSP	President's Surveillance Program
PSP	Principles, Standards, and Procedures (Trump administration)
PYD	Democratic Union Party of Syria
SAS	Special Air Service (Great Britain)
SCO	Shanghai Cooperation Organisation
SCT	single communication transaction

SERE	Survival, Evasion, Resistance, and Escape
SIGINT	Signals Intelligence
S.O.	Special Operations
SSCI	Senate Select Committee on Intelligence
TSP	Terrorist Surveillance Program
UAV	unmanned aerial vehicle
UCMJ	Uniform Code of Military Justice
USCYBERCOM	United States Cyber Command
WPR	War Powers Resolution

1

Introduction

★ ★ ★

Understanding the relationship of U.S. national security law to international law requires an appreciation of what can be called the core principles of U.S. national security law and the legal principles controlling what effect international law has on U.S. domestic law. This chapter is divided into two sections so that each of these topics can be considered separately. Both topics are concerned with U.S. domestic law: the first focuses on the respective national security powers of the three branches of the federal government; the second highlights the evolving and ambivalent way in which U.S. domestic law recognizes the "binding" character of international law. A brief review of these two introductory topics will prepare the way for the consideration of substantive topics of U.S. national security law in later chapters.

CORE PRINCIPLES OF U.S. NATIONAL SECURITY LAW

The "core principles" of U.S. national security law are based on underlying constitutional principles of separation of powers and checks and balances. The Constitution sets up three branches of government—the executive, the legislative, and the judicial—and grants each branch specific authorities. Some of these powers are unique to each branch, such as the president's pardon power, Congress's impeachment power, or the judiciary's power to decide "cases and controversies." But the Constitution also grants "overlapping authorities" that require the branches—or parts of branches—to cooperate with each other to exercise the power in question. For example, only the president can nominate "Ambassadors, other public Ministers and Consuls, [and] Judges of the Supreme Court," but the appointment is confirmed only with the "advice and consent" of the Senate of the United States. Of course, each branch can use its "unique" or "overlapping" authorities to "check" the exertions of power made by the other branches. The purpose of this complicated system of powers checking each other or refusing to cooperate with each other is to preserve liberty by preventing the monopolization of political power.

Of course, liberty cannot be preserved without adequate protection of the country's national security. These two values must be balanced against each other such that neither is sacrificed for the other. The Constitution provides a general blueprint of this balance by specifying what national security powers will be exercised by each branch, but this blueprint does not necessarily give us an accurate picture of how the Constitution functions in the real world. In the main, the Constitution grants Congress a multitude of national security powers, including the power to "lay and collect Taxes"; "provide for the common Defense"; "declare War"; "grant Letters of Marque and Reprisal"; "make Rules concerning Captures on Land and Water"; "regulate Commerce with foreign Nations"; "define and punish . . . Offenses against the Law of Nations"; "raise and support Armies"; "provide and maintain a Navy"; "make Rules for the . . . Regulation of land and naval Forces"; "provide for the calling forth the Militia to execute the Laws of the Union, suppress Insurrections and repel Invasions"; "provide for organizing, arming, and disciplining, the Militia, and for governing such Part of them as may be employed in the Service of the United States"; and "make all Laws which shall be necessary and proper for carrying into Execution the foregoing Powers, and all other Powers vested by this Constitution in the Government of the United States."[1]

In comparison to Congress, the president has relatively few constitutionally rooted national security powers. First and foremost, the president is designated the "commander in chief," that is, the president is in immediate command of the armed forces of the United States. Only Congress can bring such forces into being, but once in being, it is the president who is in command of them, subject to any laws that Congress may enact for their regulation. In addition, the president "appoints" U.S. ambassadors to foreign countries and "receives" ambassadors from them in return. The president fulfills the former function with the "advice and consent" of the Senate but the latter at his sole discretion, which means that the president largely decides which foreign governments are legitimate and which are not. The president also has the power to negotiate treaties, even if the approval of two-thirds of the Senate is required before the treaty can be ratified.

Last, the president has the duty and power to "take Care that the Laws be faithfully executed." This is an important executive power, especially in the national security field. Congress has ample legislative powers, but to exercise them, Congress has little or no choice but to enact a law, which the president would then be empowered to enforce, or delegate power to the executive branch, which the president would then be empowered to implement. In either case, although Congress retains ultimate legislative control, power shifts to the executive branch in terms of the day-to-day operations of government. In effect, since the number of federal statutes has grown enormously over the last century, the president has had ample opportunities to expand and extend the reach of executive authority by enforcing or implementing congressional legislation.

The Supreme Court's opinion in *United States v. Curtiss-Wright Export Corp.* (1936) indirectly explains why the president's power to enforce and implement federal statutes has expanded his authority in the field of national security and foreign affairs. The case arose in the 1930s when Paraguay and Bolivia went to war over disputed borderlands. Wishing to contain the conflict, Congress passed a joint resolution delegating to the executive branch the power to decide whether to prohibit American companies from selling arms to either side if certain conditions were met. President Roosevelt determined that the conditions were met, issued an embargo proclamation, and then prosecuted the Curtiss-Wright Export Corporation for conspiring to sell machine guns in violation of the embargo. The company argued that the embargo was unconstitutional because the joint resolution that delegated such excessive discretionary power to the president constituted an improper delegation of legislative power. In his majority opinion for the 7–1 Court, Justice George Sutherland discusses, in a wide-ranging opinion, the differences between the federal government's "foreign or external" powers and its "domestic or internal" authorities; whether these differences have a bearing on the legality of the delegation of legislative power to the president; and the foreign affairs role of the president in our constitutional system. Sutherland's opinion arguably explains, at least in part, why the president's national security powers have waxed significantly over the last two hundred years, while Congress's have arguably waned, if not legally at least politically.

1.1 *United States v. Curtiss-Wright Export Corp.*, 299 U.S. 304 (1936)

It will contribute to the elucidation of the question if we first consider the differences between the powers of the federal government in respect of foreign or external affairs and those in respect of domestic or internal affairs. That there are differences between them, and that these differences are fundamental, may not be doubted.

The two classes of powers are different, both in respect of their origin and their nature. The broad statement that the federal government can exercise no powers except those specifically enumerated in the Constitution, and such implied powers as are necessary and proper to carry into effect the enumerated powers, is categorically true only in respect of our internal affairs. In that field, the primary purpose of the Constitution was to carve from the general mass of legislative powers *then possessed by the states* such portions as it was thought desirable to vest in the federal government, leaving those not included in the enumeration still in the states. That this doctrine applies only to powers which the states had, is self evident. And since the states severally never possessed international powers, such powers could not have been carved from the mass of state powers but obviously were transmitted to the United States from some other source. During the colonial period, those powers were possessed exclusively by and were entirely under the control of the [British] Crown. . . .

As a result of the separation from Great Britain by the colonies acting as a unit, the powers of external sovereignty passed from the Crown not to the colonies severally, but to the colonies in their collective and corporate capacity as the United States of America. . . .

It results that the investment of the federal government with the powers of external sovereignty did not depend upon the affirmative grants of the Constitution. The power to declare and wage war, to conclude peace, to make treaties, to maintain diplomatic relations with other sovereignties, if they had never been mentioned in the Constitution, would have vested in the federal government as necessary concomitants of nationality. . . . [For example, the] power to acquire territory by discovery and occupation, the power to expel undesirable aliens, the power to make such international agreements as do not constitute treaties in the constitutional sense, none of which is expressly affirmed by the Constitution, nevertheless exist as inherently inseparable from the conception of nationality. This the court recognized . . . [and] found the warrant for its conclusions not in the provisions of the Constitution, but in the law of nations. . . .

Not only, as we have shown, is the federal power over external affairs in origin and essential character different from that over internal affairs, but participation in the exercise of the power is significantly limited. In this vast external realm, with its important, complicated, delicate and manifold problems, the President alone has the power to speak or listen as a representative of the nation. He *makes* treaties with the advice and consent of the Senate, but he alone negotiates. Into the field of negotiation the Senate cannot intrude; and Congress itself is powerless to invade it. As [John] Marshall said in his great argument of March 7, 1800 in the House of Representatives, "the President is the sole organ of the nation in its external relations and its sole representative with foreign nations." . . .

It is important to bear in mind that we are here dealing not alone with an authority vested in the President by an exertion of legislative power, but with such an authority plus the very delicate, plenary and exclusive power of the President as the sole organ of the federal government in the field of international relations—a power which does not require as a basis for its exercise an act of Congress, but which, of course, like every other governmental power, must be exercised in subordination to the applicable provisions of the Constitution. It is quite apparent that if, in the maintenance of our international relations, embarrassment—perhaps serious embarrassment—is to be avoided and success for our aims achieved congressional legislation which is to be made effective through negotiation and inquiry within the international field must often accord to the President a degree of discretion and freedom from statutory restriction which would not be admissible were domestic affairs alone involved. Moreover, he, not Congress, has the better opportunity of knowing the conditions which prevail in foreign countries, and especially is this true in time of war. He has his confidential sources of information. Secrecy in respect of information gathered by them may be highly necessary, and the premature disclosure of it productive of harmful results. . . .

When the President is to be authorized by legislation to act in respect of a matter intended to affect a situation in foreign territory, the legislator properly bears in mind the important consideration that the form of the President's action—or, indeed, whether he shall act at all—may well depend, among other things, upon the nature of the confidential information which he has or may thereafter receive, or upon the effect which his action may have upon our foreign relations. This consideration . . . discloses the unwisdom of requiring Congress in this field of governmental power to lay down narrowly definite standards by which the President is to be governed. . . .

In the light of the foregoing observations, it is evident that this court should not be in haste to apply a general rule which will have the effect of condemning legislation like that under review as constituting an unlawful delegation of legislative power. . . .

Questions

1. Are you comfortable with Justice Sutherland's position that the federal government's "foreign or external" powers are not derived from the written U.S. Constitution? Why or why not?
2. If Sutherland's account of the nature and origin of the federal government's "external and foreign" powers is persuasive, would the written Constitution's grants of authority still

be decisive in determining how these powers are distributed between the president, Congress, and the courts?

3. If the Constitution's grants of authority determine which branch has what powers, why does Sutherland claim that the president has "the very delicate, plenary, and exclusive power . . . as the sole organ of the federal government in the field of international relations"? And what is the scope of this power if, as Sutherland concedes, it "must be exercised in subordination to the applicable provisions of the Constitution"?
4. If Congress does enact foreign affairs legislation that would only be effective through "negotiation and inquiry within the international field," does it make sense for Congress to grant the president more "freedom from statutory restriction" than it would in the domestic field? Why would narrow statutory restrictions render "negotiation and inquiry" less effective?
5. According to Sutherland, why does the president's access to secret information from "confidential sources" justify fewer statutory restrictions on the delegation of legislative powers to the president in the field of foreign affairs?
6. Should Congress be cautious in the field of international relations because the president may have "confidential information" concerning how his actions will "effect" foreign relations?
7. In your opinion, how much of Sutherland's opinion is dicta, that is, how much of it is not essential to the court's holding? How would you write the opinion to eliminate the dicta?

United States v. Curtiss-Wright Export Corp. (1936) became a key Supreme Court precedent in the effort to expand presidential power during the latter half of the twentieth century, especially in terms of foreign affairs and national security. The references in the opinion to the "powers of external sovereignty" and the president's "delicate, plenary and exclusive" power as the "sole organ" of the federal government in the field of international relations, although they might have been dicta, resonated with constitutional commentators who argued that the president must have the "inherent" power in an "emergency" to meet any threat to the nation's security. Just as Lincoln, at the beginning of the Civil War, had raised troops, seized telegraph and railroad lines, blockaded Southern ports, suspended the writ of habeas corpus, and spent public funds on his own authority, all without any congressional authorization, so too any future president must have the constitutional authority to do whatever is necessary to protect American life, liberty, and property. This principle was put to the test when President Harry Truman took possession of U.S. steel mills to ensure that a strike would not disrupt the supply of steel-based war materials to U.S. forces fighting the Korean War.

Unlike the situation in *Curtiss-Wright*, Congress had not authorized the president to seize private property to resolve a labor dispute, not even in an emergency. The question was—could Truman seize the mills anyway based on his constitutional "inherent" powers? The government argued yes, relying on the fact that Article II of the Constitution proclaims that (1) "executive power shall be vested in a President of the United States of America," implying that the president has *all* the executive powers that the federal government could have; (2) "the President shall be Commander-in-Chief of the Army and Navy of the United States"; (3) the president has the duty to "take Care that the Laws be faithfully executed"; and finally, (4) the government has the "inherent" authority to do what was necessary in an emergency. The steel companies argued that the president had no "inherent" powers to do what he thought was necessary in an emergency and that the seizure of private property was a "legislative" act that was beyond the executive powers of the president.

In *Youngstown Sheet & Tube Co. v. Sawyer* (1952), the Supreme Court, in a 6–3 decision, held that Truman's seizure of the steel mills was unconstitutional. Justice Hugo Black wrote the majority opinion, which focused on the literal words of the Constitution and their logical implications, concluding that seizure of private property was a "legislative" act beyond the powers of the executive branch. Justice Felix Frankfurter wrote a concurring opinion, arguing in favor of a more historical approach, one that would permit a "systematic, unbroken, executive practice" to be treated as a "gloss" on "executive power." Last, Justice Robert Jackson, former attorney general for President Roosevelt, also wrote a concurring opinion. He argued that the issue of Truman's seizure authority should be decided in the light of the "enduring consequences" that the decision would have on "the balanced power structure" of the American republic. Although other judges issued additional opinions in this decision, excerpts from these three are included below because they reflect different and important approaches to how judges should resolve separation-of-powers cases involving difficult questions of national security.

1.2 *Youngstown Sheet & Tube Co. v. Sawyer*, 343 U.S. 579 (1952)

MR. JUSTICE BLACK delivered the opinion of the Court. . . .

It is clear that if the President had authority to issue the order he did, it must be found in some provision of the Constitution. . . .

. . . [First, we] cannot with faithfulness to our constitutional system hold that the Commander in Chief of the Armed Forces has the ultimate power as such to take possession of private property in order to keep labor disputes from stopping production. This is a job for the Nation's lawmakers, not for its military authorities.

. . . [Second,] the President's power to see that the laws are faithfully executed refutes the idea that he is to be a lawmaker. The Constitution limits his functions in the lawmaking process to the recommending of laws he thinks wise and the vetoing of laws he thinks bad. . . .

. . . The power of Congress to adopt such public policies as those proclaimed by the [Truman] order is beyond question. It can authorize the taking of private property for public use. It can make laws regulating the relationships between employers and employees, prescribing rules designed to settle labor disputes, and fixing wages and working conditions in certain fields of our economy. The Constitution does not subject this lawmaking power of Congress to presidential military supervision or control. . . .

The Founders of this Nation entrusted the lawmaking power to the Congress alone in both good and bad times. . . .

MR. JUSTICE FRANKFURTER, concurring . . .

. . . The Founders of this Nation were not imbued with the modern cynicism that the only thing that history teaches is that it teaches nothing. They acted on the conviction that the experience of man sheds a good deal of light on his nature. It sheds a good deal of light not merely on the need for effective power, if a society is to be at once cohesive and civilized, but also on the need for limitations on the power of governors over the governed. . . .

To be sure, the content of the three authorities of government is not to be derived from an abstract analysis. The areas are partly interacting, not wholly disjointed. The Constitution is a framework for government. Therefore the way the framework has consistently operated fairly establishes that it has operated according to its true nature. Deeply embedded traditional ways of conducting government cannot supplant the Constitution or legislation, but they give meaning to the words of a text or supply them. It is an inadmissibly narrow conception of American constitutional law to confine it to the words of the Constitution and to disregard the gloss which life has written upon them. In short, a systematic, unbroken, executive practice, long pursued to the knowledge of the Congress and never before questioned, engaged in by Presidents who have also sworn to uphold the Constitution, making as it were such exercise of power part of the structure of our government, may be treated as a gloss on "executive Power" vested in the President by section I of Article II. . . .

. . . [It] suffices to say that these three isolated instances [of past presidents seizing private property] do not add up, either in number, scope, duration, or contemporaneous legal justification, to the kind of executive construction of the Constitution. . . . Nor do they come to us sanctioned by long-continued acquiescence of Congress giving decisive weight to a construction by the Executive of its powers. . . .

MR. JUSTICE JACKSON, concurring . . .

That comprehensive and undefined presidential powers hold both practical advantages and grave dangers for the country will impress anyone who has served as legal advisor to a President in a time of transition and public anxiety. While an interval of detached reflection may temper teachings of that experience, they probably are a more realistic influence on my views than the conventional materials of judicial decision which seem unduly to accentuate doctrine and legal fiction. . . . [Unfortunately, the] tendency is strong to emphasize transient results upon policies—such as wages or stabilization—and lose sight of enduring consequences upon the balanced power structure of our Republic.

A judge, like an executive advisor, may be surprised at the poverty of really useful and unambiguous authority applicable to concrete problems of executive power as they actually present themselves. Just what our forefathers did envision, or would have envisioned had they foreseen modern conditions, must be divined from materials almost as enigmatic as the dreams Joseph was called upon to interpret for Pharaoh. A century and a half of partisan debate and scholarly speculation yields no net result but only supplies more or less apt quotations from respected sources on each side of any question. They largely cancel each other. And court decisions are indecisive because of the judicial practice of dealing with the largest questions in the most narrow way.

. . . We may well begin by a somewhat over-simplified grouping of practical situations in which a president may doubt, or others may challenge, his powers, and by distinguishing roughly the legal consequences of this factor of relativity.

1. When the President acts pursuant to an express or implied authorization of Congress, his authority is at its maximum, for it includes all that he possesses in his own right plus all that Congress can delegate. In these circumstances, and in these only, may he be said (for what it may be worth) to personify the federal sovereignty. If his act is held unconstitutional under these circumstances, it usually means that the Federal Government as an undivided whole lacks power. . . .

2. When the President acts in absence of either congressional grant or denial of authority, he can only rely upon his own independent

powers, but there is a zone of twilight in which he and Congress may have concurrent authority, or in which its distribution is uncertain. Therefore, congressional inertia, indifference or quiescence may sometimes, at least as a practical matter, enable, if not invite, measures on independent presidential responsibility. In this area, any actual test of power is likely to depend on the imperatives of events and contemporary imponderables rather than on abstract theories of law.

3. When the President takes measures incompatible with the expressed or implied will of Congress, his power is at its lowest ebb, for then he can rely only upon his own constitutional powers minus any constitutional powers of Congress over the matter. Courts can sustain exclusive presidential control in such a case only by disabling the Congress from acting upon the subject. Presidential claim to a power at once so conclusive and preclusive must be scrutinized with caution, for what is at stake is the equilibrium established by our constitutional system. . . .

. . . [The] current seizure [can be] . . . justified only by the severe tests under the third grouping, where it can be supported only by any remainder of executive power after subtraction of such powers as Congress may have over the subject. In short, we can sustain the President only by holding that seizure of such strikebound industries is within his domain and beyond control by Congress. . . .

. . . However, because the President does not enjoy unmentioned powers does not mean that the mentioned ones should be . . . [interpreted narrowly]. Some clauses could be made almost unworkable, as well as immutable, by refusal to indulge some latitude of interpretation for changing times. I have heretofore, and do now, give to the enumerated powers the scope and elasticity afforded by what seem to be reasonable, practical implications instead of the rigidity dictated by a doctrinaire textualism. . . .

[Justice Jackson concludes that the textual provisions of Article II that President Truman relies upon do not authorize his seizure of the steel mills.]

The Solicitor General lastly grounds support of the seizure upon nebulous inherent powers never expressly granted but said to have accrued to the office from the customs and claims of preceding administrations. The plea is for a resulting power to deal with a crisis or an emergency according to the necessities of the case, the unarticulated assumption being that necessity knows no law.

. . . [The Solicitor General] asks us to do what many think would be wise, although it is something the forefathers omitted. They knew what emergencies were, knew the pressures they engender for authoritative action, knew, too, how they afford a ready pretext for usurpation. . . . I do not think we rightfully may so amend their work, and, if we could, I am not convinced it would be wise to do so, although many modern nations have forthrightly recognized that war and economic crises may upset the normal balance between liberty and authority. Their experience with emergency powers may not be irrelevant to the argument here that we should say that the Executive, of his own volition, can invest himself with undefined emergency powers. . . .

The contemporary foreign experience . . . suggests that emergency powers are consistent with free government only when their control is lodged elsewhere than in the Executive who exercises them. That is the safeguard that would be nullified by our adoption of the "inherent powers" formula. Nothing in my experience convinces me that such risks are warranted by any real necessity, although such powers would, of course, be an executive convenience. . . .

. . . Such [inherent emergency] power either has no beginning or it has no end. If it exists, it need submit to no legal restraint. I am not alarmed that it would plunge us straightway into dictatorship, but it is at least a step in that wrong direction. . . .

Questions

1. Justice Black deduces his conclusion that Truman does not have the authority to seize the steel mills from the premise that the Constitution does not make him the "lawmaker." In your view, is the simplicity of this argument a strength or a weakness? Why?
2. Can you explain how Justice Frankfurter relates history and experience to the rule of law?
3. Justice Frankfurter argues that the authorities of the three branches of government are "not to be derived from an abstract analysis." What does he mean?
4. In your view, is Justice Frankfurter correct that the Constitution is not just a written document but also a "framework for government"?
5. Justice Jackson claims that his experiences as attorney general had more of an influence on his views than relevant judicial decisions. Is this a proper perspective for a judge?
6. Do you think Justice Jackson places too much or too little weight on the intentions of the framers to resolve "concrete problems of executive power"?
7. Justice Jackson claims that Congress in the "zone of twilight" can "invite" executive action by doing nothing. Does this claim make any sense?
8. What about Justice Jackson's claim that "contemporary imponderables rather than abstract theories of law" will be the "tests" of power in the "zone of twilight"? What does he mean?
9. Regarding the meaning of the actual grants of authority to the president in Article II, Justice Jackson argues that they should be interpreted in light of "practical implications" rather than "a doctrinaire textualism." Is he right?
10. Does Justice Jackson rely on "contemporary foreign experience" to justify his conclusion that "inherent" powers should not be vested in the executive branch? What foreign experience is he referring to? Is foreign experience a proper basis for a Supreme Court decision?

Justice Jackson's tripartite analysis of executive power in *Youngstown* has become widely accepted: executive power is at its "zenith" when it is based on an authorization by Congress, and at its "lowest ebb" when it conflicts with congressional will;[2] there is a "twilight zone" in the middle, when the president acts without congressional authorization but not against Congress's will. The Supreme Court decided an interesting case involving the "twilight zone" in *Dames & Moore v. Regan* (1981). The case focused on the question whether President Carter could suspend the judicial claims of American citizens and companies against Iranian state entities as a negotiating step with Iran to release American hostages. In his majority opinion for the court, Chief Justice William Rehnquist denied that the International Emergency Economic Powers Act (IEEPA) or the Hostage Act explicitly authorized the president to suspend such claims. However, these statutes, according to Rehnquist, were nonetheless "highly relevant" to whether Congress accepted "a broad scope for executive action in circumstances such as those presented in this case." Accordingly, the statutes were, Rehnquist concluded, a sufficient basis to conclude that Congress's "intent" was "to accord the President broad discretion" and an "invitation" to take "measures of independent presidential responsibility," at least when there was no "contrary indication of legislative intent" and there was "a history of congressional acquiescence" in comparable instances of presidential conduct.[3]

Curtiss-Wright, *Youngstown*, and *Dames & Moore* conclusively show that the judicial branch of the federal government does at times fulfill the important role of defining the respective roles that Congress and the president play in the field of foreign affairs and national security. But courts have, over the years, developed a number of legal doctrines that enable them to avoid deciding cases that implicate national security concerns. One such doctrine is that cases with national security implications often present "political questions." Many years ago the Supreme Court defined the "political question" doctrine as follows:

> Prominent on the surface of any case held to involve a political question is found a textually demonstrable constitutional commitment of the issue to a coordinate political department; or a lack of judicially discoverable and manageable standards for resolving it; or the impossibility of deciding without an initial policy determination of a kind clearly for nonjudicial discretion; or the impossibility of a court's undertaking independent resolution without expressing lack of the respect due coordinate branches of government; or an unusual need for unquestioning adherence to a political decision already made; or the potentiality of embarrassment from multifarious pronouncements by various departments on one question.[4]

Obviously, these six criteria of the "political question" doctrine are rather general in character, thereby giving courts considerable latitude in deciding whether or not to hear a case, especially in the field of national security. A good example is *El-Shifa Pharmaceutical Industries Co. v. United States* (2010), a case involving U.S. missile strikes against a Sudanese pharmaceutical company, strikes that the United States initiated in retaliation for the 1998 embassy bombings in Kenya and Tanzania. The court generalized in the following way:

> Disputes involving foreign relations . . . are "quintessential sources of political questions." Because these cases raise issues that "frequently turn on standards that defy judicial application" or "involve the exercise of a discretion demonstrably committed to the executive or legislature," "[m]atters intimately related to foreign policy and national security are rarely proper subject for judicial intervention."[5]

In the end, the court in *El-Shifa* invoked the political question doctrine on the ground that it could not lawfully second-guess "the prudence of the political branches in matters of foreign policy or national security constitutionally committed to their discretion."[6] In other words, the pharmaceutical company's lawsuit was dismissed on the ground that the judge was unable to assess whether the missile strikes were warranted or not.

Courts can also decline to hear a case, not on the ground that it is a political question, but rather on the ground that the plaintiffs are not qualified to bring the lawsuit. They are not qualified because they lack "standing," which means that the plaintiffs (1) have not shown a "concrete injury in fact" or the "imminent threat" of such an injury; (2) have not established a causal relationship between the injury and the challenged conduct; or (3) have not shown a likelihood that a favorable decision will actually redress the injury. Courts cannot decide disputes unless the parties have these characteristics because Article III limits the jurisdiction of federal courts to actual "cases and controversies."

The upshot is that citizens often cannot bring a lawsuit to challenge the lawfulness of what the government is doing because they cannot satisfy the requirements of standing. For example, a group of U.S. journalists and human rights activists challenged the legality of the National Security Agency's (NSA) program of targeting the communications of noncitizens who were reasonably believed to be outside the United States. Although the NSA's program could not legally target these journalists and activists, their communications could be collected if they communicated with noncitizens outside the United States who were targets. For this reason, the plaintiffs argued that the NSA program violated their Fourth Amendment rights, but the Supreme Court held, in *Clapper v. Amnesty International USA* (2013), that they lacked standing because, even if it was likely that their communications might be collected in the future, this type of injury was "too speculative" to qualify as an "imminent" or "impending" injury. Moreover, even if the plaintiffs had adopted "costly and burdensome measures" to avoid NSA surveillance, such as by encrypting their international communications, the court held that such injuries were not sufficient for standing. The plaintiffs could not "manufacture standing by choosing to make expenditures based on hypothetical future harm that is not certainly impending."[7]

A third type of doctrine that permits courts to avoid deciding cases involving national security issues is called the state secrets privilege. American courts have recognized this privilege for over a hundred years, but the scope of the privilege has expanded considerably since the 9/11 attacks. In *Totten v. United States* (1876), the Supreme Court considered whether the estate of a Civil War spy could sue the United States for failure to compensate the spy in accordance with a confidential agreement. The court concluded that the case was completely barred because it was based on the existence of a "contract for secret services with the government," a secret fact that was "not to be disclosed."[8]

In *United States v. Reynolds* (1953), the court reviewed whether the widows of three civilian observers killed in a crash of a military plane carrying secret electronic equipment were entitled to a copy of the air force's report of the official accident investigation and the statements of three crew members who survived the crash. Relying on the state secrets privilege, the court refused to give the plaintiffs access to the report or the statements of the crew members, but it did not dismiss the case. Instead, the court granted the plaintiffs an opportunity to establish their claims without the privileged evidence. Accordingly, the state secrets privilege can function in two ways: if the case is analogous to *Totten*, it can completely bar adjudication of a plaintiff's claims; if the case is analogous to *Reynolds*, it can exclude specific pieces of privileged evidence from a lawsuit.

In *Mohamed v. Jeppesen Dataplan, Inc.* (2010), an en banc court of the Ninth Circuit considered whether the United States could intervene in a case involving a twenty-eight-year-old Ethiopian citizen and legal resident of the United Kingdom who was suing a U.S. corporation that had provided logistical support to the CIA's rendition and interrogation program. According to the plaintiff, Jeppesen personnel knew that he would be unlawfully detained and tortured in Morocco and Afghanistan. Relying on the state secrets privilege, the United States argued that the lawsuit had to be immediately dismissed, even though Jeppesen had yet to file an answer to the plaintiff's initial complaint. In the end, the en banc court, in a 6–5 decision, upheld the government's state secrets privilege, holding that (1) in some cases *Reynolds* justified, not simply excluding specific pieces of evidence from a lawsuit, but also dismissing the case entirely; and (2) such a dismissal of a case is warranted if the defendant, not the plaintiff, might present a defense that would create an "unjustifiable" risk of revealing state secrets.

1.3 *Mohamed v. Jeppesen Dataplan, Inc.*, 614 F.3d 1070 (2010)

FISHER, Circuit Judge . . .

. . . The court must sustain a claim of [state secrets] privilege when it is satisfied, "from all the circumstances of the case, that there is a reasonable danger that compulsion of the evidence will expose . . . matters which, in the interest of national security, should not be divulged.". . .

. . . In evaluating the need for secrecy, "we acknowledge the need to defer to the Executive on matters of foreign policy and national security and surely cannot legitimately find ourselves second guessing the Executive in this arena." But "the state secrets doctrine does not represent a surrender of judicial control over access to the courts." Rather, "to ensure that the state secrets privilege is asserted no more frequently and sweepingly than necessary, it is essential that the courts continue critically to examine instances of its invocation." . . .

We have thoroughly and critically reviewed the government's public and classified declarations and are convinced that at least some of the matters it seeks to protect from disclosure in this litigation are valid state secrets, "which, in the interest of national security, should not be divulged." . . .

We are precluded from explaining precisely which matters the privilege covers lest we jeopardize the secrets we are bound to protect. . . .

Having determined that the privilege applies, we next determine whether the case must be dismissed under the *Reynolds* privilege. . . . Given plaintiffs' extensive submission of public documents and the stage of the litigation, we do not rely on the first two circumstances in which the *Reynolds* privilege requires dismissal—that is, whether plaintiffs could prove a prima facie case without privileged evidence, or whether the privilege deprives Jeppesen of evidence that would otherwise give it a valid defense to plaintiffs' claims. Instead, we assume without deciding that plaintiffs' prima facie case and Jeppesen's defenses may not inevitably depend on privileged evidence. Proceeding on that assumption, we hold that dismissal is nonetheless required under *Reynolds* because there is no feasible way to litigate Jeppesen's alleged liability *without creating an unjustifiable risk of divulging state secrets.*

We reach this conclusion because . . . certain aspects of [the broad and complex logistical support provided by Jeppesen] . . . are absolutely protected by the state secrets privilege. Notwithstanding that some information about that process has become public, Jeppesen's alleged role and its attendant liability cannot be isolated from aspects that are secret and protected. Because the facts underlying plaintiffs' claims are so infused with these secrets, *any* plausible effort by Jeppesen to defend against them would create an unjustifiable risk of revealing state secrets, even if plaintiffs could make a prima facie case on one or more claims with nonprivileged evidence.

Here, further litigation presents an unacceptable risk of disclosure of state secrets no matter what legal or factual theories Jeppesen would choose to advance during a defense. Whether or not Jeppesen provided logistical support in connection with the extraordinary rendition and interrogation programs, there is precious little Jeppesen could say about its relevant conduct and knowledge without revealing information about how the United States government does *or does not* conduct covert operations. . . . Although district courts are well equipped to wall off isolated secrets from disclosure, the challenge is exponentially greater in exceptional cases like this one, where the relevant secrets are difficult or impossible to isolate and even efforts to define a boundary between privileged and unprivileged evidence would risk disclosure by implication. . . .

Dismissal at the pleading stage under *Reynolds* is a drastic result and should not be readily granted. We are not persuaded, however, by the dissent's views that the state secrets privilege can never be "asserted during the pleading state to excise entire allegations," or that the government must be required "to make its claims of state secrets with regard to specific items of evidence or groups of such items as their use is sought in the lawsuit."

HAWKINS, Circuit Judge . . . , dissenting . . .

The majority dismisses the case in its entirety before Jeppesen has even filed an answer to Plaintiffs' complaint. Outside of the narrow *Totten* context, the state secrets privilege has never applied to prevent parties from litigating the truth or falsity of allegations, or facts, or information simply because the government regards the truth or falsity of the allegations to be secret. Within the *Reynolds* framework, dismissal is justified if and only if specific privileged evidence is itself indispensable to establishing either the truth of the plaintiffs' allegations or a valid defense that would otherwise be available to the defendant.

This is important, because an approach that focuses on specific evidence after issues are joined has the benefit of confining the operation of the state secrets doctrine so that it will sweep no more broadly than clearly necessary. The state secrets doctrine is a judicial construct without foundation in the Constitution, yet its application often trumps what we ordinarily consider to be due process of law. . . . [For example, in this case] Plaintiffs' attempt to prove their case is simply cut off. They are not even allowed to attempt to prove their case by use of nonsecret evidence in their own hands or in the hands of third parties.

It is true that, judicial construct though it is, the state secrets doctrine has become embedded in our controlling decisional law. Government claims of state secrets therefore must be entertained by the judiciary. But the doctrine is so dangerous as a means of hiding governmental misbehavior under the guise of national security, and so violative of common rights to due process, that courts should confine its application to the narrowest circumstances that still protect the government's essential secrets. When, as here, the doctrine is successfully invoked at the threshold of litigation, the claims of secret are necessarily broad and hypothetical. The result is a maximum interference with the due processes of the courts, on the most general claims of state secret privilege. It is far better to require the government to make its claims of state secrets with regard to specific items of evidence or groups of such items as their use is sought in the lawsuit. . . .

Questions

1. How do you square Judge Raymond Fisher's view that judges cannot "second guess" the executive with his position that judges must "critically examine" the government's invocation of the state secrets privilege?
2. Do you agree with Judge Fisher that he reviewed the government's invocation of the state secrets privilege in this case with a "skeptical eye"?
3. Judge Fisher assumes that the "plaintiffs' prima facie case and Jeppesen's

defenses may not inevitably depend on privileged evidence" yet concludes that "any plausible effort" by Jeppesen to defend its action "would create an unjustifiable risk of revealing state secrets." Should a lawsuit be dismissed on the basis of a "risk" of disclosing state secrets?

4. According to Judge Fisher, should a judge's role in deciding whether the government can invoke the state secrets privilege be limited to assessing the danger that the disclosure of fact X, Y, and Z will likely endanger national security, or does it include an assessment that the disclosure of unprivileged facts A, B, and C might result in the disclosure of X, a fact that would likely harm national security?
5. Why does the plaintiff in this case bear the harsh burden of dismissal if it is the defense that is creating an "unjustifiable risk of divulging state secrets"?
6. In his dissent, Judge Michael Hawkins claims that *Reynolds* can be the basis for dismissing a lawsuit in its entirety only if the state secrets are "indispensable to establishing either the truth of the plaintiffs' allegations or a valid defense that would otherwise be available to the defendant." Is this the same rule that Judge Fisher endorses?
7. Can you reconcile the state secrets privilege with the due process clause of the Fifth and Fourteenth Amendments? How does Judge Hawkins reconcile them since he is of the view that the state secret doctrine is "a judicial construct without foundation in the Constitution"? Does this reconciliation make sense?
8. Is it likely that the states secrets doctrine is at times used to hide "governmental misbehavior under the guise of national security"? If so, what should be done about it?

DOMESTIC EFFECT OF INTERNATIONAL LAW

The Supremacy Clause of the Constitution identified treaties as the "supreme Law of the Land," but it did not explicitly say whether this "supremacy" meant that judges were legally obliged to apply the provisions of all treaties to the "cases and controversies" that came before them. Could it be that a treaty was the "supreme Law of the Land" in one sense but that in another its provisions were not enforceable by courts? Chief Justice Marshall addressed this thorny question in *Foster v. Neilson*. He said that, as a general matter, a "treaty is in its nature a contract between two nations, not a legislative act," and it is therefore generally not judicially enforceable for that reason. However, Marshall continued, "a different principle is established" in the United States. "Our constitution declares a treaty to be the law of the land." U.S. courts are therefore to regard the treaty as an act of legislature, according to Marshall, "whenever it operates of itself without the aid of any legislative provision." Such a treaty is "self-executing" because the legislature does not have to enact any implementing legislation to make the treaty judicially effective. However, if a treaty does not "operate of itself without the aid of any legislative provision," then, according to Marshall, the treaty "addresses itself to the political not the judicial department; and the legislature must execute the contract [by domestic implementing legislation] before it can become a rule for the Court."[9] Such treaties are "non-self-executing."

An important implication arising from Chief Justice Marshall's distinction between a self-executing treaty that "operates of itself" and is judicially enforceable and a treaty that is addressed to the legislature, which must first enact implementation legislation before any provision of the treaty could become judicially enforceable, is that a treaty of the first sort could conflict with a law that Congress later enacted. If such a conflict occurred, what law should the court enforce—the treaty or the statute? The Constitution says that both are the "supreme Law of the Land," but obviously a court must choose one over the other if they conflict. The Supreme Court considered this question in *The Head Money Cases* (1884), a case involving a statute that imposed a customs duty on new immigrants, a duty that violated provisions of "numerous treaties of our government with friendly nations."

1.4 *The Head Money Cases*, 112 U.S. 580 (1884)

Mr. Justice Miller delivered the opinion of the Court. . . .

A treaty is primarily a compact between independent nations. It depends for the enforcement of its provisions on the interest and honor of the government which are parties to it. If these fail, its infraction becomes the subject of international negotiations and reclamations, so far as the injured party chooses to seek redress, which may in the end be enforced by actual war. It is obvious that with all this the judicial courts have nothing to do and can give no redress. But a treaty may also contain provisions which confer certain rights upon the citizens or subjects of one of the nations residing in the territorial limits of the other, which partake of the nature of municipal law, and which are capable of enforcement as between private parties in the courts of country. An illustration of this character is found in treaties, which regulate the mutual rights of citizens and subjects of the contracting nations in regard to rights of property by descent or inheritance, when the individuals concerned are aliens. The Constitution of the United States places such provisions as these in the same category as other laws of Congress by its declaration that "this Constitution and the laws made in pursuance thereof; and all treaties made or which shall be made under authority of the United States, shall be the supreme law of the land." A treaty, then, is a law of the land as an act of Congress is, whenever its provisions prescribe a rule by which the rights of the private citizen or subject may be determined. And when such rights are of a nature to be enforced in a court of justice, that court resorts to the treaty for a rule of decision for the case before it as it would to a statute.

But even in this aspect of the case there is nothing in this law which makes it irrepealable or unchangeable. The Constitution gives it no superiority over an act of Congress in this respect, which may be repealed or modified by an act of a later date. Nor is there anything in its essential character, or in the branches of the government by which the treaty is made, which gives it this superior sanctity.

A treaty is made by the President and the Senate. Statutes are made by the President, the Senate and the House of Representatives. The addition of the latter body to the other two in making a law certainly does not render it less entitled to respect in the matter of its repeal or modification than a treaty made by the other two. If there be any difference in this regard, it would seem to be in favor of an act in which all three of the bodies participate. And such is, in fact, the case in a declaration of war, which must be made by Congress, and which, when made, usually suspends or destroys existing treaties between the nations thus at war.

In short, we are of the opinion, so far as a treaty made by the United States with any foreign nation can become the subject of judicial cognizance in the courts of this country, it is subject to such acts as Congress may pass for its enforcement, modification or repeal. . . .

Questions

1. By use of the term "infraction," does Justice Samuel Miller imply that a violation of treaty that is not self-executing is nonetheless a legal violation? If it is not a legal violation, how could the injured party justifiably declare war as a means of redress?
2. Is Justice Miller in fact claiming that it does not matter whether the treaties in question are self-executing because Congress has the power to repeal by statute self-executing and non-self-executing treaties?
3. Is Justice Miller hinting that a statute is entitled to more respect than a treaty because the House of Representatives participates in the creation of the former but not the latter? Is there any validity to this suggestion? If so, should a treaty be able to repeal a statute?
4. Justice Miller relies to some extent on the fact that a declaration of war "destroys" existing treaties between the warring nations to justify his conclusion that a statute can repeal a treaty. Is this a persuasive argument? Why or why not?

Another important question was the relationship of treaties to the Constitution itself. In *Missouri v. Holland* (1920), the court considered the constitutionality of a treaty that protected birds migrating between the United States and Canada. To implement the treaty, Congress enacted the Migratory Bird Treaty Act of July 3, 1918. The state of Missouri objected that Congress had no constitutional authority to protect migratory birds and insisted that the treaty and implementing statute violated the reserved powers of the states protected by the Tenth Amendment. In a 7–2 decision, the court rejected the state's arguments, holding that the treaty power was expressly granted by the Constitution, removing any possibility that it was included within the reserved powers of the state, and that the "necessary and proper clause" of Article I, Section 8, gave Congress the power to execute all powers of the federal government, including the power to make treaties.[10] The implication was that a treaty could expand Congress's legislative power, at least if the expansion was consistent with the Constitution.

The Supreme Court in *Missouri v. Holland* did not fully clarify, however, when and how a treaty could be inconsistent with the Constitution. While Article VI of the Constitution made it clear that statutes are the "supreme Law of the Land" only if made "pursuant" to the Constitution, treaties are described as "supreme" if made "under the Authority of the United States." The court confronted this question in *Reid v. Covert* (1957), a case involving an international agreement between the United States and Britain that granted U.S. military courts exclusive jurisdiction over offenses committed in Great Britain by dependents of American servicemen. The court concluded that the international agreement could not deprive the wife of a U.S. Air Force sergeant of her Fifth Amendment right to an indictment by a grand jury and her Sixth Amendment right to a trial by jury.[11] In other words, a treaty or any other international agreement could be made "under the Authority of the United States" only if it was consistent with the Constitution.

As noted earlier, the *Charming Betsy* doctrine posits that an act of Congress "ought never to be construed to violate the law of nations if any other possible construction remains." A more recent source defends the same position and extends it to treaties: "When fairly possible, a United States statute is to be construed so as not to conflict with international law or with an international agreement of the United States."[12] Of course, both formulations of this principle imply that, if a newly enacted statute cannot be construed in any way consistent with customary international law or international agreements, then courts must enforce the statute. However, such a newly enacted statute would not nullify the United States' legal obligation to comply with either customary international law or a treaty. Its obligations under international law would remain the same even though violating international law would be lawful under domestic law.

International and domestic law are therefore two "dual" bodies of law that can potentially come into conflict with each other. Judge Abner Mikva discusses the nuances of this "dual" approach to international and domestic law in *Committee of U.S. Citizens Living in Nicaragua v. Reagan* (1988), a case involving a group of U.S. citizens living in Nicaragua challenging an appropriations statute that provided financial assistance to Contra rebels fighting the Sandinista regime of Nicaragua. At the time of this decision, the International Court of Justice (ICJ) had already ruled (see **reading 7.5**) in 1986 that such support violated both the UN Charter (a treaty) and customary international law. According to the ICJ, the United States had an obligation to abide by its decision because the United States had earlier ratified the UN Charter, including Article 94, which imposes on each member state an obligation "to comply with the decision of the International Court of Justice in any case to which it is a party."

1.5 *Committee of U.S. Citizens Living in Nicaragua v. Reagan*, 859 F.2d 929 (1988)

MIKVA, Circuit Judge . . .

. . . [T]he key question is not simply whether the United States has violated . . . [international law] but whether such violations can be remedied by an American court or whether they can only be redressed on an international level. In short, do violations of international law have domestic legal consequences? The answer largely depends on what form the "violation" takes. Here, the alleged violation is the law that Congress has enacted and that the President signed, appropriating funds for the Contras. When our government's two political branches, acting together, contravene an international legal norm, does this court have any authority to remedy the violation? The answer is "no" if the type of international obligation that Congress and the President violate is either a treaty or a rule of customary international law. If, on the other hand, Congress and the President violate a peremptory norm (or *jus cogens*), the domestic legal consequences are unclear. We need not resolve this uncertainty, however, for we find that the principles appellants characterize as peremptory norms of international law are not recognized as such by the community of nations. Thus, as we explain below in greater detail, none of the claims that appellants derive from violations of international law can succeed in the court. . . .

Our conclusion, of course, speaks not at all to whether the United States has upheld its treaty obligations under international law. . . . This conclusion reflects the United States' adoption of a partly "dualist"—rather than strictly "monist"—view of international and domestic law. "[D]ualists view international law as a discrete legal system [which] . . . operates wholly on an inter-nation plane.". . .

. . . [The] appellants also invoke the rule "of customary international law that nations must obey the rulings of an international court to whose jurisdiction they submit." We accept that some version of this rule describes a norm of customary international law. . . . For the moment, we assume *arguendo* that Congress's decision to disregard the ICJ judgment violates customary international law.

The question is whether such a violation is cognizable by domestic courts. Once again, the United States' rejection of a purely "monist" view of the international and domestic legal orders shapes our analysis. Statutes inconsistent with principles of customary international law may well lead to international law violations. But within the domestic legal realm, that inconsistent statute simply modifies or supersedes customary international law to the extent of the inconsistency. . . .

Few other courts have had occasion to consider the principles that, under domestic law, statutes supersede customary international law. But the principle is implicit in decisions that uphold the statutory abrogation of treaties, "since violation of a treaty is essentially a violation of the principle of customary international law requiring that treaties be observed." . . .

Appellants argue that the rule requiring parties who have submitted to an international court to abide by its judgment is not only a principle of customary international law but has become a form of *jus cogens*. Because such peremptory norms are nonderogable and enjoy the highest status within international law, appellants conclude that these norms are absolutely binding upon our government as a matter of domestic law as well. Indeed, appellants assert that "the obligation stemming from the ICJ judgment . . . is such that it rises to the level of a constitutional obligation, which *cannot* be overridden by statute."

Appellants cite no authority for this assertion that a peremptory norm of international law operates domestically as if it were a part of our Constitution. So far as we know, no federal court has ever considered the concept—much less the domestic effect—of *jus cogens*. . . .

[However, we] . . . need not decide whether an ICJ judgment would restrict Congress's foreign affairs power if that judgment were in fact a peremptory norm of international law. ICJ judgments simply do not meet . . . the definition of *jus cogens*. . . .

Fewer than a third of the U.N.'s member nations have filed unilateral declarations consenting to compulsory jurisdiction, and many of these have imposed significant reservations on the scope of their consent. More to the point, "[i]n the 1970s and 1980s, the Court's compulsory jurisdiction cases have been beset with non-appearing defendants." One scholar concludes that "States do not yet seem to have reached a stage where they are prepared to submit their disputes to international adjudication." . . .

Our conclusion is strengthened when we consider those few norms that arguably do meet the stringent criteria for *jus cogens*. The recent revised *Restatement* acknowledges two categories of such norms: "the principles of the United Nations Charter prohibiting the use of force," and fundamental human rights law that prohibits genocide, slavery, murder, torture, prolonged arbitrary detention, and racial discrimination.

Such basic norms of international law as the proscription against murder and slavery may well have the domestic legal effect that appellants suggest. That is, they may well restrain our government in the same way that the Constitution restrains it. If Congress adopted a foreign policy that resulted in the enslavement of our citizens or of other individuals, that policy might well be subject to challenge in domestic court under international law. . . .

We think it clear, however, that the harm that results when a government disregards or contravenes an ICJ judgment does not generate the level of universal disapprobation aroused by torture, slavery, summary execution, or genocide. . . . The ICJ judgment does not represent such a preemptory norm. . . .

Questions

1. In your view, does Judge Mikva believe that the United States has a legal obligation to comply with international law?
2. How does a "dualist" view of domestic and international law differ from a "monist" approach?
3. Is Judge Mikva correct that statutes must "supersede customary international law" since the legal obligation to comply with a treaty is ultimately derived from a customary rule? What customary rule is he referring to?
4. In your view, is Judge Mikva correct that obedience to ICJ's judgments does not meet the "definition of *jus cogens*," the set of rules that have the "highest status in international law" and that purportedly bind all governments "as a matter of domestic law"? What is his evidence for such a conclusion?
5. Judge Mikva concedes that if Congress adopted a foreign policy that truly violated *jus cogens*, such as the rules against torture, slavery, summary execution, or genocide, that policy might "well be subject to challenge in domestic court under international law." Why would the "dualist" view of domestic and international law not preclude this possibility?

There are at least two noteworthy aspects of Judge Mikva's opinion: first, he has no hesitancy in referring to the appropriation bill funding the Contras as a violation of international law, thereby implying that the United States had a legal obligation not to enact this legislation; second, he was willing to let the door open to the possibility that a future court would have jurisdiction to review whether the United States was in violation of *jus cogens*. Both of these aspects of the decision reflected an outlook on international law that echoed to some extent nineteenth-century assumptions that international law was indeed "part of our law." Academic opposition to this tradition arose during the 1990s. It was, these critics charged, undemocratic if U.S. judges based domestic judicial decisions on customary international law that evolved from the practice of foreign states without any or very little input from the political representatives of the American people.[13] The 9/11 attacks bolstered this growing opposition to the traditional outlook on international law, largely because policymakers feared that norms of international law might unduly restrict how the United States could respond to the terrorist attacks.

As the temperature of this academic debate increased, the nature and status of international law became a point of contention between the justices on the Supreme Court in *Medellín v. Texas* (2008). In this decision, the Supreme Court considered whether the ICJ's ruling in *Case Concerning Avena and Other Mexican Nationals* (2004) was judicially enforceable in U.S. courts.[14] This ICJ ruling interpreted Article 36(1)(b) of the Vienna Convention on Consular Relations, a provision of international law that was arguably self-executing, one that the United States had ratified in 1969.[15] This provision provided that, if a person was detained by a foreign country, "the competent authorities of the receiving [detaining] state shall, without delay, inform the consular post of the sending State" of the detention of one of its nationals, and the "said authorities shall inform the person concerned [the detainee] without delay of his rights" to seek various types of assistance from the consul of his native state.[16]

José Medellín, a Mexican national, was convicted of murder and sentenced to death by Texas even though he had not been informed of his right to consult with the Mexican consulate. Mexico filed suit in the ICJ, claiming that Medellín and fifty other Mexican nationals had been denied their rights under the Vienna Convention. Mexico filed the lawsuit at the ICJ because a protocol to the Vienna Convention, which was also ratified by the United States, gave the ICJ jurisdiction to decide disputes concerning the "interpretation and application" of the Vienna Convention. In *Case Concerning Avena and Other Mexican Nationals* (2004), the ICJ held that the detained Mexicans should have their convictions and sentences reconsidered. George W. Bush issued a memorandum in February 2005 that announced the United States would "discharge its international obligations" under *Avena* "by having state courts give effect to the ICJ decision."[17] Despite Bush's memorandum, the Texas Court of Appeals in 2006 rejected Bush's guidance, holding that the ICJ's ruling did not bind the state courts and that Bush's memorandum was an unlawful intrusion into the independence of state courts.

The Supreme Court affirmed the state court's decision in a 6–3 decision. Chief Justice John Roberts wrote the majority opinion, while Justice Stephen Breyer wrote a strong dissent. Roberts relied on the standard distinction between self-executing and non-self-executing treaties. In his judgment, the protocol by which the United States agreed to submit disputes concerning the Vienna Convention to the ICJ was not self-executing because, by its terms, the United States had only agreed to "submit" disputes to the ICJ's jurisdiction, not to be "bound" by the ICJ's decisions.[18] Accordingly, any obligation to abide by the ICJ's decision, Roberts argued, derived not from the protocol but from Article 94 of the UN Charter. However, according to Roberts, Article 94 only requires that each member "undertakes to comply" with the ICJ's decisions, not that they legally "must comply."[19] For this reason, ICJ's decisions can have no immediate legal effect on U.S. courts. An additional consideration is that the second paragraph of Article 94—what Roberts calls "the enforcement provision"—provides referral to the Security Council as the sole remedy for an aggrieved state injured by noncompliance with an ICJ decision, thereby precluding the possibility that ICJ's decisions were enforceable by American courts.[20] Last, according to Roberts, President Bush's memo had no force because it is up to Congress, not the president, to decide whether to transform an international obligation arising under a non-self-executing treaty or customary international law into domestic law.[21]

In his dissent, Justice Breyer argues that Chief Justice Roberts's position that the treaties in question are not self-executing is unpersuasive. First, the protocol requires disputes about the Vienna Convention to be submitted to the "*compulsory* jurisdiction" of the ICJ, which underlines the "mandatory and binding nature" of the proceedings. Second, Article 36 of the Vienna Convention is self-executing because, by granting rights to individuals, it "operates of itself." Third, since Article 36 is self-executing, it only makes sense that the protocol's provision that provides for "final" and "binding" judgments regarding the meaning of Article 36 is also self-executing.[22]

Justice Breyer's arguments assume that Chief Justice Roberts has an overly skeptical attitude toward self-executing treaties, such that he will do whatever is necessary to find a way to convert such treaties into non-self-executing treaties that have no effect on U.S. domestic law unless the political branches enact relevant implementation legislation. Roberts takes this position even though President Bush supported the *Avena* decision and even though Congress, unlike the situation reviewed by Judge Mikva in *Committee of U.S. Citizens Living in Nicaragua v. Reagan*, enacted no legislation in opposition to the ICJ's decision.

Another issue regarding the domestic effect of international law arose in the context of the detention authority that Congress had authorized under the 2001 Authorization for Use of Military Force (AUMF), which granted President Bush the authority to use "all necessary and appropriate force against those nations, organizations, or person he determines planned, authorized, committed, or aided" the 9/11 attacks.[23] The Supreme Court addressed this question in *Hamdi v. Rumsfeld* (2004) by upholding the government's authority to subject an American citizen to military detention under the AUMF if he was "'part of or supporting forces hostile to the United States or coalition partners' in Afghanistan" and was "engaged in an armed conflict against the United States" there. The fact that the AUMF did not mention military detention was of "no moment" because "detention to prevent a combatant's return to the battlefield is a fundamental incident of waging war" based on "longstanding law-of-war principles."[24] In this fashion, the Supreme Court used the law of war, a branch of international law, as a means to justify its view that the AUMF's reference to "necessary and appropriate" force included the authority to detain American citizens who were "part of" or "supporting" forces hostile to the United States in Afghanistan and who were "engaged" in armed conflict.

The Supreme Court's decision in *Hamdi* did not resolve the question whether international law set any limits to the detention authority of the president under the AUMF. Ghaleb Nassar Al-Bihani, who served as a cook for the Fifty-Fifth Arab Brigade, a group associated with the Taliban in Afghanistan during fall 2001, argued in a habeas proceeding that the United States could not subject him to military detention because "providing support" to the Fifty-Fifth Arab Brigade as a cook was not a lawful basis for detention under the law of war, a subset of international law. A panel of the Fourth Circuit Court of Appeals rejected Al-Bihani's argument, holding that Al-Bihani was a member of the Fifty-Fifth Arab Brigade and that he was detainable on that basis independently of whether he "provided support" to the Taliban. However, regarding Al-Bihani's claim that his detention violated international law, the panel added that the laws of war were "not a source of authority for U.S. courts" unless Congress had passed relevant implementation legislation.[25] Al-Bihani petitioned for a rehearing en banc, which a seven-member majority of the D.C. Circuit denied on the ground that the "role of international law-of-war principles in interpreting the AUMF . . . is not necessary to the disposition of the merits" of this case.[26] Despite this holding, three of the judges on the en banc court discussed the degree to which international law, specifically the law of war, should determine the limits of the president's detention authority under the AUMF.

1.6 *Al-Bihani v. Obama*, 619 F.3d 1 (D.C. Cir. 2010) (en banc)

BROWN, Circuit Judge, concurring . . .

. . . The idea that international norms hang over domestic law as a corrective force to be implemented by courts is not only alien to our caselaw, but an aggrandizement of the judicial role beyond the Constitution's conception of separation of powers. The aggrandizement is clear in the more extreme scholarly opinions calling for courts to ignore congressional intent in favor of international norms. And it is only slightly better disguised in the superficially restrained claims that Congress intends to conform its actions with global ideals, and that a clear statement is required if courts are to be prevented from reading international law into statutory text. . . . However, a demand that Congress clearly enunciate the inapplicability of international norms is not premised on any constitutional value; nothing in the Constitution compels the domestic incorporation of international law. Instead, what such a demand protects is a policy preference, imputing to Congress a general posture toward international restrictions and erecting the highest interpretive hurdle to the legitimate prerogative of Congress to legislate apart from them. This is a restrained search for legislative "intent" only in the most Orwellian sense—one that grants judges license to usurp the legislative role and dictate to Congress what it is supposed to think. Surprisingly, proponents of this idea actually claim it guards the separation of powers. But if that is the case, then the cure is truly worse than the disease. . . .

. . . I am unaware of any federal judicial opinion—and Judge Williams cites none—that has ever before characterized international discourse as a traditional tool of statutory interpretation on par with legislative history, usage in other domestic statutes and cases, or dictionary definitions. The varied process by which international law is made—through treaty, tribunal decision, and the constant churn of state practice and opinio juris—shares few, if any, of the qualities that give the traditional sources of interpretation their authority. . . .

The only generally applicable role for international law in statutory interpretation is the modest one afforded by the Charming Betsy canon, which counsel courts, where fairly possible, to construe ambiguous statutes so as not to conflict with international law. However, Judge Williams does not appear to confine international law to such a narrow space. By including international discourse among the traditional tools available to courts when interpreting statutes, Judge Williams is not limiting the application of international law to ambiguous statutory text. . . .

There is no indication that the AUMF placed any international legal limits on the President's discretion to prosecute the war and, in light of the challenge our nation faced after September 11, 2001, that makes eminent sense. Confronted with a shadowy, non-traditional foe that succeeded in bringing a war to our doorstep by asymmetric means, it was (and still is) unclear how international law applies in all respects to this new context. The prospect is very real that some tradeoffs traditionally struck by the laws of war no longer make sense. That Congress wished the President to retain the discretion to recalibrate the military's strategy and tactics in light of circumstances not contemplated by our international obligations is therefore sensible and reflects the traditional sovereign prerogative to violate international law or terminate international agreements. . . .

KAVANAUGH, Circuit Judge, concurring . . .

In sum, a federal court lacks legitimate authority to interfere with the American war effort by ordering the President to comply with international-law principles that are not incorporated into [domestic] statutes, regulations, or self-executing treaties.

. . . I emphasize three overarching points about the position advanced in this separate opinion.

First, this opinion recognizes and reinforces the traditional roles of Congress, the President, and the Judiciary in national-security-related matters. . . . Courts enforce constitutionally permissible constraints imposed by Congress on the President's war powers. . . . But courts may not interfere with the President's exercise of war powers based on international-law norms that the political branches have not seen fit to enact into domestic U.S. law.

Second, the limited authority of the Judiciary to rely on international law to restrict the American war effort does not imply that the political branches should ignore or disregard international-law norms. The principles of the international laws of war (and of international law more generally) deserve the respect of the United States. Violating international-law norms and breaching international obligations may trigger serious consequences, such as subjecting the United States to sanctions, undermining U.S. standing in the world community, or encouraging retaliation against U.S. personnel abroad. . . .

But in our constitutional system of separated powers, it is for Congress and the President—not the courts—to determine in the first instance whether and how the United States will meet its international obligations. When Congress and the President have chosen not to incorporate international-law norms into domestic U.S. law, bedrock principles of judicial restraint and separation of powers counsel that courts respect that decision.

Third, consistent with that constitutional division of authority, Congress has enacted a significant body of legislation to prohibit certain wartime actions by the Executive and military that contravene American values. For example, Congress has adopted a detailed and extensive Uniform Code of Military Justice, which governs many aspects of military conduct. . . .

In his thoughtful opinion in connection with the denial of rehearing, Judge Williams says that it "would be an odd member of Congress who supposed that in authorizing the use of military force he was embracing uses equivalent to *all* such uses that have ever occurred: think Nanking 1937–38; Katyn 1940; Lidice 1942; My Lai 1968." I agree entirely with Judge Williams on that point, but not because I believe Congress intended for U.S. courts to enforce international-law norms against the Executive. Rather, when Congress authorized war in 2001, it did so knowing that domestic U.S. law already prohibited a variety of improper wartime conduct. Judge Williams' worrisome hypotheticals are thus already taken care of—by the domestic U.S. laws of war—and do not support his suggestion that the AUMF incorporates international-law norms. Notably, Judge Williams points to no examples of violations of international law that would be contrary to fundamental American values but that are not already independently prohibited by domestic U.S. law. There is a good deal of overlap between the international laws of war and domestic U.S. laws regulating war. When there is divergence, however, Congress and the President—not the courts—have the authority in the first instance to decide whether and how to conform U.S. law to international law. . . .

WILLIAMS, Senior Circuit Judge . . .

Judge Kavanaugh, I think, fails to adequately distinguish between treatment of international law norms as "judicially enforceable limits" on Presidential authority or as "domestic U.S. law" and use of such norms as a "basis for courts to alter their interpretation of federal statutes." By "alter their interpretation," I take Judge Kavanaugh to mean (as I said above) for a court to allow international law to persuade it to adopt a narrower interpretation of the President's authority than it would otherwise have chosen. I will assume that Judge Kavanaugh is correct as to the impropriety of the stronger use of international law (treating it as "domestic law"), but I believe him incorrect on the weaker (allowing it to affect a court's statutory interpretation).

Courts use a wide range of information outside the words of a statute to find those words' meaning. This reflects the simple truth that the question of a word's meaning is an empirical one: what have persons in the relevant community actually meant when using the words that appear in a statute? Among the most obvious outside sources to resolve that question are legislative history, usage in other laws and in judicial decisions, and dictionaries. Courts use all three incessantly. Dictionaries, of course, are only scholars' claims as to how people have historically used the words in question. Because military conflict is commonly an international phenomenon, words relating to such conflict are used in international discourse, of which international law is a subset. That international law has a normative element is nothing special; virtually all laws do—yet laws represent widely known public uses of language that legislatures often repackage in novel combinations and contexts. It would be an odd member of Congress who supposed that in authorizing the use of military force he was embracing uses equivalent to all such uses that have ever occurred: think Nanking 1937–38; Katyn 1940; Lidice 1942; My Lai 1968. More generally, it seems improbable that in authorizing the use of all "necessary and appropriate force" Congress could have contemplated employment of methods clearly and unequivocally condemned by international law.

Judge Kavanaugh agrees with that conclusion, but argues that we infer such limits on Congress's grant of power simply from penalties or prohibitions in domestic law. He is surely correct that this is one source for finding limits on an authorization of military force, but that does not make it the only legitimate source of such limits. In some circumstances, Judge Kavanaugh's "domestic U.S. law of war" may have relatively little to say on a question that international practice has addressed for centuries. It obviously seemed so to the Supreme Court in *Hamdi v. Rumsfeld* (2004) where the plurality looked to international norms on the question of whom the President may detain pursuant to the AUMF, and for how long. . . .

Questions

1. Is Judge Janice Rogers Brown right that judges who assume that Congress intends to conform its legislative action to global ideals are really trying to aggrandize their judicial roles?
2. Brown also claims that this type of judicial aggrandizement is "truly worse than the disease." What is the "disease" that she is referring to?
3. Why does Judge Brown endorse the use of legislative history, usage in domestic statutes and judicial decisions, and dictionaries as "tools" of statutory interpretation but rejects the use of international law?
4. How would you articulate the difference between the "Charming Betsy canon," which Judge Brown accepts, and the assumption that Congress's laws conform to international law unless Congress "clearly states" that they do not, which she rejects?
5. Is it likely that Congress intended the president to have some discretion to fight a new type of foe after the 9/11 attacks in ways inconsistent with international law?
6. Judge Brett Kavanaugh argues that "domestic U.S. laws of war" prohibit a "variety of improper wartime conduct." Where are these "domestic U.S. laws of war" to be found? Statutes? Judicial decisions? Would Congress have authority to change these "domestic U.S. laws of war" at its discretion? Does this mean Congress could authorize a massacre during wartime that would be comparable to the Vietnam My Lai Massacre in 1968?
7. Judge Stephen Williams distinguishes between using international law as "judicially enforceable limits" on presidential authority and using it as a "basis for courts to alter their interpretation of federal statutes." Does this distinction have much value if the statute in question is about the scope of presidential war powers?

Despite the D.C. Court of Appeal's opinion in *Al-Bihani v. Obama*, the administration of President Obama was relatively supportive of the role of international law in world affairs. On March 25, 2010, Harold Koh, the State Department's legal adviser, delivered a speech to the annual meeting of the American Society of International Law, one that articulated a "strategic vision of international law" that he and his colleagues were trying to implement. The "strategic vision" consisted of four core commitments: "**principled engagement**," a belief in "the interdependence of the global community; "**smart power**," a blend of principle and pragmatism to promote "democracy, development, technology, and human rights and international law"; "**strategic multilateralism**," based on the premise that the challenges of the twenty-first century "can't be met by any one leader or any one nation"; and "**living our values by respecting the rule of law**," a recognition that law "legitimates and gives credibility to governmental action."[27]

The 2016 presidential election brought on a sharp change of outlook. President Donald Trump entered the Oval Office with what appears to be a decidedly negative attitude toward international law. On the fourth day of his administration, for example, he signed an executive order withdrawing from the Trans-Pacific Partnership. He repeatedly cited his campaign promise to abandon the Iran nuclear deal, drafted executive orders that drastically reduced the United States' role at the United Nations and other international organizations, and established a process for the review and abrogation of multilateral treaties, such as the Paris climate agreement and NAFTA. Perhaps these draft executive orders were a mere negotiating technique, but they cast a pall over the world's perception of the United States as an international leader and a proponent of international law.

Trump also issued two executive orders on immigration, one of which subjected illegal immigrants seeking asylum to tougher screenings, longer periods of detention, summary processing, and expedited asylum adjudications, arguably in violation of U.S. treaty obligations relating to refugees.[28] Lastly, in December 2017, Trump recognized Jerusalem as Israel's capital, despite numerous Security Council resolutions (which arguably have the force of international law) proclaiming that Israel's claim of sovereignty over Jerusalem was invalid and that the city's final status had to be decided by the Israelis and Palestinians through negotiations.[29] Although these executive agreements and declarations may not constitute clear and indisputable violations of international law, Trump's actions do reflect a different presidential outlook from that of the Obama administration, one that could lead to a process of U.S. disengagement and withdrawal from international commitments and institutions. It is interesting to note, however, that Koh has recently argued that Trump's nationalistic and isolationist approach will likely be short lived if only because it is, in comparison to international engagement, smart power, and multilateralism, contrary to long-term U.S. interests.[30] In his view, it is only a matter of time—and not much more time is needed—that voters will figure this out and vote accordingly.

NOTES

1. U.S. Constitution, Article I, Section 8.
2. A recent Supreme Court case, *Zivotofsky v. Kerry*, 135 S. Ct. 2076 (2015), confirms that, when the president acts contrary to the will of Congress, his powers may be at their "lowest

ebb," but that does not mean they are nonexistent. In this case, the court held that Section 214 of a statute titled "United States Policy with Respect to Jerusalem as the Capital of Israel," which allowed U.S. citizens born in Israel to list their place of birth as "Israel," was unconstitutional because it intruded upon the president's exclusive power to grant formal recognition to a foreign sovereign. In short, Congress cannot interfere with the exercise of the president's exclusive constitutional powers.

3. *Dames & Moore v. Regan*, 453 U.S. 654, 677–78 (1981).

4. *Baker v. Carr*, 369 U.S. 186, 217 (1962).

5. *El-Shifa Pharmaceutical Industries Co. v. United States*, 607 F.3d 836, 841 (2010) (en banc).

6. *El-Shifa Pharmaceutical Industries Co.*, 607 F.3d at 842.

7. *Clapper v. Amnesty International USA*, 568 U.S. 398, 411–12, 416 (2013).

8. *Totten v. United States*, 92 U.S. 105, 107 (1876).

9. *Foster v. Neilson*, 27 U.S. 253, 314 (1829).

10. *Missouri v. Holland*, 252 U.S. 416 (1920).

11. *Reid v. Covert*, 354 U.S. 1 (1957).

12. *Restatement (Third) of Foreign Relations Law* §114 (1987).

13. See Curtis A. Bradley and Jack L. Goldsmith, "Customary International Law as Federal Common Law: A Critique of the Modern Position," *Harvard Law Review* 110 (1999): 815, 857; John C. Yoo, "Globalism and the Constitution: Treaties, Non-Self-Execution, and the Original Understanding," *Columbia Law Review* 99 (1999): 1955, 1962, 2092–93.

14. *Mexico v. United States*, 2004 ICJ 1 (Mar 31).

15. *Medellín v. Texas*, 552 U.S. 491 (2008).

16. The Vienna Convention, which the United States ratified in 1969, is available at http://www.fuech.eu/pdf/viennaconvention.pdf.

17. George W. Bush, memorandum for the attorney general, "Compliance with the International Court of Justice in Avena," White House Archives, February 28, 2005, https://georgewbush-whitehouse.archives.gov.

18. *Medellín v. Texas*, 552 U.S. 491 at 507.

19. *Medellín v. Texas*, 552 U.S. 491 at 508.

20. *Medellín v. Texas*, 552 U.S. 491 at 509.

21. *Medellín v. Texas*, 552 U.S. 491 at 526.

22. *Medellín v. Texas*, 552 U.S. 491 at 551–58. Justice Breyer has additional criticisms of Chief Justice Roberts's opinion beyond those described here.

23. Public Law 107-40, September 18, 2001, Congress.gov, https://www.congress.gov.

24. *Hamdi v. Rumsfeld*, 542 U.S. 507, 516, 521 (2004).

25. *Al-Bihani v. Obama*, 590 F.3d 866, 871, 872–73 (D.C. Cir. 2010).

26. *Al-Bihani v. Obama*, 619 F.3d 1,1 (D.C. Cir. 2010) (en banc).

27. Harold Koh, "The Obama Administration and International Law," U.S. Department of State Archives, March 25, 2010, https://2009-2017.state.gov.

28. Human Rights First, "Asylum under Threat: Impact of President Trump's Immigration Executive Order and the Department of Homeland Security's Memoranda on Asylum Seekers," February 22, 2017, https://www.humanrightsfirst.org.

29. Rick Gladstone and Mark Landler, "Defying Trump, U.N. General Assembly Condemns U.S. Decree on Jerusalem," *New York Times,* December 21, 2017, https://www.nytimes.com/2017/12/21/world/middleeast/trump-jerusalem-united-nations.html.

30. See Harold Koh, "The Trump Administration and International Law: A Counter-Strategy," an address delivered at the Geneva Centre for Security Policy, March 26, 2018, available at https://www.gcsp.ch/News-Knowledge/News/Professor-Koh-inaugurates-new-GCSP-series-Security-and-Law-A-Reality-Check. The address is based on Koh's forthcoming book, *The Trump Administration and International Law*, which Oxford University Press will publish in September 2018.

2

The Right to Make War—*Jus ad Bellum*

★ ★ ★

Whether a state has the right to make war depends upon two underlying questions. First, under what conditions may a state lawfully initiate armed hostilities and, second, who decides whether these conditions have been met? As the Latin expression *jus ad bellum* suggests, there is a long tradition of religious, philosophical, and ethical speculation regarding these two fundamental questions. St. Thomas Aquinas summed up this "just war" tradition in the thirteenth century in the following way:

> In order for a war to be just, three things are necessary. First, the authority of the sovereign by whose command the war is to be waged. . . . Secondly, a just cause is required, namely that those who are attacked should be attacked because they deserve it on account of some fault. . . . Thirdly, it is necessary that the belligerents should have a right intention, so that they intend the advancement of good, or the avoidance of evil.[1]

Aquinas's first requirement—that only a public sovereign could initiate war—underlined his understanding that a "just" war could only be initiated by a state, not a private person or group. This condition is fairly clear and straightforward. In contrast, Aquinas's second and third requirements of a "just cause"—"some fault" and "right intention"—are fairly hard to measure in any objective way. These vague notions would have left the sovereigns of Aquinas's day with considerable flexibility regarding whether to go to war or not.

In the seventeenth century, Hugo Grotius, often referred to as the father of modern international law, gave the "just war" tradition a more legal character by relating "just cause" to private legal causes of action. "The grounds of war are as numerous," he wrote, "as those of judicial actions. For where the power of law ceases, there war begins." In other words, if a private party could bring a judicial action for a wrong, then a sovereign could initiate armed hostilities if it suffered a comparable harm. Compared to Aquinas, Grotius focused less on the necessity of a "right intention" and more on whether the sovereign had been harmed in a manner recognized by law. He subsumed these types of harms under three "just causes" of war; they were the "right to defend, to recover, and the encroachment on which it is right to punish."[2] Eighteenth-century jurists of international law, such as Emer de Vattel and Jean-Jacques Burlamaqui, followed Grotius's approach.[3] At the time of the founding of the United States, it was therefore generally understood that a sovereign state, under *jus ad bellum* standards of international law, had the right to wage war to prevent harms to its citizens or subjects, to recover damages for any injuries suffered, and to punish proportionately any state that violated its rights.

Although international law established these vague guidelines that limited when a state could go to war in the eighteenth century, it had very little to say regarding how a state should go about deciding whether these conditions were met. This question was left up to the domestic law of individual states. In many countries of that time, such as Great Britain, France, and Russia, it was the monarch who made the decision to wage war. Of course, the Constitution of the United States took a different approach. As mentioned in chapter 1, Article I grants Congress the power to "declare War, grant Letters of Marque and Reprisal, and make Rules concerning Captures on Land and Water," while Article II confers on the president the powers of the "Commander in Chief of the Army and navy of the United States, and of the Militia of the several States, when called into the actual Service of the United States." During the Constitutional Convention, an initial draft of the Constitution gave Congress the power to "make" war, but it was changed to "declare" for two reasons. First, the change would make it clearer that the president had the power "to repel sudden attacks," even if Congress had not yet declared war. Second, giving Congress the power to "make" war might be understood to mean that Congress had the power to "conduct" war, which would be a congressional intrusion into the president's power as commander in chief.[4]

The Constitution therefore, in a very vague and general way, allocated to the Congress and the president different dimensions of the authority to decide if the conditions of *jus ad bellum* were met. The president had the constitutional authority to decide if the armed forces were to be used for defensive purposes to repel an attack. In all other cases, Congress had the authority to decide if some other nation had violated the rights of the United States such that armed force should be used to punish the violator proportionate to the extent of the harm. However, the constitutional text was obscure on certain points. First, while it was clear that Congress could grant "Letters of Marque and Reprisal," which are commissions authorizing the owners of private ships (privateers) to attack and capture enemy vessels, the Constitution's text did not explicitly grant Congress the power to authorize the use of the military forces of the United States without declaring war. Second, if Congress can initiate an undeclared war, it was unsettled whether it could also impose restrictions on how the executive branch could prosecute it. Would such restrictions be legally valid, or would they violate the president's powers as commander in chief?

Such questions arose during the 1790s when the United States was engaged in a limited war with France, primarily one on the high seas. During this conflict, Congress enacted a number of statutes, including a 1798 statute that required owners of U.S. merchant ships recaptured from the French to pay as salvage one-eighth the value of the ship to the recaptors. A 1799 statute changed the amount of salvage the owner had to pay to one-half the value of the ship if the ship was recaptured from "the enemy" (a term that was not used in the 1798 statute) after ninety-six hours of its initial capture. An owner of a merchant ship recaptured from the French following the enactment of the 1799 statute objected to paying one-half the value of his ship on the ground that the French were not "enemies" because Congress had not declared war on France.

In *Bas v. Tingy* (1800), the Supreme Court held that the French were in fact "enemies" even though Congress had not declared war. The court explained that there were two types of wars: a "solemn" or "general" declared war that was "perfect" in character versus an "imperfect" or "limited" nondeclared war, one in which Congress had imposed restrictions, whether on "where" it could be fought, "what" objects could be seized, or "when" fighting could occur. However, despite this distinction between the two types of war, the court concluded that both types were "public wars" because they were both authorized by legitimate powers, and for that reason, the citizens or subjects of each state were the "enemies" of the other.[5]

In February 1799, during the undeclared war with France, Congress made it illegal for any vessel "owned, hired or employed, wholly or in part, by any person resident within the United States" to travel to "any port or place within the territory of the French republic," including any French territories, colonies, or dependencies. To enforce this law, Congress gave President John Adams the power to use the ships of the U.S. Navy to stop and search any U.S. merchant ship that appeared to be sailing *to* a French port. In December 1789, Captain Little, who commanded the U.S. frigate *Boston*, captured the *Flying Fish* and brought her into the port of Boston. Little mistakenly thought the *Flying Fish* was an American vessel, when in fact she was Danish. The trial judge held that the *Flying Fish* had to be restored to its owners because it was neutral property, but refused to impose damages on Captain Little since there was probable cause to believe that the *Flying Fish* was an American vessel. On appeal, the circuit court reversed on the ground that the *Flying Fish* was not subject to seizure under the law, even if she were an American ship, because she was not sailing *to* a French port. Although the *Flying Fish* sailed *from* Jeremie, a port in Haiti, then a French colony, her destination was St. Thomas in the Virgin Islands, which at the time was a crown colony of Denmark.

The Supreme Court affirmed the circuit court in an opinion written by Chief Justice John Marshall. Although Marshall initially thought that Captain Little could not be liable for damages since President Adams had ordered him to seize ships sailing both to and *from* French ports, he changed his mind on the ground that the president's instructions could not "legalize" an unlawful act. The decision is noteworthy because it clearly supports Congress's power to limit how the president could prosecute the undeclared war against France, notwithstanding the commander-in-chief clause.

2.1 *Little v. Barreme*, 6 U.S. 170 (1804)

Chief Justice MARSHALL delivered the opinion of the court. . . .

. . . [Since t]he fifth section [of the 1799 statute] gives a special authority to seize on the high seas, and limits that authority to the seizure of vessels bound or sailing to a French port, the legislature seem to have prescribed that the manner in which this law shall be carried into execution, was to exclude a seizure of any vessel not bound to a French port. [Whatever circumstances] . . . induced Captain Little to suspect the Flying Fish to be an American vessel, they could not excuse the detention of her, since he would not have been authorized to detain her had she been really American.

It was so obvious, that if only vessels sailing to a French port could be seized on the high seas, that the law would be very often evaded, that this act of congress appears to have received a different construction from the executive of the United States; a construction much better calculated to give it effect.

A copy of this act was transmitted by the secretary of the navy to the captains of the armed vessels, who were ordered to consider the fifth section as a part of their instructions. The same letter contained the following clause. "A proper discharge of the important duties enjoined on you, arising out of this act, will require . . . [you to be] vigilant that vessels or cargoes really American, but covered by Danish or other foreign papers, and bound to or from French ports, do not escape you."

These orders, given by the executive under the construction of the act of congress made by the department to which its execution was assigned, enjoin the seizure of American vessels sailing from a French port. Is the officer who obeys them liable for damages sustained by this misconstruction of the act, or will his orders excuse him? . . .

I confess the first bias of my mind was very strong in favour of the opinion that though the instructions of the executive could not give a right, they might yet excuse from damages. I was much inclined to think that a distinction ought to be taken between acts of civil and those of military officers; and between proceedings within the body of the country and those on the high seas. That implicit obedience which military men usually pay to the orders of their superiors, which indeed is indispensably necessary to every military system, appeared to me strongly to imply the principle that those orders, if not to perform a prohibited act, ought to justify the person whose general duty it is to obey them, and who is placed by the laws of his country in a situation which in general requires that he should obey them. I was strongly inclined to think that where, in consequence of orders from the legitimate authority, a vessel is seized with pure intention, the claim of the injured party for damages would be against that government from which the orders proceeded, and would be a proper subject for negotiation. But I have been convinced that I was mistaken, and I have receded from this first opinion. I acquiesce in that of my brethren, which is, that the instructions cannot change the nature of the transaction, or legalize an act which without those instructions would have been a plain trespass.

It becomes therefore unnecessary to inquire whether the probable cause afforded by the conduct of the Flying Fish to suspect her of being an American, would excuse captain Little from damages for having seized and sent her into port, since had she actually been an American, the seizure would have been unlawful.

Captain Little then must be answerable in damages to the owner of this neutral vessel. . . .

Questions

1. Do you agree with Chief Justice Marshall that Captain Little should be liable for damages to the owner of the *Flying Fish*? Wasn't he just obeying the orders of his commander in chief? Should that be an excuse to engage in what was an illegal action—"a plain trespass"? Is it relevant that Marshall says obedience is "indispensably necessary to every military system"?
2. How do you understand Chief Justice Marshall's remark that it was "obvious" the 1799 law would "be very often evaded" if seizures on the high seas were limited to American vessels sailing *to* French ports? If that were so, could it not be argued that President Adams was simply correcting Congress's mistake?
3. Does it matter that the 1799 statute authorizes the president to seize American vessels sailing *to* French ports, but it does not explicitly prohibit the president from seizing American vessels sailing *from* French ports? In undeclared wars, does the president have any constitutional authority under the commander-in-chief clause to go beyond the statutory war powers granted to him or her by Congress?
4. Of what significance is it that the Constitution empowers Congress to make "Rules concerning Captures on Land and Water"? What if the president went beyond the statutory war powers Congress granted to him or her in circumstances that did *not* involve captures on land and sea?

The Supreme Court's holding in *Little v. Barreme* is somewhat in tension with *Durand v. Hollins*, an 1860 decision by the Circuit Court of the Southern District of New York. In this latter case, the circuit court considered the conduct of Captain George N. Hollins, who responded to a local mob engaged in theft and destruction of American property in Greytown, Nicaragua. Captain Hollins ordered his ship, the U.S.S. *Cyrene*, to bombard the small port city. Calvin Durand, an American citizen whose property was destroyed by the bombardment, sued Hollins for trespass. In defense, Hollins claimed he was bound to obey the orders of the president of the United States and the secretary of the navy, but Durand argued that neither the president nor the secretary had the authority to order the shelling. The circuit court decided the case in favor of Hollins based on the president's constitutional duty to protect the lives and property of American citizens, even if they are abroad. In somewhat of an ironic twist, an American citizen, whose property is destroyed by the actions of U.S. military personnel, is denied relief based on the president's constitutional authority to protect American property abroad.

2.2 *Durand v. Hollins*, 8 F. Cas. 111 (C.C.S.D.N.Y. 1860)

NELSON, Circuit Justice.

The principal ground of objection to the pleas, as a defense of the action, is, that neither the president nor the secretary of the navy had authority to give the orders relied on to the defendant, and, hence, that they afford no ground of justification.

The executive power, under the constitution, is vested in the president of the United States. . . . He is commander-in-chief of the army and navy . . . and [the Constitution] has imposed upon him the duty to "take care that the laws be faithfully executed.". . .

As the executive head of the nation, the president is made the only legitimate organ of the general government, to open and carry on correspondence or negotiations with foreign nations, in matters concerning the interests of the country or of its citizens. It is to him, also, the citizens abroad must look for protection of person and of property, and for the faithful execution of the laws existing and intended for their protection. For this purpose, the whole executive power of the country is placed in his hands, under the constitution, and the laws passed in pursuance thereof; and different departments of government have been organized, through which this power may be most conveniently executed, whether by negotiation or by force—a department of state and a department of the navy.

Now, as it respects the interposition of the executive abroad, for the protection of the lives or property of the citizen, the duty must, of necessity, rest in the discretion of the president. Acts of lawless violence, or of threatened violence to the citizen or his property, cannot be anticipated and provided for; and the protection, to be effectual or of any avail, may, not unfrequently, require the most prompt and decided action. Under our system of government, the citizen abroad is as much entitled to protection as the citizen at home. The great object and duty of government is the protection of the lives, liberty, and property of the people composing it, whether abroad or at home; and any government failing in the accomplishment of the object, or the performance of the duty, is not worth preserving.

I have said, that the interposition of the president abroad, for the protection of the citizen, must necessarily rest in his discretion; and it is quite clear that, in all cases where a public act or order rests in executive discretion neither he nor his authorized agent is personally civilly responsible for the consequences. . . . The question whether it was the duty of the president to interpose for the protection of the citizens at Greytown against an irresponsible and marauding community that had established itself there, was a public political question, in which the government, as well as the citizens whose interests were involved, was concerned, and which belonged to the executive to determine; and his decision is final and conclusive, and justified the defendant in the execution of his orders given through the secretary of the navy. . . .

Questions

1. Although Circuit Justice Samuel Nelson refers to the commander-in-chief clause in his opinion, does this clause have any relevance if there is not a state of armed conflict between the United States and Nicaragua?
2. Circuit Justice Nelson also claims that the president is the "only legitimate organ of the general government, to open and carry on correspondence or negotiations with foreign nations." Even if this statement is true, can this authority be the lawful basis for shelling a foreign town on the theory that the bombardment is a form of negotiation?
3. The third constitutional basis for the president's authority to order the bombardment that Circuit Justice Nelson mentions is the duty to "take care that the laws be faithfully executed," but does the scope of this duty include the protection of the property of American citizens abroad, or is it confined to executing the laws of the United States inside the United States?
4. Do you agree with Circuit Justice Nelson that a government that fails in its duty of protecting the lives, liberty, and property of Americans abroad "is not worth preserving"? How does the performance of this duty relate to the sovereignty of other states?
5. Circuit Justice Nelson argues that the protection of the lives or property of citizens abroad "must, of necessity, rest in the discretion of the president," and for that reason, "neither he nor his authorized agent is personally civilly responsible for the consequences." What does he mean by "necessity"? Why doesn't Congress have a role to play? Is this conclusion consistent with Chief Justice Marshall's reasoning in *Little v. Barreme*?

In 1861, the year after *Durand v. Hollins* was decided, President Abraham Lincoln took several strong measures in response to the shelling of Fort Sumter at the beginning of the Civil War on April 12, 1861. He called into federal service seventy-five thousand men from the state militias, he began to enroll volunteers into the federal army and navy, and he issued a proclamation of a naval blockade of the ports of the Southern states that were "in insurrection." Lincoln did these things without congressional authorization because Congress was in recess and would not reconvene in a special emergency session until July. The blockade, which authorized the U.S. Navy to seize Southern and neutral merchant ships that tried to run the blockade, was particularly controversial because it was an act of war under international law and Lincoln initially imposed the blockade solely on his authority as commander in chief. Blockade runners captured by the U.S. Navy were subject to condemnation as prizes, which meant that the ship and cargo would be sold, with some of the proceeds distributed to the crew of the capturing ship. The owners of several ships that were seized in this manner in May–June of 1861, prior to Congress's special session in July, objected to the legality of the blockade, claiming in part that Southern resistance to the federal government was an "insurrection," not a war, and that only Congress, not the president, could declare war. Although Congress in the emergency July session ratified all of Lincoln's actions, the owners of the seized ships nonetheless filed suit. In 1863, while the Civil War raged on, the Supreme Court decided in a 5–4 decision that Lincoln's blockade was lawful because, as commander in chief, it was his constitutional duty to decide if the Southern resistance was of such a nature that a state of war existed between the federal government and the Southern states that were attempting to secede from the Union. The dissent argued that the president had the constitutional and statutory power to resist those Southerners who were engaged in insurrection but that only Congress could declare war and thereby permit a blockade in accordance with international law and the laws of war.

2.3 *The Prize Cases*, 67 U.S. 635 (1863)

Mr. Justice GRIER.

. . . The right of prize and capture has its origin in the "jus belli," and is governed and adjudged under the law of nations. To legitimate the capture of a neutral vessel or property on the high seas, a war must exist de facto, and the neutral must have a knowledge or notice of the intention of one of the parties belligerent to use this mode of coercion against a port, city, or territory, in possession of the other.

Let us enquire whether, at the time this blockade was instituted, a state of war existed which would justify a resort to these means of subduing the hostile force.

War has been well defined to be, "That state in which a nation prosecutes its right by force."

The parties belligerent in a public war are independent nations. But it is not necessary to constitute war, that both parties should be acknowledged as independent nations or sovereign States. A war may exist where one of the belligerents, claims sovereign rights as against the other.

Insurrection against a government may or may not culminate in an organized rebellion, but a civil war always begins by insurrection against the lawful authority of the Government. A civil war is never solemnly declared; it becomes such by its accidents—the number, power, and organization of the persons who originate and carry it on. When the party in rebellion occupy and hold in a hostile manner a certain portion of territory; have declared their independence; have cast off their allegiance; have organized armies; have commenced hostilities against their former sovereign, the world acknowledges them as belligerents, and the contest a war. They claim to be in arms to establish their liberty and independence, in order to become a sovereign State, while the sovereign party treats them as insurgents and rebels who owe allegiance, and who should be punished with death for their treason. . . .

If a war be made by invasion of a foreign nation, the President is not only authorized but bound to resist force by force. He does not initiate the war, but is bound to accept the challenge without waiting for any special legislative authority. And whether the hostile party be a foreign invader, or States organized in rebellion, it is none the less a war, although the declaration of it be "unilateral." . . .

This greatest of civil wars was not gradually developed by popular commotion, tumultuous assemblies, or local unorganized insurrections. However long may have been its previous conception, it nevertheless sprung forth suddenly from the parent brain, a Minerva in the full panoply of war. The President was bound to meet it in the shape it presented itself, without waiting for Congress to baptize it with a name; and no name given to it by him or them could change the fact. . . .

The law of nations is also called the law of nature; it is founded on the common consent as well as the common sense of the world. It contains no such anomalous doctrine as that which this Court are now for the first time desired to pronounce, to wit: That insurgents who have risen in rebellion against their sovereign, expelled her Courts, established a revolutionary government, organized armies, and commenced hostilities, are not enemies because they are traitors; and a war levied on the Government by traitors, in order to dismember and destroy it, is not a war because it is an "insurrection."

Whether the President in fulfilling his duties, as Commander in-chief, in suppressing an insurrection, has met with such armed hostile resistance, and a civil war of such alarming proportions as will compel him to accord to them the character of belligerents, is a question to be decided by him, and this Court must be governed by the decisions and acts of the political department of the Government to which this power was entrusted. "He must determine what degree of force the crisis demands." The proclamation of blockade is itself official and conclusive evidence to the Court that a state of war existed which demanded and authorized a recourse to such a measure, under the circumstances peculiar to the case. . . .

Mr. Justice NELSON, dissenting.

In the case of a rebellion or resistance of a portion of the people of a country against the established government, there is no doubt, if in its progress and enlargement the government thus sought to be overthrown sees fit, it may by the competent power recognize, or declare the existence of a state of civil war, which will draw after it all the consequences and rights of war between the contending parties as in the case of a public war. . . . It is not to be denied, therefore, that if a civil war existed between that portion of the people in organized insurrection to overthrow this Government at the time this vessel and cargo were seized, and if she was guilty of a violation of the blockade, she would be lawful prize of war. But before this insurrection against the established Government can be dealt with on the footing of a civil war, within the meaning of the law of nations and the Constitution of the United States, and which will draw after it belligerent rights, it must be recognized or declared by the war-making power of the Government. No power short of this can change the legal status of the Government or the relations of its citizens from that of peace to a state of war, or bring into existence all those duties and obligations to neutral third parties growing out of a state of war. The war power of the Government must be exercised before this changed condition of the Government and people and of neutral third parties can be admitted. There is no difference in this respect between a civil or a public war. . . .

. . . [Actual resistance to the government] may be a war of the most extensive and threatening dimensions and effects, but it is a statement simply of its existence in a material sense, and has no relevancy or weight when the question is what constitutes war in a legal sense, in the sense of the law of nations, and of the Constitution of the United States? For it must be a war in this sense to attach to it all the consequences that belong to belligerent rights. Instead, therefore, of inquiring after armies and navies, and victories lost and won, or organized rebellion against the general Government, the inquiry should be into the law of nations and into the municipal fundamental laws of the Government. For we find there that to constitute a civil war in the sense in which we are speaking, before it can exist, in contemplation of law, it must be recognized or declared by the sovereign power of the State, and which sovereign power by our Constitution is lodged in the Congress of the United States—civil war, therefore, under our system of government, can exist only by an act of Congress, which requires the assent of two of the great departments of the Government, the Executive and Legislative. . . .

Upon the whole, after the most careful consideration of this case which the pressure of other duties has admitted, I am compelled to the conclusion that no civil war existed between this Government and the States in insurrection till recognized by the Act of Congress 13th of July, 1861; that the President does not possess the power under the Constitution to declare war or recognize its existence within the meaning of the law of nations, which carries with it belligerent rights, and thus change the country and all its citizens from a state of peace to a state of war; that this power belongs exclusively to the Congress of the United States, and, consequently, that the President had no power to set on foot a blockade under the law of nations, and that the capture of the vessel and cargo in this case, and in all cases before us in which the capture occurred before the 13th of July, 1861, for breach of blockade, or as enemies' property, are illegal and void, and that the decrees of condemnation should be reversed and the vessel and cargo restored. . . .

Questions

1. According to Justice Robert Grier, what factors are relevant to deciding when an insurrection turns into a civil war according to international law and *jus belli*? Is it a matter of fact or law? Does Justice Samuel Nelson agree or disagree?
2. According to Justice Grier, did the North "unilaterally" declare war on the South? In his view, how was the American Civil War "declared"?
3. Is Grier saying that Lincoln can lawfully establish a blockade because a state of war existed in April 1861 and a state of war between the federal government and the Southern states existed at that time because Lincoln issued his proclamation of a blockade on April 19, 1861? Is this a circular argument? Are such arguments convincing?
4. According to Nelson, the Constitution and laws of the United States give the president the means to respond to emergencies but not the authority to proclaim a blockade. Why? Is it because a blockade could potentially harm Southerners who are not actively involved with the insurrection?

Following *Durand* and *The Prize Cases*, a major issue left unresolved is whether the president has the constitutional authority to use military force in any circumstances where the lives, liberties, and properties of U.S. citizens are *not* threatened. Must Congress authorize the use of U.S. military forces in such circumstances, or can the president act unilaterally, at least in certain circumstances? This question is complicated by the fact that international law during the twentieth century has seemingly narrowed the conditions under which a state can legitimately invoke the *jus ad bellum*. While Grotius, it will be recalled, identified three just causes of war—the "right to defend, to recover and the encroachment on which it is right to punish"—twentieth-century treaties have sharply limited the conditions under which a state may legitimately wage war. For example, Article 10 of the Covenant of the League of Nations (1919) required all high contracting parties "to respect and preserve as against external aggression the territorial integrity and political independence of all Members of the League," and Articles 12 and 13 required all members to submit their disputes about international law "either to arbitration or judicial settlement."[6] Moreover, in 1928, the Kellogg-Briand Pact condemned "recourse to war for the solution to international controversies" and insisted that the "settlement or solution of all disputes or conflicts of whatever nature or of whatever origin they may be . . . shall never be sought except by pacific means."[7] The Nuremberg trials following World War II established the principle that waging a war of aggression was a violation of international law and a war crime. Last, the United Nations Charter, initially signed by fifty countries in San Francisco on June 26, 1945, firmly denounced "acts of aggression or other breaches of peace" and established a new legal framework for the settlement of international disputes that significantly altered the traditional understanding of *jus ad bellum*.

2.4 The Charter of the United Nations (1945)

CHAPTER I: PURPOSES AND PRINCIPLES

Article 1

1. To maintain international peace and security, and to that end: to take effective collective measures for the prevention and removal of threats to the peace, and for the suppression of acts of aggression or other breaches of the peace, and to bring about by peaceful means, and in conformity with the principles of justice and international law, adjustment or settlement of international disputes or situations which might lead to a breach of the peace;
2. To develop friendly relations among nations based on respect for the principle of equal rights and self-determination of peoples, and to take other appropriate measures to strengthen universal peace. . . .

Article 2

The Organization and its Members, in pursuit of the Purposes stated in Article 1, shall act in accordance with the following Principles.

1. The Organization is based on the principle of the sovereign equality of all its Members.
2. All Members, in order to ensure to all of them the rights and benefits resulting from membership, shall fulfill in good faith the obligations assumed by them in accordance with the present Charter.
3. All Members shall settle their international disputes by peaceful means in such a manner that international peace and security, and justice, are not endangered.
4. All Members shall refrain in their international relations from the threat or use of force against the territorial integrity or political independence of any state, or in any other manner inconsistent with the Purposes of the United Nations.
5. All Members shall give the United Nations every assistance in any action it takes in accordance with the present Charter, and shall refrain from giving assistance to any state against which the United Nations is taking preventive or enforcement action.
6. The Organization shall ensure that states which are not Members of the United

Nations act in accordance with these Principles so far as may be necessary for the maintenance of international peace and security.

7. Nothing contained in the present Charter shall authorize the United Nations to intervene in matters which are essentially within the domestic jurisdiction of any state or shall require the Members to submit such matters to settlement under the present Charter; but this principle shall not prejudice the application of enforcement measures under Chapter VII. . . .

CHAPTER V: THE SECURITY COUNCIL

Article 23

1. The Security Council shall consist of fifteen Members of the United Nations. [China, France, the USSR, Great Britain, and the United States shall be permanent members of the council, while the general assembly will elect ten nonpermanent members to two-year terms.] . . .

Article 27

1. Each member of the Security Council shall have one vote.
2. Decisions of the Security Council on procedural matters shall be made by an affirmative vote of nine members.
3. Decisions of the Security Council on all other matters shall be made by an affirmative vote of nine members including the concurring votes of the permanent members. . . .

CHAPTER VII: ACTION WITH RESPECT TO THREATS TO THE PEACE, BREACHES OF THE PEACE, AND ACTS OF AGGRESSION

Article 39

The Security Council shall determine the existence of any threat to the peace, breach of the peace, or act of aggression and shall make recommendations, or decide what measures shall be taken in accordance with Articles 41 and 42, to maintain or restore international peace and security. . . .

Article 41

The Security Council may decide what measures not involving the use of armed force are to be employed to give effect to its decisions, and it may call upon the Members of the United Nations to apply such measures. These may include complete or partial interruption of economic relations and of rail, sea, air, postal, telegraphic, radio, and other means of communication, and the severance of diplomatic relations.

Article 42

Should the Security Council consider that measures provided for in Article 41 would be inadequate or have proved to be inadequate, it may take such action by air, sea, or land forces as may be necessary to maintain or restore international peace and security. Such action may include demonstrations, blockade, and other operations by air, sea, or land forces of Members of the United Nations. . . .

Article 51

Nothing in the present Charter shall impair the inherent right of individual or collective self-defense if an armed attack occurs against a Member of the United Nations, until the Security Council has taken measures necessary to maintain international peace and security. Measures taken by Members in the exercise of this right of self-defense shall be immediately reported to the Security Council and shall not in any way affect the authority and responsibility of the Security Council under the present Charter to take at any time such action as it deems necessary in order to maintain or restore international peace and security. . . .

Questions

1. The charter's purpose is not only to suppress "acts of aggression" but also to prevent "other breaches of the peace" and "threats to peace." What

do these latter terms mean? What is a "breach of peace" that is not an "act of aggression"? What would qualify as a "threat to peace"?

2. Although the charter endorses the principle of the sovereign equality of all its members, it also creates five permanent members of the Security Council whose concurrence is required for all nonprocedural matters, which effectively gives each permanent member a veto on the council's substantive decisions. Is the charter therefore inconsistent in its commitment to sovereign equality? Why is there this inconsistency? Would you support changes to the Security Council that would more fully realize the goal of sovereign equality?
3. The charter denies that it authorizes the United Nations to intervene in matters that are "essentially within the domestic jurisdiction of any state." Does this mean that the Security Council has absolutely no role to play in civil wars or insurgencies? Could a civil war pose a "threat to international peace"? Would that be a civil war that was not "essentially" within the domestic jurisdiction of the state?
4. Would Congress have a legal obligation to support military measures approved by the Security Council under Article 42?
5. Article 51 seems to limit the right of the United States to engage in defensive war to cases involving an armed attack on the United States. Does this conflict with the president's domestic constitutional authority to defend the lives, liberties, and properties of Americans abroad? Which rule should the president follow?
6. Does Article 51 also imply that the right of individual or collective self-defense disappears if and when the Security Council has made a decision on how to maintain or restore international peace and security?
7. Why is the Security Council authorized to use military force in response to "threats to peace" or "breaches of the peace," while a state can only respond in self-defense in case of an "armed attack"? Should this difference exist? Why?

Despite all the hopes and aspirations embodied in the language of the UN Charter, the Security Council since World War II has had limited success maintaining international peace and security through the use of military force. One major reason the Security Council has been largely ineffective is because the Cold War made it almost impossible for the permanent members of the Security Council to reach unanimity about the use of military force to resolve international disputes.[8] One exception was the Korean War (1950–1953), but the Security Council was able to act in this instance only because the Soviets were boycotting the council as a way to protest the United Nations' refusal to give the People's Republic of China the permanent seat on the Security Council that was then occupied by the Republic of China (Taiwan). Moreover, the Security Council did not invoke Article 42 and take military action itself but instead adopted a resolution under Article 39 that only "recommended" that member states should furnish "such assistance" to South Korea "as may be necessary to repel the armed attack and to restore international peace and security in the area."[9] In response, President Harry S. Truman immediately began sending U.S. military forces to South Korea without any declaration of war or explicit congressional authorization for the use of military force, although Congress did extend the draft and increase the size of the armed forces. In what was called a "UN police action," rather than a "war," more than a dozen countries provided assistance to South Korea, but it was the United States who led the effort and provided the lion's share of manpower and military resources. Approximately thirty-four thousand Americans died and more than one hundred thousand Americans were wounded in the Korean "police action."

In response to critics, the Truman administration defended its actions by claiming that sending troops "abroad is certainly one of the powers which the President may exercise in carrying out such a treaty as . . . the United Nations Charter."[10] Given the fact that the Security Council only "recommended" that member states aid South Korea, it is not clear whether this argument is convincing. Arguably, since the attack by North Korea did not trigger the president's constitutional duty to protect the lives of Americans abroad, President Truman needed congressional authorization before he could commit military forces to the defense of South Korea. However, if the Security Council had taken action under Article 42, would Truman have been legally justified in committing troops to the defense of South Korea without congressional authorization, or would he still have needed some sort of explicit congressional approval? And what if Congress refused to give the requisite approval? Would Congress be violating its obligations under international law by not complying with a Security Council directive issued under Article 42? Could such a failure to act by Congress constitute a "threat to peace"?

In contrast to the Korean War, Congress explicitly authorized the use of military force during the Vietnam War by passing the Gulf of Tonkin Resolution on August 7, 1964, while the UN Security Council did nothing since Russia or China would block any resolution in favor of U.S. involvement in the conflict. The above resolution was Congress's response to an alleged attack by North Vietnam PT boats on two U.S. destroyers in the Gulf of Tonkin. It authorized President Johnson "to take all measures to repel any armed attack against the forces of the United States and to prevent further aggression" and "to take all necessary steps, including the use of armed force, to assist any member or protocol state of the Southeast Asia Collective Defense Treaty requesting assistance in defense of its freedom."[11] Relying on this regional treaty enabled the Johnson administration to sidestep the need for the approval of the Security Council because Article 51 of the charter recognized the "inherent right" of "individual" and "collective" self-defense. If the Saigon government was deemed to be the legitimate government of the Republic of Vietnam, which was a judgment that was arguably within the president's Article II authority to "receive Ambassadors and other public Ministers," then the United States would not be in violation of the UN Charter, so long as the Saigon government requested assistance and consented to the use of U.S. armed forces on its sovereign territory.

Political support for the Vietnam War began to dissipate following North Vietnam's TET offensive in early 1968. Elected later that year, President Nixon began to withdraw U.S. troops, but at the same time he broadened the war into Cambodia and Laos. Having little trust that Nixon would quickly end the war, Congress repealed the Gulf of Tonkin Resolution by attaching a rider to a Foreign Military Sales Act, which Nixon signed in January 1971. Despite this withdrawal of the key domestic authorization of the war, courts nevertheless refused to consider the legality of the conflict on the ground that it was a "political question," one not subject to judicial resolution.[12] In the fall of 1971 Congress passed and Nixon signed the Mansfield Amendment, which declared that it was the policy of the United States to end "at the earliest possible date all military operations" in Indochina, but the war nevertheless dragged on. On May 31, 1973, Congress passed a bill that cut off all funds for combat activities in Cambodia and Laos, but Nixon vetoed the bill. A month later, however, Nixon signed a bill into law that required the end of all U.S. military involvement in Southeast Asia by August 15, 1973. Frustrated by these delays in ending the war and by Nixon's intransigence, Congress enacted the War Powers Resolution over Nixon's veto in November 1973. In the words of the resolution, its central purpose was "to fulfill the intent of the framers of the Constitution of the United States" by ensuring "that the collective judgment of both the Congress and the President will apply to the introduction of United States Armed Forces into hostilities, or into situations where imminent involvement in hostilities is clearly indicated by the circumstances, and to the continued use of such forces in hostilities or such situations."

2.5 The War Powers Resolution (WPR)

SEC. 2. PURPOSE AND POLICY

(c) The constitutional powers of the President as Commander-in-Chief to introduce United States Armed Forces into hostilities, or into situations where imminent involvement in hostilities is clearly indicated by the circumstances, are exercised only pursuant to (1) a declaration of war, (2) specific statutory authorization, or (3) a national emergency created by attack upon the United States, its territories or possessions, or its armed forces.[13]

SEC. 3. CONSULTATION

The President in every possible instance shall consult with Congress before introducing United States Armed Forces into hostilities or into situations where imminent involvement in hostilities is clearly indicated by the circumstances, and after every such introduction shall consult regularly with the Congress until United States Armed Forces are no longer engaged in hostilities or have been removed from such situations.

SEC. 4. REPORTING

SEC. 4. (a) In the absence of a declaration of war, in any case in which United States Armed Forces are introduced [into situations involving hostilities or into foreign countries equipped for combat, including substantial increases of the number of such forces] . . . the president shall submit within 48 hours to the Speaker of the House of Representatives and to the President pro tempore of the Senate a report, in writing, setting forth . . . [the circumstances that required the introduction of U.S. forces; the constitutional and legislative authority for the introduction; and the scope and duration of the involvement].

SEC. 5. CONGRESSIONAL ACTION

(b) Within sixty calendar days after a report is submitted or is required to be submitted pursuant to section 4(a)(1), whichever is earlier, the President shall terminate any use of United States Armed Forces with respect to which such report was submitted (or required to be submitted), unless the Congress (1) has declared war or has enacted a specific authorization for such use of United States Armed Forces, (2) has extended by law such sixty-day period, or (3) is physically unable to meet as a result of an armed attack upon the United States. Such sixty-day period shall be extended for not more than an additional thirty days if the President determines and certifies to the

Congress in writing that unavoidable military necessity respecting the safety of United States Armed Forces requires the continued use of such armed forces in the course of bringing about a prompt removal of such forces.
(c) Notwithstanding subsection (b), at any time that United States Armed Forces are engaged in hostilities outside the territory of the United States, its possessions and territories without a declaration of war or specific statutory authorization, such forces shall be removed by the President if the Congress so directs by concurrent resolution. . . .

SEC. 8. INTERPRETATION OF JOINT RESOLUTION

SEC. 8. (a) Authority to introduce United States Armed Forces into hostilities or into situations wherein involvement in hostilities is clearly indicated by the circumstances shall not be inferred [from any treaty or from any law or appropriation act unless it "specifically authorizes" the introduction of such forces and states that it is "intended" to constitute specific statutory authorization "within the meaning of this joint resolution."]

Questions

1. Section 2 of the WPR says that the president can introduce U.S. military forces into hostilities only in three situations, but Section 5 arguably recognizes a sixty-day window during which time the president can introduce U.S. forces into hostilities without congressional authorization. Are the two sections consistent? If not, which section should be controlling?
2. How can a president "consult" with 535 members of Congress? Does the president fulfill the consultation requirement by keeping a few congressional leaders informed? Is the consultation requirement consistent with the need for the United States to act decisively in an international crisis? How should one interpret the requirement that the president should consult with Congress "in every possible instance"?
3. Would the sixty-day deadline in the WPR be unconstitutional if the president introduced U.S. military forces abroad for the purpose of saving the lives, liberties, and properties of Americans? Would the deadline encourage an adversary not to negotiate for peace during the sixty days? Why?
4. In *INS v. Chadha* (1983), the Supreme Court invalidated a law that delegated power to an executive branch agency but reserved to either house of Congress the right to "veto" how the agency was interpreting or implementing its delegated power.[14] Since Section 5(c) requires the president to remove troops from situations involving hostilities if Congress "so directs by concurrent resolution," is this provision an unconstitutional "legislative veto" comparable to the one in *Chadha*? In what sense does the WPR "delegate" power to the executive branch?
5. If the president must be given the opportunity to veto any congressional action requiring the removal of U.S. forces from situations of hostilities abroad, is it easier under the Constitution for the United States to get into war than it is to get out of one? Is that what the framers intended?

In general, the WPR has not been effective in fostering a "collective judgment" between the Congress and the president regarding when and where U.S. military forces should be lawfully introduced into hostilities in foreign countries. In fact, no president has formally acknowledged a legal obligation to comply with the WPR. They have at times filed the reports required by Section 4 of the WPR, but the reports note that they are filed "consistent with," not "in compliance with," the WPR. The degree to which presidents have "consulted" with Congress has varied considerably, depending largely on the political and tactical circumstances of the military operation. In 1975, President Ford unilaterally ordered troops to rescue the *Mayaguez*, a U.S. merchant ship seized in international waters by Cambodia's Khmer Rouge government. In 1980, without consulting Congress, President Carter launched a military operation to rescue the American hostages seized by the Iranian government of Ayatollah Khomeini, but the operation ended in failure after several helicopters were disabled. In 1982, President Reagan sent troops to Lebanon to help maintain a semblance of order in the midst of fighting between various Lebanese factions, the PLO, Syria, and Israel. In 1983, Reagan ordered the invasion of Grenada after a communist takeover of that country purportedly endangered the welfare of hundreds of American students attending medical school on the island. In 1986, in response to the bombing of a discotheque in West Berlin that killed two American servicemen, Reagan directed air strikes against Libya, including specific strikes against Colonel Muammar Gaddafi's residential compound, one of which killed Hanna Gaddafi, the baby daughter of the Libyan leader. In 1989, President George H. W. Bush committed tens of thousands of troops to arrest Manual Noriega, the military dictator of Panama, on drug charges and to protect the American community living in that country.

In 1991, with prior congressional authorization, an international coalition under U.S. leadership expelled Saddam Hussein's Iraqi army from Kuwait. In 1992 Bush authorized the dispatch of troops to Somalia to provide humanitarian relief and to maintain the peace between various warlords, but President Bill Clinton pulled the troops out after two Black Hawk helicopters were shot down over Mogadishu and eighteen U.S. soldiers were killed. In 1993 Clinton launched cruise missiles against Iraq in response to an Iraqi assassination attempt on the life of former president George H. W. Bush. That same year Clinton authorized the U.S. military to cooperate with a NATO air campaign against the Bosnian Serb Army, which was attacking UN-designated "safe areas" in Bosnia and Herzegovina. In 1998, Clinton launched cruise missile strikes against al-Qaeda bases in Afghanistan and a pharmaceutical factory in Sudan in response to the bombings of the American embassies in Kenya and Tanzania. In 1999, Clinton ordered U.S. military forces to cooperate with NATO-led air strikes against Yugoslavia to end ethnic cleansing and force the Serbian forces to withdraw from Kosovo.

It is, of course, difficult to apply the WPR to these military operations that are so different from one another in terms of congressional approval, size of the operation, risk to American ground forces, and possible threat to American lives. Obviously, the military operation becomes more legally controversial from a domestic law perspective to the degree that the president refuses to consult with Congress, that the size of the operation constitutes a significant U.S. commitment of military forces, that a large number of U.S. ground forces are deployed where hostilities are ongoing or imminent, and that the lives of no U.S. citizens are threatened. But U.S. domestic law is not the only body of law relevant to assessing the legality of U.S. military operations. The standards of contemporary international law require that these military operations either have the approval of the UN Security Council or are necessary for the national defense of the United States or its allies (collective self-defense). For example, the UN Security Council approved Reagan's deployment of U.S. troops to Lebanon in 1982, the 1991 Gulf War to expel Iraq from Kuwait, the 1992 peacekeeping and humanitarian mission in Somalia, and the 1993 NATO mission in Bosnia and Herzegovina.

Military operations that were not sanctioned by the Security Council were consistent with international law only if they were legitimately justified on grounds of national or collective self-defense. In light of decisions by the UN's International Court of Justice (ICJ), the right of self-defense could be lawfully invoked only if (1) there was an "armed attack" against the United States or against an ally who requested assistance from the United States; and (2) the military operation was "necessary" and "proportionate" to the nature of the initial attack.[15] In other words, even if a military operation was in response to an "armed attack" on the United States, it would be lawful only if there was no other nonmilitary alternative that would have remedied the dispute and only if the military response was not disproportionate to the injury suffered by the United States or its ally.

The ICJ elaborated on these principles in *Oil Platforms*, a 2003 case involving the Islamic Republic of Iran suing the United States because, during the last year of the Iran-Iraq war, the U.S. Navy launched armed attacks against Iranian oil platforms in the Persian Gulf on October 19, 1987, and April 18, 1988. Iran argued that the attacks were "fundamental breaches" of a 1955 treaty and violated customary international law. In response, the United States claimed it did not violate the 1955 treaty because it was acting in self-defense in both attacks: in the first instance, the United States claimed it was responding to an Iranian missile strike against *Sea Isle City*, a Kuwaiti tanker sailing under a U.S. flag; in the second instance, it claimed it was reacting to a mine explosion that severely damaged an American frigate, the USS *Samuel B. Roberts*, while it was in international waters near Bahrain. The United States filed a counterclaim at the ICJ, arguing that Iran was in breach of its obligations under the 1955 treaty because it was responsible for more than two hundred attacks against neutral shipping in the Persian Gulf during the Iraq-Iran war.

In regard to Iran's claim, the ICJ held that the United States breached the 1955 treaty only if its actions did not meet the standards of self-defense under customary international law. Turning to this latter question, the court found a number of problems with the United States' claim of self-defense. First, the United States had failed to prove that Iran was responsible for the missile strike on the *Sea Isle City* or the damage done to the USS *Samuel B. Roberts*. Second, the ICJ held that, even if Iran was responsible for the two "incidents," they did not qualify as an "armed attack" that would justify self-defense. Last, even if the two "incidents" did qualify as an "armed attack," the U.S. attacks on the oil platforms were neither "necessary" nor "proportionate."

2.6 *Oil Platforms (Iran v. United States)*, 2003 I.C.J. 161 (November 6)

51. . . . [I]n order to establish that it was legally justified in attacking the Iranian platforms in exercise of the right of individual self-defense, the United States has to show that attacks had been made upon it for which Iran was responsible; and that those

attacks were of such a nature as to be qualified as "armed attacks" within the meaning of that expression in Article 51 of the United Nations Charter, and as understood in customary law on the use of force. As the Court observed in the case concerning Military and Paramilitary Activities in and against Nicaragua [see **reading 7.5**], it is necessary to distinguish "the most grave forms of the use of force (those constituting an armed attack) from other less grave forms," since "In the case of individual self-defense, the exercise of this right is subject to the State concerned having been the victim of an armed attack." The United States must also show that its actions were necessary and proportional to the armed attack made on it, and that the platforms were a legitimate military target open to attack in the exercise of self-defense. . . .

61. . . . [T]he Court has examined with great care the evidence and arguments presented on each side, and finds that the evidence indicative of Iranian responsibility for the attack on the *Sea Isle City* is not sufficient to support the contentions of the United States. The conclusion to which the Court has come on this aspect of the case is thus that the burden of proof of the existence of an armed attack by Iran on the United States, in the form of the missile attack on the *Sea Isle City*, has not been discharged. . . .

71. As in the case of the attack on the *Sea Isle City*, the first question is whether the United States has discharged the burden of proof that the USS *Samuel B. Roberts* was the victim of a mine laid by Iran. . . . The main evidence that the mine struck by the USS *Samuel B. Roberts* was laid by Iran was the discovery of moored mines in the same area, bearing serial numbers matching other Iranian mines, in particular those found aboard the vessel *Iran Air*. This evidence is highly suggestive, but not conclusive. . . .

72. The Court notes further that, as on the occasion of the earlier attack on oil platforms, the United States in its communication to the Security Council, claimed to have been exercising the right of self-defense in response to the "attack" on the USS *Samuel B. Roberts*. . . . The question is therefore whether that incident sufficed in itself to justify action in self-defense, as amounting to an "armed attack." The Court does not exclude the possibility that the mining of a single military vessel might be sufficient to bring into play the "inherent right of self defense," but in view of all the circumstances, including the inconclusiveness of the evidence of Iran's responsibility for the mining of the USS *Samuel B. Roberts*, the Court is unable to hold that the attacks on the Salman and Nasr platforms have been shown to have been justifiably made in response to an "armed attack" on the United States by Iran, in the form of the mining of the USS *Samuel B. Roberts*.

73. . . . [I]n the present case a question of whether certain action is "necessary" arises both as an element of international law relating to self-defense and on the basis of the actual terms . . . of the 1955 Treaty. . . . [T]he United States claims that it considered in good faith that the attacks on the platforms were necessary to protect its essential security interests, and suggests that "A measure of discretion should be afforded to a party's good faith application of measures to protect its essential security interests." Iran was prepared to recognize some of the interests referred to by the United States—the safety of United States vessels and crew, and the uninterrupted flow of maritime commerce in the Persian Gulf—as being reasonable security interests of the United States, but denied that the United States actions against the platforms could be regarded as "necessary" to protect those interests. The Court does not however have to decide whether the United States . . . is correct, since the requirement of international law that measures taken avowedly in self-defense must have been necessary for that purpose is strict and objective, leaving no room for any "measure of discretion." The Court will therefore turn to the criteria of necessity and proportionality in the context of international law on self-defense.

74. In its decision in the case concerning Military and Paramilitary Activities in and against

Nicaragua, the Court endorsed the shared view of the parties to that case that in customary law "whether the response to the [armed] attack is lawful depends on observance of the criteria of the necessity and the proportionality of the measures taken in self-defense. One aspect of these criteria is the nature of the target of the force used avowedly in self-defense. In its communications to the Security Council, in particular in that of 19 October 1987, the United States indicated the grounds on which it regarded the Iranian platforms as legitimate targets for an armed action in self-defense. In the present proceedings, the United States has continued to maintain that they were such, and has presented evidence directed to showing that the platforms collected and reported intelligence concerning passing vessels, acted as a military communication link coordinating Iranian naval forces and served as actual staging bases to launch helicopter and small boat attacks on neutral commercial shipping. . . . On the other hand, the forces that attacked the Salman and Nasr complexes were not able to board the platforms containing the control centers, and did not therefore seize any material (if indeed such existed) tending to show the use of those complexes for military purposes.

75. Iran recognizes the presence of limited military personnel and equipment on the Reshadat platforms, but insists that their purpose was exclusively defensive and justified by previous Iraqi attacks on its oil production facilities. Iran further challenges the evidence adduced by the United States in this regard. It alleges that documents found aboard the *Iran Air* and the Reshadat platforms are read out of their proper context, incorrectly translated and actually consistent with the platforms' purely defensive role; and that military expert analysis relied on by the United States is hypothetical and contradictory. . . .

76. The Court is not sufficiently convinced that the evidence available supports the contentions of the United States as to the significance of the military presence and activity on the Reshadat oil platforms; and it notes that no such evidence is offered in respect of the Salman and Nasr complexes. However, even accepting those contentions, for the purposes of discussion, the Court is unable to hold that the attacks made on the platforms could have been justified as acts of self-defense. . . . In the case both of the attack on the *Sea Isle City* and the mining of the USS *Samuel B. Roberts*, the Court is not satisfied that the attacks on the platforms were necessary to respond to these incidents. In this connection, the Court notes that there is no evidence that the United States complained to Iran of the military activities of the platforms, in the same way as it complained repeatedly of minelaying and attacks on neutral shipping, which does not suggest that the targeting of the platforms was seen as a necessary act. The Court would also observe that in the case of the attack of 19 October 1987, the United States forces attacked the R-4 platform as a "target of opportunity," not one previously identified as an appropriate military target.

77. As to the requirement of proportionality, the attack of 19 October 1987 might, had the Court found that it was necessary in response to the *Sea Isle City* incident as an armed attack committed by Iran, have been considered proportionate. In the case of the attacks of 18 April 1988, however, they were conceived and executed as part of a more extensive operation entitled "Operation Praying Mantis." The question of the lawfulness of other aspects of that operation is not before the Court, since it is solely the action against the Salman and Nasr complexes that is presented as a breach of the 1955 Treaty; but the Court cannot assess in isolation the proportionality of that action to the attack to which it was said to be a response; it cannot close its eyes to the scale of the whole operation, which involved, inter alia, the destruction of two Iranian frigates and a number of other naval vessels and aircraft. As a response to the mining, by an unidentified agency, of a single United States warship, which was severely damaged but not sunk, and without loss of life, neither "Operation Praying Mantis" as a whole, nor even that part of it that destroyed the Salman and Nasr platforms, can be regarded, in the circumstances of this case, as a proportionate use of force in self-defense. . . .

Questions

1. Why does the ICJ place the burden of proving that Iran was responsible for the two attacks on the United States? Should the victim of an attack always bear this burden?
2. What is the proper standard for assessing whether the burden of proof has been met? The ICJ says at one point that the evidence submitted by the United States "is highly suggestive, but not conclusive." Is this the right standard? What would constitute "conclusive" evidence of Iran's responsibility?
3. Do you agree with the ICJ that, even if Iran was responsible for the two incidents involving the *Sea Isle City* and the USS *Samuel B. Roberts*, neither "incident" qualified as an "armed attack" that would trigger the right of national self-defense under Article 51 of the UN Charter?
4. Was the ICJ correct in its view that the "necessity" required for a valid claim of self-defense under international law "is strict and objective, leaving no room for any 'measure of discretion'"? Can any military response meet the requirement of "necessity" if no discretion is permitted regarding the selection of the military target?
5. The United States claims that at least one of the oil platforms collected intelligence, served as a military communication facility, and functioned as a staging base for attacks on neutral shipping, while Iran responded that the military personnel and equipment on the platform was "exclusively defensive" in character. Which of these factors is relevant to whether the U.S. attack on the oil platforms was "necessary"?
6. The ICJ justifies its conclusion that the U.S. attacks were not "necessary" in part on the fact that the United States did not complain to Iran about their military activities on the oil platforms. Is this argument persuasive?
7. Regarding whether the U.S. attack on April 18 was "proportionate," the ICJ claims that it cannot "isolate" the attacks on the oil platforms from other contemporaneous U.S. military operations, even though the legality of these other U.S. military operations was "not before the Court." Do you agree with the ICJ? How would you criticize this reasoning?
8. Despite its claim that it could not "isolate" the April 18 attacks from other U.S. military operations, the ICJ concludes that the destruction of two oil platforms was not "proportionate" to the severe damage done to one single U.S. warship when there was no loss of life. Do you agree with the ICJ's assessment?

The ICJ's decision in *Oil Platforms* (2003) followed the reasoning of the court's earlier decisions in *Military and Paramilitary Activities in and against Nicaragua* (1986) (see **reading 7.5**) and *Legality of the Threat or Use of Nuclear Weapons* (1996), but it was an important decision because it sharpened the criteria of self-defense under international law. In summary, any presidential exertion of military power that was not sanctioned by the Security Council was legally justified by national self-defense only if there was an "armed attack" and only if the response was "necessary" and "proportionate." Of course, following the 9/11 attacks, the United States lawfully engaged in military action against al-Qaeda consistent with these standards of international law. There was an "armed attack" that clearly justified a "necessary" and "proportionate response" and the Security Council approved military action against those responsible for the attacks. Moreover, in terms of domestic law, Congress quickly enacted an Authorization for Use of Military Force (AUMF) that granted President George

W. Bush authority to use "all necessary and appropriate" force against individuals and groups "he determines" to be responsible for the attacks or who "harbored" such organizations or individuals. The 2001 AUMF was, and continues to be, a crucial statutory foundation of domestic law for U.S. military activities against radical Islamic groups.

2.7 Authorization for Use of Military Force (AUMF) (2001)

Whereas, on September 11, 2001, acts of treacherous violence were committed against the United States and its citizens[16] and

Whereas, such acts render it both necessary and appropriate that the United States exercise its rights to self-defense and to protect United States citizens both at home and abroad; and

Whereas, in light of the threat to the national security and foreign policy of the United States posed by these grave acts of violence; and

Whereas, such acts continue to pose an unusual and extraordinary threat to the national security and foreign policy of the United States; and

Whereas, the President has authority under the Constitution to take action to deter and prevent acts of international terrorism against the United States: Now, therefore, be it

Resolved by the Senate and House of Representatives of the United States of America in Congress assembled . . .

. . . That the president is authorized to use all necessary and appropriate force against those nations, organizations, or persons he determines planned, authorized, committed, or aided the terrorist attacks that occurred on September 11, 2001, or harbored such organizations or persons, in order to prevent any future acts of international terrorism against the United States by such nations, organizations, or persons. . . .

. . . [T]he Congress declares that this section is intended to constitute specific statutory authorization within the meaning of . . . the War Powers Resolution. . . .

Questions

1. Since the AUMF says it is appropriate for the United States to exercise its rights to self-defense and recognizes that the president has *constitutional* authority to both "deter" and "prevent" acts of international terrorism, does it imply that the president has the unilateral authority to use military force against any terrorist groups without congressional approval?
2. The AUMF says it is "necessary" to protect U.S. citizens "both at home and abroad." Is the president's constitutional duty to protect U.S. citizens abroad consistent with the requirement of international law that self-defense can be lawfully invoked only if there is an "armed attack"? Does the president's duty as commander in chief take precedence over any conflicting obligation of international law to refrain from a military response unless there is an "armed attack"?
3. How do you understand the phrase "necessary and appropriate force"? Is this a limitation on the president's AUMF-based authority to attack terrorist groups responsible for the 9/11 attacks or a recognition that the president has discretion to use any type of force consistent with the laws of war? What about types of force inconsistent with the laws of war?
4. Since the AUMF does not explicitly authorize the use of military force against groups or persons "associated" with "nations, organizations, or persons" responsible for the 9/11 attacks, can the president use force against such "associated" groups or

persons based on the fact that they have become co-belligerents in the conflict, or would Congress have to approve the extension of the authorization to these "associated" groups or persons?

5. If the president can act unilaterally against "associated" groups and persons, what kind of "association" must be established before military force could legally be used? Must the "association" be of a military character, such that the president cannot use military force against an "associated" group or person unless that group or person applies military force against U.S. personnel or American citizens first?
6. What if a group "associates" with al-Qaeda but the group's members are not all combatants? What if some of the members of the group are dedicated to humanitarian work or simply provide financial support for the group's military activities against the United States but do not take up arms themselves? Can the president target such noncombatants on the authority granted by the AUMF? Would it be consistent with the international law of co-belligerency?

A number of events have complicated the extent and nature of U.S. military activities in the Middle East/North Africa following the 9/11 attacks, at times raising the question whether the 2001 AUMF legally justifies such military operations. First, President George W. Bush's decision to invade Iraq in 2003 was a major development. Bush ordered the invasion with the approval of Congress and the Security Council on the ground that Saddam Hussein refused to destroy his weapons of mass destruction—weapons that were never found after the overthrow of Hussein's Sunni-based Baathist regime. In December 2005, elections were held under a new Iraqi Constitution that culminated in a Shia-dominated government that in turn fueled a growing Sunni insurgency. The invasion therefore produced a violent sectarian division internal to Iraq at the same time that it aggravated Sunni-Shia relations throughout the Middle East, in particular drawing Iran and Saudi Arabia into a regional power struggle. President Bush responded to these developments in 2007 with a 20,000-plus troop surge, but President Barack Obama withdrew combat troops from Iraq in 2011, though U.S. special forces continued to train and advise the Iraqi military, even to the point of accompanying Iraqi troops on specific military operations. Since these troops performed these functions at the request of the Iraqi government, there is little doubt they are in compliance with both domestic and international law.

While the United States was militarily involved in Iraq and Afghanistan, a new international principle slowly emerged: the "responsibility to protect," sometimes called R2P. This principle was a reaction to the atrocities that occurred during the Rwandan genocide of 1994 and the Balkan Wars of the 1990s. In response to the latter tragedy, NATO, along with the United States, launched a bombing campaign against Yugoslav armed forces to protect Kosovo Albanians from ethnic cleansing, war crimes, and crimes against humanity. Since NATO did not have the approval of the UN Security Council, the military operation's legality was doubtful, even though it was perceived by many to be morally "legitimate," if not "praiseworthy." The UN, therefore, took up the issue of when the international community could intervene in a state if it was "unwilling" or "unable" to fulfill its obligation to protect its own people. The end result was that the UN General Assembly adopted, on September 16, 2005, a resolution endorsing the "responsibility to protect," but it also affirmed that the Security Council had to approve any "use of force" undertaken by the international community in support of this principle.

2.8 2005 World Summit Outcome, para. 138–40

138. Each individual State has the responsibility to protect its populations from genocide, war crimes, ethnic cleansing and crimes against humanity.[17] This responsibility entails the prevention of such crimes, including their incitement, through appropriate and necessary means. We accept that responsibility and will act in accordance with it. The international community should, as appropriate, encourage and help States to exercise this responsibility and support the United Nations in establishing an early warning capability.

139. The international community, through the United Nations, also has the responsibility to use appropriate diplomatic, humanitarian and other peaceful means, in accordance with Chapters VI and VIII of the Charter, to help to protect populations from genocide, war crimes, ethnic cleansing and crimes against humanity. In this context, we are prepared to take collective action, in a timely and decisive manner, through the Security Council, in accordance with the Charter, including Chapter VII, on a case-by-case basis and in cooperation with relevant regional organizations as appropriate, should peaceful means be inadequate and national authorities are manifestly failing to protect their populations from genocide, war crimes, ethnic cleansing and crimes against humanity. We stress the need for the General Assembly to continue consideration of the responsibility to protect populations from genocide, war crimes, ethnic cleansing and crimes against humanity and its implications, bearing in mind the principles of the Charter and international law. We also intend to commit ourselves, as necessary and appropriate, to helping States build capacity to protect their populations from genocide, war crimes, ethnic cleansing and crimes against humanity and to assisting those which are under stress before crises and conflicts break out. . . .

Questions

1. In your view, is this type of resolution of the UN General Assembly "legally binding" or is it simply a "recommendation" to member states? Should it be "legally binding"? Would it make any difference if it were?
2. Is it likely that each member state, by this resolution, is recognizing its responsibility to protect its citizens from genocide, war crimes, ethnic cleansing, and crimes against humanity committed by other states (and perhaps by nonstate actors), but not any sort of responsibility of protecting its citizens from its own conduct, regardless if the conduct consists of atrocities? Is that a viable, coherent interpretation of the resolution?
3. Paragraph 139 of the resolution seems to contemplate a role for the "international community" to protect populations from atrocities "in a timely and decisive manner," but only if it acts through the Security Council. Is it possible for the "international community" to act "in a timely and decisive manner" if any of the five permanent members of the Security Council can veto any remedial measure, including the use of military force? What does history suggest regarding this question?
4. The resolution also states that any measure undertaken by the "international community" to protect vulnerable populations must be in accordance with the charter, but the charter permits the use of military force only if the Security Council has approved it or if it is undertaken in the exercise of a state's right of self-defense. Does this mean that Security Council approval is always required for any effort to

protect vulnerable populations from the atrocities identified in the resolution, or could an individual state claim that such atrocities trigger its right to self-defense because they pose an imminent danger and threat to international peace?

5. The resolution permits the "international community" to use force through the Security Council, but only if a national authority is "manifestly failing" to protect its population from genocide, war crimes, ethnic cleansing, and crimes against humanity. How would you interpret the phrase "manifestly failing"? Is the bar set too high or too low? If a state is killing a segment of its own population, would that be a clear case of a "manifest failure" to protect?
6. Article 2.1 of the charter recognizes the principle of "the sovereign equality of all its Members" (see **reading 2.4**). If any action undertaken by the 'international community" to protect a vulnerable population must be in conformity with the principle of the "sovereign equality" of each member state, then how could any such remedial action ever be undertaken? Would not the use of military force to protect a population from the actions of its own government necessarily be an intrusion upon that state's "equal sovereignty"?

By the time the UN General Assembly endorsed the "responsibility to protect," a significant number of terrorist groups around the world, but particularly in the Middle East and North Africa, had "associated" themselves with al-Qaeda. In response to this development, the U.S. military and the CIA began to target alleged terrorists in various countries. The Congressional Research Service (CRS) reported in 2013 that the Bush and Obama administrations had invoked the 2001 AUMF thirty times to justify the use of U.S. military forces in the Philippines, Georgia, Yemen (al-Qaeda in the Arabian Peninsula [AQAP]), Djibouti, Kenya, Ethiopia, Eritrea, Iraq, and Somalia (al-Shabab). The purpose of these military operations was, according to the CRS, to fight terrorists "around the world" and "on the high seas."[18] With this geographical extension of the 2001 AUMF, the U.S. conflict with terrorist groups "associated" with al-Qaeda has become global in scope. Although it is not at all clear that Congress intended the 2001 AUMF to have this geographical reach, it never clarified the situation by enacting a broader authorization. Both the Bush and Obama administrations simply "shoehorned" new terrorist groups into the 2001 authorization as the need arose.

The 2010 revolutionary wave of protests, riots, and civil wars that swept the Arab world—often referred to as the Arab Spring or the Arab Awakening—is another factor that has affected U.S. military policy in the Middle East/North Africa region. Responding to Muammar Gaddafi's brutal treatment of his own people during Libya's 2011 civil war, President Barack Obama, without congressional approval, ordered U.S. military forces to cooperate with a NATO-led air campaign against the Gaddafi regime. To justify his actions, Obama chiefly relied on a Security Council resolution that imposed a no-fly zone on Libya and demanded an immediate cease-fire and "a complete end to violence and all attacks against, and abuses of, civilians."[19] It is debatable whether the NATO-led air campaign went beyond the Security Council's mandate since it contributed to the destruction of the Gaddafi regime and the death of its leader. Vladimir Putin, then prime minister of Russia, certainly thought that it did, claiming that the NATO operation was nothing less than a "crusade," one that clearly violated Libya's sovereignty.[20]

And even if the NATO campaign did not exceed the parameters of the Security Council's resolution, could Obama rely on his Article II powers to legally justify U.S. involvement in terms of domestic law? It might seem plausible that the president has a duty to enforce Security Council resolutions on the grounds that the UN Charter is a treaty ratified by the Senate and therefore is, under Article VI of the Constitution, "the supreme Law of the Land." But an equally defensible position is that the president's executive power and duty to enforce valid treaties only extends to the limits of his or her constitutional and statutory powers. In other words, if a military operation (such as the attacks on the Gaddafi regime) required congressional authorization according to domestic law, then a president can enforce a treaty that authorizes such an operation, but only up to the limits of the Article II power. If the president's Article II war powers are only "defensive" in character, then a treaty cannot "expand" this power beyond that limit and the president would need an authorization from Congress before the military operation could be lawfully initiated. Which of these approaches to presidential Article II war powers is more persuasive?

A civil war in Syria also broke out in 2011. It pitted various oppositional Sunni groups supported by Saudi Arabia and its allies against the Shia-based government of Bashar al-Assad, which was backed in turn by Iran, the Shia community of Iraq, Hezbollah, and Russia. Through the CIA, the United States provided military aid to the Free Syrian Army, a so-called moderate opposition group, but little progress was made in bringing down the Assad government. Instead the chaos of the war enabled a radical Sunni-based terrorist group, commonly known as the Islamic State of Iraq and Syria (ISIS) or the Islamic State of Iraq and the Levant (ISIL) to take over a broad swath of Iraqi and Syrian territory. ISIS had evolved from a 2006 merger of several Sunni-based insurgent groups fighting Iraq's Shia government into the organization known as al-Qaeda in Iraq (AQI). However, because of ISIS's indiscriminate brutality, including beheadings, killings, and floggings of Muslims, Ayman al-Zawahiri, Osama bin Laden's former associate and current titular leader of al-Qaeda, publicly disowned ISIS and cut all ties with the organization in February 2014. Despite the rupture, ISIS declared the establishment of a caliphate in June 2014. At the time, the CIA estimated that ISIS had approximately thirty thousand fighters.

In reaction to the rise of ISIS, the Obama administration and a number of international partners, such as Saudi Arabia and Bahrain, launched air strikes in Syria and Iraq against ISIS and other radical Islamic terrorist groups. The Obama administration took this action even though neither Congress nor the Security Council expressly authorized the action and even though Syria had not consented to the use of U.S. military forces on its sovereign territory. As of August 2017, the United States and coalition partners have conducted 24,566 air strikes, 11,235 of which were conducted in Syria and 13,331 in Iraq. These strikes, along with complementary ground action by local U.S. allied groups, have taken a heavy toll on ISIS, both in Syria and Iraq, forcing the group to abandon a great deal of territory by the end of 2017, including its capital, Raqqa, Syria, and important

Iraqi cities, such as Fallujah, Mosul, and Tikrit. Despite ISIS's loss of status, from a caliphate to a loosely organized insurgency, U.S. air strikes continue, with six engagements from March 16 to March 22, 2018.[21]

Meanwhile, as ISIS has retreated into isolated pockets of resistance, Assad's government, with Russian assistance, has regained a considerable amount of territory from the rebels. Moreover, Turkey's military entered northern Syria in January 2018 to attack the YPG, the armed wing of the Kurdish-led Democratic Union Party (PYD) of Syria, a party Turkey believes to be indistinguishable from the Kurdistan Workers' Party (PKK), a designated terrorist organization. Turkey has been in a state of armed conflict with the PKK since the 1980s because its ultimate goal is an independent Kurdish state, one that likely would to some extent be carved out of Turkey's sovereign territory. In short, the military situation in Syria is as confused as ever, as is U.S. strategy in the region, but the threat posed by ISIS has been considerably alleviated, at least at this point in time

The U.S. military actions in Syria of the Obama and Trump administrations pose difficult legal questions. In terms of international law, there is the argument that the United States can legally attack a nonstate terrorist group, such as ISIS, if the group "threatens" American lives or the lives of U.S. allies and if the government of the country in which it operates is either "unable or unwilling" to prevent the group from committing terrorist acts. This argument is very controversial since it clearly expands the right of individual and collective self-defense beyond what the ICJ recognized in *Oil Platforms* (see **reading 2.6**). In what sense could the ISIS "threats" to American lives qualify as an "armed attack" or as an "imminent" threat thereof? In what sense are U.S. air attacks and "kill or capture" missions "necessary" or "proportionate" to ISIS "threats" to American lives? Are ISIS attacks on Iraqis in Iraq a sufficient justification for the United States to attack ISIS groups in Syria? Of course, these questions become even more difficult to the degree that ISIS's military capabilities have been degraded over time, especially in light of the fact—which bears repeating—that the Assad government has not consented to any U.S. military presence in Syria.

In terms of domestic law, the president arguably, as commander in chief, might have the authority to strike at ISIS since this terrorist group has beheaded Americans and inspired attacks here in the United States, such as the attack in San Bernardino in December 2015. However, it is unclear whether such incidents, as tragic as they are, can legally justify a multi-year air campaign across a large area of Syria. Obviously, such an extensive military operation will inevitably produce a significant number of civilian casualties. Perhaps because of the weakness of this constitutional argument, a senior Obama administration official in 2014 pointed to the 2001 AUMF as the legal basis for Obama's military activities in Syria, despite the fact that ISIL did not even exist when this authorization was passed by Congress. The unnamed official argued that

> based on ISIL's longstanding relationship with al-Qa'ida (AQ) and Usama bin Laden; its long history of conducting, and continued desire to conduct, attacks against U.S. persons and interests, the extensive history of U.S. combat opera-

> tions against ISIL dating back to the time the group first affiliated with AQ in 2004; and ISIL's position—supported by some individual members and factions of AQ-aligned groups—that it is the true inheritor of Usama bin Laden's legacy, the President may rely on the 2001 AUMF as statutory authority for the use of force against ISIS, notwithstanding the recent public split between AQ's senior leadership and ISIL.[22]

This interpretation of the scope of the 2001 AUMF gives the president a broad statutory basis to conduct military operations against terrorist groups in the twenty-first century. As discussed above, the 2001 AUMF had earlier been stretched geographically to cover military actions around the world, including in the Philippines and Georgia. This unnamed official's interpretation is arguably stretching the 2001 AUMF in a temporal fashion, authorizing the president to conduct military activities in the future against terrorist groups that have a minimal connection to those who were actually responsible for the 9/11 attacks. An important question is whether the 2001 AUMF does in fact provide the legal authority for what could be called a new form of "light-footprint warfare," a form of warfare that is indefinite in duration and conducted largely in secret at the discretion of the president without risk of substantial U.S. casualties.[23] Does this new type of warfare pose dangers to our constitutional system, to the principle of democratic accountability, and to the norms of international law governing the right to wage war? Congress has declined to clarify the legal situation by enacting a more precise AUMF. Should it do so? Does it have a constitutional responsibility to do so? Is it possible that a new AUMF would make matters worse? Why?

In May 2016, Captain Nathan Michael Smith, a twenty-eight-year-old military officer, sued Obama, claiming that he did not have the authority to wage war against ISIS under the 2001 AUMF. Citing his obligation to uphold the Constitution, Smith argued that Congress had not authorized the armed conflict against ISIS and that Obama had no Article II authority to constitutionally justify it. In Smith's view, even though the fight against ISIS was a "good war," the 2001 AUMF could not be applied to an organization that did not exist in 2001 and that operated far from Afghanistan. But Congress in 2016 did pass military appropriations bills that explicitly provided funds for military operations against ISIS, raising the question whether providing funds for the conflict constituted an authorization.[24] Meanwhile, a federal district court ruled that Smith could not bring his lawsuit because he lacked "standing" to sue and because Congress and the president, not courts, should resolve disputes about war powers.[25] As President Trump took office in 2017, the case—now *Smith v. Trump*—went up on appeal to the D.C. Circuit Court of Appeals, which heard oral argument on October 27, 2017. Despite the apparent conflict between Smith's statutory duty to obey the commands of his superiors and his officer's oath to preserve and defend the Constitution, it is not clear whether the D.C. Circuit will grant him "standing" to bring his lawsuit or that it will not rule that the issue of whether Trump can lawfully use military force in Syria is a "political question."[26] Lastly, Trump's announcement on March 30, 2018, that U.S. military forces would be out of Syria "very soon" raises the additional question whether the D.C. Circuit will "moot" Smith's case.[27]

On April 6, 2017, in response to the Assad regime's use of chemical weapons against Syrian civilians, President Trump ordered 59 cruise-missile strikes against a Syrian air base. He did so without seeking permission from the Security Council of the UN or asserting a self-defense justification, one of which was required by the UN Charter for the strikes to be in accordance with international law. Whatever its legality, the attack had little impact because Assad continued to use chemical weapons against his own people during the rest of 2017 and early 2018.[28] Finally, on April 7, 2018, another chemical attack (involving chlorine gas and possibly a sarin nerve agent) took place in Douma, Syria, reportedly killing at least 70 people and injuring hundreds more. Although the Assad government denied responsibility, the Trump administration, in cooperation with Great Britain and France, launched over 100 missile attacks against three chemical weapons storage and research facilities near Damascus and Homs. Defense Department officials claimed the strikes had taken out the "heart" of the Assad regime's chemical weapons program but, at the same time, conceded that the regime likely retained a residual capacity to use chemical agents.[29] Only time will tell whether the April 2018 attack will be any more effective than 2017's.

Whether effective or not, the 2017 and 2018 attacks on Syria were likely in violation of international law. No clear-cut U.S. claim could be made that the attacks were justified on the basis of self-defense, and the UN Security Council never authorized either attack. It is true that Syria's use of chemical weapons did violate the Chemical Weapons Convention, which Syria had joined in 2013, the same year it agreed to an international plan to destroy its stockpile of chemical weapons. UN Security Resolution 2118 not only sanctioned this plan but also "determined" that Syria's use of chemical weapons was "a threat to international peace and security" and "decided" to "impose measures under Chapter VII of the United Nations Charter" if Syria did not comply with the agreement.[30] However, it is doubtful whether this resolution justified the Trump administration's attacks on Syria because a decision to "impose" measures in the future, based on a contingency of Syrian noncompliance, is not itself an "authorization" of the use of military force. After all, the Security Council could have decided to "impose" nonmilitary measures, such as economic sanctions, in the event that Syria did not comply with its agreement not to use chemical weapons. It is therefore very difficult, if not impossible, to argue that Resolution 2118 authorized Trump's strikes against Syria.

Another alternative is to claim that Resolution 2118's identification of Syria's use of chemical weapons as a "threat to international peace and security" is itself an implicit recognition that the right of self-defense is not completely irrelevant to whether the missile attacks on Syria were lawful. However, what is curious is that the Trump administration did little to address the issue of whether the attacks were justifiable based on international law, whether in terms of an implicit UN Security Council resolution or in terms of self-defense. Instead, Trump focused on the humanitarian purpose of the attack: regarding the 2017 attack, he said, "When you kill innocent children, innocent babies, babies, little babies, with a chemical gas that is so lethal . . . [that] crosses many, many lines, beyond a red line, many, many lines."[31] In regard to the 2018 strike, he added, "The evil and the despicable attack left mothers and fathers, infants and children, thrashing in pain and gasping for air. These are not the actions of a man; they are crimes of a monster instead."[32] Such remarks implicitly reinforced a version of the emerging "responsibility to protect" principle of customary international law, a version that would legitimate the use of military force without the UN Security Council in egregious circumstances. Although the majority of nations do not formally accept this humanitarian exception to the UN Charter's restrictions on the use of military force, the principle does seem to be gaining ground, at least in the human rights community. In the end, perhaps Trump's missile attacks on Syria, like NATO's attacks on Kosovo in 1999, will be perceived not only as technical violations of international law but also as morally and politically legitimate, if not praiseworthy.

A completely separate question, of course, is whether Trump's 2017 and 2018 missile attacks on Syria are consistent with U.S. domestic law. In a March 2018 "transparency" report, the Trump administration referred to the 2017 missile attacks as follows:

> For example, on April 6, 2017, the President directed a military strike against the Shayrat military airfield in Syria pursuant to his authority under Article II of the Constitution to conduct foreign relations and as Commander in Chief and Chief Executive. United States intelligence indicated that Syrian military forces operating from that airfield were responsible for the chemical weapons attack on Syrian civilians in southern Idlib Province, Syria. The President directed this strike in order to degrade the Syrian military's ability to conduct further chemical weapons attacks and to dissuade the Syrian government from using or proliferating chemical weapons, thereby promoting regional stability and averting a worsening of the region's current humanitarian catastrophe. In directing this strike, the President acted in the vital national security and foreign policy interest of the United States.[33]

The tenor of the language suggests that it is the current administration's view that Trump can use military force to promote "regional stability" around the world, to avert or ameliorate "humanitarian catastrophes," and to protect "the vital national security and foreign policy interest of the United States." Following the 2018 attacks, Secretary of Defense James Mattis argued that, as commander in chief, "the president has the authority under Article II of the Constitution to use military force overseas to defend important United States national interests" and that the "United States has vital national interest in averting a worsening catastrophe in Syria, and specifically deterring the use and proliferation of chemical weapons."[34] Obviously, these claims of presidential Article II war powers are in tension with the assumptions and language of the War Powers Resolution (see **reading 2.5**) and converts the traditional "defensive" understanding of presidential war powers (see **reading 2.3**) into a legal basis for what could arguably be called "offensive" military operations. Despite these legal controversies, the vast majority of Republicans in Congress applauded Trump's Syrian attacks, while some Democrats expressed concern that Trump acted without congressional approval but did not criticize the attacks themselves.[35]

Trump's approach to presidential war power under Article II is important for many reasons, but especially because North Korea is near or at the threshold of developing nuclear intercontinental ballistic missiles that could hit cities in the United States. In response to this emerging threat, Trump in September 2017 warned Kim Jong-un, the Supreme Leader of North Korea, that "fire and fury like the world has never seen" would rain down on his country if it continued to threaten the United States.[36] Trump doubled down in a speech at the UN by claiming that the United States would "totally destroy North Korea" to defend itself or its allies and mocking Kim as a "Rocket Man" on a "suicide mission for himself." Kim responded in kind, calling Trump a "mentally deranged U.S. dotard."[37]

As the crisis escalated in late 2017, diplomatic solutions receded into the background, leaving two apparent options on the table: a conventional attack against North Korea's missile sites (the so-called bloody nose option) or a preemptive nuclear strike. In terms of international law, both options required either authorization by the UN Security Council, which is extremely unlikely because either China or Russia would veto any such authorization, or a credible claim of self-defense, which would be very difficult to substantiate unless the United States could convincingly show that North Korea was planning an "imminent" attack on the territorial United States, its possessions (such as Guam), or military bases located in South Korea or Japan. North Korea's possession of intercontinental missiles with nuclear warheads would presumably not be enough to justify a U.S. armed response, if only because a number of U.S. adversaries have such weapons, including China and Russia, and that fact alone has never been considered a sufficient basis for an armed attack on them.

In terms of domestic law, unless the language of the "transparency" report discussed earlier gains acceptance among members of Congress, executive officials, and military leaders, it is doubtful whether Trump could lawfully initiate either a conventional war or a preemptive nuclear attack without congressional authorization unless there was sufficient evidence to trigger the president's Article II power and duty to defend the country and its citizens from an actual imminent North Korean attack. However, the situation was worrisome in late 2017 because President Trump gave no indication that he would consult with Congress or abide by its decisions regarding how to respond to North Korea's provocative actions when he repeatedly asserted that the "era of strategic patience" in dealing with North Korea was "over."[38]

Fortunately, the drumbeat for war began to recede in 2018. The easing of tensions began in February 2018 when North Korea agreed to participate in the 2018 Winter Olympics, which were held in PyeongChang, South Korea. South Korean president Moon Jae-in, reaching out to the North Korean delegation, advocated dialogue between North Korea and the United States. Following the Olympics, North and South Korea met in Pyongyang, the capital of North Korea, to discuss ways to improve relations and maintain peace on the peninsula.[39] A South Korean delegation to the United States then relayed to President

Trump a suggestion from Kim that they should meet to discuss denuclearization of the Korean peninsula. With the understanding that North Korea would suspend all missile tests, Trump agreed to the meeting, tweeting, "Now there is a good chance that Kim Jong Un will do what is right for his people and for humanity."[40] However, in late March 2018 Trump appointed John Bolton, a conservative nationalist and former U.S. ambassador to the United Nations, to be his new national security advisor. Bolton, who has remarked that North Koreans are lying whenever their "lips are moving," has argued for a first strike, claiming that it would be "perfectly legitimate" as an act of "self-defense."[41]

Whether the Trump-Kim meeting (now scheduled for some time in May 2018) will occur and what its outcome will be are, at the time of this writing, very uncertain. Kim might very well be stalling for time, giving his nuclear program the opportunity to increase plutonium production, improve rockets and launchers, and develop a reentry vehicle that would not burn up when it reentered the atmosphere. If the meeting is cancelled or ends in failure, an embarrassed Trump will be back to square one, with Bolton by his side. What he will do at that point is anyone's guess. However, even if the threat of a U.S. attack against North Korea subsides, the underlying domestic legal question remains: Can the president, without congressional authorization, rely on his Article II powers to justify either a conventional or preemptive nuclear attack on a regime like North Korea, one that is close to developing nuclear intercontinental ballistic missiles that can hit U.S. cities and one whose leaders are often provocative, bellicose, and prone to taking risks? Can the president do so if he or she thinks the attack is "in the vital national security and foreign policy interest of the United States"? If the president has such powers, can Congress limit them in any way? Should it? What restrictions does international law impose on the use of such military force? Would these restrictions have an important impact?

NOTES

1. Thomas Aquinas, *Summa Theologica: War (Secunda Secundae Partis, Q. 40)*, https://dhspriory.org/thomas/summa/SS/SS040.html#SSQ40OUTP1.

2. Hugo Grotius, *The Rights of War and Peace* (M. Walter Dunne, 1901), 2:75.

3. See Emer de Vattel, *The Law of Nations* (1758); and Jean-Jacques Burlamaqui, *The Principles of Natural and Politic Law* (1748).

4. See James Madison's notes of the convention, included in *The Records of the Federal Convention of 1787*, ed. Max Farrand (New Haven, CT: Yale University Press, 1911), 2:318–19.

5. *Bas v. Tingy*, 4 U.S. 37 (1800).

6. League of Nations, "Covenant of the League of Nations," April 28, 1919, UNHCR refworld, http://www.refworld.org.

7. "Kellogg-Briand Pact 1928," Yale Law School, Lillian Goldman Law Library, http://avalon.law.yale.edu.

8. Since World War II, the Security Council has sponsored peacekeeping and humanitarian missions, but these missions are not considered military actions approved under Chapter VII of the UN Charter, even if military forces are involved in the operation. For example, a UN peacekeeping force is authorized only if all the main parties of the conflict consent to the presence of the peacekeeping force, if the peacekeeping force can maintain "impartiality" between

the parties, and if force is used only as a last resort, usually in self-defense or the defense of innocent civilians not involved with the conflict. Since 1948, the UN Security Council has authorized more than seventy such peacekeeping and humanitarian missions. See "60 Years of United Nations Peacekeeping," UN Information Service (UNIS), http://www.unis.unvienna.org; and United Nations, "United Nations Peacekeeping Operations: Principles and Guidelines," 2008, https://www.un.org.

9. Security Council Resolution 83 (1950), United Nations, http://www.un.org.

10. Curtis A. Bradley and Jack L. Goldsmith, *Foreign Relations Law*, 5th ed. (New York: Wolters Kluwer, 2014), 615, quoting from Joint Comm. of the Comms. on Foreign Relations and on Armed Services, 82 Cong., 1st Sess., Powers of the President to Send the Armed Forces Outside the United States 20 (1951).

11. Pub. L. No. 88-408, 78 Stat. 384 (1964).

12. See *DaCosta v. Laird*, 448 F.2d 1368 (2d Cir. 1971).

13. The War Powers Resolution, Pub. L. No. 93-148 (November 7, 1973), 50 U.S.C. 33, https://www.law.cornell.edu.

14. *INS v. Chadha*, 462 U.S. 919 (1983).

15. See *Military and Paramilitary Activities in and against Nicaragua (Nicaragua v. United States)*, 1986 I.C.J. 14 (June 27) (see **reading 7.5**); and *Legality of the Threat or Use of Nuclear Weapons*, Advisory Opinion, 1996 I.C.J. 226 (July 8).

16. "S.J.Res.23: Authorization for Use of Military Force," Congress.gov, 2001–2002, https://www.congress.gov.

17. UN General Assembly, Resolution 60/1. 2005 World Summit Outcome, September 16, 2005, A/RES/60/1.

18. Matthew Weed, congressional research analyst in Foreign Policy Legislation, memorandum to Barbara Lee, "The 2001 Authorization for Use of Military Force: A Background in Brief," July 10, 2013, Federation of American Scientists, https://fas.org.

19. Security Council, Resolution 1973, March 17, 2011, United Nations, http://www.un.org.

20. Ellen Barry, "Putin Criticizes West for Libyan Incursion," *New York Times*, April 26, 2011, https://www.nytimes.com/2011/04/27/world/europe/27putin.html.

21. U.S. Department of Defense, "Airstrike Updates: Details" and "Inherent Resolve Officials Report Details of Latest Strikes against ISIS in Syria, Iraq," http://www.defense.gov.

22. Quoted in Spencer Ackerman, "Obama's Legal Rationale for Isis Strikes: Shoot First, Ask Congress Later," *Guardian*, September 10, 2014, https://www.theguardian.com.

23. See Jack Goldsmith and Matthew Waxman, "The Legal Legacy of Light-Footprint Warfare," *Washington Quarterly* 39 (Summer 2016): 7–21.

24. Charlie Savage, "An Army Captain Takes Obama to Court over ISIS Fight," *New York Times*, May 4, 2016, https://www.nytimes.com.

25. *Smith v. Obama*, 217 F. Supp. 3d 283 (DCDC 2016).

26. See Bruce Ackerman, "Smith v. Trump in the D.C. Circuit: A Guided Tour of the Oral Argument," *Lawfare* (blog), November 1, 2017, https://lawfareblog.com.

27. Steve Holland, "Trump Tells Advisers He Wants U.S. out of Syria," Reuters, March 30, 2018, https://www.reuters.com/article/us-usa-trump-syria/trump-tells-advisers-he-wants-u-s-out-of-syria-senior-officials-idUSKBN1H61J0.

28. See White House Statement, "United States Assessment of the Assad Regime's Chemical Weapons Use," April 13, 2018, https://www.defense.gov/portals/1/features/2018/0418_syria/img/United-States-Assessment-of-the-Assad-Regime%E2%80%99s-Chemical-Weapons-Use.pdf.

29. Helene Cooper and Ben Hubbard, "Pentagon Says Syria Strikes Hit 'Heart' of Chemical Weapons Program," *New York Times*, April 13, 2018, https://www.nytimes.com/2018/04/14/world/middleeast/syria-airstrikes-analysis.html.

30. Un Security Council Resolution 2118, S/RES/2118 (2013), September 27, 2013, http://unscr.com/en/resolutions/doc/2118.

31. Julian Berger, David Smith, and Jennifer Rankin, "Syria Chemical Attack Has Changed My View of Assad, Says Trump," *Guardian*, April 6, 2017, https://www.theguardian.com/us-news/2017/apr/05/syria-chemical-gas-attack-donald-trump-nikki-haley-assad.

32. "Statement by President Trump on Syria," *Lawfare* (blog), April 13, 2018, https://www.lawfareblog.com/transcript-president-trumps-remarks-syria-airstrikes.

33. "Report on the Legal and Policy Frameworks Guiding the United States' Use of Military Force and Related National Security Operations," (undated), transmitted to Congress on March 12, 2018, available at https://lawfareblog.com/document-white-house-legal-and-policy-frameworks-use-military-force. The language of this report seems to track the claims made in an opinion issued by the Office of Legal Counsel in October 2002, a year after the 9/11 attacks. See Memorandum Opinion for the Counsel to the President, "Authority of the President under Domestic and International Law to Use Military Force Against Iraq," October 23, 2002, 150–52, https://www.justice.gov/sites/default/files/olc/opinions/2002/10/31/op-olc-v026-p0143_0.pdf.

34. "Briefing by Secretary Mattis on U.S. Strikes in Syria," April 13, 2018, https://www.defense.gov/News/Transcripts/Transcript-View/Article/1493658/briefing-by-secretary-mattis-on-us-strikes-in-syria/.

35. Stephanie Ebbs and Ali Rogin, "Members of Congress React to US Strike on Syria," ABC News, April 13, 2018, http://abcnews.go.com/International/members-congress-react-us-strike-syria/story?id=54459343.

36. Julian Borger, "North Korea's Latest Nuclear Test Reflects Failure of Trump's Bellicose Rhetoric," *Guardian*, September 3, 2017, https://www.theguardian.com.

37. Austin Ramzy, "Kim Jong-un Called Trump a 'Dotard.' What Does That Even Mean?" *New York Times*, September 22, 2017, https://www.nytimes.com/2017/09/22/world/asia/trump-north-korea-dotard.html.

38. Kevin Liptak and Jeremy Diamond, "Trump Says 'Era of Strategic Patience Is Over' for North Korea," CNN, November 6, 2017, http://www.cnn.com.

39. Joshua Berlinger and Sophie Jeong, "Kim Jong Un Wants to 'Write New History' on South Korea Reunification," CNN, March 7, 2018, https://www.cnn.com/2018/03/05/asia/north-korea-south-korea-talks-intl/index.html.

40. Shane Croucher, "Trump: Good Chance North Korea Will Denuclearize after Kim Jong Un Meeting," *Newsweek*, March 28, 2018, http://www.newsweek.com/trump-good-chance-north-korea-will-denuclearize-after-kim-jong-un-meeting-863203.

41. Uri Friedman, "John Bolton's Radical Views on North Korea," *Atlantic*, March 23, 2018, https://www.theatlantic.com/international/archive/2018/03/john-bolton-north-korea/556370/.

3

The Laws of War—*Jus in Bello*

★ ★ ★

The laws of war, or *jus in bello*, refer to the norms that govern how war can be morally or legally waged—rules that are today often referred to as the law of armed conflict or international humanitarian law. These rules are conceptually distinct from the rules governing when war can morally or legally be initiated, the *jus ad bellum*, the subject of the preceding chapter. Prior to the rise of Christianity, there were few, if any, rules limiting how war could be conducted. The Old Testament of the Bible records many instances of victorious armies pillaging and razing cities and killing all the inhabitants, including noncombatants, such as women and children. Thucydides in his *History of the Peloponnesian War* recalls the tragic end of the city of Melos in 416 BC. Athens attacked Melos because the Melians refused either to pay tribute or to join Athens's war against Sparta; killed all the adult men regardless of whether they were civilians or not; and sold the women and children into slavery. As is well known, the Romans were no less cruel in their manner of war. Following the siege of Carthage, Rome completely sacked and destroyed the city (146 BC), leaving not one stone on top another, and sold approximately fifty thousand people into slavery. Although Cicero (106–43 BC) later lamented Carthage's fate, commenting that "when the victory is won, we should spare those who have not been blood-thirsty and barbarous in their warfare,"[1] Rome often failed to live up to this principle. Defeated enemy soldiers often suffered crucifixion, while civilians, including women and children, were typically enslaved.

Augustine (AD 354–430) admired Roman courage and discipline, but he deplored the lust for power and the desire for glory that he thought were at the heart of the expansion of the Roman Empire. Wars of this kind—characterized by love of violence, revenge, cruelty, hatred, and the lust of power—were evil, according to Augustine, because they were not undertaken for the sake of justice and peace. In his view, Christians need not be pacifists. They could take up arms, but the war had to be conducted in a manner that was consistent with the goal of a just and lasting peace. For that reason, razing cities and crucifying enemy soldiers were incompatible with the Christian conception of *jus in bello*. St. Thomas Aquinas (AD 1225–1274) endorsed Augustine's view that the goal of a "just" war precluded certain types of conduct because such a war must be conducted with the "right intention," which, as we saw in the preceding chapter, was Aquinas's third criterion of a "just" war. Accordingly, Aquinas joined Augustine in condemning the "'passion for inflicting harm, the cruel thirst for vengeance, . . . [and] the lust of power.'"[2] By deriving *jus in bello* from his third criterion of *jus ad bellum* in this manner, Aquinas inevitably came up with principles that were largely moral in character, that were general and vague in tone and application, and that largely related to the intentions and motives of the belligerents.

In the seventeenth century, Hugo Grotius gave the *jus in bello* a more legal character and separated it more clearly from *jus ad bellum*. After he discussed the circumstances "under which war may be undertaken" in the first two books of *De Jure Belli ac Pacis*, he dedicated the entire third book to the subject of "the extent" to which war may be carried on and "the manner" in which its rights may be enforced. All of these matters, he insisted, "may be viewed in the light of privileges resulting simply from the law of nature and of nations, or as the effects of some prior treaty or promise." Regarding the law of nature, the first principle Grotius mentions is that any means of war, "provided they be lawful," can be used if they are "necessary" to the attainment of any rightful military objective.[3]

Grotius's principle of "necessity" is logically related to a second general principle of the laws of war, the principle of humanity, which requires that belligerents avoid causing unnecessary suffering. For example, Grotius claims that during war no harm should intentionally be inflicted on the priesthood, those devoted to the pursuit of letters and other studies, farmers, merchants, artisans, and others "whose subsistence depends upon cultivating the arts of peace." In the same spirit, Grotius insists that "civilized manners" have "abolished the barbarous practice of putting prisoners to death."[4] In this passage, Grotius is delineating the third principle of the laws of war, the principle of distinction, which confines war's violence to the active combatants on each side and, at the same time, immunizes those active combatants from any legal liability for their violent acts. Accordingly, in war violence can only lawfully be directed at combatants who are in turn not subject to criminal liability as long as they abide by the laws of war.[5]

Grotius discusses additional rules limiting what can lawfully be done during war, such as rules relating to captures of enemy property and the degree to which an enemy's country can be despoiled. In the eighteenth century, Emer de Vattel, Cornelis van Bijnkershoek, and Jean-Jacques Burlamqui further defined and clarified the substance of *jus in bello*. One question that perplexed these writers was whether a belligerent state could immediately seize enemy property located within its borders.

Vattel's view was as follows:

> The sovereign declaring war, can neither detain the persons nor the property of those subject of the enemy who are within his dominions at the time of the

> declaration. They came into his country under the public faith. By permitting them to enter and reside in his territories, he [the sovereign] tacitly promised them full liberty and security for their return. He is therefore bound to allow them a reasonable time for withdrawing with their effects; and if they stay beyond the time prescribed, he has a right to treat them as enemies, though as enemies unarmed.[6]

Despite Vattel's rule, a U.S. attorney during the War of 1812 seized 550 tons of pine timber that belonged to a British subject. It was not at all clear whether Vattel's rule applied to the above seizure because the British owners of the property were not inside the United States at the time but were instead acting through an agent, who was an American citizen. In *Brown v. United States*, Chief Justice John Marshall and Justice Joseph Story consider the status and content of *jus in bello*, including the validity of Vattel's rule, in the context of a debate whether the declaration of war, by itself, grants the executive branch the authority to seize the property in question.

3.1 *Brown v. United States*, 12 U.S. 110 (1814)

MARSHALL, Chief Justice delivered the opinion of the Court . . .

Vattel says, that "the sovereign can neither detain the persons nor the property of those subjects of the enemy who are within his dominions at the time of the declaration."

It is true that this rule is, in terms, applied by Vattel to the property of those only who are personally within the territory at the commencement of hostilities; but it applies equally to things in action and to things in possession; and if war did, of itself, without any further exercise of the sovereign will, vest the property of the enemy in the sovereign, his presence could not exempt it from this operation of war. Nor can a reason be perceived for maintaining that the public faith is more entirely pledged for the security of property trusted in the territory of the nation in time of peace, if it be accompanied by its owner, than if it be confided to the care of others. . . .

The modern rule then would seem to be, that tangible property belonging to an enemy and found in the country at the commencement of war, ought not to be immediately confiscated. . . .

This rule appears to be totally incompatible with the idea, that war does of itself vest the property in the belligerent government. It may be considered as the opinion of all who have written on the jus belli, that war gives the right to confiscate, but does not itself confiscate the property of the enemy; and their rules go to the exercise of this right.

The constitution of the United States was framed at a time when this rule, introduced by commerce in favor of moderation and humanity, was received throughout the civilized world. In expounding that constitution, a construction ought not lightly to be admitted which would give to a declaration of war an effect in this country it does not possess elsewhere, and which would fetter that exercise of entire discretion respecting enemy property, which may enable the government to apply to the enemy the rule that he applies to us. . . .

It is urged that in executing the laws of war, the executive may seize and the courts condemn all property which, according to the modern law of nations, is subject to confiscation. . . .

This argument must assume for its basis the position that modern usage constitutes a rule which acts directly upon the thing itself by its own force, and through the sovereign power. This position is not allowed. This usage is a guide which the sovereign follows or abandons at his will. The rule, like other precepts of morality, of humanity, and even of wisdom, is addressed to the judgment of the sovereign, and although it cannot be disregarded by him without obloquy, yet it may be disregarded. . . .

Commercial nations, in the situation of the United States, have always a considerable quantity of property in the possession of their neighbors. When war breaks out, the question, what shall be done with enemy property in our country, is a question rather of policy than of law. The rule which we apply to the property of our enemy, will be applied by him to the property of our citizens. Like all other questions of policy, it is proper for the consideration of a department which can modify it at will; not for the consideration of a department which can pursue only the law as it is written. It is proper for the consideration of the legislature, not of the executive or judiciary. . . .

STORY Justice, dissenting . . .

. . . Vattel has indeed contended . . . that the sovereign declaring war, can neither detain the persons nor the property of those subjects of the enemy who are within his dominions at the time of the declaration, because they came into the country upon the public faith. This exception (which, in terms, is confined to the property of persons who are within the country,) seems highly reasonable in itself. . . . But, even limited as it is, it does not seem followed in practice. . . . [For example,] it is very certain that Great Britain has uniformly seized, as prize, all vessels and cargoes of her enemies found afloat in her ports at the commencement of war. . . . Of the right of Great Britain thus to seize vessels and cargoes found in her ports on the breaking out of war, I do not find any denial in authorities which are entitled to much weight; and I, therefore, consider the rule of the law of nations to be, that every such exercise of authority is lawful, and rests in the sound discretion of the sovereign of the nation. . . .

. . . By the constitution, the executive is charged with the faithful execution of the laws; and the language of the act declaring war authorizes him to carry it into effect. In what manner, and to what extent, shall he carry it into effect? What are the legitimate objects of the warfare which he is to wage? There is no act of the legislature defining the powers, objects or mode of warfare: by what rule, then, must he be governed? I think the only rational answer is by the law of nations as applied to a state of war. Whatever act is legitimate, whatever act is approved by the law, or hostilities among civilized nations, such he may, in his discretion, adopt and exercise; for with him the sovereignty of the nation rests as to the execution of the laws. If any of such acts are disapproved by the legislature, it is in their power to narrow and limit the extent to which the rights of war shall be exercised; but until such limit is assigned, the executive must have all the right of modern warfare vested in him, to be exercised in his sound discretion, or he can have none. . . .

It has been supposed that my opinion assumes for its basis the position, that modern usage constitutes a rule which acts directly on the thing itself by its own force, and not through the sovereign power. Certainly I do not admit this supposition to be correct. My argument proceeds upon the ground, that when the legislative authority, to whom the right to declare war is confided, has declared war in its most unlimited manner, the executive authority, to whom the execution of the war is confided, is bound to carry it into effect. He has a discretion vested in him, as to the manner and extent; but he cannot lawfully transcend the rules of warfare established among civilized nations. He cannot lawfully exercise powers or authorize proceedings which the civilized world repudiates and disclaims. The sovereignty, as to declaring war and limiting its effects, rests with the legislature. The sovereignty, as to its execution, rests with the president. If the legislature do not limit the nature of the war, all the regulations and rights of general war attach upon it. . . .

Questions

1. If "war gives the right to confiscate" enemy property, as Chief Justice Marshall asserts, why should Congress's declaration of war not trigger this right? What is Marshall's answer?
2. How is Marshall's rule concerning the confiscation of enemy property different from Vattel's? How is it different from Justice Story's?
3. How does Marshall's rule regarding the confiscation of enemy property grant Congress the discretion to decide what to do with enemy property, while Justice Story's position grants the president the discretion if Congress is silent? Which position is preferable? Why?
4. Marshall refers to international law, presumably including *jus in bello*, as "modern usage" and a "guide which the sovereign follows or abandons at his will." Does this mean that Congress is under no legal obligation to obey international law? If so, why does Marshall say a sovereign cannot disregard international law "without obloquy"?
5. What is Justice Story's position on the binding character of "modern usage"? Does he think the president can violate the laws of warfare if Congress declares war?

Prior to the nineteenth century, *jus in bello* consisted primarily of customary international law—that is, the customs and practices of states. In the 1850s, however, states began to make treaties with one another regarding how war could be waged legally. Some of the provisions of these treaties defined more specifically and explicitly what customary international law required, but other provisions broke new ground. The most important of these treaties was the 1856 Declaration of Paris, which was ratified by fifty-five states, including many of the major powers of the day, such as France, Austria, Russia, Prussia, the United Kingdom, and the Ottoman Empire. The declaration, which focused on issues related to maritime law during war, abolished privateering; prohibited the confiscation of enemy goods on neutral vessels and neutral goods on enemy vessels if the goods in question were not war contraband; and concluded that blockades were legally binding only if they were maintained "by a force sufficient really to prevent access to the enemy's coastline."[7]

The first attempt to codify the rules of land warfare took place during the American Civil War. At the request of General Henry W. Halleck, Francis Lieber, a German legal scholar who taught at Columbia University, drafted a code of warfare for the Union armies. On April 24, 1863, President Abraham Lincoln promulgated the code as General Orders No. 100, Instructions for the Government of the Armies of the United States in the Field, but it became commonly known as the Lieber Code. In this code, Lieber explored the meaning of military necessity; elaborated on the distinction between combatants and civilians in war (a topic explored more in depth in the next chapter); and insisted that retaliation for violations of *jus in bello* was lawful and necessary but should be used only as a last resort. Unlike earlier treatises on *jus in bello* by Grotius and Vattel, Lieber's code was written in a plain style that could readily be understood by Union military commanders. It was the first code of armed conflict of its kind.

3.2 The Lieber Code (1863)

Art. 14.[8] Military necessity, as understood by modern civilized nations, consists in the necessity of those measures which are indispensable for securing the ends of the war, and which are lawful according to the modern law and usages of war.

Art. 15. Military necessity admits of all direct destruction of life or limb of armed enemies, and of other persons whose destruction is incidentally unavoidable in the armed contests of the war; it allows of the capturing of every armed enemy, and every enemy of importance to the hostile government, or of peculiar danger to the captor; it allows of all destruction of property, and obstruction of the ways and channels of traffic, travel, or communication, and of all withholding of sustenance or means of life from the enemy; of the appropriation of whatever an enemy's country affords necessary for the subsistence and safety of the army, and of such deception as does not involve the breaking of good faith either positively pledged, regarding agreements entered into during the war, or supposed by the modern law of war to exist. Men who take up arms against one another in public war do not cease on this account to be moral beings, responsible to one another and to God.

Art. 16. Military necessity does not admit of cruelty—that is, the infliction of suffering for the sake of suffering or for revenge, nor of maiming or wounding except in fight, nor of torture to extort confessions. It does not admit of the use of poison in any way, nor of the wanton devastation of a district. It admits of deception, but disclaims acts of perfidy; and, in general, military necessity does not include any act of hostility which makes the return to peace unnecessarily difficult. . . .

Art. 22. . . . [A]s civilization has advanced during the last centuries, so has likewise steadily advanced, especially in war on land, the distinction between the private individual belonging to a hostile country and the hostile country itself, with its men in arms. The principle has been more and more acknowledged that the unarmed citizen is to be spared in person, property, and honor as much as the exigencies of war will admit.

Art. 23. Private citizens are no longer murdered, enslaved, or carried off to distant parts, and the inoffensive individual is as little disturbed in his private relations as the commander of the hostile troops can afford to grant in the overruling demands of a vigorous war. . . .

Art. 27. The law of war can no more wholly dispense with retaliation than can the law of nations, of which it is a branch. Yet civilized nations acknowledge retaliation as the sternest feature of war. A reckless enemy often leaves to his opponent no other means of securing himself against the repetition of barbarous outrage.

Art. 28. Retaliation will, therefore, never be resorted to as a measure of mere revenge, but only as a means of protective retribution, and moreover, cautiously and unavoidably; that is to say, retaliation shall only be resorted to after careful inquiry into the real occurrence, and the character of the misdeeds that may demand retribution.

Unjust or inconsiderate retaliation removes the belligerents farther and farther from the mitigating rules of regular war, and by rapid steps leads them nearer to the internecine wars of savages.

Art. 29. . . . Peace is . . . [the] normal condition; war is the exception. The ultimate object of all modern war is a renewed state of peace.

The more vigorously wars are pursued, the better it is for humanity. Sharp wars are brief. . . .

Art. 56. A prisoner of war is subject to no punishment for being a public enemy, nor is any revenge wreaked upon him by the intentional infliction of any suffering, or disgrace, by cruel imprisonment, want of food, by mutilation, death, or any other barbarity.

Art. 57. So soon as a man is armed by a sovereign government and takes the soldier's oath of fidelity, he is a belligerent; his killing, wounding, or other warlike acts are not individual crimes or offenses. No belligerent has a right to declare that enemies of a certain class, color, or condition, when properly organized as soldiers, will not be treated by him as public enemies. . . .

Art. 75. Prisoners of war are subject to confinement or imprisonment such as may be deemed necessary on account of safety, but they are to be subjected to no other intentional suffering or indignity. The confinement and mode of treating a prisoner may be varied during his captivity according to the demands of safety. . . .

Art. 82. Men, or squads of men, who commit hostilities, whether by fighting, or inroads for destruction or plunder, or by raids of any kind, without commission, without being part and portion of the organized hostile army, and without sharing continuously in the war, but who do so with intermitting returns to their homes and avocations, or with the occasional assumption of the semblance of peaceful pursuits, divesting themselves of the character or appearance of soldiers—such men, or squads of men, are not public enemies, and, therefore, if captured, are not entitled to the privileges of prisoners of war, but shall be treated summarily as highway robbers or pirates. . . .

Art. 88. A spy is a person who secretly, in disguise or under false pretense, seeks information with the intention of communicating it to the enemy.

The spy is punishable with death by hanging by the neck, whether or not he succeed in obtaining the information or in conveying it to the enemy. . . .

Art. 148. The law of war does not allow proclaiming either an individual belonging to the hostile army, or a citizen, or a subject of the hostile government, an outlaw, who may be slain without trial by any captor, any more than the modern law of peace allows such intentional outlawry; on the contrary, it abhors such outrage. The sternest retaliation should follow the murder committed in consequence of such proclamation, made by whatever authority. Civilized nations look with horror upon offers of rewards for the assassination of enemies as relapses into barbarism. . . .

Questions

1. According to the Lieber Code, "military necessity" consists of only those measures that are both "indispensable" for victory in war and are "lawful according to the modern law and usages of war." Does this mean that lawful methods of war are not permitted if they are not "indispensable" for victory? What do you think Lieber meant by "indispensable"?
2. At one point, Lieber claims that "military necessity does not include any act of hostility which makes the return to peace unnecessarily difficult." How is this claim to be understood? Are there acts of hostility that are lawful in war and indispensable for victory but also make the return to peace more difficult? How would you balance these different factors?
3. Lieber recognizes the distinction between civilians and combatants, and endorses the rule that the unarmed civilian's person, property, and honor should be spared in war "as much as the exigencies of war will admit." Does this mean that "military necessity" and the law of war might justify some degree of oppression of civilians? How much oppression would be legally tolerable according to Lieber?
4. Does Lieber's concept of retaliation permit a belligerent to violate the laws of war if the enemy violates them first? Why does Lieber defend this position if it is generally thought that two wrongs don't make a right? Does the state of war render the two-wrongs principle inapplicable?

5. Do you agree with Lieber that "sharp" wars are "brief" and are better for "humanity" for that reason?
6. According to Lieber, prisoners of war cannot be punished or intentionally made to suffer, but those (Art. 82) who assume "the character or appearance of soldiers" are to be temporarily treated "summarily as highway robbers or pirates." What explains this radical difference in treatment?

Article 148 of the Lieber Code prohibited assassinations, although it is not entirely clear whether the rule was confined to the murder of prisoners or whether it extended to the murder of enemy noncombatants, in particular the murder of high government enemy officials far from a battlefield. Would this type of murder qualify as an "assassination" that violated the laws of war? This question came to the fore following the assassination of Abraham Lincoln on April 14, 1865, just five days after Confederate general Robert E. Lee surrendered at Appomattox. Lincoln's assailant, John Wilkes Booth, was shot and killed on April 26, but eight of his alleged associates were arrested, including Mary Surratt. Secretary of War Edwin Stanton favored giving these individuals a quick military trial, rather than turning them over to civilian authorities for prosecution in a civilian court. Stanton's approach was controversial since the Constitution requires grand jury indictments and jury trials for federal crimes. It is true that Washington, D.C., was under martial law at the time of the assassination, but the civilian courts were open and functioning.

Another key question regarding the legality of a military trial was whether the eight conspirators were in some way associated with the rapidly crumbling Confederate government, which fled Richmond, Virginia, on April 7 in advance of the Union occupation. Several of the eight defendants were known Confederate sympathizers and former Confederate prisoners of war. It is also relevant that the conspiracy was to kill not just Lincoln but also Vice President Andrew Johnson, Secretary of State William Seward (who was severely injured), and General Ulysses S. Grant. Confronting the difficult question of how to proceed, President Johnson asked his attorney general, James Speed, for a legal opinion on whether it would be lawful to have a military commission try the alleged conspirators. Speed advised Johnson that such a trial would be lawful. The trial before nine military officers began on May 9; the military commission found all the conspirators guilty and sentenced four of them to death. In July, Speed issued a written opinion that explained why the commission was lawful. The key to his argument was that a conspiracy "to assassinate" was an offense against the laws of war.

3.3 Attorney General James Speed, "Opinion on the Constitutional Power of the Military to Try and Execute the Assassins of the President" (1865)

That the laws of nations constitute a part of the laws of the land is established from the face of the Constitution, upon principle and by authority.[9] But the laws of war constitute much the greater part of the law of nations. Like the other laws of nations, they exist and are of binding force upon the departments and citizens of the Government, though not defined by any law of Congress. . . .

Congress can declare war. When war is declared, it must be, under the Constitution, carried on according to the known laws and usages of war among civilized nations. Under the power to define those laws, Congress cannot abrogate them or authorize their infraction. The Constitution does not permit this Government to prosecute a war as an uncivilized and barbarous people. . . .

But enemies with which an army has to deal are of two classes:

1. Open, active participants in hostilities, as soldiers who wear the uniform, move under the flag, and hold the appropriate commission from their government. Openly assuming to discharge the duties and meet the responsibilities and dangers of soldiers, they are entitled to all belligerent rights, and should receive all the courtesies due to soldiers. . . .
2. Secret, but active participants, as spies, brigands, bushwhackers, jayhawkers, war rebels and assassins. In all wars, and especially in civil wars, such secret, active enemies . . . must be met and put down by the army. When lawless wretches become so impudent and powerful as to not be controlled and governed by the ordinary tribunals of a country, armies are called out, and the laws of war invoked. . . .

. . . [To] act as spy is an offence against the laws of war, and the punishment of which in all ages has been death, and yet it is not a [civil] crime; to violate a flag of truce is an offence against the laws of war, and yet not a crime of which a civil court can take cognizance; to unite with banditti, jayhawkers, guerillas, or any other unauthorized marauder is a high offence against the laws of war; the offence is complete when the band is organized or joined. The atrocities committed by such a band do not constitute the offence, but make the reasons, and sufficient reasons they are, why such banditti are denounced by the laws of war. . . .

. . . If the prisoner be a regular unoffending soldier of the opposing party to the war, he should be treated with all the courtesy and kindness consistent with his safe custody; if he has offended against the laws of war, he should have such trial and be punished as the laws of war require. A spy, though a prisoner of war, may be tried, condemned and executed by a military tribunal without a breach of the Constitution. A bushwhacker, a jayhawker, a bandit, a war rebel, an assassin, being public enemies, may be tried, condemned and executed as offenders against the laws of war. The soldier that would fail to try a spy or bandit after his capture, would be as derelict in duty as if he were to fail to capture; he is as much bound to try and to execute, if guilty, as he is to arrest; the same law that makes it his duty to pursue and kill or capture, makes it his duty to try according to the usages of war. The judge of a civil court is not more strongly bound under the Constitution and the law to try a criminal than is the military to try an offender against the laws of war. . . .

. . . Obedience to the Constitution and the law, then, requires that the military should do their whole duty; they must not only meet and fight the enemies of the country in open battle, but they must kill or take the secret enemies of the country, and try and execute them according to the laws of war. The civil tribunals of the country can not rightfully interfere with the military in the performance of their high, arduous and perilous, but lawful duties. That Booth and his associates were secret active public enemies, no mind that contemplates the facts can doubt. The exclamation used by him when he escaped from the box on to the stage, after he had fired the fatal shot, sic semper tyrannis, and his dying message, "Say to my mother that I died for my country," show that he was not an assassin from private malice, but that he acted as a public foe. . . .

My conclusion, therefore, is, that if the persons who are charged with the assassination of the President committed the deed as public enemies, as I believe they did, and whether they did or not is a question to be decided by the tribunal before which they are tried, they not only can, but ought to be tried before a military tribunal. If the persons charged have offended against the laws of war, it would be as palpably wrong of the military to hand them over to the civil courts, as it would be wrong in a civil court to convict a man of murder who had, in time of war, killed another in battle. . . .

Questions

1. Attorney General James Speed argues forcefully that Congress cannot "abrogate" the laws of war. Is he right? Is his view consistent with Chief Justice Marshall's (see **reading 3.1**)?
2. Is it Speed's view that military commissions can only try "secret active public enemies," such as "spies, brigands, bushwhackers, jayhawkers, war rebels and assassins"? What if a regular soldier violated the laws of war?
3. What evidence did Speed use to justify his conclusion that Booth and his associates were "secret active public enemies"? Did Speed require any evidence of communications between the assassins and the Confederate government or army? Do you agree with Speed's analysis of this question?
4. Speed argues that a conspiracy to kill an enemy political leader far from a battlefield is a war crime and that the "offense is complete when the band is organized or joined." Is that statement true? What if Booth organized his "band" but was never able to assassinate Lincoln? Could a military commission have nonetheless tried the conspirators because they violated the laws of war?
5. Did Speed go so far as to say that the United States had a duty to try Lincoln's assassins by military commission?

During and after the American Civil War, European countries continued to ratify treaties and declarations that codified the law of armed conflict. For example, the first Geneva Convention for the Amelioration of the Condition of the Wounded in Armies in the Field was signed in 1864, and the 1868 St. Petersburg Declaration banned the use of bullets (weighing less than four hundred grams) that exploded upon impact, a type of ammunition that sharply increased the severity of wounds. This trend of written treaties, however, did not abandon the principle that customary international law was also a legitimate source of the *jus in bello*. Indeed, the preamble to the 1899 Convention with Respect to the Laws and Customs of War on Land (Hague II) included a statement that became known as the "Martens Clause" in honor of the Russian lawyer who drafted it. This clause, which reappeared in treaties of the twentieth century, argued that the laws of war extended beyond the specific treaty provisions that the countries had ratified.

> Until a more complete code of the laws of war is issued, the High Contracting Parties think it right to declare that in cases not included in the Regulations adopted by them, populations and belligerents remain under the protection and empire of the principles of international law, as they result from the usages established between civilized nations, from the laws of humanity, and the requirements of the public conscience.[10]

A year after the 1899 Hague conference, the validity of the Martens principle was debated by two Supreme Court justices in *The Paquete Habana*, a case dealing with the seizure of two Cuban coastal fishing vessels by the United States during the Spanish-American War. Congress declared war against Spain on April 25, 1898, after the U.S. Navy battleship *Maine* inexplicably sank in Havana's harbor. Seized in the early days of the war in a U.S. blockade of Cuba, the two fishing vessels were condemned as prizes of war in Key West, Florida.

3.4 *The Paquete Habana*, 175 U.S. 677 (1900)

MR. JUSTICE GRAY delivered the opinion of the court. . . .

International law is part of our law, and must be ascertained and administered by the courts of justice of appropriate jurisdiction, as often as questions of right depending upon it are duly presented for their determination. For this purpose, where there is no treaty, and no controlling executive or legislative act or judicial decision, resort must be had to the customs and usages of civilized nations; and, as evidence of these, to the works of jurists and commentators, who by years of labor, research and experience, have made themselves peculiarly well acquainted with the subjects of which they treat. Such works are resorted to by judicial tribunals, not for the speculations of their authors concerning what the law ought to be, but for trustworthy evidence of what the law really is. . . .

. . . [A] review of the precedents and authorities on the subject appears to us abundantly to demonstrate that at the present day, by the general consent of the civilized nations of the world, and independently of any express treaty or other public act, it is an established rule of international law, founded on considerations of humanity to a poor and industrious order of men, and of the mutual convenience of belligerent States, that coast fishing vessels, with their implements and supplies, cargoes and crews, unarmed, and honestly pursuing their peaceful calling of catching and bringing in fresh fish, are exempt from capture as prize of war.

The exemption, of course, does not apply to coast fishermen or their vessels, if employed for a warlike purpose, or in such a way as to give aid or information to the enemy; nor when military or naval operations create a necessity to which all private interests must give way. . . .

This rule of international law is one which prize courts, administering the law of nations, are bound to take judicial notice of, and to give effect to, in the absence of any treaty or other public act of their own government in relation to the matter. . . .

. . . [I]t is the duty of this court, sitting as the highest prize court of the United States, and administering the law of nations, to declare and adjudge that the capture was unlawful, and without probable cause. . . .

MR. CHIEF JUSTICE FULLER . . . , dissenting. . . .

In truth, the exemption of fishing craft is essentially an act of grace, and not a matter of right, and it is extended or denied as the exigency is believed to demand. . . .

It is needless to review the speculations and repetitions of the writers on international law. Ortolan, De Boeck and others admit that the custom relied on as consecrating the immunity is not so general as to create an absolute international rule; Heffter, Calvo and others are to the contrary. Their lucubrations may be persuasive, but are not authoritative.

In my judgment, the rule is that exemption from the rigors of war is in the control of the Executive. He is bound by no immutable rule on the subject. It is for him to apply, or to modify, or to deny altogether such immunity as may have been usually extended.

Exemptions may be designated in advance, or granted according to circumstances, but carrying on war involves the infliction of the hardships of war at least to the extent that the seizure or destruction of enemy's property on sea need not be specifically authorized in order to be accomplished. . . .

Questions

1. Is Justice Horace Gray correct in his view that "international law is part of our law" and, for that reason, judges in federal courts should decide cases based on the "customs and usages of civilized nations"? Is this a vague stan-

dard? Is it the vagueness of customary international law that bothers Chief Justice Melville Fuller? Would it be better to limit federal judges to treaties ratified by the Senate?

2. If coastal fishing vessels are "employed for a warlike purpose" or are used in a way to "give aid or information to the enemy," then their exemption from seizure is, according to Gray, suspended. Should federal judges be the ones deciding whether these exceptions apply to specific seizures during wartime?
3. Gray implies that judges have a duty to apply the rule against seizure of coastal fishing vessels during war "in the absence of any treaty or other public act of their own government." Does this imply that a treaty or a law enacted by Congress could set aside the rule against seizing coastal fishing vessels during armed conflict? If so, to what extent is Congress legally obliged to respect international law?
4. Does Fuller's view that the "exemption from the rigors of war is in the control of the Executive" mean that Congress cannot prohibit the Executive from seizing coastal fishing vessels in a declared war? Would Fuller's position be the same if the rule against seizure had the clear and definite support of customary international law?

Following 1899, an even larger Hague peace conference was held in 1907, one that produced ten conventions on the law of war. Topics covered by these conventions included the opening of hostilities, the rights and duties of neutral powers, the status of enemy merchant ships, the use of mines, naval bombardment, maritime warfare, and the laws and customs of war on land. This last convention, known as Hague IV, explained in its preamble that the goal was to "revise the general laws and customs of war, either with a view to defining them with greater precision or to confining them within such limits as would mitigate their severity as far as possible."[11] Hague IV included an annex that discussed in fairly specific terms how prisoners of war were to be treated and what a belligerent could or could not do when occupying the territory of the enemy state. Articles 22 to 28 listed specific types of conduct that were prohibited by the convention and the laws of war.

3.5 Hague Convention (IV), Annex

Art. 22.[12] The right of belligerents to adopt means of injuring the enemy is not unlimited.

Art. 23. In addition to the prohibitions provided by special Conventions, it is especially forbidden

a. To employ poison or poisoned weapons;
b. To kill or wound treacherously individuals belonging to the hostile nation or army;
c. To kill or wound an enemy who, having laid down his arms, or having no longer means of defense, has surrendered at discretion;
d. To declare that no quarter will be given;
e. To employ arms, projectiles, or material calculated to cause unnecessary suffering;
f. To make improper use of a flag of truce, of the national flag or of the military insignia and uniform of the enemy, as well as the distinctive badges of the Geneva Convention;
g. To destroy or seize the enemy's property, unless such destruction or seizure be imperatively demanded by the necessities of war;
h. To declare abolished, suspended, or inadmissible in a court of law the rights and actions of the nationals of the hostile party. A belligerent is likewise forbidden

to compel the nationals of the hostile party to take part in the operations of war directed against their own country, even if they were in the belligerent's service before the commencement of the war.

Art. 24. Ruses of war and the employment of measures necessary for obtaining information about the enemy and the country are considered permissible.

Art. 25. The attack or bombardment, by whatever means, of towns, villages, dwellings, or buildings which are undefended is prohibited.

Art. 26. The officer in command of an attacking force must, before commencing a bombardment, except in cases of assault, do all in his power to warn the authorities.

Art. 27. In sieges and bombardments all necessary steps must be taken to spare, as far as possible, buildings dedicated to religion, art, science, or charitable purposes, historic monuments, hospitals, and places where the sick and wounded are collected, provided they are not being used at the time for military purposes.

It is the duty of the besieged to indicate the presence of such buildings or places by distinctive and visible signs, which shall be notified to the enemy beforehand.

Art. 28. The pillage of a town or place, even when taken by assault, is prohibited. . . .

Questions

1. Do these rules substantiate the conclusion that Hague IV successfully mitigated the severity of *jus in bello* "as far as possible"? What additional restrictions on warfare could have been added?
2. Why is poison or poisoned weapons prohibited?
3. Does Hague IV limit the right to destroy enemy property more than the Lieber Code did?
4. Since Article 24 permits "ruses" of war, why does Article 23(f) prohibit the improper use of a flag of truce, the national flag of the enemy, or a badge of the Geneva Convention?
5. If employing "measures necessary for obtaining information about the enemy and the country" are permissible, why did the Lieber Code treat spying as a war crime punishable by death? Which is the more defensible view?

Even though the belligerents in World War I failed to live up to the standards enunciated in the Annex to the Hague Convention (IV), in particular the rule prohibiting the use of poisonous gas, the trend in favor of using treaties and protocols to mitigate the harshness and cruelty of war continued. The Protocol for the Prohibition of the Use in War of Asphyxiating, Poisonous or other Gases, and of Bacteriological Methods of Warfare was signed in 1925 and a Convention for the Amelioration of the Condition of the Wounded and Sick in Armies in the Field and a Convention Relative to the Treatment of Prisoners of War were signed in 1929, both in Geneva. However, despite these steps in the direction of humanizing warfare, the rise of Hitler's fascist Germany during the 1930s threatened to take the world in the opposite direction. That threat became a reality with the German invasions of Poland in 1939, of France in 1940, and of the USSR in 1941. Committed to the concept of "total war," Hitler's war machine engaged in war crimes on a vast scale. Prisoners of war and civilians were tortured and murdered; civilians from occupied territories were transported to Germany to work as slaves in German arms industries; hostages were taken and frequently shot; and concentration camps were set up, along with camps that implemented Hitler's plan to exterminate the Jewish race.

Following Hitler's suicide and Nazi Germany's surrender in May 1945, the United States, Great Britain, the USSR, and France signed the London Agreement, which established an International Military Tribunal to investigate and try three types of crimes committed during the war: (1) crimes against peace, such as waging a war of aggression or a war in violation of treaties; (2) war crimes, such as murder, ill-treatment, slave labor, plunder, wanton destruction of towns and cities; and (3) crimes against humanity, such as extermination, enslavement, deportation, and persecution on political, racial, or religious grounds.[13] The tribunal's first trial addressed the crimes of the top officials of the Nazi regime, including Hermann Göring, a longtime political associate of Hitler who became the head of the Luftwaffe (German Air Force) in 1935 and Hitler's designated successor in 1941. The Nuremberg Tribunal convicted Göring and his fellow defendants of crimes against peace, war crimes, and crimes against humanity, along with the crime of conspiring to commit all of these offenses. The following excerpt is from the section of the tribunal's opinion that discusses war crimes and crimes against humanity, with a focus on the Jewish holocaust.

3.6 *In re: Göring and Others*, International Military Tribunal (1946)

The evidence relating to War Crimes has been overwhelming in its volume and its detail.[14] It is impossible for this Judgment adequately to review it, or to record the mass of documentary and oral evidence that has been presented. The truth remains that War Crimes were committed on a vast scale, never before seen in the history of war. They were perpetrated in all the countries occupied by Germany, and on the high seas, and were attended by every conceivable circumstance of cruelty and horror. There can be no doubt that the majority of them arose from the Nazi conception of "total war," with which the aggressive wars were waged. For in this conception of "total war," the moral ideas underlying the conventions which seek to make war more humane are no longer regarded as having force or validity. Everything is made subordinate to the over-mastering dictates of war. Rules, regulations, assurances and treaties all alike are of no moment; and so, freed from the restraining influence of International Law, the aggressive war is conducted by the Nazi leaders in the most barbaric way. Accordingly, War Crimes were committed when and wherever the Führer and his close associates thought them to be advantageous. They were for the most part the result of cold and criminal calculation. . . .

. . . Prisoners of war were ill-treated and tortured and murdered, not only in defiance of the well-established rules of International Law, but in complete disregard of the elementary dictates of humanity. Civilian populations in occupied territories suffered the same fate. Whole populations were deported to Germany for the purposes of slave labor on defense works, armament production and similar tasks connected with the war effort. Hostages were taken in very large numbers from the civilian populations in all the occupied countries and were shot as suited the German purposes. Public and private property was systematically plundered and pillaged in order to enlarge the resources of Germany at the expense of the rest of Europe. Cities and towns and villages were wantonly destroyed without military justification or necessity. . . .

The persecution of the Jews at the hands of the Nazi Government has been proved in the greatest detail before the Tribunal. It is a record of consistent and systematic inhumanity on the greatest scale. . . .

. . . The Nazi persecution of Jews in Germany before the war, severe and repressive as it was, cannot compare . . . with the policy pursued during the war in the occupied territories. Originally the policy was similar to that which had been in force inside Germany. Jews were required to register, were forced to live in ghettoes, to wear the yellow star, and were used as slave laborers. In the summer of 1941, however, plans were made for the "final solution" of the Jewish question in all of Europe. This "final solution" meant the extermination of the Jews, which early in 1939 Hitler had threatened would be one of the consequences of an outbreak of war, and a special section in the Gestapo under Adolf Eichmann . . . was formed to carry out the policy. . . .

. . . Part of the "final solution" was the gathering of Jews from all German-occupied Europe in concentration camps. Their physical condition was the test of life or death. All who were fit to work were used as slave laborers in the concentration camps; all who were not fit to work were destroyed in gas chambers and their bodies burnt. Certain concentration camps such as Treblinka and Auschwitz were set aside for this main purpose. With regard to Auschwitz, the Tribunal heard the evidence of Hoess, the commandant of the camp from 1st May, 1940, to 1st December, 1943. He estimated that in the camp of Auschwitz alone in that time 2,500,000 persons were exterminated, and that a further 500,000 died from disease and starvation. . . .

Beating, starvation, torture, and killing were general. The inmates were subjected to cruel experiments at Dachau in August, 1942[;] victims were immersed in cold water until their body temperature was reduced to 28 degrees Centigrade, when they died immediately. Other experiments included high-altitude experiments in pressure chambers, experiments to determine how long human beings could survive in freezing water, experiments with poison bullets, experiments with contagious diseases, and experiments dealing with sterilization of men and women by x-rays and other methods.

Evidence was given of the treatment of the inmates before and after their extermination. It was testified that the hair of woman victims was cut off before they were killed, and shipped to Germany, there to be used in the manufacture of mattresses. The clothes, money and valuables of the inmates were also salvaged and sent to the appropriate agencies for disposition. After the extermination the gold teeth and fillings were taken from the heads of the corpses and sent to the Reichsbank.

After the cremation the ashes were used for fertilizer, and in some instances attempts were made to utilize the fat from the bodies of the victims in the commercial manufacture of soap. Special groups travelled through Europe to find Jews and subject them to the "final solution." German missions were sent to such satellite countries as Hungary and Bulgaria to arrange for the shipment of Jews to extermination camps, and it is known that by the end of 1944, 400,000 Jews from Hungary had been murdered at Auschwitz. Evidence has also been given of the evacuation of 110,000 Jews from part of Roumania for "liquidation." Adolf Eichmann, who had been put in charge of this programme by Hitler, has estimated that the policy pursued resulted in the killing of 6,000,000 Jews, of whom 4,000,000 were killed in the extermination institutions. . . .

Questions

1. Is "total war" incompatible with the view that war can be regulated by law? Is "total war" a possibility in today's world? Would nuclear war be a form of "total war"? Should nuclear weapons be banned?
2. Was Germany's war of aggression linked to its persecution of the Jews? Do wars of aggression tend to lead to racial genocide? Why or why not?
3. Why would Hitler's regime insist on the shipment of Jews from other coun-

tries, such as Hungary or Bulgaria, to the extermination camps? Why did these countries cooperate?

4. Does the treatment of the dead Jewish corpses, such as the extraction of gold teeth and fillings, magnify the enormity of this war crime to the point that no type of punishment is commensurate to the underlying culpability? Does it bother you that Göring escaped the hangman's noose by taking cyanide the night before his scheduled execution?

In 1949, representatives from around the world met in Geneva to consider how the law of armed conflict should be revised in light of the horrors and calamities of World War II. This conference produced four conventions—two dealing with conditions of wounded in the field (first) and at sea (second), one on the treatment of prisoners of war (third), and one on the protection of civilians (fourth). The Geneva Conventions incorporated many of the rules of earlier treaties, and nearly all of the sovereign nations of the world quickly ratified them. Since so many states have accepted the laws of war contained in these treaty provisions, it is understood that the Geneva Conventions are obligatory for all contemporary states, whether they ratified them or not, based on their status as customary international law. For that reason, these conventions contain the principles of *jus in bello* that are valid today. The first three articles of each of the Geneva Conventions are identical in substance. The reading below includes excerpts from these three common articles as well as additional excerpts from the Third Convention on the treatment of prisoners and the Fourth on the treatment of civilians.

3.7 The Geneva Conventions of 1949

COMMON ARTICLES:

Art. 1: The High Contracting Parties undertake to respect and to ensure respect for the present Convention in all circumstances.[15]

Art. 2: . . . [T]he present Convention shall apply to all cases of declared war or of any other armed conflict which may arise between two or more of the High Contracting Parties, even if the state of war is not recognized by one of them.

The Convention shall also apply to all cases of partial or total occupation of the territory of a High Contracting Party, even if the said occupation meets with no armed resistance. . . .

Art. 3: In the case of armed conflict not of an international character occurring in the territory of one of the High Contracting Parties, each Party to the conflict shall be bound to apply, as a minimum, the following provisions:

1. Persons taking no active part in the hostilities, including members of armed forces who have laid down their arms and those placed "hors de combat" by sickness, wounds, detention, or any other cause, shall in all circumstances be treated humanely, without any adverse distinction founded on race, colour, religion or faith, sex, birth or wealth, or any other similar criteria. To this end, the following acts are and shall remain prohibited at any time and in any place whatsoever with respect to the above-mentioned persons:
   a. violence to life and person, in particular murder of all kinds, mutilation, cruel treatment and torture;
   b. taking of hostages;
   c. outrages upon personal dignity, in particular humiliating and degrading treatment;
   d. the passing of sentences and the carrying out of executions without previous judgment pronounced by a regularly constituted court, affording all the

judicial guarantees which are recognized as indispensable by civilized peoples. . . .

THIRD CONVENTION RELATIVE TO THE TREATMENT OF PRISONERS OF WAR:

Art. 4: . . . Prisoners of war . . . are persons belonging to one of the following categories, who have fallen into the power of the enemy:

1. Members of the armed forces of a Party to the conflict as well as members of militias or volunteer corps forming part of such armed forces.
2. Members of other militias and members of other volunteer corps . . . [who] fulfill the following conditions:
   a. that of being commanded by a person responsible for his subordinates;
   b. that of having a fixed distinctive sign recognizable at a distance;
   c. that of carrying arms openly;
   d. that of conducting their operations in accordance with the laws and customs of war. . . .

Art. 5: . . . Should any doubt arise as to whether persons, having committed a belligerent act and having fallen into the hands of the enemy, belong to any of the categories enumerated in Article 4, such persons shall enjoy the protection of the present Convention until such time as their status has been determined by a competent tribunal. . . .

Art. 13: Prisoners of war must at all times be humanely treated. Any unlawful act or omission by the Detaining Power causing death or seriously endangering the health of a prisoner of war in its custody is prohibited, and will be regarded as a serious breach of the present Convention. In particular, no prisoner of war may be subjected to physical mutilation or to medical or scientific experiments of any kind which are not justified by the medical, dental or hospital treatment of the prisoner concerned and carried out in his interest.

Likewise, prisoners of war must at all times be protected, particularly against acts of violence or intimidation and against insults and public curiosity. . . .

Art. 15: The Power detaining prisoners of war shall be bound to provide free of charge for their maintenance and for the medical attention required by their state of health. . . .

Art. 17: . . . No physical or mental torture, nor any other form of coercion, may be inflicted on prisoners of war to secure from them information of any kind whatever. Prisoners of war who refuse to answer may not be threatened, insulted, or exposed to any unpleasant or disadvantageous treatment of any kind. . . .

Art. 26: The basic daily food rations shall be sufficient in quantity, quality and variety to keep prisoners of war in good health and to prevent loss of weight or the development of nutritional deficiencies. . . .

Art. 28: The Detaining Power shall be bound to take all sanitary measures necessary to ensure the cleanliness and healthfulness of camps and to prevent epidemics. . . .

Also, apart from the baths and showers with which the camps shall be furnished, prisoners of war shall be provided with sufficient water and soap for their personal toilet and for washing their personal laundry; the necessary installations, facilities and time shall be granted them for that purpose. . . .

Art. 38: . . . [T]he Detaining Power shall encourage the practice of intellectual, educational, and recreational pursuits, sports and games amongst prisoners, and shall take the measures necessary to ensure the exercise thereof by providing them with adequate premises and necessary equipment.

Prisoners shall have opportunities for taking physical exercise, including sports and games, and for being out of doors. Sufficient open spaces shall be provided for this purpose in all camps. . . .

FOURTH CONVENTION RELATIVE TO THE PROTECTION OF CIVILIANS:

Art. 16: The wounded and sick, as well as the infirm, and expectant mothers, shall be the object of particular protection and respect. . . .

Art. 27: Protected persons are entitled, in all circumstances, to respect for their persons, their honor, their family rights, their religious convictions and practices, and their manners and customs. They shall at all times be humanely treated, and shall be protected especially against all acts of violence or threats thereof and against insults and public curiosity.

Women shall be especially protected against any attack on their honor, in particular against rape, enforced prostitution, or any form of indecent assault.

Without prejudice to the provisions relating to their state of health, age and sex, all protected persons shall be treated with the same consideration by the Party to the conflict in whose power they are, without any adverse distinction based, in particular, on race, religion or political opinion.

However, the Parties to the conflict may take such measures of control and security in regard to protected persons as may be necessary as a result of the war. . . .

Art. 42: The internment or placing in assigned residence of protected persons may be ordered only if the security of the Detaining Power makes it absolutely necessary. . . .

Art. 91: Every place of internment shall have an adequate infirmary, under the direction of a qualified doctor, where internees may have the attention they require, as well as an appropriate diet. Isolation wards shall be set aside for cases of contagious or mental diseases.

Maternity cases and internees suffering from serious diseases, or whose condition requires special treatment, a surgical operation or hospital care, must be admitted to any institution where adequate treatment can be given and shall receive care not inferior to that provided for the general population. . . .

Treatment, including the provision of any apparatus necessary for the maintenance of internees in good health, particularly dentures and other artificial appliances and spectacles, shall be free of charge to the internee. . . .

Art. 94: The Detaining Power shall encourage intellectual, educational and recreational pursuits, sports and games amongst internees, whilst leaving them free to take part in them or not. It shall take all practicable measures to ensure the exercise thereof, in particular by providing suitable premises.

All possible facilities shall be granted to internees to continue their studies or to take up new subjects. The education of children and young people shall be ensured; they shall be allowed to attend schools either within the place of internment or outside.

Internees shall be given opportunities for physical exercise, sports and outdoor games. For this purpose, sufficient open spaces shall be set aside in all places of internment. Special playgrounds shall be reserved for children and young people. . . .

Art. 146: The High Contracting Parties undertake to enact any legislation necessary to provide effective penal sanctions for persons committing, or ordering to be committed, any of the grave breaches of the present Convention defined in [Article 147]. . . .

Art. 147: Grave breaches to which [Article 146] . . . relates shall be those involving any of the following acts, if committed against persons or property protected by the present Convention: willful killing, torture or inhuman treatment, including biological experiments, willfully causing great suffering or serious injury to body or health, unlawful deportation or transfer or unlawful confinement of a protected person, compelling a protected person to serve in the forces of a hostile Power, or willfully depriving a protected person of the rights of fair and regular trial prescribed in the present Convention, taking of hostages and extensive destruction and appropriation of property, not justified by military necessity and carried out unlawfully and wantonly. . . .

Questions

1. Was one of the goals of the 1949 Geneva Conventions to broaden the scope of the *jus in bello* by broadening the definition of war? If so, how did the conventions go about accomplishing this goal?
2. Common Article 3 refers to "non-international armed conflicts." What types of conflicts are these? Do the Geneva Conventions impose fewer restrictions on these types of conflict than on conflicts between nations? Why?
3. Does Article 4 of the Third Convention expand Hague IV's definition of a "belligerent"? Why is this definition so important? In cases of doubt, Article 5 of the Third Convention requires that a "competent tribunal" decide the "belligerent" status of the prisoner. What type of tribunal should this be? A court? A panel of military officers?
4. Does the Third Convention grant rights to prisoners of war that are surprising to you?
5. Article 27 of the Fourth Geneva Convention not only grants many rights to protected civilian persons during wartime but also gives a belligerent state the right to "take such measures of control and security in regard to protected persons as may be necessary as a result of the war." Is this an exception that swallows the rule? Who decides what measures are necessary?
6. Internment of protected civilian persons is justified under the Fourth Convention only if it is "absolutely necessary" for security. How do you understand this requirement? In your view, what would have to occur before internment would be "absolutely necessary"?
7. Does the Fourth Convention grant any rights to civilians that are surprising to you?

The four 1949 Geneva Conventions are the foundation for today's law of armed conflict. As of 2006, all of the world's nations have ratified these conventions, and much of their substance has been deemed customary international law and thereby obligatory on any new nation that might refuse to ratify it. At the same time, *jus in bello* has also continued to evolve. One influence has been the human rights movement, which was born when the United Nations General Assembly proclaimed the Universal Declaration of Human Rights on December 10, 1948. This movement, a reaction to the horrors and brutalities of World War II, resulted in the ratification of many human rights treaties, including the International Covenant on Civil and Political Rights (1966), the Convention against Torture and Other Cruel, Inhuman or Degrading Treatment or Punishment (1984), and the International Convention for the Protection of All Persons from Enforced Disappearance (2006). Though not every country ratified these human rights treaties and though they arguably only apply in times of peace, human rights law has had a pervasive impact on *jus in bello* over the last fifty years. It has been at the center of the trend in favor of humanization of the law of armed conflict.

Another major factor in the evolution of *jus in bello* following World War II has been the changing nature of warfare itself. Many of the conflicts that have arisen since 1960 are not large-scale conflicts between the armed forces of states but rather colonial revolutions, insurgencies, or what have been called "wars of national liberation." During the 1970s, experts from more than a hundred countries met in Geneva to consider how the 1949 conventions could be modernized or supplemented to meet the contingencies of these new types of conflict in the context of an expanding human rights movement. The result was that two additional protocols were drafted in 1977: Additional Protocol I (AP I) addressed the protection of victims of international armed conflicts, while Additional Protocol II (AP II) did the same for victims of noninternational conflicts. The United States never ratified either of these protocols, but many of the provisions of both protocols are binding on all states because they have achieved the status of customary international law. For example, in *Hamdan v. Rumsfeld* (2006), a four-justice plurality of the Supreme Court endorsed the view that the trial and court protections of Article 75 of AP I were customary law.[16] The following excerpts focus on the key paragraphs of Article 75 that have since become customary international law.

3.8 Additional Protocol I (AP I) (1977)

Art. 75. Fundamental Guarantees[17]

1. . . . [P]ersons who are in the power of a Party to the conflict and who do not benefit from more favorable treatment under the Conventions or under this Protocol shall be treated humanely in all circumstances and shall enjoy, as a minimum, the protection provided by this Article. . . .
2. The following acts are and shall remain prohibited at any time and in any place whatsoever, whether committed by civilian or by military agents:
   a. violence to the life, health, or physical or mental well-being of persons, in particular:
      i. murder;
      ii. torture of all kinds, whether physical or mental;
      iii. corporal punishment; and
      iv. mutilation;
   b. outrages upon personal dignity, in particular humiliating and degrading treatment, enforced prostitution and any form of indecent assault;
   c. the taking of hostages;
   d. collective punishments; and
   e. threats to commit any of the foregoing acts. . . .
3. No sentence may be passed and no penalty may be executed on a person found guilty of a penal offence related to the armed conflict except pursuant to a conviction pronounced by an impartial and regularly constituted court respecting the generally recognized principles of regular judicial procedure. . . .

Questions

1. Article 75 provides a safety net for persons who are not protected under the 1949 Conventions or AP I. Who are these persons? Prisoners of war? Civilians? Civilians who take part in hostilities? Unlawful enemy combatants? Unlawful enemy combatants who commit war crimes?
2. Does Article 75 extend the duty of "humane treatment" to all persons in the power of a party to the conflict? Is there a reason such a rule should apply to "wars of national liberation"?
3. Article 75 prohibits both "military agents" and "civilians" from engaging in certain prohibited conduct. Why

should the laws of war prohibit what civilians can do?

4. Article 75 prohibits "outrages upon personal dignity" and "humiliating and degrading treatment." Is this prohibition too vague to be enforceable? Can you identify a type of offensive conduct that would not be prohibited by this provision?

The UN Security Council has created several tribunals to prosecute war crimes in specific armed conflicts. One of these is the International Criminal Tribunal for the former Yugoslavia (ICTY), which was established in 1993 to prosecute genocide, war crimes, and crimes against humanity committed in the violent aftermath of the dissolution of Yugoslavia. Even though ICTY's decisions are binding only on the parties of a case, they nonetheless constitute an authoritative source of *jus in bello*, and the ICTY has handed down a number of significant decisions relevant to the law of armed conflict. One of the more important cases decided by the ICTY is *Prosecutor v. Tadić*. In this lengthy case, the ICTY clarified the criteria of what constitutes an international versus noninternational armed conflict and discussed the nexus that had to exist between an offense and an armed conflict to qualify as a war crime. The former question is fundamental because a war crime can only occur in the context of an "armed conflict," whether the conflict is an "international" one between states or a "non-international" one, for example, between a state and an internal insurgency group. While the ICTY assumes that any conflict between states is an "armed conflict" that triggers international humanitarian law, it holds that a noninternational conflict qualifies as an "armed conflict" that triggers Common Article 3 of the Geneva Conventions only if the "intensity" of the conflict and the "organization" of the parties to the conflict distinguish it from "banditry, unorganized and short-lived insurrections, or terrorist activities." If the conflict does not satisfy the criteria of either type of armed conflict, then there is no armed conflict and the ICTY would not have jurisdiction to hear the case. The alleged offense would have to be prosecuted as a domestic crime in local courts. The second issue is of a similar character. Even if it is indisputable that an "armed conflict" exists, not every criminal offense committed during the conflict will necessarily qualify as a war crime. The offense must in some way be "closely related" to the armed conflict if it is to constitute a "war crime."

3.9 *Prosecutor v. Tadić* (IT-94-1T), Opinion and Judgment (May 7, 1997)

561. According to the Appeals Chamber Decision, the test for determining the existence of such a conflict is that[18]

> an armed conflict exists whenever there is a resort to armed force between States or protracted armed violence between governmental authorities and organized armed groups or between such groups within a State. . . .

562. The test applied by the Appeals Chamber to the existence of an armed conflict for the purposes of the rules contained in Common Article 3 focuses on two aspects of a conflict; the intensity of the conflict and the organization of the parties to the conflict. In an armed conflict of an internal or mixed character, these closely related criteria are used solely for the purpose, at a minimum, of distinguishing an armed conflict from banditry, unorganized and short-lived insurrections, or terrorist activities, which are not subject to international humanitarian law. . . .

568. Having regard then to the nature and scope of the conflict in the Republic of Bosnia and Herzegovina and the parties involved in that conflict . . . the Trial Chamber finds that, at all relevant times, an armed conflict was taking place between the parties to the conflict in the Republic of Bosnia and Herzegovina of sufficient scope and intensity for the purposes of the application of the laws or customs of war embodied in Article 3 common to the four Geneva Conventions of 12 August 1949, applicable as it is to armed conflicts in general, including armed conflicts not of an international character. . . .

572. The existence of an armed conflict or occupation and the applicability of international humanitarian law to the territory is not sufficient to create international jurisdiction over each and every serious crime committed in the territory of the former Yugoslavia. For a crime to fall within the jurisdiction of the International Tribunal, a sufficient nexus must be established between the alleged offence and the armed conflict which gives rise to the applicability of international humanitarian law.

573. In relation to the applicability of international humanitarian law to the acts alleged in the Indictment, the Appeals Chamber has held that:

> Even if substantial clashes were not occurring in the Prijedor region at the time and place the crimes allegedly were committed—a factual issue on which the Appeals Chamber does not pronounce—international humanitarian law applies. It is sufficient that the alleged crimes were closely related to the hostilities occurring in other parts of the territories controlled by the parties to the conflict.

For an offence to be a violation of international humanitarian law, therefore, this Trial Chamber needs to be satisfied that each of the alleged acts was in fact closely related to the hostilities. It would be sufficient to prove that the crime was committed in the course of or as part of the hostilities in, or occupation of, an area controlled by one of the parties. It is not, however, necessary to show that armed conflict was occurring at the exact time and place of the proscribed acts alleged to have occurred, as the Appeals Chamber has indicated, nor is it necessary that the crime alleged takes place during combat, that it be part of a policy or of a practice officially endorsed or tolerated by one of the parties to the conflict, or that the act be in actual furtherance of a policy associated with the conduct of war or in the actual interest of a party to the conflict; the obligations of individuals under international humanitarian law are independent and apply without prejudice to any questions of the responsibility of States under international law. The only question, to be determined in the circumstances of each individual case, is whether the offences were closely related to the armed conflict as a whole.

574. In any event, acts of the accused related to the armed conflict in two distinct ways. First, there is the case of the acts of the accused in the take-over of Kozarac and the villages. . . . Given the nature of the armed conflict as an ethnic war and the strategic aims of the Republika Srpska to create a purely Serbian State, the acts of the accused during the armed take-over and ethnic cleansing of Muslim and Croat areas . . . were directly connected with the armed conflict.

575. Secondly, there are the acts of the accused in the camps run by the authorities of the Republika Srpska. Those acts clearly occurred with the connivance or permission of the authorities running these camps and indicate that such acts were part of an accepted policy towards prisoners in the camps. . . . Indeed, such treatment effected the objective of the Republika Srpska to ethnically cleanse, by means of terror, killings or otherwise, the areas of the Republic of Bosnia and Herzegovina controlled by Bosnian Serb forces. Accordingly, those acts too were directly connected with the armed conflict. . . .

Questions

1. Is the ICTY claiming that any type of conflict between states qualify as "armed conflict" subject to international humanitarian law, but that conflict between states and armed groups qualify as armed conflicts only if the conflict is sufficiently "intense" and if the parties to the conflict are well "organized"? Why is there this difference between the two types of armed conflict?
2. The ICTY argues that international humanitarian law does not apply to terrorist groups. Can this position be defended following the 9/11 attacks? What if a state's conflict with a terrorist group is sufficiently intense and the terrorist group is well organized?
3. Is the ICTY correct that a criminal act can constitute a war crime even if it does not occur at a time or place of active hostilities?
4. The ICTY concludes that a criminal act only needs to be "closely related to the armed conflict" to qualify as a war crime, but is this criterion too vague to be applied in any consistent way?
5. The ICTY argues that the criminal offense need not be "authorized" by one of the parties of the conflict or in "furtherance of a policy" of a party to qualify as a war crime. Is this position defensible, especially since the ICTY underlines the fact that the defendant in this case was working toward the strategic goal of the war—that is, ethnic cleansing—and that he "connived" with the authorities running the prison camps? Do you have any suggestions as to how to make the ICTY's criteria of "closely related to the armed conflict" more precise?

Five years after *Tadic*, the ICTY, in *Prosecutor v. Kunarac* (2002), elaborated on the nexus that must exist between a crime and an "armed conflict" before the former can qualify as a "war crime." The court's definition of "armed conflict" remained unchanged: any "resort to armed force between States" was sufficient, while armed violence between governmental authorities and "organized armed groups" or between such groups had to be "protracted" in character. In either type of conflict, a crime had to be "closely related" to an "armed conflict" before it could qualify as a "war crime." Obviously, this criterion is somewhat vague in character, but the court underlined the fact that the law of war extended to the "whole territory of the warring states" or the "whole territory under the control of a party to the conflict." What this meant in practice was that a war crime need not be directly linked to or associated with actual combat for it to be "closely related to hostilities," whether these hostilities were occurring in the immediate area or in "other parts of the territory controlled by the parties to the conflict." Moreover, the court's understanding of when an alleged crime was "closely related" to an armed conflict was not a particularly high standard. One of the court's formulations posits that a domestic offense could constitute a "war crime" if it is "shaped by or dependent upon" the underlying environment of the "armed conflict"—a fairly malleable and flexible standard.

3.10 *Prosecutor v. Kunarac et al.* (IT-96-23 and 23/1-A) (June 12, 2002)

57. There is no necessary correlation between the area where the actual fighting is taking place and the geographical reach of the laws of war.[19] The laws of war apply in the whole territory of the warring states or, in the case of internal armed conflicts, the whole territory under the control of a party to the conflict, whether or not actual combat takes

place there, and continue to apply until a general conclusion of peace or, in the case of internal armed conflicts, until a peaceful settlement is achieved. A violation of the laws or customs of war may therefore occupy a time when and in a place where no fighting is actually taking place. . . . [T]he requirement that the acts of the accused must be closely related to the armed conflict would not be negated if the crimes were temporally and geographically remote from the actual fighting. It would be sufficient, for instance, for the purpose of this requirement, that the alleged crimes were closely related to hostilities controlled by the parties to the conflict.

58. What ultimately distinguishes a war crime from a purely domestic offence is that a war crime is shaped by or dependent upon the environment—the armed conflict—in which it is committed. It need not have been planned or supported by some form of policy. The armed conflict need not have been causal to the commission of the crime, but the existence of an armed conflict must, at a minimum, have played a substantial part in the perpetrator's ability to commit it, his decision to commit it, the manner in which it was committed or the purpose for which it was committed. Hence, if it can be established, as in the present case, that the perpetrator acted in furtherance of or under the guise of the armed conflict, it would be sufficient to conclude that his acts were closely related to the armed conflict. . . .

59. In determining whether or not the act in question is sufficiently related to the armed conflict, the Trial Chamber may take into account, *inter alia*, the following factors: the fact that the perpetrator is a combatant; the fact that the victim is a non-combatant; the fact that the victim is a member of the opposing party; the fact that the act may be said to serve the ultimate goal of a military campaign; and the fact that the crime is committed as part of or in the context of the perpetrator's official duties.

60. The Appellant's proposition that the laws of war only prohibit those acts which are specific to actual wartime situations is not right. The laws of war may frequently encompass acts which, though they are not committed in the theater of conflict, are substantially related to it. The laws of war can apply to both types of acts. The Appeals Chamber understands the Appellant's argument to be that if an act can be prosecuted in peacetime, it cannot be prosecuted in wartime. This betrays a misconception about the relationship between the laws of war and the laws regulating a peacetime situation. The laws of war do not necessarily displace the laws regulating a peacetime situation; the former may add elements requisite to the protection which needs to be afforded to victims in a wartime situation. . . .

Questions

1. Should the ICTY have recognized some geographical limit to the laws of war other than the territory of the warring states or parties? Does the ICTY's rule mean that a crime within the United States could conceivably be a "war crime" since the United States is in an armed conflict with al-Qaeda or ISIS? What if a U.S. citizen engaged in credit card theft for the purpose of sending the proceeds to al-Qaeda? Is that arguably a possible war crime?
2. The ICTY rejects the view that one of the parties to the conflict must have "planned" or "supported" the criminal act as a matter of "policy" for it to be a war crime. Would there be any advantages to limiting the scope of war crimes to those that are sanctioned by one of the parties to the conflict? Are there any disadvantages?
3. The ICTY also argues that a war crime need not be "caused" by the armed conflict. Would there be some value in requiring some sort of causal linkage between the armed conflict and a crime prior to prosecuting it as a war crime? Would you support the rule

that a crime can be considered a war crime only if it would not have happened "but for" the armed conflict?

4. The ICTY concludes that, at a minimum, a "war crime" requires that the armed conflict played a "substantial part" in the perpetrator's "ability" to commit the crime, his "decision" to commit it, the "manner" in which it was committed, or the "purpose" for which it was done. Can you imagine scenarios that would satisfy one of these four criteria but where, in your view, the perpetrator's crime did not qualify as a "war crime"? Would you revise any of these four criteria? Do you reject any of them as an insufficient basis for classifying a crime as a "war crime"? To what extent does the requirement that the armed conflict play a "substantial part" in one of the identified dimensions of the crime remedy any problem with the four criteria?
5. The ICTY also lists five factors that a trial court may take into account to determine if a crime "is sufficiently related to the armed conflict." How do these five factors relate to the four criteria discussed above? Would it be fair to assume, from the fact that the victim "is a member of the opposing party," that this factor adds weight to the conclusion that the armed conflict had a bearing on the perpetrator's "decision" to commit the crime or on his "purpose" in committing it?
6. The ICTY implies that there are crimes during an armed conflict that can be tried in either domestic criminal courts or war crime tribunals. Should prosecutors have this option? Does it permit prosecutors to engage in what is called "forum shopping"? Does this bifurcated approach inevitably raise questions of fairness?

The ICTY's jurisdiction is confined to the conflict arising from the dissolution of Yugoslavia, and its mandate is drawing to a close. However, an international treaty—called the Rome Statute—was signed in 1998 that created the International Criminal Court (ICC). The ICC is the first permanent international criminal court that has jurisdiction to prosecute all cases involving genocide, crimes against humanity, and war crimes. Obviously, with jurisdiction over these types of crimes, the likelihood is very high that the ICC will often be handling cases arising out of armed conflicts. The Rome Statute's list of war crimes incorporates relevant provisions of the Geneva Conventions and Additional Protocols I and II. However, the ICC can take jurisdiction over a case only if the country where the alleged crime occurred is either "unwilling or unable" to prosecute individuals involved or if the UN Security Council refers a case to the court. The ICC began operating in 2002, and currently more than 120 states have ratified the Rome Statute and the ICC has indicted almost forty persons, of which three have been convicted and sentenced.

The United States has consistently opposed the creation of the ICC because of fears that members of the U.S. military and other U.S. nationals would be more likely to end up as defendants given the active role that the United States plays in conflict-ridden areas of the world and because U.S. policymakers are confident that the U.S. military will more than adequately prosecute American personnel involved with crimes within the ICC's jurisdiction. Whether the latter assumption is a reasonable one, given that no high-level American official has been held criminally accountable for detention and interrogation practices in Afghanistan, is a sensitive issue. In any case, the United States has refused to ratify the Rome Statute or join the ICC. In addition, in 2002, Congress enacted the Servicemembers' Protection Act, which provided for the withdrawal of U.S. military assistance from countries that ratified the Rome Statute, made U.S. support for peacekeeping missions contingent on immunity from ICC prosecution for all U.S. personnel, and included a provision that authorized the use of military force to liberate any American or citizen of a U.S.-allied country detained by the ICC in The Hague—the so-called Hague invasion clause.

The Obama administration, despite its internationalist orientation, has had at best an ambivalent attitude toward the ICC. It supported the ICC's efforts to arrest Joseph Kony, the leader of the Lord's Resistance Army, a guerilla group that operated in Uganda that exploited children by using them as "child soldiers" and "sex slaves," and it voted at the UN Security Council in favor of referring Libya and the Gaddafi regime to the ICC for "war crimes" against civilians in February 2011. However, when it came to the deployment of American troops in foreign countries, Obama followed the practice of the Bush administration by using Bilateral Immunity Agreements (BIAs) to immunize U.S. troops from prosecution by the ICC. Article 98 of the Rome Statute prohibited the ICC from proceeding with a prosecution if it required a state to act "inconsistently" with its international agreements. Accordingly, before sending troops to Mali in 2014, Obama issued a legal memorandum stating that U.S. military personnel "are without risk of criminal prosecution or other assertion of jurisdiction by the International Criminal Court (ICC) because the Republic of Mali has entered into an agreement in accordance with Article 98 of the Rome Statute preventing the ICC from proceeding against members of the Armed Forces of the United States present in that country."[20] The use of such BIAs has become the typical way by which the United States avoids the jurisdiction of the ICC.

Other countries and regional entities have also expressed their reservations about the jurisdiction of the ICC. Based on its view that the ICC unfairly targeted African governments, the African Union called for a mass withdrawal from the ICC, following which Burundi, South Africa, and Gambia enacted laws with that effect in October 2016. The following month Russia, a permanent member of the UN Security Council, withdrew its signature from the Rome Statute, putting to rest any chance that it would become a member of the ICC. The atrocities committed during the Syrian civil war highlighted the apparent ineffectiveness of the ICC for there was little likelihood that the perpetrators of these "war crimes" would ever be held accountable for their actions. A few weeks before the 2016 U.S. presidential election, the prosecutor of the ICC, Fatou Bensouda, released her latest update on the ongoing inquiry into the conflict in Afghanistan, noting that U.S. personnel "may be" responsible for war crimes.[21] The ICC Pre-Trial Chamber of judges is currently considering whether Bensouda's proposed investigation will go forward. It may not be an easy decision since Afghanistan has both conceded to the ICC jurisdiction over crimes "committed on the territory of Afghanistan or by its nationals from 1 May 2003 onwards"[22] and signed a confidential Status of Forces Agreement with the United States in 2002 that presumably precludes ICC jurisdiction over U.S. personnel, an international agreement that Afghanistan might think is "inconsistent" with ICC jurisdiction.[23]

Bensouda's proposal for an investigation of possible U.S. war crimes in Afghanistan did little to endear the ICC to the newly elected president, Donald Trump. Perhaps in response to the ICC prosecutor's November update, the Trump administration drafted an executive order that would decrease funding for international organizations by 40 percent and charged the committee that would implement the order to examine in particular the role of the ICC.[24] In March 2018, Trump appointed John Bolton to be his new national security advisor. Bolton, a former United States ambassador to the United Nations, has written that "America should welcome the opportunity . . . to strangle the ICC in its cradle" because it was "toxic to democratic sovereignty." He also suggested that the White House should write "a terse note" to the ICC prosecutor: "You are dead to us. Sincerely, the United States."[25] John Bellinger, former legal advisor for the Department of State, has argued that it would be "especially unwise" for the ICC prosecutor to launch an "investigation of U.S. activities in Afghanistan and elsewhere," claiming that it would be a "self-defeating action" that "would hurt the Court and its overall mission."[26] The current drift of events is clearly not in favor of the ICC and its mission of prosecuting genocide, crimes against humanity, and "war crimes" at the international level. Only future elections and events will show whether U.S. hostility to the ICC is part of an irreversible long-term nationalist trend or rather a temporary pause in the further internationalization of criminal prosecutions of crimes involving genocide, crimes against humanity, and war crimes. How should the ICC Pre-Trial Chamber balance the political and legal factors in play regarding an investigation of possible U.S. war crimes in Afghanistan? If the goal is to preserve the role that international law has played in the context of armed conflict, what should the ICC do?

The Trump administration has also confronted a different question regarding the law of armed conflict or the *jus in bello*. The question has arisen in the context of the emerging intercontinental ballistic missile crisis with North Korea discussed briefly in the preceding chapter. If, as President Trump insists, the "era of strategic patience" is over, there are arguably only two options or threats that the administration can pursue: a conventional war with North Korea (the so-called bloody nose option) or a preemptive nuclear strike. There is little doubt that the former option can be lawfully pursued consistent with *jus in bello* if the conditions of *jus ad bellum* are clearly satisfied—that is, for example, if the conflict is a lawful exercise of the right of self-defense and Congress has authorized the use of military force.

However, regarding a preemptive nuclear strike, there is some controversy regarding whether nuclear weapons would ever be consistent with *jus in bello* principles. Even if justified by self-defense, could a preemptive nuclear strike or the threat thereof ever be "necessary"? Could the loss of innocent civilian lives ever be "proportionate" to the military advantage gained by such a devastating attack. The UN General Assembly requested the International Court of Justice (ICJ) to address this question in an advisory opinion in 1994. The court acknowledged that specific treaties explicitly prohibited the use of certain weapons, such as poisonous, bacteriological, and chemical weapons, but concluded that no treaty or principle of customary law explicitly prohibited the threat or use of nuclear weapons. However, despite the lack of an explicit prohibition, the ICJ insisted that the threat or use of nuclear weapons would "generally be contrary to the rules of international law applicable in armed conflict." However, it could not "conclude definitively whether the threat or use of nuclear weapons would be lawful or unlawful in an extreme act of self-defense, in which the very survival of a State would be at stake."[27] The implication of the ICJ's decision was that the threat or use of nuclear weapons is generally inconsistent with principles of *jus in bello* unless a state finds itself in the direst of circumstances. A fundamentally important question for every American citizen to consider is how the ICJ's decision applies to the circumstances of the ongoing crisis between the United States and North Korea.

NOTES

1. *De Officiis*, book I, XI, http://www.constitution.org/rom/de_officiis.htm.
2. St. Thomas Aquinas, *Summa Theologica: War (Secunda Secundae Partis, Q 40)*, https://dhspriory.org/thomas/summa/SS/SS040.html#SSQ40OUTP1.
3. *De Jure Belli ac Pacis*, book III, chap. 1, http://www.constitution.org/gro/djbp.htm.
4. *De Jure Belli ac Pacis*, book III, chap. 11.
5. For Grotius's view that violence between combatants is lawful, see *De Jure Belli ac Pacis*, book III, chap. 4.
6. Vattel, *The Law of Nations*, book 3, para. 63, http://oll.libertyfund.org.
7. Declaration of Paris, April 16, 1856, http://oll.libertyfund.org.
8. "General Orders No. 100: The Lieber Code," April 24, 1863, Yale Law School, Lillian Goldman Law Library, http://avalon.law.yale.edu.
9. James Speed, "Opinion on the Constitutional Power of the Military to Try and Execute the Assassins of the President," July 1865, UMKC School of Law, https://law.umkc.edu.
10. "Laws of War: Laws and Customs of War on Land (Hague II)," July 29, 1899, Yale Law School, Lillian Goldman Law Library, http://avalon.law.yale.edu.
11. "Hague Convention (IV) Respecting the Laws and Customs of War on Land," October 18, 1907, preamble, International Committee of the Red Cross (ICRC), https://ihl-databases.icrc.org.
12. "Hague Convention (IV)."
13. See Charter of the International Military Tribunal, Art. 6, Yale Law School, Lillian Goldman Law Library, http://avalon.law.yale.edu.
14. See the complete opinion at "International Military Tribunal (Nuremberg): Judgment of 1 October 1946," Global Campaign for Ratification and Implementation of the Kampala Amendments on the Crime of Aggression, http://crimeofaggression.info/documents/6/1946_Nuremberg_Judgement.pdf (see pp. 58–79).
15. All four 1949 Geneva Conventions can be found at "Geneva Conventions and Commentaries," International Committee of the Red Cross (ICRC), https://www.icrc.org.
16. See Justice Stevens's opinion in *Hamdan v. Rumsfeld*, 548 U.S. 557, 633 (2006).
17. The formal names for the two protocols are Protocol Additional to the Geneva Conventions of 12 August 1949, and relating to the Protection of Victims of International Armed Conflicts (Protocol I), 8 June 1977; and Protocol Additional to the Geneva Conventions of 12 August 1949, and relating to the Protection of Victims of Non-International Armed Conflicts (Protocol II), 8 June 1977. Both protocols can be found at "Geneva Conventions and Commentaries," cited in n. 15.

18. United Nations, "International Tribunal for the Prosecution of Persons . . . ," IT-94-1-T, May 7, 1997, UN International Criminal Tribunal for the former Yugoslavia (ICTY), http://www.icty.org.

19. United Nations, "International Tribunal for the Prosecution of Persons . . . ," IT-96-23 and 23/1-A, June 12, 2002, UN International Criminal Tribunal for the former Yugoslavia (ICTY), http://www.icty.org.

20. Barack Obama, "Certification concerning U.S. Participation in the United Nations Multidimensional Integrated Stabilization Mission in Mali . . . ," January 31, 2014, White House Archives, https://obamawhitehouse.archives.gov.

21. "Report on Preliminary Examination Activities," November 14, 2016, p. 47, para. 211, International Criminal Court, https://www.icc-cpi.int.

22. "Afghanistan: Preliminary Examination," International Criminal Court, https://www.icc-cpi.int/afghanistan.

23. Luis Moreno Ocampo, "The ICC's Afghanistan Investigation: The Missing Option," *Lawfare* (blog), April 24, 2017, https://www.lawfareblog.com/iccs-afghanistan-investigation-missing-option.

24. Max Fisher, "Trump Prepares Orders Aiming at Global Funding and Treaties," *New York Times*, January 25, 2017, https://www.nytimes.com.

25. John Bolton, "The Hague Aims for U.S. Soldiers," *Wall Street Journal*, November 20, 2017, https://www.wsj.com/articles/the-hague-tiptoes-toward-u-s-soldiers-1511217136.

26. John Bellinger, "The International Criminal Court and the Trump Administration," *Lawfare* (blog), March 27, 2018, https://www.lawfareblog.com/international-criminal-court-and-trump-administration.

27. "Legality of the Threat or Use of Nuclear Weapons: Advisory Opinion of 8 July 1996," International Court of Justice, para. 105, http://www.un.org/law/icjsum/9623.htm.

4

Combatant Status

★ ★ ★

The issue of combatant status, a topic briefly touched upon in the preceding chapter, addresses two fundamental questions regarding the law of war. First, there is the critical distinction between a civilian and a combatant. As the law of war has evolved over the last two hundred years, only combatants and civilians who directly participate in hostilities can be lawfully targeted during an armed conflict. Combatants can be targeted based on their status as combatants, while civilians are only targetable based on their conduct, that is, if they "directly participate in hostilities." Second, not all combatants are equal in terms of their legitimacy to participate in armed conflict. Regular members of the armed forces of a party to a conflict have the right of combatant immunity, which means they cannot lawfully be punished for their warlike actions so long as they have complied with the laws of war and they are entitled to prisoner-of-war status if the enemy captures them. The enemy can lawfully detain such prisoners of war, but this detention is nonpunitive in character and it can last only for the duration of the hostilities. So-called irregular fighters in an armed conflict do not have combatant immunity and are not entitled to prisoner-of-war status. If captured, they can lawfully be punished for their warlike acts because their very participation in the armed conflict is considered a violation of the laws of war.

As an initial matter, it is worth noting that detention of lawful enemy combatants was not always the norm. Prior to the sixteenth century, prisoners were killed, enslaved, impressed into the military service of the captor, or if extremely lucky, granted their freedom, but they generally were not detained for the duration of hostilities. Beginning in the seventeenth century, prisoner exchanges between the belligerent parties became more commonplace, as did "release on parole," which gave prisoners freedom if they promised not to return to the conflict. The Peace of Westphalia (1648), which ended the Thirty Years' War and established the principle of the sovereignty of national states, included a provision that all prisoners should be released at the end of hostilities, implicitly denying the older view that the victor had a right to kill and enslave the vanquished.

The rise of nationalist armies and the realities of warfare during the French Revolution and Napoleonic Era undermined the legitimacy and practicality of prisoner exchanges, "release on parole," and impressment into the captor's military service. Almost by default, nonpunitive detention of enemy prisoners of war until the end of hostilities gradually became the new norm. For example, during the American Revolution, both sides detained thousands of enemy soldiers, while it is estimated that Britain during the Napoleonic Wars detained more than one hundred thousand French soldiers and sailors.[1]

As the above principles gained acceptance during the late eighteenth century, the important question arose about what was to be done with "irregular fighters," such as the bands of Spanish insurgents or "guerillas" (derived from the Spanish word for war: *guerra*) that surreptitiously attacked Napoleon's French forces during the Peninsular War (1808–1814). Although there was initially no uniform response to such "irregular fighters," the conviction steadily grew that they were not lawful combatants or "*justus hostis*" (just enemies) but were rather "brigands," "rebels," or "banditti" who could be summarily executed if captured. Five decades later, during the American Civil War, Professor Francis Lieber wrote a legal memorandum on the lawful status of southern "guerrilla forces." He concluded that "spies," "armed prowlers," and "conspirators" could be summarily dealt with, that members of "partisan groups" and "free-corps" were lawful combatants, and that the status of "guerrilla parties" depended on the circumstances. Lieber's discussion of these complex issues is the first American attempt to introduce some clarity into the distinction between lawful ("regular") combatants and unlawful ("irregular") combatants.

4.1 Francis Lieber, "Guerilla Parties: Law and Usages of War" (1862)

. . . Both partisan-corps and free-corps designate bodies detached from the main army; but the former term refers to the action of the troop, the latter to the composition.[2] The partisan leader commands a corps whose object is to injure the enemy by action separate from that of his own main army; the partisan acts chiefly upon the enemy's lines of connection and communication, and outside of or beyond the lines of operation of his own army, in the rear and on the flanks of the enemy. Rapid and varying movements and surprises are the chief means of his success; but he is part and parcel of the army, and, as such, considered entitled to the privileges of the law of war, so long as he does not transgress it. Free-corps, on the other hand, are troops not belonging to the regular army, consisting of volunteers, generally raised by individuals authorized to do so by the government, used for petty war, and not incorporated with the *Ordre de bataille*. . . . They were generally in bad repute, given to pillage and other excesses; but this is incidental. There were many free-corps in Germany opposed to Napoleon, when that country rose against the French, but the men composing them were entitled to the benefits of the law of war, and generally received them when taken prisoner. These free-corps were composed, in many cases, of high-minded patriots. The difficulty regarding free-corps and partisans arises from the fact that their discipline is often lax, and used to be so especially in the last century, so that frequently they cannot cumber themselves with prisoners; and that, even for their own support, they are often obliged to pillage or to extort money from the places they occupy. They are treated, therefore, according to their deserts, on the principle of retaliation; but there is nothing inherently lawless or brigand-like in their character.

The Spy, the Rebel, and Conspirator deserve notice in this place simply with reference to persons acting as such, and belonging to the population of the country or district occupied by a hostile force. A person dwelling in a district under military occupation, and giving information to the government of which he was subject, but which has been expelled by the victorious invader, is universally treated as a spy—a spy of a peculiarly dangerous character. The most patriotic motives would not shield such a person from the doom of the spy. There have been high-minded and self-sacrificing spies, but, when captured, even if belonging to the armies themselves, they have never been treated otherwise than as common spies. Even mere secret correspondence of a person in an occupied district with the enemy, though the contents of the correspondence may have been innocent, has subjected the correspondent to serious consequences, and sometimes to the rigor of martial law, especially if the offence be committed after a proclamation to the contrary. . . .

The rising *en masse*, or "the arming of peasants," as it used to be called, brings us nearer to the subject of the guerilla parties. . . .

I believe it can be said that the most recent publicists and writers on international law agree that the rising of the people to repel invasion entitled them to the full benefits of the law of war, and that the invader cannot well inquire into the origin of the armed masses opposing him; that is to say, he will be obliged to treat the captured citizens in arms as prisoners of war, so long as they openly oppose him in respectable numbers, and have risen in the yet uninvaded or unconquered portions of the hostile country.

Their acting in separate bodies does not necessarily give them a different character. Some entire wars have been carried on by separate bands or capitaneries, such as the recent war of independence of Greece. . . .

It does not seem that, in the case of a rising *en masse*, the absence of a uniform can constitute a difference. There are cases, indeed, in which the absence of a uniform may be taken as very serious *prima facie* evidence against an armed prowler or marauder, but it must be remembered that a uniform dress is a matter of impossibility in a levy *en masse*; and in some cases regulars have had no uniforms, at least for a considerable time. . . . It makes a great difference, however, whether the absence of the uniform is used for the purpose of concealment or disguise, in order to get by stealth within the lines of the invader, for destruction of life or property, or for pillage, and whether the parties have no organization at all, and are so small that they cannot act otherwise than by stealth. Nor can it be maintained in good faith, or with any respect for sound sense and judgment, that an individual—an armed prowler—(now frequently called a bushwhacker) shall be entitled to the protection of the law of war, simply because he says that he has taken up his gun in defense of his country, or because his government or his chief has issued a proclamation by which he calls upon the people to infest the bushes and commit homicides which every civilized nation will consider murders. Indeed, the importance of writing on this subject is much diminished by the fact that the soldier generally decides these cases for himself. The most disciplined soldiers will execute on the spot an armed and murderous prowler found where he could have no business as a peaceful citizen. . . .

It is different, if we understand by guerilla parties, self-constituted sets of armed men, in times of war, who form no integrant part of the army, or are not paid at all, take up arms and lay them down at intervals, and carry on petty war (guerrilla) chiefly by raids, extortion, destruction, and massacre, and who cannot encumber themselves with many prisoners, and will therefore generally give no quarter.

They are peculiarly dangerous, because they easily evade pursuit, and by laying down their arms become insidious enemies; because they cannot otherwise subsist than by rapine, and almost always degenerate into simple robbers or brigands. . . .

But when guerrilla parties aid the main army of a belligerent, it will be difficult for the captor of guerrilla-men to decide at once whether they are regular partisans, distinctly authorized by their own government; and it would seem that we are borne out by the conduct of the most humane belligerents in recent times, and by many of the modern writers, if the rule be laid down, that guerrilla-men, when captured in fair fight and open warfare, should be treated as the regular partisan is, until special crimes, such as murder, or the killing of prisoners, or the sacking of places, are proved upon them; leaving the question of self-constitution unexamined.

The law of war, however, would not extend a similar favor to small bodies of armed country people, near the lines, whose very smallness shows that they must resort to occasional fighting and the occasional assuming of peaceful habits, and to brigandage. The law of war would still less favor them when they trespass within the hostile lines to commit devastation, rapine, or destruction. Every European army has treated such persons, and it seems to me would continue, even in the improved state of the present usages of war, to treat them as brigands, whatever prudential mercy might decide upon in single cases. . . .

It has been stated already, that the armed prowler, the so-called bushwhacker, is a simple assassin, and will thus always be considered by soldier and citizen; and we have likewise seen that the armed bands that rise in a district fairly occupied by military force, or in the rear of an army, are universally considered, if captured, brigands, and not prisoners of war. They unite the fourfold character of the spy, the brigand, the assassin, and the rebel, and cannot—indeed, it must be supposed, will not—expect to be treated as a fair enemy of the regular war. They know what a hazardous career they enter upon when they take up arms, and that, were the case reversed, they would surely not grant the privileges of regular warfare to persons who should thus rise in their rear. . . .

Questions

1. How does Lieber think a "partisan group" or a "free-corps" differs from a "guerrilla group"?
2. What does Lieber mean when he says that "partisans" and "free-corps" are not lawless in themselves but they can and should be treated "according to their deserts"? How is this different from or similar to how an occupying force can lawfully treat a "guerrilla group"?
3. Lieber argues that a *levee en masse*, that is, a "rising of the people to repel invasion," is fully protected by the law of war, even if the *levee* acts independently of the regular army and is not in uniform. Why do you think he treats such a *levee* so differently from a "guerrilla group"? Is it because a *levee en masse* does not use the lack of uniform for purposes of "concealment or disguise"? Is it the greater size of the *levee* over a "guerrilla group"? Is it both? In Lieber's view, how are these characteristics related?
4. Lieber seems to suggest that soldiers can lawfully execute "on the spot" a "bushwhacker," a "prowler," or a "spy." Why does Lieber extend to the soldier this degree of discretion? Do you think he is right?
5. When does Lieber think that certain "guerrilla men" should be treated as prisoners of war? Why does he take this position?
6. Lieber expresses no sympathy for small groups of fighters conducting operations near a battlefield or groups that form in areas already occupied by military force. Do these distinctions make sense? If a people can "rise to repel an invasion," why can't they "rise to expel an occupying force"? Why should the law of war necessarily disfavor small groups of fighters near a battlefield? Can they be denied prisoner-of-war status, if captured, even if they have not engaged in "devastation, rapine, or destruction"?

The principles that Lieber articulated in his 1862 legal memorandum reappeared in the Lieber Code that Abraham Lincoln issued in 1863 as General Orders No. 100. First, the code took a severe stance toward "spies," who could be executed summarily, while "armed prowlers" and "war-rebels" (defined as persons inside occupied territory who "rise in arms" against the occupying army) were denied prisoner-of-war status. Although the code deemed captured partisans "prisoners of war," it defined "partisans" somewhat narrowly as "soldiers armed and *wearing the uniform of their army* but belonging to a corps which acts detached from the main body" (emphasis added). Article 82 of the order addressed the status of groups that were called "guerrilla parties" in Lieber's 1862 memorandum.

> Men, or squads of men, who commit hostilities, whether by fighting, or [by] inroads for destruction or plunder, or by raids of any kind, without commission, without being part and portion of the organized hostile army, and without sharing continuously in the war, but who do so with intermitting returns to their homes and avocations, or with the occasional assumption of the semblance of peaceful pursuits, divesting themselves of the character or appearance of soldiers—such men, or squads of men, are not public enemies, and, therefore, if captured, are not entitled to the privileges of prisoners of war, but shall be treated summarily as highway robbers or pirates.[3]

This language denies prisoner-of-war status to Confederate guerrillas who act without a commission from the Confederate government, who are not part of the Confederate Army, and who engage in hostilities only intermittently. It is not clear whether such guerrilla captives could be summarily executed or whether they were to be given some sort of military trial. Does Lieber assume that the result would be the same in either case?

The Lieber Code also briefly discussed the status of the civilian. Article 25 states the general principle: "In modern regular wars of the Europeans, and their descendants in other portions of the globe, protection of the inoffensive citizen of the hostile country is the rule; privation and disturbance of private relations are the exceptions." However, Article 155 added a qualification if the armed conflict was a civil war:

> The military commander of the legitimate government, in a war of rebellion, distinguishes between the loyal citizen in the revolted portion of the country and the disloyal citizen. The disloyal citizens may further be classified into those citizens known to sympathize with the rebellion without precisely aiding it, and those who, without taking up arms [and becoming an unlawful combatant], give positive aid and comfort to the rebellious enemy without being bodily forced thereto.

Article 156 makes it clear that the military commander "will throw the burden of the war, as much as lies within his power, on the disloyal citizens, . . . subjecting them to a stricter police than the noncombatant enemies have to suffer in regular war," such that the commander might "expel, transfer, imprison, or fine the revolted citizens who refuse to pledge themselves anew as citizens obedient to the law and loyal to the government." Lieber's language comes close to identifying such disloyal Southern citizens as "unlawful combatants," highlighting the slippery distinction between "disloyal" civilians and "irregular" combatants.

Questions about the status of "irregular" military forces resurfaced in Europe during the Franco-Prussian War (1870–1871). The German High Command reacted harshly to French guerrillas called *francs-tireurs* (literally "free shooters") who bitterly contested the German occupation. Following the war, fifteen European states in 1874 adopted the Brussels Declaration, which focused in part on who qualified as a legitimate belligerent entitled to prisoner-of-war status if captured. Although the Brussels Declaration was never ratified, its approach to the definition of a lawful combatant was incorporated into the Hague Conventions of 1899 and 1907,[4] both of which were multilateral treaties that gave the definition the full sanction of international law.

4.2 Hague Convention IV, Annex, Regulations Respecting the Laws and Customs of War on Land (1907)

Article 1.[5] The laws, rights, and duties of war apply not only to armies but also to militia and volunteer corps fulfilling the following conditions:

1. To be commanded by a person responsible for his subordinates;
2. To have a fixed distinctive emblem recognizable at a distance;
3. To carry arms openly; and
4. To conduct their operations in accordance with the laws and customs of war.

In countries where militia or volunteer corps constitute the army, or form part of it, they are included under the denomination "army."

Art. 2. The inhabitants of a territory which has not been occupied, who, on the approach of the enemy, spontaneously take up arms to resist the invading troops without having had time to organize themselves in accordance with Article 1, shall be regarded as belligerents if they carry arms openly and if they respect the laws and customs of war.

Art. 3. The armed forces of the belligerent parties may consist of combatants and non-combatants. In the case of capture by the enemy, both have a right to be treated as prisoners of war.

Art. 4. Prisoners of war are in the power of the hostile Government, but not of the individuals or corps who capture them.

They must be humanely treated.

All their personal belongings, except arms, horses, and military papers, remain their property.

Art. 5. Prisoners of war may be interned in a town, fortress, camp, or other place, and bound not to go beyond certain fixed limits; but they cannot be confined except as an indispensable measure of safety and only while the circumstances which necessitate the measure continue to exist. . . .

Questions

1. The Lieber Code defined "partisans" or "free-corps" as a "detachment from the main army," while the Hague Convention regards any "militia" or "volunteer corps" as lawful combatants if they satisfy Article 1's four stated criteria. Does this change broaden or narrow the category of lawful combatant?
2. In your view, is each of Article 1's four stated criteria necessary? Why?

3. According to the Hague Convention, if a country has a "militia" or a "volunteer corps" as an "army," would its members qualify as lawful combatants even if they do not satisfy the four criteria? Why or why not?
4. Why does the Hague Convention classify the inhabitants of an unoccupied territory who "spontaneously take up arms to resist the invading troops" (a *levee en masse*) as lawful combatants even if the group has no military chain of command or any "fixed distinctive emblem recognizable at a distance"? Why does a "militia" or "volunteer corps" need to satisfy these two criteria to qualify as groups of lawful combatants but a *levee en masse* does not?
5. Does the lawfulness of a *levee en masse* depend on the fact that it occurs in unoccupied territory? Why is there this requirement? Would the Hague Convention classify a *levee en masse* that occurs in a territory occupied by the enemy as an unlawful act of war? Should the law of war encourage inhabitants of occupied territories not to take up arms against the enemy occupying forces? Why?
6. Is it logical for Article 3 to say that noncombatants might be a part of the armed forces of a belligerent party? Would these noncombatants be civilians? If so, why should they be considered prisoners of war? Should they instead be released?
7. Does Article 5 set too high of a standard for the detention of prisoners of war? Is detention of prisoners of war always "indispensable," or can you imagine circumstances in which they need not be detained? According to this article, would it be unlawful to detain a prisoner if you believed he or she would not return to the battlefield?

The Hague Conventions of 1899 and 1907 were the controlling multilateral treaties of international law that were in effect during World War I (1914–1918) and II (1939–1945). Although "irregular forces" did not play a major role in World War I, it is worth noting that German forces executed thousands of civilians identified as *francs-tireurs* in Belgium and France at the beginning of the conflict. These alleged atrocities underlined the difficulty of precisely distinguishing between a civilian and an "irregular" fighter. Of course, atrocities occurred to a much greater degree during World War II. Apart from the unprecedented horrors of the Jewish holocaust, occupying German military forces brutally suppressed Russian, Polish, Yugoslavian, Greek, and French partisans, even those who arguably satisfied the four criteria of a lawful combatant outlined in the Hague Convention, and summarily shot large numbers of "irregular" partisans, lawful combatants, and civilians. Following the war, a U.S. military tribunal convicted German soldiers who had participated in such executions as war criminals.[6]

The third Geneva Convention of 1949, which addressed the subject of how prisoners of war must be treated, responded to the German suppression of partisans by expanding the category of "lawful combatants" by including within it members of "organized resistance movements." Article 4 described such "movements" as follows:

> Members of other militias and members of other volunteer corps, including those of organized resistance movements, belonging to a Party to the conflict and operating in or outside their own territory, even if this territory is occupied, provided such militias or volunteer corps, including such organized resistance

> movements, fulfill . . . [the four conditions identified in Article 1 of the annex of Hague Convention IV—chain of command, distinctive emblem, carrying arms openly, and obeying laws of war].[7]

Accordingly, an "organized resistance movement" that fulfilled the four Hague conditions was lawful even if it was fighting an occupying military force. This constituted a significant departure from the Lieber Code, which referred to members of such an "organized resistance" as "war rebels" who could legally be executed if captured.[8] The Hague Convention did not explicitly address the lawfulness of an "organized resistance movement" fighting an enemy occupational force, but Article 2 did limit the *levee en masse*, the right of inhabitants to spontaneously take up arms, to groups operating in unoccupied territories. Article 4 of Geneva III was therefore a significant change in the law of war, one that recognized the important role "organized resistance movements" played in World War II.

Common Article 3 of the Geneva Conventions also clarified the distinction between a civilian and an "irregular" combatant, although this clarification was limited to armed conflicts "not of an international character occurring in the territory of one of the High Contracting Parties." It will be recalled that the Lieber Code sanctioned harsh treatment of civilians during a civil war if they sympathized with the rebel cause. Common Article 3 arguably prohibited such treatment, at least in regard to civilians who did not take an "active part in hostilities."

> Persons taking no active part in the hostilities, including members of armed forces who have laid down their arms and those placed "hors de combat" [outside of combat] by sickness, wounds, detention, or any other cause, shall in all circumstances be treated humanely, without any adverse distinction founded on race, colour, religion or faith, sex, birth or wealth, or any other similar criteria.

Civilians who were "actively" taking part in hostilities could be targeted, killed, and detained, but civilians who only sympathized with the enemy were to be treated "humanely." In addition, if civilians who "actively" participated in hostilities "laid down their arms" or were "hors de combat" because they were captured, they could no longer be summarily shot as unlawful "irregular" combatants as the Lieber Code had suggested. They too were to be treated "humanely."

Following World War II, "wars of national liberation" erupted, pitting indigenous nationalist forces against European colonial powers and their local allies, including colonial administrators, security forces, and European settlers. Examples include the Malayan Emergency (1948–1960), the Mau Mau uprising in Kenya (1952–1960), both of which involved territories within the British Empire, and the Algerian War of Independence against France (1954–1962). Great Britain and France insisted that the Geneva Conventions were not applicable to these situations, primarily on the ground that they were not "wars" or "armed conflicts" but were rather "domestic emergencies," "riots," or "acts of terrorism." Accordingly, the legal protections accorded by the Geneva Conventions to "organized resistance movements," to civilians who only sympathized with anticolonial forces, and to captured civilians were often not respected in these conflicts by either side. Summary executions of captured combatants and civilians, regardless of whether they were taking an active part in hostilities, were commonplace. Nevertheless, victory by the nationalist forces in all three of these contests ushered in a new era, one that led to the dismantling of colonial empires and a demand that the Geneva Conventions be revised so that they were explicitly applicable to "wars of national liberation." An international conference met in Geneva from 1974 to 1977, including representatives from newly constituted states recently liberated from colonial powers. The result was Additional Protocols I and II to the Geneva Conventions of 1949.

The first protocol dealt with "international conflicts," a category Article 1 defined to include "conflicts in which peoples are fighting against colonial domination and alien occupation and against racist regimes in the exercise of their right of self-determination." In contrast, the second protocol applied to all other "armed conflicts" occurring within the territory of one of the "High Contracting Parties" between its armed forces and "dissident armed forces or other organized armed groups," but only if the "dissident armed forces" were under "responsible command" and exercised such control over a part of its territory "as to enable them to carry out sustained and concerted military operations." Internal "disturbances and tensions, such as riots, isolated and sporadic acts of violence" were excluded from the scope of the second protocol because they did not qualify as "armed conflicts."[9] The first protocol addressed key issues relating to lawful combatants, prisoner-of-war status, the rights of "irregular fighters," and civilian status.

4.3 Additional Protocol I (AP I) (1977)

Article 43—Armed forces[10]

1. The armed forces of a Party to a conflict consist of all organized armed forces, groups and units which are under a command responsible to that Party for the conduct of its subordinates, even if that Party is represented by a government or an authority not recognized by an adverse Party. Such armed forces shall be subject to . . . the rules of international law applicable in armed conflict.
2. Members of the armed forces of a Party to a conflict . . . have the right to participate directly in hostilities. . . .

Article 44—Combatants and prisoners of war

1. Any combatant, as defined in Article 43, who falls into the power of an adverse Party shall be a prisoner of war.
2. While all combatants are obliged to comply with the rules of international law applicable in armed conflict, violations of these rules shall not deprive a combatant of his right to be a combatant or, if he falls into the power of an adverse Party, of his right to be a prisoner of war, except as provided in paragraphs 3 and 4.
3. In order to promote the protection of the civilian population from the effects of hostilities, combatants are obliged to distinguish themselves from the civilian population while they are engaged in an attack or in a military operation preparatory to an attack. Recognizing, however, that there are situations in armed conflicts where, owing to the nature of the hostilities an armed combatant cannot so distinguish himself, he shall retain his status as a combatant, provided that, in such situations, he carries his arms openly:

a. during each military engagement, and
b. during such time as he is visible to the adversary while he is engaged in a military deployment preceding the launching of an attack in which he is to participate. . . .

4. A combatant who falls into the power of an adverse Party while failing to meet the requirements set forth in the second sentence of paragraph 3 shall forfeit his right to be a prisoner of war, but he shall, nevertheless, be given protections equivalent in all respects to those accorded to prisoners of war by the Third Convention and by this Protocol. . . .
5. Any combatant who falls into the power of an adverse Party while not engaged in an attack or in a military operation preparatory to an attack shall not forfeit his rights to be a combatant and a prisoner of war by virtue of his prior activities. . . .
6. This Article is not intended to change the generally accepted practice of States with respect to the wearing of the uniform by combatants assigned to the regular, uniformed armed units of a Party to the conflict. . . .

Article 45—Protection of persons who have taken part in hostilities

1. A person who takes part in hostilities and falls into the power of an adverse Party shall be presumed to be a prisoner of war, and therefore shall be protected by the Third Convention, if he claims the status of prisoner of war, or if he appears to be entitled to such status, or if the Party on which he depends claims such status on his behalf by notification to the detaining Power or to the Protecting Power. Should any doubt arise as to whether any such person is entitled to the status of prisoner of war, he shall continue to have such status and, therefore, to be protected by the Third Convention and this Protocol until such time as his status has been determined by a competent tribunal.
2. If a person who has fallen into the power of an adverse Party is not held as a prisoner of war and is to be tried by that Party for an offence arising out of the hostilities, he shall have the right to assert his entitlement to prisoner-of-war status before a judicial tribunal and to have that question adjudicated. Whenever possible under the applicable procedure, this adjudication shall occur before the trial for the offence. . . .
3. Any person who has taken part in hostilities, who is not entitled to prisoner-of-war status and who does not benefit from more favorable treatment in accordance with the Fourth Convention shall have the right at all times to the protection of Article 75 of this Protocol. . . .

Questions

1. Do you agree with AP I that all conflicts against colonial powers, alien occupations, and racist regimes should be considered "international conflicts"? Should there be any exceptions? How should the terms "colonial," "alien," and "racist" be defined? Do these terms introduce a subjective or ethical factor into determining whether a conflict is an "international" one?
2. Do you have any concerns that Article 44.2 of AP I generally grants prisoner-of-war status to combatants who violate the laws of war?
3. Would Article 44.3 endanger civilians by encouraging combatants to hide among civilians when they are not engaged in or preparing for an attack?
4. Does the second sentence of Article 44.3 mean that combatants can dress as civilians as long as they carry their arms openly during military engagements or when they are "visible" to their adversary? How would this rule operate if armed conflict took place in a country where civilians usually carried arms openly? Does this rule place a regular soldier in uniform at a disadvantage?
5. Does Article 44.4 go a step further? Is it saying that combatants who dress as civilians and do not carry their weapons

openly during military engagements are nonetheless granted the protections "accorded to prisoners of war," even if they do not have the "right" to be prisoners of war? Does this rule give combatants an incentive not to comply with the laws of armed conflict?

6. Does Article 45 grant de facto prisoner-of-war status to civilians who take an active part in hostilities? Does this rule confuse the categories of civilian, "irregular" combatant, and combatant? Should these categories be abandoned?

More than 150 countries ratified Additional Protocols I and II, but the United States, along with a handful of other nations, refused to ratify either. On January 29, 1987, in a letter to the Senate, President Ronald Reagan objected to Protocol I's "vague, subjective, politicalized terminology" and its grant of combatant status to "irregular" forces that did not distinguish themselves from the civilian population.[11] Although the United States has never formally ratified either protocol, over the years some of the provisions of both protocols have been deemed to be valid customary international law. The uncertainty of which provisions of the protocols were valid international law complicated the legal questions that arose following the 9/11 attacks, including the legal status of al-Qaeda and Taliban detainees captured by U.S. forces in Afghanistan. Congress quickly passed an Authorization for Use of Military Force (AUMF) that granted President George W. Bush the authority to use "all necessary and appropriate" military force against those "he determines planned, authorized, committed, or aided the terrorist attacks that occurred on September 11, 2001, or harbored such organizations or persons."[12] Although the phrase "necessary and appropriate" force arguably included the use of military detention, the joint resolution was vague about who was in fact subject to the "force" the resolution authorized, seemingly leaving these issues to the discretion of the president.

President George W. Bush first addressed the issue of who could be detained under the authority of the AUMF in a military order titled "Detention, Treatment, and Trial of Certain Non-Citizens in the War against Terrorism" that he issued on November 13, 2001. The order identified three groups of noncitizens who fell within the scope of its provisions: any person who

(i) is or was a member of the organization known as al Qaida;
(ii) has engaged in, aided or abetted, or conspired to commit, acts of international terrorism, or acts in preparation therefor, that have caused, threaten to cause, or have as their aim to cause, injury to or adverse effects on the United States, its citizens, national security, foreign policy, or economy; or
(iii) has knowingly harbored one or more individuals described . . . [in (i) or (ii)].[13]

In a memorandum issued on February 7, 2002, Bush provided further clarification by designating both al-Qaeda and Taliban captives as "unlawful combatants" who were subject to military detention but lacked combatant immunity and were not entitled to "prisoner-of-war" status under the Geneva Conventions. In addition, Bush concluded that Common Article 3 was not applicable to the conflict with al-Qaeda and the Taliban since the conflict was "international" in scope, extending beyond the borders of Afghanistan.[14] In the context of the United States' conflict with al-Qaeda, the Taliban, and associated forces, Bush's memorandum indirectly highlighted the significance of the distinction between "unlawful" combatants and al-Qaeda sympathizers who were simply civilians.

The Supreme Court gave its first assessment of the scope of the AUMF's detention authority in *Hamdi v. Rumsfeld* (2004), a case dealing with an American citizen affiliated with a Taliban military unit who was captured in Afghanistan by the Northern Alliance, transferred to the custody of U.S. military forces, and who eventually ended up in a navy brig in Charleston, South Carolina. A majority of the court ultimately concluded that the government had violated Hamdi's Fifth Amendment right to due process because it had not granted him a meaningful opportunity to rebut the evidence regarding his status as an "enemy combatant" before a "neutral decision maker." The court therefore remanded the case for further proceedings. However, a number of justices issued opinions in the case that discussed the scope of legitimate military detention under the AUMF. In her plurality opinion, Justice Sandra Day O'Connor argued that the AUMF, in light of the laws of war, authorized military detention of a citizen who was "'part of or supporting forces hostile to the United States or coalition partners' in Afghanistan and who 'engaged in an armed conflict against the United States' there," so long as adequate process was granted to the citizen-detainee to challenge his designation as an "enemy combatant." Justice Antonin Scalia insisted that, so long as the writ of habeas corpus was not suspended, the government could not subject to military detention a citizen who joined an enemy military force, but could only subject him or her to criminal prosecution. In contrast, Justice David Souter's opinion was that the AUMF did not clearly and unmistakably authorize the detention of citizens and that such authority could not be inferred from the laws of war because the Bush administration was arguably violating the laws of war by holding Yaser Esam Hamdi incommunicado at the South Carolina naval brig. Only Justice Clarence Thomas accepted the government's position that it had the responsibility of determining if a citizen was an "enemy combatant" subject to military detention and that the federal judiciary had no authority whatsoever to interfere with these determinations.

4.4 *Hamdi v. Rumsfeld*, 542 U.S. 507 (2004)

JUSTICE O'CONNOR . . . delivered an opinion, in which THE CHIEF JUSTICE, JUSTICE KENNEDY, and JUSTICE BREYER join . . .

The threshold question before us is whether the Executive has the authority to detain citizens who qualify as "enemy combatants." There is some debate as to the proper scope of this term, and the Government has never provided any court with the full criteria that it uses in classifying individuals as such. It has made clear, however, that, for purpose of this case, the "enemy combatant" that it is seeking to detain is an individual who, it alleges, was "part of or supporting forces hostile to the United States or coalition partners" in Afghanistan and who "engaged in an armed conflict against the United States" there. We therefore answer only the narrow question before us: whether the detention of citizens falling within that definition is authorized. . . .

The capture and detention of lawful combatants and the capture, detention, and trial of unlawful combatants, by "universal agreement and practice," are "important incident[[s]] of war." The purpose of detention is to prevent captured individuals from returning to the field of battle and taking up arms once again.

There is no bar to this Nation's holding one of its own citizens as an enemy combatant. In [Ex parte] *Quirin* [1942] [see **reading 6.2**], . . . we held that "[[c]]itizens who associate themselves with the military arm of the enemy government, and with its aid, guidance and direction enter this country bent on hostile acts, are enemy belligerents within the meaning of . . . the law of war." . . . A citizen, no less than an alien, . . . if released, would pose the same threat of returning to the front during the ongoing conflict.

In light of these principles, it is of no moment that the AUMF does not use specific language of detention. Because detention to prevent a combatant's return to the battlefield is a fundamental incident of waging war, in permitting the use of "necessary and appropriate force," Congress has clearly and unmistakably authorized detention in the narrow circumstances here. . . .

Hamdi contends that the AUMF does not authorize indefinite or perpetual detention. Certainly, we agree that indefinite detention for the purpose interrogation is not authorized. . . .

Ex parte Milligan [1866] does not undermine our holding about the Government's authority to seize enemy combatants, as we define that term today. In that case, the Court made repeated reference to the fact that its inquiry into whether the military tribunal had jurisdiction to try and punish Milligan turned in large part on the fact that Milligan was not a prisoner of war, but a resident of Indiana [a civilian living in a Union state] arrested while at home there. . . .

[Regarding the process required for a designation of a citizen detainee as an "enemy combatant," we] . . . hold that a citizen-detainee seeking to challenge his classification as an enemy combatant must receive notice of the factual basis for this classification, and a fair opportunity to rebut the Government's factual assertions before a neutral decisionmaker. . . .

At the same time, the exigencies of the circumstances may demand that, aside from these core elements, enemy combatant proceedings may be tailored to alleviate their uncommon potential to burden the Executive at a time of ongoing military conflict. Hearsay, for example, may need to be accepted as the most reliable available evidence from the Government in such a proceeding. Likewise, the Constitution would not be offended by a presumption in favor of the Government's evidence, so long as that presumption remained a rebuttable one and fair opportunity for rebuttal were provided. . . .

. . . The parties agree that initial captures on the battlefield need not receive the process we have discussed here; that process is due only when the determination is made to *continue* to hold those who have been seized. . . .

. . . Plainly the "process" Hamdi has received is not that to which he is entitled under the Due Process Clause.

There remains the possibility that the standards we have articulated could be met by an appropriately authorized and properly constituted military tribunal. Indeed, it is notable that military regulations already provide for such process in related instances, dictating that tribunals be made available to determine the status of enemy detainees who assert prisoner-of-war status under the Geneva Convention. In the absence of such process, however, a court that receives a petition for a writ of habeas corpus from an alleged enemy combatant must itself ensure that the minimum requirements of due process are achieved. . . .

JUSTICE SCALIA, with whom JUSTICE STEVENS joins, dissenting . . .

JUSTICE O'CONNOR, writing for a plurality of this Court, asserts that captured enemy combatants (other than those suspected of war crimes) have traditionally been detained until the cessation of hostilities and then released. That is probably an accurate description of wartime practice with respect to enemy aliens. The tradition with respect to American citizens, however, has been quite different. Citizens aiding the enemy have been treated as traitors subject to criminal process. . . .

There are times when military exigency renders resort to the traditional criminal process impracticable. English law accommodated such exigencies by allowing legislative suspension of the writ of habeas corpus for brief periods. . . .

The Suspension Clause was by design a safety valve, the Constitution's only "express provision for exercise of extraordinary authority because of a crisis." . . .

. . . In *Quirin* it was uncontested that the petitioners were members of enemy forces. They were "*admitted* enemy invaders," and it was "undisputed" that they had landed in the United States in service of German forces. The specific holding of the Court was only that, "upon the conceded facts," the petitioners were "plainly within [the] boundaries" of military jurisdiction. But where those jurisdictional facts are not conceded—where the petitioner insists that he is not a belligerent—*Quirin* left the pre-existing law in place: Absent suspension of the writ, a citizen held where the courts are open is entitled either to criminal trial or to a judicial decree requiring his release.

It follows from what I have said that Hamdi is entitled to a habeas decree requiring his release unless (1) criminal proceedings are promptly brought, or (2) Congress has suspended the writ of habeas corpus. . . .

Several limitations give my views in this matter a relatively narrow compass. They apply only to citizens, accused of being enemy combatants, who are detained within the territorial jurisdiction of a federal court. . . .

. . . To be sure, suspension is limited by the Constitution to cases of rebellion or invasion. But whether the attacks of September 11, 2001, constitute an "invasion," and whether those attacks still justify suspension several years later, are questions for Congress rather than this Court. If civil rights are to be curtailed during wartime, it must be done openly and democratically, as the Constitution requires, rather than by silent erosion through an opinion of this Court. . . .

JUSTICE SOUTER, with whom JUSTICE GINSBURG joins, concurring in part, dissenting in part, and concurring in the judgment . . .

The threshold issue is how broadly or narrowly to read the Non-Detention Act [1971], the tone of which is severe: "No citizen shall be imprisoned or otherwise detained by the United States, except pursuant to an Act of Congress." Should the severity of the Act be relieved when the Government's stated factual justification for incommunicado detention is a war on terrorism, so that the Government may be said to act "pursuant" to congressional terms that fall short of explicit authority to imprison individuals? With one possible though important qualification, the answer has to be no. . . .

Because the Force Resolution [the AUMF] authorizes the use of military force in acts of war by the United States, the argument goes, it is reasonably clear that the military and its Commander in Chief are authorized to deal with enemy belligerents according to the treaties and customs known collectively as the laws of war. Accordingly, the United States may detain captured enemies, and *Ex parte Quirin* may perhaps be claimed for the proposition that the American citizenship of such a captive does not as such limit the Government's power to deal with him under the usages of war. . . .

[However] . . . the Government's stated legal position in its campaign against the Taliban (among whom Hamdi was allegedly captured) is apparently at odds with its claim here to be acting in accordance with customary law of war and hence to be within the terms of the Force Resolution in its detention of Hamdi. . . .

By holding him [Hamdi] incommunicado . . . the Government obviously has not been treating him as a prisoner of war, and in fact the Government claims that no Taliban detainee is entitled to prisoner of war status. This treatment appears to be a violation of the Geneva Convention provision that even in case of doubt, captives are entitled to be treated as prisoners of war "until such time as their status has been determined by a competent tribunal." The Government answers that the President's determination that Taliban detainees do not qualify as prisoners of war is conclusive as to Hamdi's status and removes any doubt that would trigger application of the Convention's tribunal requirement. But reliance on this categorical pronouncement to settle doubt is apparently at odds with the military regulation, adopted to implement the Geneva Convention, and setting out a detailed procedure for a military tribunal to determine an individual's status. . . .

. . . Thus, there is reason to question whether the United States is acting in accordance with the laws of war it claims as authority.

[Therefore] . . . the Government has not made out its claim that in detaining Hamdi in the manner described, it is acting in accord with the laws of war authorized to be applied against citizens by the Force Resolution. I conclude accordingly that the Government has failed to support the position that the Force Resolution authorizes the described detention of Hamdi for purposes of § 4001(a). . . .

JUSTICE THOMAS, dissenting.

The Executive Branch, acting pursuant to the powers vested in the President by the Constitution and with explicit congressional approval, has determined that Yaser Hamdi is an enemy combatant and should be detained. This detention falls squarely within the Federal Government's war powers, and we lack the expertise and capacity to second-guess that decision. As such, petitioners' habeas challenge should fail, and there is no reason to remand the case. . . .

Questions

1. Did the AUMF clearly authorize military detention of U.S. citizens fighting alongside the Taliban in Afghanistan? Does Justice O'Connor or Justice Souter have the better argument? Does it matter if the citizen is an "unlawful," rather than a "lawful," combatant?
2. Should this authority be limited to citizens who are in Afghanistan fighting U.S. military forces, or can this authority be broadened to include citizens fighting U.S. forces in Yemen or Somalia?
3. If the AUMF permits the military detention of citizens to prevent them from returning to the battlefield, why does it not, according to Justice O'Connor, also permit such detention for the purpose of interrogation?
4. Justice Scalia believes that military detention of citizens, even those that "could" be called "enemy belligerents," is lawful only if the writ of habeas corpus is suspended or if the citizen concedes his or her belligerent status. What is the value of this rule? If it is Congress that suspends the writ, why should Congress not be able to authorize military detention of citizens by some other method? Why should it matter whether the citizen concedes his or her belligerency?
5. Justice Thomas argues that federal judges have no authority or expertise to determine who is an "enemy combatant." Does he have a point? Why is it that no other justice agrees with him?
6. Justice Souter claims that the executive branch cannot rely on the law

of war to justify its position that the AUMF grants it authority to detain a citizen "enemy combatant" because it arguably has not respected all aspects of the law of war. Does this position make sense? Is it a better argument that the authority to detain depends exclusively on the status of the detainee rather than the conduct of the government?

After the Supreme Court remanded the case, the Bush administration declined to subject Hamdi to continued military detention. Instead, it released him to his family in Saudi Arabia on condition that he renounce his U.S. citizenship, abandon terrorism, waive any civil claim against the United States, and accept restrictions on his right to travel. In addition, on July 7, 2004, a week or so after the Supreme Court decided *Hamdi*, deputy secretary of defense Paul Wolfowitz issued an order that established Combatant Status Review Tribunals for more than six hundred alien detainees held at Guantanamo Bay Naval Base (GBNB). The order was a response to two developments: (1) Justice O'Connor's suggestion in *Hamdi* that a military tribunal might be able to fulfill the role of a "neutral decision maker," one that could make individualized determinations of whether specific detainees were "enemy combatants"; and (2) the Supreme Court's holding in *Rasul v. Bush*, a companion case to *Hamdi*, that federal judges did have statutory-based jurisdiction to consider petitions for writs of habeas corpus from detainees held at GBNB. Wolfowitz's order defined an enemy combatant as a foreign national "who was part of or supporting Taliban or al Qaeda forces, or associated forces that are engaged in hostilities against the United States or its coalition partners. This includes any person who has committed a belligerent act or has directly supported hostilities in aid of enemy armed forces."[15] Wolfowitz's definition generally tracked the understanding that the government had relied on in *Hamdi*, but there was one major difference: the Supreme Court limited the AUMF's detention authority to citizens who were "engaged in an armed conflict" in Afghanistan, while Wolfowitz designated "foreign nationals" enemy combatants if they were "part of" or "supporting" Taliban, al-Qaeda, or associated forces engaged in hostilities against the United States and its partners without any geographic limitation.

The definition of "unlawful enemy combatant" had special relevance to the case of José Padilla, a U.S. citizen who was arrested on May 8, 2002, upon his arrival at O'Hare International Airport in Chicago, and Ali Saleh Kahlah al-Marri, a lawful resident alien who entered the United States the day before the 9/11 attacks and who resided in Preoria, Illinois, when he was arrested in December 2001. Padilla and al-Marri were initially held as material witnesses, but President Bush eventually designated both of them "enemy combatants" and placed them in military detention at the navy brig in Charleston, South Carolina. The justification for Padilla's military detention was that he, like Hamdi, had fought with al-Qaeda and the Taliban against U.S. forces in Afghanistan. In turn, the government identified al-Marri as an al-Qaeda "sleeper agent" who was planning to facilitate terrorist attacks inside the United States and disrupt the country's financial system through computer hacking. Padilla filed for a writ of habeas corpus, first in the southern district of New York, where he had been initially held as a material witness. The Second Circuit granted Padilla the writ in 2003, holding that his military detention was illegal, but the Supreme Court reversed this decision on the ground that Padilla should have filed his petition in South Carolina, where he was being detained as an "unlawful enemy combatant."[16]

Following the Supreme Court's decision in *Hamdi* in 2004, the Fourth Circuit, in an opinion written by Judge J. Michael Luttig, upheld the legality of Padilla's military detention, largely arguing that there was no significant difference between Padilla and Hamdi. According to Luttig, there was no question that Padilla had associated with al-Qaeda and Taliban military forces in Afghanistan during an armed conflict with the United States. Those facts were sufficient to justify his military detention. It did not matter that Padilla was captured inside the United States or that Padilla could be criminally prosecuted. Last, according to Luttig, *Ex parte Milligan* was no bar to Padilla's military detention because Milligan was a civilian living in Indiana during the Civil War. He was unaffiliated with the Confederate Army, while Padilla had associated himself with enemy forces fighting the United States.

4.5 *Padilla v. Hanft*, 423 F.3d 386 (4th Cir. 2005)

Judge Luttig . . .

. . . Padilla principally argues that his case does not fall within the "narrow circumstances" considered by the [Supreme] Court . . . [in *Hamdi*] because, although he too stood alongside Taliban forces in Afghanistan, he was seized on American soil, whereas Hamdi was captured on a foreign battlefield.[17] In other words, Padilla maintains that capture on a foreign battlefield was one of the "narrow circumstances" to which the plurality in *Hamdi* confined its opinion. We disagree. When the plurality articulated the "narrow question" before it, it referred simply to the permissibility of detaining "an individual who . . . was "'part of or supporting forces hostile to the United States or coalition partners' in Afghanistan and who 'engaged in an armed conflict against the United States' there." Nowhere in its framing of the "narrow question" presented did the plurality even mention the locus of capture.

The actual reasoning that the plurality thereafter employed is consistent with the question having been framed so as to render locus of capture irrelevant. That reasoning was that Hamdi's detention was an exercise of "necessary and appropriate force" within the meaning of the AUMF because "detention to prevent a combatant's return to the battlefield is a fundamental incident of waging war." This reasoning simply does not admit of a distinction between an enemy combatant captured abroad and detained in the United States, such as Hamdi, and an enemy combatant who escaped capture abroad but was ultimately captured domestically and detained in the United States, such as Padilla. As we previously explained, Padilla poses the same threat of returning to the battlefield as Hamdi posed at the time of the Supreme Court's adjudication of Hamdi's petition. Padilla's detention is thus "necessary and appropriate" to the same extent as Hamdi's. . . .

As to the fact that Padilla can be prosecuted, the availability of criminal process does not distinguish him from Hamdi. If the mere availability of criminal prosecution rendered detention unnecessary within the meaning of the AUMF, then Hamdi's detention would have been unnecessary and therefore unauthorized, since he too was detained in the United States and amenable to criminal prosecution. We are convinced, in any event, that the availability of criminal process cannot be determinative of the power to detain, if for no other reason than that criminal prosecution may well not achieve the very purpose for which detention is authorized in the first place—the prevention of return to the field of battle. Equally important, in many instances criminal prosecution would impede the Executive in its efforts to gather intelligence from the detainee and to restrict the detainee's communication with confederates so as to ensure that the detainee does not pose a continuing threat to national security even as he is confined—impediments that would render military detention not only an appropriate, but also the necessary, course of action to be taken in the interest of national security. . . .

Finally, Padilla argues that, even if his detention is authorized by the AUMF, it is unlawful under *Ex parte Milligan*. In *Milligan*, the Supreme Court held that a United States citizen associated with an anti-Union secret society but unaffiliated with the Confederate army could not be tried by a military tribunal while access to civilian courts was open and unobstructed. *Milligan* purported to restrict the power of Congress as well as the power of the President. *Quirin*, however, confirmed that *Milligan* does not extend to enemy combatants. As the Court in *Quirin* explained, the *Milligan* Court's reasoning had "particular reference to the facts before it," namely, that Milligan was not "a part of or associated with the armed forces of the enemy." The *Hamdi* plurality in turn reaffirmed this limitation on the reach of *Milligan*, emphasizing that *Quirin*, a unanimous opinion, "both postdates and clarifies *Milligan*." Thus confined, *Milligan* is inapposite here because Padilla, unlike Milligan, associated with, and has taken up arms against the forces of the United States on behalf of, an enemy of the United States. . . .

Questions

1. Did the Supreme Court place more weight on the fact that Hamdi was captured in Afghanistan than Judge Luttig allows? Did Padilla in fact engage "in an armed conflict" against the United States in Afghanistan?
2. Even if the purpose of military detention is to "prevent a combatant's return to the battlefield," does that rationale clarify who is a "combatant"? Does Judge Luttig conflate this rationale with the definition of an "enemy combatant"?
3. How can the military detention of Padilla be "necessary" if the United States could prosecute him in a civilian court?
4. Does Judge Luttig hint that the purpose of military detention is not only to prevent a combatant's return to the battlefield but also to interrogate the detainee? Is interrogation a legitimate purpose for military detention?
5. Does Padilla resemble Quirin more than he resembles Milligan? Why or why not?

While Padilla's appeal of the Fourth Circuit's decision was pending at the Supreme Court, the executive branch transferred him back to civilian custody and prosecuted him for conspiracy to commit murder and providing material support to terrorist groups. He was convicted and sentenced to seventeen years in prison in 2007. Although al-Marri was not a U.S. citizen, he had the constitutional rights of a citizen since he was a lawful resident alien living inside the United States at the time President Bush designated him an "enemy combatant" and transferred him to military custody. Al-Marri filed a petition for a writ of habeas corpus in South Carolina. He lost at the district court level, but on appeal a three-judge panel of Fourth Circuit judges, a panel different from the one that had denied the writ to Padilla, reversed the lower court decision in 2007.[18] In response, the government requested an *en banc* rehearing of the case, and the Fourth Circuit granted this request. Nine judges of the Fourth Circuit participated in the *en banc* decision handed down in July of 2008. Five of the judges held that, if the government's contentions about al-Marri were true, then he could lawfully be subject to military detention. However, one judge in the majority joined the four dissenters to conclude that the government had violated al-Marri's rights to due process by not giving him a sufficient opportunity to challenge his designation as an enemy combatant.

The following excerpts reveal sharply contrasting perspectives regarding whether al-Marri is or is not an "enemy combatant," assuming that the government allegations against him are true. Judge Diana Gribbon Motz, who argued that al-Marri was not an "enemy combatant," relied heavily on the Supreme Court's ruling in *Hamdan v. Rumsfeld* (2006)[19] that Common Article 3 was applicable to the United States' conflict with al-Qaeda, a holding that conflicted with President Bush's earlier position that it was not applicable because the conflict was "international" in character. In the Supreme Court's view, the conflict was not "international" in character because it was not a conflict between nations, and for that reason, Common Article 3 applied. Based on this assumption, Motz argued al-Marri could not be an "enemy combatant" because Common Article 3 neither defined this term nor recognized its existence and al-Marri was never affiliated with the armed forces of an enemy nation and never fought against the United States on any battlefield. Five judges on the Fourth Circuit found this argument unconvincing. In their view, reflected in three of the excerpts that follow, the laws of war and the AUMF authorize military detention of persons who are affiliated with al-Qaeda and enter the United States for the purpose of facilitating acts of terrorism and engaging in conduct that could potentially disrupt financial markets.

4.6 *Al-Marri v. Pucciarelli*, 534 F.3d 213 (4th Cir. 2008)

MOTZ, Circuit Judge, . . . concurring in the judgment . . .

. . . [T]he holding of *Hamdi* and *Padilla* share two characteristics: (1) they look to law-of-war principles to determine who fits within the "legal category" of enemy combatant; and (2) following the law of war, they rest enemy combatant status on affiliation with the military arm of an enemy nation [that is, affiliation with Taliban forces, which are "Afghanistan's government forces"].

In view of the holdings in *Hamdi* and *Padilla*, we find it remarkable that the Government contends that they "compel the conclusion" that the President may detain al-Marri as an enemy combatant. For unlike Hamdi and Padilla, al-Marri is not alleged to have been part of a Taliban unit, not alleged to have stood alongside the Taliban or the armed forces of any other enemy nation, not alleged to have been on the battlefield during the war in Afghanistan, not alleged to have even been in Afghanistan during the armed conflict there, and not alleged to have engaged in combat with United States forces anywhere in the world.

In place of the "classic wartime detention" that the Government argued justified Hamdi's detention as an enemy combatant or the "classic battlefield" detention it maintained justified Padilla's, here the Government argues that al-Marri's seizure and indefinite detention by the military in this country are justified "because he engaged in, and continues to pose a very real threat of carrying out . . . acts of international terrorism." . . .

. . . Our dissenting colleagues . . . contend that the definition of enemy combatant has somehow expanded to permit a person to be so classified because of his criminal conduct on behalf of a terrorist organization. We have searched extensively for authority that would support the dissents' position; we have found none.

First, the Supreme Court's most recent terrorism cases—*Hamdan* and *Boumediene*—provide no support for the dissenters' position. In *Hamdan*, the Court held that because the conflict between the United States and al Qaeda in Afghanistan is not "between nations," it is a "'conflict not of an international character'"—and so is governed by Common Article 3 of the Geneva Conventions [see **reading 3.7**]. Common Article 3 and other Geneva Convention provisions applying to non-international conflicts (in contrast to those applying to international conflicts) simply do not recognize the "legal category" of enemy combatant. As the International Committee of the Red Cross explains, "an 'enemy combatant' is a person who, either lawfully or unlawfully, engages in hostilities for the opposing side in an international armed conflict"; in contrast, "[[i]]n non-international armed conflict combatant status does not exist."

. . . Because the legal status of enemy combatant does not exist in non-international conflicts, the law of war leaves the detention of persons in such conflicts to the applicable law of the detaining country. In al-Marri's case, the applicable law is our Constitution. Under our Constitution, even if the Supreme Court should hold that the Government may detain indefinitely Boumediene, Hamdan, and others like them, who were captured outside the United States and lack substantial and voluntary connections to this country, that holding would provide no support for approving al-Marri's military detention. For not only was al-Marri seized and detained within the United States, he also has substantial connection to the United States and so plainly is protected by the Due Process Clause. . . .

To sanction such presidential authority to order the military to seize and indefinitely detain civilians, even if the President calls them "enemy combatants," would have disastrous consequences for the Constitution—and the country. For a court to uphold a claim to such extraordinary power would . . . effectively undermine all of the freedoms guaranteed by the Constitution. . . . We refuse to recognize a claim to power that would so alter the constitutional foundation of our Republic. . . .

TRAXLER, Circuit Judge, concurring in the judgment: . . .

I am . . . unpersuaded by the claim that because al Qaeda itself is an international terrorist organization instead of a "nation state" or "enemy government," the AUMF cannot apply, consistent with the laws of war and our constitutional guarantees, to such persons. The premise of that claim seems to be that because al Qaeda is not technically in control of an enemy nation or its government, it cannot be considered as anything other than a criminal organization whose members are entitled to all the protections and procedures granted by our Constitution. I disagree.

In my view, al Qaeda is much more and much worse than a criminal organization. And while it may be an unconventional enemy force in a historical context, it is an enemy force nonetheless. The fact that it allied itself with an enemy government of a foreign nation only underscores this point, rendering attempts to distinguish its soldiers or operatives as something meaningfully different from military soldiers in service to the Taliban government (or al Qaeda operatives such as Hamdi and Padilla, who fought beside them) equally strained. The President attacked the Taliban in Afghanistan as retaliation for al Qaeda's strike upon our nation because al Qaeda was centralized there and allied with the Taliban, and it also strains credulity to assert that while we are legitimately at war with the Taliban government, we cannot be at war with al Qaeda. . . .

WILLIAMS, Chief Judge, concurring in part and dissenting in part . . .

A distillation of these precedents [*Milligan*, *Quirin*, and *Hamdi*], I believe, yields a definition of an enemy combatant subject to detention pursuant to Congressional authorizations [the AUMF] as an individual who meets two criteria: (1) he attempts or engages in belligerent acts against the United States, either domestically or in a foreign combat zone; (2) on behalf of an enemy force.

Given the specific allegations against al-Marri, I have little difficulty concluding that he satisfies the first criterion. First, the allegations . . . clearly show that al-Marri was on United States soil to commit acts of belligerency against the United States. . . . [A]l-Marri also meets what I view as the second requirement of an enemy combatant: that the belligerent acts be carried out on behalf of an enemy force. Unlike the plurality, I cannot accept al-Marri's contention that because he allegedly has ties only to al Qaeda, a terrorist organization that does not control any nation, he does not meet this portion of the definition of enemy combatant.

The plurality opinion may very well be correct that under traditional "law of war," persons not affiliated with the military of a nation-state may not be considered enemy combatants. And I recognize the respect domestic courts have long afforded the "law of nations." Here, however, Congress has, through the AUMF, addressed precisely this question by clearly authorizing the President to use force against "organizations," as well as against nation-states. As a specific and targeted congressional directive, the AUMF controls the question of who may be detained, for the purposes of domestic law—at least with respect to those individuals that fall within its scope. . . . Al Qaeda is obviously an "organization" that "planned, authorized, committed, or aided in" the September 11 attacks. Thus, in my view, the AUMF has labeled al Qaeda an enemy force. Indeed, "read in light of its purpose clause . . . and its preamble . . . the AUMF applies even more clearly and unmistakably to [[al-Marri]] than to Hamdi." . . .

WILKINSON, Circuit Judge, concurring in part and dissenting in part: . . .

. . . Having . . . considered the recent changes in warfare and international relations, I believe that three criteria best identify who qualifies as an enemy combatant in the current conflict. . . .

. . . The first two criteria determine who constitutes an "enemy." . . .

. . . [A]n "enemy" is any individual who is (1) a member of (2) an organization or nation against whom Congress has declared war or authorized the use of military force. Taken together, these two criteria closely track traditional law of war concepts that distinguish enemies from non-enemies. At the same time, they recognize that modern military threats include those posed by non-state actors. I first address the criterion of membership. While the traditional requirement of residency or other affiliation with an enemy nation still applies, the advent of enemy organizations requires a functional equivalent to residency for this new stateless actor. . . . Such indicia of membership may include: self-identification with the organization through verbal or written statements; participation in the group's hierarchy or command structure; or knowingly taking overt steps to aid or participate in the organization's activities. Thus, for example, someone who sends money to "a nonprofit charity that feeds Afghan orphans" that unknowingly makes "its way to al Qaeda" would not be a member of the al Qaeda organization, and it is beyond hyperbole for the plurality to suggest otherwise. Furthermore, the membership requirement is important because it aids in distinguishing those who are the enemy from those who merely sympathize with the enemy.

The second criterion—congressional authorization—recognizes that Congress may authorize the use of military force against non-state actors, such as terrorist organizations, as it has already with the AUMF. . . .

If the first two criteria address who in modern warfare is the enemy, the third criterion addresses who is the combatant. Historically, this distinction has separated those with military aims from those who do not present a threat to opposing forces. . . . In light of today's realities, a "combatant" is a person who knowingly plans or engages in conduct that harms or aims to harm persons or property for the purpose of furthering the military goals of an enemy nation or organization. Like the first two criteria, this requirement closely tracks the relevant traditional law of war rules.

Under this criterion, those who use military-like force against American soldiers or civilians obviously qualify as combatants. Similarly, members of an enemy sleeper terrorist cell that have taken steps, even if preliminary in nature, toward an act of destruction are also considered combatants. Conversely, persons traditionally considered civilians, such as members of the enemy organization who do not possess hostile or military designs, are non-combatants and may not be detained by the military. This includes persons who would clearly be non-combatants, such as a "physician who treated a member of al Qaeda," because they intend no harm to persons or property. Such persons would not be subject to military detention. . . .

Based on the criteria identified and the facts alleged, al-Marri easily qualifies as an enemy combatant. . . .

. . . It matters not that al-Marri was not in uniform, that he was not on some foreign battlefield, or that he was not in the service of a nation's armed forces. It matters not that his status was that of a lawful alien, that he was arrested on American soil where the threat of belligerency may be greatest, or that he was detained militarily rather than prosecuted by civil authority. To hold that these things mandate a grant of the writ [of habeas corpus] requires this country to face contemporary threats of grave dimension shackled by outmoded notions of the law of war. . . .

Questions

1. Is Judge Motz's claim that "enemy combatants" do not exist in noninternational conflicts convincing? Why or why not? According to her, can an al-Qaeda member arrested abroad be subject to military detention?
2. How does Judge William Traxler's position differ from Judge Motz's in regard to how the AUMF applies to members of al-Qaeda?
3. If the AUMF authorizes the military detention of al-Marri, but the laws of war do not, which law should prevail? Which of the above judges support your view? Which oppose it?
4. Why does Chief Judge Karen Williams believe that the AUMF applies more "unmistakably" to al-Marri than to Hamdi?
5. Is Judge Harvie Wilkinson correct that the law of war, including the definition of "enemy combatant," must evolve? Does Judge Motz disagree? Do these judges differ on the role that judges should play in the evolution of the law of war?
6. Chief Judge Williams has two criteria for defining an "enemy combatant," while Judge Wilkinson has three. How are their definitions similar? How are they different?
7. Is Judge Wilkinson arguing that members of al-Qaeda who are not combatants cannot lawfully be subject to military detention? Do you agree?

Following the Fourth Circuit's *en banc* decision, the Supreme Court agreed to hear al-Marri's appeal, but the new Obama administration sidestepped the appeal by shifting al-Marri back to civilian authorities in early 2009. The Supreme Court then dismissed al-Marri's appeal and vacated the Fourth Circuit's decision that had narrowly upheld the president's AUMF-based authority to subject a noncitizen captured inside the United States to military detention if sufficient due process was granted to the detainee. Al-Marri pleaded guilty to one count of conspiracy to provide material support to a foreign terrorist organization in April 2009, was sentenced to eight years in prison in October of that year, and was repatriated to Qatar in January 2015.

Hamdi, Padilla, and al-Marri were the only persons militarily detained inside the United States after the 9/11 attacks. However, the Bush administration subjected hundreds of noncitizens to military detention at the Guantanamo Bay Naval Base (GBNB) in Cuba, a military facility where the United States was de facto sovereign. It was unclear for several years whether these detainees had any right to challenge the lawfulness of their detention. Not until the Supreme Court decided *Boumediene v. Bush* in 2008 was this question finally resolved. A majority of the Supreme Court held that detainees at GBNB did have a constitutional right to challenge the lawfulness of their detention by petitioning for a writ of habeas corpus in the federal district court in Washington, D.C. This ruling led to dozens of habeas petitions focusing on the scope of lawful military detention of GBNB detainees. In March 2009, the Obama administration offered the following definition of who qualified as an "enemy combatant," one that slightly revised the Bush administration's earlier formulations.

> The President has the authority to detain persons that the President determines planned, authorized, committed, or aided the terrorist attacks that occurred on September 11, 2001, and persons who harbored those responsible for those attacks. The President also has the authority to detain persons who were part of, or substantially supported, Taliban or al-Qaida forces or associated forces that are engaged in hostilities against the United States or its coalition partners, including any person who has committed a belligerent act, or has directly supported hostilities, in aid of such enemy armed forces.[20]

This definition did not resolve the question whether it was consistent with international law to detain militarily those who "substantially" or "directly" supported the Taliban, al-Qaeda, or associated forces. In *Gherebi v. Obama*, Judge Reggie B. Walton argued that "support" was a valid basis for military detention,[21] but Judge John D. Bates in *Hamlily v. Obama* could find "no authority in domestic law or the law of war . . . to justify the concept of 'support' as a valid ground for detention."[22] The Court of Appeals of the District of Columbia addressed the controversy in *Al-Bihani v. Obama*, a case dealing with the military detention of a cook in the Fifty-Fifth Arab Brigade, a group allied with the Taliban against the Northern Alliance in Afghanistan. The court found that both "membership" and "support" were both valid grounds for military detention and, in the form of dicta, added that Congress could, if it was so inclined, expand the scope of detention beyond what was permitted by international law.

4.7 *Al-Bihani v. Obama*, 590 F.3d 866 (D.C. Cir. 2010)

BROWN, Circuit Judge: . . .

. . . [What Al-Bihani] does not dispute is that he eventually accompanied and served a paramilitary group allied with the Taliban, known as the 55th Arab Brigade, which included Al-Qaeda members within its command structure and which fought on the front lines against the Northern Alliance. He worked as the brigade's cook and carried a brigade-issued weapon, but never fired it in combat. Combat, however—in the form of bombing by the U.S.-led Coalition that invaded Afghanistan in response to the attacks of September 11, 2001—forced the 55th to retreat from the front lines in October 2001. At the end of this protracted retreat, Al-Bihani and the rest of the brigade surrendered, under orders, to Northern Alliance forces, and they kept him in custody until his handover to U.S. Coalition forces in early 2002. The U.S. military sent Al-Bihani to Guantanamo for detention and interrogation. . . .

Al-Bihani challenges the statutory legitimacy of his detention by advancing a number of arguments based upon the international laws of war. He first argues that relying on "support," or even "substantial support" of Al Qaeda or the Taliban as an independent basis for detention violates international law. . . . Al-Bihani interprets international law to mean anyone not belonging to an official state military is a civilian, and civilians, he says, must commit a direct hostile act, such as firing a weapon in combat, before they can be lawfully detained. Because Al-Bihani did not commit such an act, he reasons his detention is unlawful. . . .

. . . [Al-Bihani's argument relies] heavily on the premise that the war powers granted by the AUMF and other statutes are limited by the international laws of war. This premise is mistaken. There is no indication in the AUMF . . . that Congress intended the international laws of war to act as extra-textual limiting principles for the President's war powers under the AUMF. The international laws of war as a whole have not been implemented domestically by Congress and are therefore not a source of authority for U.S. courts. . . . Therefore, putting aside that we find Al-Bihani's reading of international law to be unpersuasive, we have no occasion here to quibble over the intricate application of vague treaty provisions and amorphous customary principles. The sources we look to for resolution of Al-Bihani's case are the sources courts always look to: the text of relevant statutes and controlling domestic caselaw. . . .

. . . The 2006 MCA [Military Commissions Act] authorized the trial of an individual who "engaged in hostilities or who has purposefully and materially supported hostilities against the United States or its co-belligerents who is not a lawful enemy combatant (including a person who is part of the Taliban, al-Qaeda, or associated forces)." In 2009, Congress enacted a new version of the MCA with a new definition that authorized the trial of "unprivileged enemy belligerents," a class of persons that includes those who "purposefully and materially supported hostilities against the United States or its coalition partners." The provisions of the 2006 and 2009 MCAs are illuminating in this case because the government's detention authority logically covers a category of persons no narrower than is covered by its military commission authority. . . . But for this case, it is enough to recognize that any person subject to a military commission trial is also subject to detention, and that category of persons includes those who are part of forces associated with Al Qaeda or the Taliban or those who purposefully and materially support such forces in hostilities against U.S. Coalition partners.

In light of these provisions of the 2006 and 2009 MCAs, the facts . . . place Al-Bihani within the "part of" and "support" prongs of the relevant statutory definition. The district court found Al Qaeda members participated in the command structure of the 55th Arab Brigade, making the brigade an Al Qaeda-affiliated outfit, and it is unquestioned that the 55th fought alongside the Taliban while the Taliban was harboring Al Qaeda. Al-Bihani's evidence confirmed these points, establishing that the 55th "supported the Taliban against the Northern Alliance," a Coalition partner, and that the 55th was "aided, or even, at times, commanded, by al-Qaeda members." Al-Bihani's connections with the 55th therefore render him detainable. His acknowledged actions—accompanying the brigade on the battlefield, carrying a brigade-issued weapon, cooking for the unit, and retreating and surrendering under brigade orders—strongly suggest, in the absence of an official membership card, that he was part of the 55th. Even assuming, as he argues, that he was a civilian "contractor" rendering services, those services render Al-Bihani detainable under the "purposefully and materially supported" language of both versions of the MCA. That language constitutes a standard whose outer bounds are not readily identifiable. But wherever the outer bounds may lie, they clearly include traditional food operations essential to a fighting force and the carrying of arms. Viewed in full, the facts show Al-Bihani was part of and supported a group—prior to and after September 11—that was affiliated with Al-Qaeda and Taliban forces and engaged in hostilities against a U.S. Coalition partner. Al-Bihani, therefore, falls squarely within the scope of the President's statutory detention powers. . . .

WILLIAMS, Senior Circuit Judge, concurring in part and concurring in the judgment . . .

. . . For purposes of both my analysis and the majority's, the petitioner has conceded facts that render his detention lawful. . . .

Within the portion of the opinion addressing the petitioner's substantive argument that his activities in Afghanistan do not put him in the class of people whom the President may detain pursuant to the AUMF, the majority unnecessarily . . . [claims] that "the premise that the war powers granted by the AUMF and other statutes are limited by the international laws of war . . . is mistaken." The paragraph appears hard to square with the approach that the Supreme Court took in *Hamdi*. In any event, there is no need for the court's pronouncements, divorced from application to any particular argument. Curiously, the majority's dictum goes well beyond what even the government has argued in this case. . . .

Questions

1. Is Judge Brown correct that international law does not place limits on the scope of detention authorized by the AUMF? Does Judge Williams agree or disagree?
2. Does Judge Brown think that Al-Bihani's detention is sanctioned by international law because his "reading" of international law is "unpersuasive"? If international law authorizes Al-Bihani's detention, why does Judge Brown reject its relevance?
3. Does Judge Brown assume that Al-Bihani can be lawfully detained because he can be tried by a military commission under the 2006 and 2009 MCAs? Is this assumption valid?
4. Although Judge Brown concedes that the "outer bounds" of the "purposefully and materially support" standard of detention "are not readily identifiable," she thinks they "clearly include traditional food operations." If a "cook" is lawfully subject to military detention on this basis, would a food truck driver also be detainable? A restaurant owner who donated food to the group? A dishwasher at the restaurant?
5. The D.C. Circuit justifies Al-Bihani's detention by relying on "facts" conceded by him, not on "facts" alleged by the government. Does this approach have a built-in tendency to widen and expand the scope of lawful military detention?
6. According to Judge Williams, the opinion of the court granted a broader authority to detain persons militarily than the government had requested. Does this feature of the case raise any concerns?

The full D.C. Circuit Court of Appeal denied an *en banc* review of the three-judge panel's decision in *Al-Bihani*. Although a majority of the court's judges indicated that Judge Brown's remarks on the role of international law-of-war principles were "not necessary to the disposition of the merits" of the case, three judges nonetheless engaged in an extended debate on the degree to which international law limited the scope of military detention under the AUMF and other relevant statutes. Only one of the three—Judge Williams—was willing to endorse the view that judges could legitimately use norms of international law as a basis for interpreting the meaning of federal statutes (see **reading 1.6**).[23]

Congress again addressed the issue of the scope of legitimate military detention in the National Defense Authorization Act (NDAA) for fiscal year 2012. In this law, Congress said that the government may subject to military detention any non-U.S. person

> (1) . . . who planned, authorized, committed, or aided the terrorist attacks that occurred on September 11, 2001, or harbored those responsible for those attacks[; or]
> (2) . . . who was a part of or substantially supported al-Qaeda, the Taliban, or associated forces that are engaged in hostilities against the United States or its coalition partners, including any person who has committed a belligerent act or has directly supported such hostilities in aid of such enemy forces.[24]

The NDAA clearly authorized military detention solely on the basis of "substantial" or "direct" support. The rationale for this legislative action was somewhat unclear since the government has never justified detention in any of the GBNB habeas cases solely on this basis. In all of the GBNB habeas cases, the government had always included the claim that the detainee was a "member" or "part of" al-Qaeda, the Taliban, "or associated forces."

A group of U.S. citizens, lawful permanent residents, and noncitizens challenged the provision of the NDAA authorizing detention solely on the basis of "substantial" or "direct" support, arguing that they could be detained militarily based on their activities as investigative reporters researching radical Islamic groups, advocates for various human rights organizations, or lawyers representing clients with alleged ties to terrorist groups. The district court granted the injunction,[25] but the Second Circuit quashed it in 2013, holding that plaintiffs did not have standing to challenge the constitutionality of the law. Noncitizens who were not lawful permanent residents and who were abroad did not have standing because they had not shown a "sufficient threat" that the U.S. government would detain them. The court came to this conclusion even though it was unwilling to hold that the laws of war limited the detention authority granted by the NDAA. In other words, even if the NDAA granted authority to detain the noncitizen plaintiffs, they did not have standing to contest such detention since the threat of such detention had not yet materialized.

Citizens and lawful permanent residents inside the United States, in contrast, did not have standing because NDAA did not apply to them. In the court's view, the NDAA left the president's authority to detain citizens and lawful permanent residents inside the United States as it was prior to its passage.[26] Whatever it was, it still is, which meant that, more than sixteen years after the 9/11 attacks, it was still not clear whether the president had authority to subject a U.S. citizen or lawful permanent resident residing in the United States to military detention in the armed conflict against al-Qaeda, the Taliban, and associated forces. Why have U.S. courts left this question unresolved? Are there good reasons why a court should address this question only if there is no other option? What are these reasons?

On or about September 14, 2017, a Syrian rebel militia captured a dual U.S.-Saudi citizen fighting for ISIS near the Syrian border with Turkey. The Trump administration could have prosecuted the individual in federal court, but it is likely that the evidence the government had against him was not admissible in a court of law and that a public prosecution would disclose U.S. sources and methods of gathering military intelligence. Accordingly, the administration chose to detain the individual militarily in Iraq without disclosing his name to the public or giving him access to a lawyer. In October, the American Civil Liberties Union (ACLU), without ever having met the unnamed detainee, filed a habeas corpus petition on his behalf, referring to him as John Doe. The government argued that the ACLU lacked standing to file the habeas action on Doe's behalf and the district court had no power to ascertain Doe's wishes or intentions since he was detained in Iraq, not in the United States. The *Washington Post* reported on October 29 that Doe at some point in his interrogation had refused to answer any more questions and demanded to speak to a lawyer.[27] At a hearing in late November, when pressed by district court judge Tanya Chutkan, the government conceded that Doe had invoked his constitutional right to an attorney on September 25 and that the government had not honored his request for two months.

After a *New York Times* story reported on December 20, 2017, that the administration was considering transferring Doe to the custody of Saudi Arabia,[28] district court judge Tanya Chutkan ordered the government, first, to provide ACLU lawyers with "temporary, immediate, unmonitored" access to Doe to find out if he wanted the ACLU or a court-appointed lawyer to represent him, and, second, not to transfer Doe to any other country. In late January 2018, Judge Chutkan relaxed the latter order, requiring the government only to provide her and the ACLU with 72 hours' notice prior to any transfer of Doe, but she indicated that the purpose of the notice requirement was to allow the court to review the lawfulness of any transfer. Regarding the merits of Doe's habeas petition, Judge Chutkan might have to consider two key issues: one statutory, the other, constitutional. The statutory question is whether the 2001 AUMF or the 2002 AUMF provides statutory authority for the military detention of an American citizen who is a "member" or "direct supporter" of ISIS. Such statutory authority is arguably required because the Non-Detention Act (18 U.S.C. § 4001) prohibits detention of U.S. citizens unless authorized by statute, and the 2012 NDAA was not relevant because it only applied to "non-U.S. persons."

The issue of whether the AUMFs cover ISIS is complicated because this organization did not formally exist until 2013, although it evolved from al-Qaeda in Iraq (AQI), an organization led by Abu Musab al-Zarqawi, who had pledged loyalty to Osama bin Laden in 2003. A U.S air strike killed Zarqawi in 2006, and Abu Bakr al-Baghdadi became his successor in 2010. When the Syrian conflict broke out in 2011, Baghdadi established a base of operations there and renamed his organization the Islamic State of Iraq and Syria (ISIS). Meanwhile,

U.S. military forces left Iraq at the end of 2011, which arguably terminated the 2002 AUMF. Ayman al-Zawahiri, who assumed the leadership of al-Qaeda after bin Laden's death in 2011, distrusted ISIS leadership, goals, and methods and, therefore, ordered Baghdadi to confine his operations to Iraq. Baghdadi refused, which led Zawahiri to publicly disavow him and his organization in February 2014, thereby ending the affiliation between ISIS and al-Qaeda. It is worth noting that the government concedes Doe did not join ISIS until July 2014, approximately four months after the two organizations had formally separated.[29] Accordingly, the statutory issue in *Doe v. Mattis* is a difficult one. The executive branch has adopted an expansive interpretation of the scope of military detention authorized under the AUMFs, but is it within the competence and the expertise of a federal judge to assess what terrorist groups are "associated" with al-Qaeda and the Taliban? Is this a judicial or a "political question," or is it both? In your view, how should Judge Chutkan balance these difficult tradeoffs?

However, if Judge Chutkan eventually decides that the AUMFs do not authorize military action against ISIS, she will then have to confront an even more controversial issue because the government is also arguing that President Trump has Article II authority to subject Doe to military detention, even if he is an American citizen, a position the ACLU vigorously contests. The following reading is composed of excerpts that focus on this constitutional question; they are taken from documents filed by the government and ACLU at the district court.

4.8 *Doe v. Mattis* (D.D.C. 2018)

GOVERNMENT'S FACTUAL RETURN TO DOE'S HABEAS PETITION

46. In addition to relying on the statutory authority Congress provided in the 2001 and 2002 AUMFs, Presidents have long directed the use of military force overseas in defense of the nation pursuant to their authority under Article II of the U.S. Constitution.[30] . . . [T]he Executive Branch . . . has inherent authority to direct the deployment of military forces and, as part of that authority, the power to detain combatants captured on the battlefield for as long as U.S. troops are engaged in active hostilities on that battlefield.

47. The President's power to employ military force abroad derives from his constitutional responsibility as Commander in Chief and Chief Executive for foreign and military affairs, and it has been confirmed by "the historical gloss on the 'executive power' vested in Article II of the Constitution." This authority "has long been recognized as extending to the dispatch of armed forces outside the United States, either on missions of goodwill or rescue, or for the purpose of protecting American lives or property or American interests."

48. Indeed, there are over two centuries of Executive Branch practice in support of this authority. Examples from recent decades in which Presidents directed the use of military force without specific prior authorization legislation include "bombing in Libya (1996), an intervention in Panama (1989), troop deployments to Somalia (1992), Bosnia (1995), and Haiti (twice, 1994 and 2004), air patrols and airstrikes in Bosnia (1993–1995), and a bombing campaign in Yugoslavia (1999)." President Obama authorized the use of military force against Libya in 2011. President Trump similarly did so against a Syrian military airfield following a 2017 chemical weapons attack by the Syrian regime.

49. In considering the President's authority to use military force in Libya in 2011, the Department of Justice's Office of Legal Counsel (OLC) asked whether the operations would "serve sufficiently important interests

to permit the President's action as Commander in Chief and Chief Executive and pursuant to his authority to conduct U.S. foreign relations." In that opinion, OLC noted that defense of the United States to repel a direct and immediate military attack is one basis—but not the exclusive one—on which the President may use military force without congressional approval.

50. This constitutional authority is likewise sufficient basis to exercise military force against ISIL, a hostile organization that has both inspired and aided attacks on United States soil and that has attacked U.S. military forces overseas. And "[b]ecause detention to prevent a combatant's return to the battlefield is a fundamental incident of waging war," the President's constitutional authority to use military force against ISIL includes the power to detain individuals who are part of or substantially support ISIL "for the duration of these hostilities." There can be no dispute that U.S. operations against ISIL continue given the ongoing deployment of forces in Iraq and Syria. While the 2001 and 2002 AUMF provide clear statutory authorization for those operations, even absent those provisions, the United States would have the authority to conduct operations against ISIL and detain ISIL combatants apprehended by the United States or its co-belligerents in that military theater of operations.

51. Finally, for purposes of this case, the fact remains that United States forces are currently engaged in hostilities in Syria. Regardless of the specific authorization for such hostilities, the Executive necessarily has the inherent power under Article II to detain enemy combatants captured on a battlefield where U.S. forces are deployed and in harm's way. Just as the U.S. military has the inherent authority to defend itself using deadly force on a battlefield, it has the inherent authority to detain enemy combatants captured on that battlefield. While this inherent detention authority likely exists throughout the "duration of hostilities," it certainly exists until U.S. forces either leave the military theater of operations (and are out of harm's way), or are able to arrange for release of a battlefield detainee in a manner that does not endanger U.S. forces (such as by relinquishing custody of the detainee to another sovereign). . . .

PETITIONER'S RESPONSE TO RESPONDENT'S FACTUAL RETURN[31]

. . . [T]he government argues that the president has "inherent" authority under Article II of the Constitution to detain Petitioner indefinitely without congressional authorization. No court has ever suggested, let alone held, that the president has unilateral authority to imprison an American citizen without trial—unless Congress suspends habeas corpus, which of course it has not done. This Court should reject this extraordinary assertion of executive power.

Because Congress has not authorized Petitioner's military detention, and because Congress expressly prohibited any such unauthorized detention in the Non-Detention Act, the president's "power is at its lowest ebb." The president may therefore "rely only on his own constitutional powers minus any powers of Congress over the matter." To sustain the government's claim of Article II power here, therefore, would "disabl[e] Congress" from protecting the right of American citizens against executive detention without trial. Not even the most expansive reading of the president's Article II authority can justify the power claimed here. . . .

Time and again, the Supreme Court has therefore affirmed Alexander Hamilton's oft-cited observation that the powers conferred on the president by the Commander-in-Chief Clause "amount to nothing more than the supreme command and direction of the military and naval forces." In *Youngstown*, the Supreme Court rejected the president's claim of Article II authority to seize the nation's steel mills, despite his impassioned plea that it was vital to the war effort. As Justice Jackson explains, "[a]side from suspension of the privilege of the writ of habeas corpus in time of rebellion or invasion," the Framers "made no express provision for exercise of extraordinary authority because of a crisis." For such "emergency powers" to remain "consistent with free government," their control must be "lodged elsewhere than in the Executive who exercises them."

Even assuming that in "a moment of genuine emergency, when the Government must act with no time for deliberation, the Executive may be able to detain a citizen if there is reason to fear he is an imminent threat to the safety of the Nation and its people," no such circumstances exist here. Petitioner has been detained for nearly five months, and the federal courts have, of course, remained open throughout Petitioner's detention. During this time, moreover, the government has sought to engage in law-enforcement interrogations of Petitioner. As in *Hamdi*, there is no genuine emergency that remotely justifies Petitioner's indefinite military detention by executive fiat. . . .

The government cannot sustain its radical contention that the president, acting in contravention of congressional legislation, and absent a compelling military exigency warranting suspension of the writ, can condemn an American citizen to indefinite military detention without charge. . . . The government . . . cites instances in which the president authorized the use of military force without prior specific authorization legislation. But these presidential actions are irrelevant here. Whatever the scope of the president's Article II authority to use military force in Syria or elsewhere, that authority does not give the president *carte blanche* to imprison American citizens indefinitely in defiance of the Constitution's explicit protection of habeas corpus and the essential requirement that detention be pursuant to the law of the land. . . .

Questions

1. Is the Trump administration inferring a right to detain combatants on a battlefield from the executive branch's "inherent authority to direct the deployment of military forces"? If so, is this inference valid? What does the ACLU say about this contention?
2. Why does the administration's brief claim that the Article II power "to employ military force abroad" is based on the president's responsibility not only as commander in chief but also as chief executive for foreign and military affairs? What does the latter responsibility add to the force of the government's argument?
3. Is the government claiming that the president's power "to employ military force abroad" includes "missions of good will or rescue" and not only for the purpose of protecting American lives but also American "property" and "interests"? If it is making this claim, do you agree or disagree with the government's understanding of the scope of the president's Article II powers to employ U.S. military forces abroad?
4. The Trump administration claims that "two centuries" of Executive practice support its understanding of the scope of the president's Article II powers but cites no historical example of the use of such powers earlier than the 1989 intervention in Panama. What do you make of this omission? Does it matter that many of the recent examples the government cites only involve air strikes, which typically do not involve issues of military detention?
5. The government cites an Office of Legal Counsel (OLC) opinion supporting the position that repelling a "direct and immediate attack" on the United States is not the "exclusive" basis on which the president may use military force without congressional approval. To what degree does this OLC opinion support the Trump administration's understanding of the scope of presidential war powers under Article II?
6. Even if the president's Article II powers imply a right to detain enemy combatants on the battlefield, would that right necessarily include the authority to detain a person who was not a member of ISIS, but only someone who "substantially supported" it? What if the international laws of war denied that anyone could be classified as an "enemy combatant" on this basis?

Should it make any difference if such a "supporter" of ISIS was an American citizen?

7. The government's brief also seems to infer an Article II power to detain enemy combatants from the U.S. military's "inherent authority to defend itself using deadly force on a battlefield." Is this a valid inference? What if a group of U.S. soldiers found themselves on a "hot" battlefield, perhaps because of a helicopter crash, without any authorization by Congress or the president? Could these soldiers start taking prisoners because they have a right to use deadly force to defend themselves if attacked?
8. The ACLU's position seems to be that the executive branch, barring a "genuine emergency," cannot detain an American citizen without trial unless Congress has explicitly authorized the detention or has suspended the writ of habeas corpus. Is this rule preferable to the Trump administration's reliance on Article II powers? Is the ACLU's rule consistent with the Supreme Court's decision in *Hamdi v. Rumsfeld* (see **reading 4.4**)?
9. Based on its understanding of *Youngstown*, the ACLU argues that the court can uphold the Trump administration's Article II argument only if Congress has no legislative power to protect "the right of American citizens against executive detention without trial." Is this a convincing argument? Does it ignore that Doe's capture took place on a "battlefield" in the context of an "armed conflict"? On the other hand, Doe is an American citizen who has, as of April 1, 2018, been detained for about seven months. How long can this kind of detention go on without any judicial review of his status as an "enemy combatant"?
10. According to the ACLU, the government has tried to engage in "law-enforcement interrogations" of Doe. If this allegation is correct and the government at some point initiated a criminal investigation, can the Trump administration nonetheless rely on its Article II powers relating to war and foreign relations to justify the indefinite detention of an American citizen? Would such a scenario permit the government to use indefinite military detention as leverage to encourage Doe to renounce his right to an attorney and his right to remain silent and confess to crimes that will put him in federal prison for many years? Would such a result be consistent with "due process"?
11. If the Trump administration is correct and the president can subject an American citizen captured overseas on a battlefield in the context of an armed conflict to indefinite military detention, could he or she do the same regarding an American citizen inside the United States who is planning terrorist attacks? Why or why not?

In February 2018, the Trump administration appealed the seventy-two-hours' notice requirement to the D.C. Circuit. While this appeal was pending, the administration gave notice to the district court that it intended to transfer Doe to Saudi Arabia, but Judge Chutkan issued an injunction against the transfer, concluding that the government had no legal authority under any statute or treaty to transfer a citizen from one country to another. The administration appealed to the D.C. Circuit, claiming that the injunction was unwarranted. The D.C. Circuit handed down its decision on May 7, 2018, upholding the district court's view that the administration had no authority to transfer Doe to Saudi Arabia. The D.C. Circuit added, however, that if it was established that Doe was an enemy combatant, then the administration could make the transfer. But Doe's status as an enemy combatant is exactly what he is contesting in his habeas petition at the district court. Therefore Doe cannot be transferred, the D.C. Circuit reasoned, without first giving him a full opportunity to establish that he is not an enemy combatant. Of course, in Doe's future habeas litigation, it is likely that the scope of the 2001 AUMF, in particular whether it includes ISIS, as well as the scope of President Trump's Article II detention authority, are both likely to be points of contention. However, whether this litigation will produce any clarity on either or both of these issues is unknown at this time.[32]

NOTES

1. See Gavin Daly, "Napoleon's Lost Legions: French Prisoners of War in Britain, 1803–1814," *History* 89 (2004): 361–80.
2. Francis Lieber, "Guerrilla Parties," August 1862, Google Books, https://ia802701.us.archive.org/17/items/guerrillapartie00liebgoog/guerrillapartie00liebgoog.pdf.
3. "General Orders No. 100: The Lieber Code," April 24, 1863, Yale Law School, Lillian Goldman Law Library, http://avalon.law.yale.edu, esp. Articles 81–85.
4. For example, see regulations 1 and 2 of the annex to the Hague Convention (IV) of 1907.
5. Available at "Convention IV Respecting the Laws and Customs of War on Land and Its Annex," October 18, 1907, International Committee of the Red Cross (ICRC), Treaties, State Parties and Commentaries, https://ihl-databases.icrc.org.
6. *United States v. Ohlendorf* (Einsatzgruppen case), 4 U.S. Trials of War Crim. 1 (1949).
7. "Geneva Convention (III) Relative to the Treatment of Prisoners of War," August 12, 1949, International Committee of the Red Cross (ICRC), https://ihl-databases.icrc.org.
8. See Article 85 of "General Orders No. 100."
9. Article 1 of Additional Protocol II. The formal names for the two protocols are Protocol Additional to the Geneva Conventions of 12 August 1949, and relating to the Protection of Victims of International Armed Conflicts (Protocol I), 8 June 1977; and Protocol Additional to the Geneva Conventions of 12 August 1949, and relating to the Protection of Victims of Non-International Armed Conflicts (Protocol II), 8 June 1977. Both protocols are available at "Geneva Conventions and Commentaries," International Committee of the Red Cross (ICRC), https://www.icrc.org.
10. Article 1 of Additional Protocol II.
11. See Ronald Reagan, letter of transmittal, January 29, 1987, Library of Congress, https://www.loc.gov.
12. Public Law 107-40, Authorization for Use of Military Force, September 18, 2001, Congress.gov, https://www.congress.gov.
13. "Military Order of November 13, 2001," Executive Orders, Federal Register, Federation of American Scientists, https://fas.org.
14. See George W. Bush, "Humane Treatment of Taliban and al Qaeda Detainees," February 7, 2002, Project to Enforce the Geneva Conventions, http://www.pegc.us.
15. "Memorandum from Deputy Secretary Paul Wolfowitz re: *Order Establishing Combatant Status Review Tribunals*," July 7, 2004, U.S. Department of Defense, http://www.dod.mil.
16. See *Rumsfeld v. Padilla*, 542 U.S. 426 (2004) and *Padilla v. Rumsfeld*, 352 F.3d 695 (2d Cir. 2003).
17. *Padilla v. Hanft*, 423 F.3d 386 (4th Cir. 2005).
18. *Al-Marri v. Wright*, 487 F.3d 160 (4th Cir. 2007).
19. *Hamdan v. Rumsfeld*, 548 U.S. 557 (2006).
20. Respondents' Memorandum regarding the Government's Detention Authority Relative to Detainees Held at Guantanamo Bay, *In re: Guantanamo Bay Detainee Litigation*,

March 13, 2009, https://assets.documentcloud.org/documents/1369994/march-13-2009-detention-definition.pdf.

21. *Gherebi v. Obama*, 609 F. Supp. 2d 43, 70 (D.D.C. Apr. 22, 2009).

22. *Hamlily v. Obama*, 616 F. Supp. 2d 63, 69 (D.D.C. May 19, 2009).

23. See, generally, *Al-Bihani v. Obama*, 619 F.3d 1 (D.C. Cir. 2010).

24. Pub. L. No. 112-81, §1021(b), 125 Stat. 1298, 1562 (2011).

25. *Hedges v. Obama*, 890 F. Supp. 2d 424 (S.D.N.Y. 2012).

26. *Hedges v. Obama*, 724 F.3d 170 (2nd Cir. 2013).

27. Davlin Barrett and Matt Zapotsky, "Case of Suspected American ISIS Fighter Captured in Syria Vexes U.S.," *Washington Post*, October 29, 2017.

28. Charlie Savage, Eric Schmitt, and Adam Goldman, "Officials Weigh Sending American Detainee to Saudi Arabia," *New York Times*, December 20, 2017.

29. *Doe v. Mattis*, "Government's Factual Return: Redacted Version for Public Filing," (D.D.C.) (Civil Action No. 1:17-cv-2069 [TSC]), filed on February 14, 2018, 36, https://www.documentcloud.org/documents/4379676-Govt-factual-return-John-Doe-US-citizen-enemy.html.

30. Ibid., 25–28.

31. *Doe v. Mattis*, "Petitioner's Response to Respondent's Factual Return," (D.D.C.) (No. 17-cv-2069 [TSC]), filed on February 9, 2018, 36–40, https://www.aclu.org/legal-document/doe-v-mattis-aclu-response-governments-factual-return.

32. See *Doe v. Mattis*, 18-5032 (slip opinion) (D.C. Cir. May 7, 2018), available at https://www.lawfareblog.com/document-dc-circuit-opinion-transfer-injunction-doe-v-mattis. The ACLU's and the government's filings at the D.C. Circuit are available at the ACLU's *Doe v. Mattis* webpage.

5

Torture and Interrogation

★ ★ ★

Torture has been widely practiced throughout much of human history. In the Greek and Roman world, slaves and foreigners were routinely tortured to force confessions or punish them for their crimes. The medieval Catholic Church relied heavily on trial by ordeal to separate the guilty from the innocent, a form of fact finding that tended to be lethal for the accused. During the Inquisition, torture was extensively used to uncover heresy, witchcraft, and political crimes, a method of discovery that almost guaranteed a finding of culpability. The spread of the ideas of Voltaire, Rousseau, and Montesquieu during the eighteenth century's Age of Enlightenment initiated a reassessment of the utility and morality of torture. Cesare Beccaria, an Italian jurist, published his influential work *On Crimes and Punishment* in 1764. This treatise contributed to the slow but steady demise of torture in European criminal proceedings, but not in other contexts, such as the interrogation of prisoners during an armed conflict. In 1798, Napoleon condemned the use of torture for this purpose, writing that the "barbarous custom of having men beaten who are suspected of having important secrets to reveal must be abolished. It has always been recognized that this way of interrogating men, by putting them to torture, produces nothing worthwhile. The poor wretches say anything that comes into their mind and what they think the interrogator wishes to know."[1] The fact that Napoleon refers to the use of torture as a "custom" in the context of armed conflicts is noteworthy, even if he personally thought it produced "nothing worthwhile." At the end of the eighteenth century, torture was still thought to be a useful means to gather intelligence in the context of war and national security.

Sixty some years after Napoleon's remarks, attitudes toward torture during wartime had shifted considerably. In his code of war, promulgated as General Orders Number 100 in 1863, Francis Lieber explicitly prohibited the use of cruelty or torture as a means to extract information from prisoners. In absolute fashion, Article 16 posited that "military necessity does not admit of cruelty . . . , nor of maiming or wounding except in fight, nor of torture to extort confessions."[2] It was not entirely clear whether Lieber's ban on the use of torture was limited to lawful combatants who were legitimate prisoners of war. Although Lieber prohibited all forms of revenge in war, he also concluded that the law of war could not "wholly dispense" with the principle of "retaliation," that is, the punishment of the enemy for their violations of the law of war. Accordingly, Lieber advised that "retaliation shall only be resorted to" as a means of protective retribution . . . "after careful inquiry into the real occurrence, and the character of the misdeeds that may demand retribution."[3] It is therefore possible that Lieber would have permitted harsh interrogations of unlawful combatants he called "armed prowlers," "war rebels," or "guerrillas" as a form of punishment, especially if these unlawful combatants had used such techniques on regular northern troops.[4]

Lieber's general prohibition of torture in war was indirectly incorporated into the Hague Convention of 1907 (Hague IV). Article 4 of the annex to this multilateral treaty required that all prisoners of war be "humanely treated."[5] Following World War II, the United Nations Universal Declaration of Human Rights and the Geneva Conventions took an even more definite stand against the use of torture during armed conflicts.[6] Article 13 of Geneva III, the convention that dealt with the treatment of prisoners of war, prohibited all forms of "physical mutilation" or "acts of violence or intimidation."[7] Common Article 3 of the Geneva Conventions, so called because it is included in each of the four conventions, required that all persons "taking no active part in hostilities" shall be "treated humanely" and that they should not be subjected "at any time and in any place" to any "violence to life and person, in particular murder of all kinds, mutilation, cruel treatment and torture" or to any "outrages upon personal dignity, in particular humiliating and degrading treatment."[8] Although Common Article 3 technically only applied to armed conflicts "not of an international character," its principles were quickly recognized as a part of customary international law applicable to all types of armed conflict.

Despite the Geneva Conventions, torture was commonly practiced during the Algerian War of Independence (1954–1962). The French argued that the conflict was not legally a "war" but rather a "police action" against the terrorism of the National Liberation Front (FLN). For this reason, according to the French, the Geneva Conventions did not apply and FLN detainees did not have the rights of lawful belligerents. Accordingly, the French used torture, in conjunction with summary executions and forced disappearances, not only as a method of acquiring information from detainees about FLN's structure and operations, but also as a systematic means to break the morale of the counterinsurgency. In the end, these brutal methods had the opposite effect by eroding French political support for the war and encouraging international opposition to France's Algerian policy. In the end, despite opposition by French Algerians and the French army, a referendum was held on July 1, 1962, at which point Algerians voted overwhelmingly in favor of independence.

While torture flourished in the Algerian War, the Council of Europe adopted the European Convention on Human Rights, which went into effect on September 3, 1953. Article 3 of the convention read as follows: "No one shall be subjected to torture or to inhuman or degrading treatment or punishment."[9] Nevertheless, during the Troubles in Northern Ireland (1970s), the British military used the following five interrogation techniques against fourteen suspected members of the Irish Republican Army (IRA): prolonged wall-standing, hooding, loud noise, sleep deprivation, and deprivation of food and water. In 1976, the European Commission of Human Rights concluded that the five techniques amounted to torture and, in conjunction with the Irish government, referred the case to the European Court of Human Rights (ECHR). The ECHR handed down its decision on January 18, 1978, holding generally that the British government had engaged in "inhuman and degrading treatment" of the IRA suspects but that the treatment did not qualify as "torture."

5.1 *Ireland v. United Kingdom*, ECHR, 5310/71 (1978)

162. As was emphasized by the Commission, ill-treatment must attain a minimum level of severity if it is to fall within the scope of Article 3 (art. 3).[10] The assessment of this minimum is, in the nature of things, relative; it depends on all the circumstances of the case, such as the duration of the treatment, its physical or mental effects and, in some cases, the sex, age and state of health of the victim, etc.

163. The Convention prohibits in absolute terms torture and inhuman or degrading treatment or punishment, irrespective of the victim's conduct. Unlike most of the substantive clauses of the Convention . . . , Article 3 makes no provision for exceptions and . . . there can be no derogation therefrom even in the event of a public emergency threatening the life of the nation. . . .

167. The five techniques were applied in combination, with premeditation and for hours at a stretch; they caused, if not actual bodily injury, at least intense physical and mental suffering to the persons subjected thereto and also led to acute psychiatric disturbances during interrogation. They accordingly fell into the category of inhuman treatment within the meaning of Article 3. The techniques were also degrading since they were such as to arouse in their victims feelings of fear, anguish and inferiority capable of humiliating and debasing them and possibly breaking their physical or moral resistance. . . .

In order to determine whether the five techniques should also be qualified as torture, the Court must have regard to the distinction, embodied in Article 3, between this notion and that of inhuman or degrading treatment.

In the Court's view, this distinction derives principally from a difference in the intensity of the suffering inflicted.

. . . [I]t was the intention that the Convention, with its distinction between "torture" and "inhuman or degrading treatment," should by the first of these terms attach a special stigma to deliberate inhuman treatment causing very serious and cruel suffering. . . .

Although the five techniques, as applied in combination, undoubtedly amounted to inhuman and degrading treatment, although their object was the extraction of confessions, the naming of others and/or information and although they were used systematically, they did not occasion suffering of the particular intensity and cruelty implied by the word torture as so understood.

168. The Court concludes that recourse to the five techniques amounted to a practice of inhuman and degrading treatment, which practice was in breach of Article 3. . . .

Separate Opinion of Judge Zekia . . .

Admittedly the word "torture" . . . is not capable of an exact and comprehensive definition. It is undoubtedly an aggravated form of inhuman treatment causing intense physical and/or mental suffering. Although the degree of intensity and the length of such suffering constitute the basic elements of torture, a lot of other relevant factors had to be taken into account. Such as: the nature of ill-treatment inflicted, the means and methods employed, the repetition and duration of such treatment, the age, sex and health condition of the person exposed to it, the likelihood that such treatment might injure the physical, mental and psychological condition of the person exposed and whether the injuries inflicted caused serious consequences for short or long duration are all relevant matters to be considered together and arrive at a conclusion whether torture has been committed.

It seems to me permissible, in ascertaining whether torture or inhuman treatment has been committed or not, to apply not only the objective test but also the subjective test.

As an example I can refer to the case of an elderly sick man who is exposed to a harsh treatment—after being given several blows and beaten to the floor, he is dragged and kicked on the floor for several hours. I would say without hesitation that the poor man has been tortured. If such treatment is applied on a wrestler or even a young athlete, I would hesitate a lot to describe it as an inhuman treatment and I might regard it as a mere rough handling. . . .

It is significant that stress has been laid on the severity of physical and/or mental pain or suffering and that . . . [Article 3 does not] qualify the word "severe" with an adjective denoting a high degree of severity in the pain or suffering inflicted.

I do not share the view that extreme intensity of physical or mental suffering is a requisite for a case of ill-treatment to amount to "torture" within the purport and object of Article 3 of the Convention. The nature of torture admits gradation in its intensity, in its severity and in the methods adopted. . . .

Separate Opinion of Judge Sir Gerald Fitzmaurice . . .

21. . . . I shall now give the reasons why I cannot agree . . . that the use of the five techniques constituted "inhuman" treatment . . . [or] "degrading" treatment." . . .

22. According to my idea of the correct handling of languages and concepts, to call the treatment involved by the use of the five techniques "inhuman" is excessive and distorting, unless the term is being employed loosely and merely figuratively . . . and it is clearly not in any such lax or light-hearted sense that Article 3 intends it. Subjection to the five techniques was certainly harsh treatment, ill-treatment, maltreatment, and other descriptions could be found; but the "inhuman" involves a totally different order or category of concept to which, in my opinion, the five techniques, even used in combination, do not properly belong. To regard them as doing so is to debase the currency of normal speech, because there is then no way left in which to differentiate or distinguish, or to describe instances of truly inhuman treatment. If anything that causes an appreciable amount of aching, strain, discomfort, distress, etc., or of deprivation of sleep or sustenance, is to be regarded as "inhuman," what words shall be found to characterize the much graver treatment that could without serious question be considered inhuman? To give concrete examples, if standing someone against a wall in a strained position over a considerable period, or keeping him with a hood over his head for a certain time, amounts to "inhuman" treatment, what language should be used to describe kicking a man in the groin, or placing him in a blacked-out cell in the company of a bevy of starving rats? That would also be merely inhuman treatment presumably?—and I say "merely" because, although the latter instances would clearly constitute inhuman treatment, they would apparently be rated no differently from, and as no worse than, the former relatively minor ones, if these also are to be characterized as "inhuman." If the extreme term is to be used for any infliction of physical or mental harm or stress, no way of marking out or attaching the necessary weight to the genuine case remains—for to employ such locutions as "very inhuman" or "severely inhuman"

would obviously be ridiculous. Thus, pretty well everything physically or mentally injurious becomes "inhuman"—which is to reduce the whole concept to an absurdity—just as, supposing that one subscribed to that view of humanity that seems to underlie Burns' well-known couplet about "Man's inhumanity to man," one would be forced to the pessimistic conclusion that there is nothing so inhuman as the human. . . .

27. Much of what I have said about exaggeration and distortion in relation to inhuman treatment applies equally . . . to the notion of degrading treatment, though less strongly. . . . [A]lmost anything that is personally unpleasant or disagreeable can be regarded as degrading by those affected. In the present context it can be assumed that it is, or should be, intended to denote something seriously humiliating, lowering as to human dignity, or disparaging, like having one's head shaved, being tarred and feathered, smeared with filth, pelted with muck, paraded naked in front of strangers, forced to eat excreta, deface the portrait of one's sovereign or head of State, or dress up in a way calculated to provoke ridicule or contempt—although here one may pause to wonder whether Christ was really degraded by being made to don a purple robe and crown of thorns and to carry His own cross. Be that as it may, the examples I have given justify asking where exactly the degradation lies in being deprived of sleep and nourishment for limited periods, in being placed for a time in a room where a continuous noise is going on, or even in being "hooded"—(after all, it has never been suggested that a man is degraded by being blindfolded before being executed although, admittedly, this is supposed to be for his benefit). . . .

Separate Opinion of Judge Evrigenis . . .

. . . [T]he judgment appears to reserve the category of "torture" exclusively for treatment which causes suffering of extreme intensity. I cannot agree with this interpretation.

The notion of torture which emerges from the judgment is in fact too limited. By adding to the notion of torture the notions of inhuman and degrading treatment, those who drew up the Convention wished . . . to extend the prohibition in Article 3 of the Convention—in principle directed against torture . . . to other categories of acts causing intolerable suffering to individuals or affecting their dignity rather than to exclude from the traditional notion of torture certain apparently less serious forms of torture and to place them in the category of inhuman treatment which carries less of a "stigma"—to use the word appearing in the judgment. The clear intention of widening the scope of the prohibition in Article 3 by adding, alongside torture, other kinds of acts cannot have the effect of restricting the notion of torture. I might advance the hypothesis that, if Article 3 of the Convention referred solely to the notion of torture, it would be difficult not to accept that the combined use of the five techniques in the present case fell within its scope. I do not see why the fact that the Convention, with the sole aim of increasing protection of the individual, condemns not only torture but also other categories of acts should lead to a different conclusion.

The Court's interpretation in this case seems also to be directed to a conception of torture based on methods of inflicting suffering which have already been overtaken by the ingenuity of modern techniques of oppression. Torture no longer presupposes violence, a notion to which the judgment refers expressly and generically. Torture can be practiced—and indeed is practiced—by using subtle techniques developed in multidisciplinary laboratories which claim to be scientific. By means of new forms of suffering that have little in common with the physical pain caused by conventional torture it aims to bring about, even if only temporarily, the disintegration of an individual's personality, the shattering of his mental and psychological equilibrium and the crushing of his will. I should very much regret it if the definition of torture which emerges from the judgment could not cover these various forms of technologically sophisticated torture. Such an interpretation would overlook the current situation and the historical prospects in which the European Convention on Human Rights should be implemented. . . .

Questions

1. Do you agree with the ECHR that "torture" and "inhuman or degrading" conduct requires a "minimal level of severity" and that this level is "relative," implying that an interrogation technique might constitute "torture" if it were applied to an old, sick woman but might not if it were applied to a young healthy man?
2. If "torture" and "inhuman or degrading" treatment are "relative" concepts, why is their prohibition "absolute," not subject to "derogation," even in a "public emergency threatening the life of the nation"? In other words, if the status of the victim can determine whether an interrogation technique is or is not torture, why shouldn't the circumstances of the interrogation have a comparable impact?
3. Should the ECHR have relied on the fact that the five interrogation techniques caused "intense physical and mental suffering" to conclude that they were "inhuman"?
4. Should the court have relied on the fact that the five techniques aroused in their victims "feelings of fear, anguish and inferiority" to the point of "breaking their physical or moral resistance" to conclude that they were "degrading"?
5. Did the ECHR properly conclude that the five interrogation techniques, even if they were used in combination with one another, did not constitute "torture" because they did not "attach a special stigma to deliberate inhuman treatment causing very serious and cruel suffering"? What sort of "stigma" is the court referring to? Why doesn't "intense physical and mental suffering" qualify as "serious and cruel suffering"?
6. What is "subjective" about Judge M. Zekia's test for "torture"? Is it more "subjective" than the majority's test? Of what significance is it that Judge Zekia takes into account other factors besides the intensity and length of suffering to decide if some form of harsh treatment qualifies as "torture"?
7. What is to be made of the fact that, although Judge Zekia concludes that the five interrogation techniques qualify as torture, Judge Gerald Fitzmaurice rejects the view that they even qualify as "inhuman" or "degrading" treatment? Is Judge Fitzmaurice correct that, if the five interrogation techniques constitute "inhuman" treatment, then anything "injurious becomes inhuman," thereby reducing the concept to an "absurdity"? Why or why not?
8. Since Judge D. Evrigenis appreciates the "ingenuity of modern techniques of oppression," does he rightly object to the majority's position that "torture" requires "suffering of extreme intensity"? Does he too quickly assume that the "new forms of suffering" caused by the "subtle" interrogation techniques of the contemporary world are as intolerable as the suffering caused by more traditional coercive interrogation techniques? Can the "new forms" be as "intolerable" if the suffering caused by them is not as "intense" as the suffering caused by coercive techniques?

During the 1960s and 1970s, the international community took additional steps to bolster its position that "torture" and "inhuman and degrading" treatment were illegal, whether in the context of an armed conflict or during peacetime. Article 7 of the International Covenant on Civil and Political Rights (ICCPR), which entered into force in 1977, categorically stated the following: "No one shall be subjected to torture or to cruel, inhuman or degrading treatment or punishment."[11] In the same year, two additional protocols were added to the Geneva Convention. Article 75 of the First Protocol prohibited "torture of all kinds, whether physical or mental" and all "outrages upon personal dignity, in particular humiliating and degrading treatment."[12] And Article 4 of the Second Protocol prohibited "cruel treatment, such as torture, mutilation or any form of corporal punishment."[13] The international community's crowning achievement in terms of outlawing torture and other forms of physical and mental abuse was the Convention against Torture and Other Cruel, Inhuman or Degrading Treatment or Punishment (CAT), which was adopted by the United Nations General Assembly on December 10, 1984. The convention went into force on June 26, 1987, after twenty countries had ratified it. Today more than 160 countries, including the United States, have ratified this convention, strongly supporting the conclusion that its principles have the sanction of customary international law.

5.2 Convention against Torture and Other Cruel, Inhuman or Degrading Treatment or Punishment (1987)

ARTICLE 1

1. For the purposes of this Convention,[14] the term "torture" means any act by which severe pain or suffering, whether physical or mental, is intentionally inflicted on a person for such purposes as obtaining from him or a third person information or a confession, punishing him for an act he or a third person has committed or is suspected of having committed, or intimidating or coercing him or a third person, or for any reason based on discrimination of any kind, when such pain or suffering is inflicted by or at the instigation of or with the consent or acquiescence of a public official or other person acting in an official capacity. It does not include pain or suffering arising only from, inherent in or incidental to lawful sanctions. . . .

ARTICLE 2

1. Each State Party shall take effective legislative, administrative, judicial or other measures to prevent acts of torture in any territory under its jurisdiction.
2. No exceptional circumstances whatsoever, whether a state of war or a threat of war, internal political instability or any other public emergency, may be invoked as a justification of torture.
3. An order from a superior officer or a public authority may not be invoked as a justification of torture.

ARTICLE 3

1. No State Party shall expel, return ("refouler") or extradite a person to another State where there are substantial grounds for believing that he would be in danger of being subjected to torture.
2. For the purpose of determining whether there are such grounds, the competent authorities shall take into account all relevant considerations including, where applicable, the existence in the State concerned of a consistent pattern of gross, flagrant or mass violations of human rights.

ARTICLE 4

1. Each State Party shall ensure that all acts of torture are offences under its criminal law. The same shall apply to an attempt to commit torture and to an act by any person which constitutes complicity or participation in torture.
2. Each State Party shall make these offences punishable by appropriate penalties which take into account their grave nature.

ARTICLE 5

1. Each State Party shall take such measures as may be necessary to establish its jurisdiction over the offences referred to in article 4 in the following cases:
   a. When the offences are committed in any territory under its jurisdiction or

on board a ship or aircraft registered in that State;

b. When the alleged offender is a national of that State;

c. When the victim is a national of that State if that State considers it appropriate.

2. Each State Party shall likewise take such measures as may be necessary to establish its jurisdiction over such offences in cases where the alleged offender is present in any territory under its jurisdiction and it does not extradite him. . . .

ARTICLE 16

1. Each State Party shall undertake to prevent in any territory under its jurisdiction other acts of cruel, inhuman or degrading treatment or punishment which do not amount to torture as defined in article I, when such acts are committed by or at the instigation of or with the consent or acquiescence of a public official or other person acting in an official capacity. . . .

Questions

1. Is there much substantive content to Article 1's definition of "torture" as "severe pain or suffering, whether physical or mental"? Should this definition be revised? How?
2. Such "pain or suffering" must be "intentionally inflicted on a person for such purposes as" obtaining information, punishing or intimidating the victim, or for any reason "based on discrimination of any kind." Is this requirement of a "comparable purpose" too open-ended? What purpose for inflicting "severe pain or suffering" would not qualify as "torture"?
3. Why must torture be inflicted "by or at the instigation of or with the consent or acquiescence of a public official"? Does this mean that a private person acting without public authority cannot commit torture? What is the justification for this rule?
4. If torture does not include pain or suffering "inherent in or incidental to lawful sanctions," does this mean that any state can circumvent the torture prohibition by legally authorizing the "pain and suffering" that would otherwise qualify as "torture"?
5. Article 2 proclaims that there are no exceptions to the prohibition against torture, but is the absolute character of the prohibition workable? Can you imagine circumstances that in your view would justify torture?
6. Article 16 requires state parties to prevent "cruel, inhuman or degrading treatment or punishment" if committed "by or at the instigation of or with the consent or acquiescence of a public official," but it does not explicitly require criminal prosecution or preclude the possibility that a state party may make exceptions. Are these omissions significant? Are they justifiable?

The United States signed the Convention against Torture in 1988 and ratified the treaty in 1994 but added a number of significant reservations. First, the United States restricted the definition of torture to acts that must be "specifically intended" to inflict severe physical or mental pain or suffering. Second, "mental pain or suffering" would qualify as torture only if it was a "prolonged mental harm" resulting from one of four factors: "(1) the intentional infliction or threatened infliction of severe physical pain or suffering; (2) the administration or application, or threatened administration of application, of mind-altering substances or other procedures calculated to disrupt profoundly the senses or the personality; (3) the threat of imminent death; or (4) the threat that another person will imminently be subjected to death, severe physical pain or suffering, or the administration or application of mind-altering substances or other procedures calculated to disrupt profoundly the senses or personality." Third, Article 3's prohibition of returning a person to another state if there are "substantial grounds" that the person would be tortured prohibits the return only "if it is more likely than not that he would be tortured." Last, the duty of the United States to prevent "cruel, inhuman or degrading treatment or punishment" was limited to conduct "prohibited by the Fifth, Eighth, and/or Fourteenth Amendments to the Constitution of the United States."[15]

Following its ratification of the CAT, the United States fulfilled its obligation to take "effective legislative, administrative, judicial or other measures to prevent acts of torture" by quickly enacting a criminal federal torture statute, one that incorporated the above reservations.

5.3 *Federal Torture Statute* (1994)

§ 2340. DEFINITIONS

As used in this chapter[16]—

(1) "torture" means an act committed by a person acting under the color of law specifically intended to inflict severe physical or mental pain or suffering (other than pain or suffering incidental to lawful sanctions) upon another person within his custody or physical control;
(2) "severe mental pain or suffering" means the prolonged mental harm caused by or resulting from—
  (A) the intentional infliction or threatened infliction of severe physical pain or suffering;
  (B) the administration or application, or threatened administration or application, of mind-altering substances or other procedures calculated to disrupt profoundly the senses or the personality;
  (C) the threat of imminent death; or
  (D) the threat that another person will imminently be subjected to death, severe physical pain or suffering, or the administration or application of mind-altering substances or other procedures calculated to disrupt profoundly the senses or personality; and
(3) "United States" means the several States of the United States, the District of Columbia, and the commonwealths, territories, and possessions of the United States.

§ 2340A. TORTURE

a. OFFENSE.—Whoever outside the United States commits or attempts to commit torture shall be fined under this title or imprisoned not more than 20 years, or both, and if death results to any person from conduct prohibited by this subsection, shall be punished by death or imprisoned for any term of years or for life.
b. JURISDICTION.—There is jurisdiction over the activity prohibited in subsection (a) if—
  (1) the alleged offender is a national of the United States; or
  (2) the alleged offender is present in the United States, irrespective of the nationality of the victim or alleged offender.
c. CONSPIRACY.—A person who conspires to commit an offense under this section shall be subject to the same penalties (other than the penalty of death) as the penalties prescribed for the offense, the commission of which was the object of the conspiracy. . . .

Questions

1. Does the Federal Torture Statute's requirement that a defendant must "specifically intend" to inflict severe physical or mental pain or suffering

significantly narrow the definition of "torture"? Can you give an example of a case of torture where such a "specific intention" is missing?

2. It is the position of the United States that "severe mental pain or suffering" qualifies as "torture" only if it is a "prolonged mental harm." Why does the United States take this position? Does it make any sense? Why doesn't brief intense mental pain or suffering qualify as torture?
3. A "prolonged mental harm" constitutes torture only if it is caused by one of the four listed factors. Why is there this additional requirement? Can you think of a "prolonged mental harm" that is not caused by one of these four factors? Should the infliction of such a harm be considered "torture"?
4. A "prolonged mental harm" caused by the threat of "severe physical pain or suffering" constitutes "torture" but not if the "prolonged mental harm" is caused by a threat of "severe mental pain or suffering." Why is there this difference? Is mental pain or suffering intrinsically less serious than physical pain or suffering?
5. Why does the United States only punish acts of torture committed outside the United States?
6. Federal courts have jurisdiction to try an act of "torture" committed outside the United States if the offender is a U.S. national or if the offender is found inside the United States. Does this jurisdictional limit satisfy the obligation of the United States to prosecute acts of torture under Article 5 of the CAT?

During the 1990s, the European Court of Human Rights (ECHR) decided a number of cases dealing with the prohibition against torture contained in the European Convention on Human Rights. In *Askoy v. Turkey* (1996), the ECHR considered the case of an applicant who was suspended from his arms ("Palestinian hanging"), which caused paralysis in both of the effected limbs. The court held that "[i]ll-treatment was of such a serious and cruel nature that it can only be described as torture."[17] In *Aydin v. Turkey* (1997), the ECHR reviewed an alleged rape and ill-treatment of a female detainee, along with the failure of the authorities to conduct an adequate investigation of her complaints. The court concluded that, "given the fundamental importance of the prohibition of torture and the especially vulnerable position of torture victims," the state had an obligation "to carry out a thorough and effective investigation of incidents of torture."[18] Last, in *Selmouni v. France* (1999), a Netherlands and Moroccan national complained that the French police had repeatedly punched, kicked, and hit him with objects; urinated on him; threatened him with a blowlamp and a syringe; and, finally, allegedly raped him with a small black truncheon after he was told, "You Arabs enjoy being screwed." The ECHR upheld Selmouni's claim that he was tortured.[19] Although all three of these decisions by the ECHR addressed cases not involving "armed conflicts," they were nonetheless relevant to how international law understood "torture" in the field of human rights law.

Also in 1999, the Israeli High Court of Justice considered the legality of a number of interrogation techniques used by Israel's General Security Services (GSS) against suspected Palestinian terrorists in *Public Committee against Torture in Israel v. Israel*. The techniques included "shaking" ("the forceful and repeated shaking of the suspect's upper torso, in a manner which causes the neck and head to swing rapidly, . . . [which] is likely to cause serious brain damage, harm the spinal cord, cause the suspect to lose consciousness, vomit and urinate uncontrollably and suffer serious headaches"); use of the "shabach" position (in which the suspect is "seated on a small and low chair, whose seat is tilted forward, towards the ground," with one hand "tied behind the suspect, and placed inside the gap between the chair's seat and back support," the other is "tied behind the chair, against its back support," the suspects' head "is covered by a sack that falls down to his shoulders," and "loud music is played" for a "long period of time"); the "frog crouch" (in which the suspect is forced into "consecutive, periodical crouches on the tips of one's toes, each lasting for five minute intervals"); the utilization of excessively tight handcuffs; and, finally, sleep deprivation.

The Israeli High Court held that no statute granted the GSS the authority to use such "physical means" of interrogation. In addition, although the court declined to base its decision on any international standard of "torture" or "inhuman or degrading treatment or punishment," it also held that the interrogation techniques in general violated Israel's basic law of human dignity and liberty. However, the court also concluded that any GSS interrogator who used such "physical means" of interrogation could invoke the "necessity defense" if criminally prosecuted. Inherited from the common law, the "necessity defense" excuses a defendant who has committed a criminal act (1) if the purpose of the criminal act was to avoid a harm; (2) if there was no lawful means by which the harm could have been avoided; and, last, (3) if the avoided harm was greater than the harm caused by violating the law. In the Israeli High Court's view, the "necessity defense" did not authorize the use of coercive interrogation techniques but was potentially a valid excuse for their use if they were necessary to prevent "serious harm to human life or limb."[20]

The International Criminal Tribunal for the former Yugoslavia (ICTY) reviewed a number of cases involving "torture" in terms of the laws of war, also known as international humanitarian law. In *Prosecutor v. Delalic* ("The Celebici Case"; 1998), the ICTY held that the prohibition of torture was not only a norm of customary international law but also a norm of *jus cogens*, which implied that the prohibition was "absolute" and "non-derogable" even in the context of an "armed conflict." The court cited the definition of "torture" contained in the CAT but declined to endorse a specific definition or an exhaustive list of tortuous acts since either would only serve to challenge "the ingenuity" of torturers. Traditionally, the act of torture had to be committed by or at the instigation of a public official, but the ICTY abandoned this requirement because, in its judgment, the prohibition had to be applicable to nonstate parties in either internal armed conflicts or international conflicts involving nonstate actors. Last, the ICTY held that rape in the context of an "armed conflict" qualified as torture if the rapist's purpose was to intimidate, degrade, humiliate, discriminate, punish, or destroy.[21] The ICTY elaborated on these holdings three years later in *Prosecutor v. Kunarac et al.* (2001), a decision in which the court concluded that the definition of torture contained in the CAT was not applicable to circumstances involving an armed conflict.

5.4 *Prosecutor v. Kunarac et al.*, IT-96-23 and 23/1-A-T (February 22, 2001)

482. . . . [T]he Trial Chamber is of the view that the definition of torture contained in the Torture Convention cannot be regarded as the definition of torture under customary international law which is binding regardless of the context in which it is applied. . . . The Trial Chamber, therefore, holds that the definition of torture contained in Article 1 of the Torture Convention can only serve, for present purposes, as an interpretational aid.

483. Three elements of the definition of torture contained in the Torture Convention are, however, uncontentious and are accepted as representing the status of customary international law on the subject:

(i) Torture consists of the infliction, by act or omission, of severe pain or suffering, whether physical or mental.
(ii) This act or omission must be intentional.
(iii) The act must be instrumental to another purpose, in the sense that the infliction of pain must be aimed at reaching a certain goal.

484. On the other hand, three elements remain contentious:

(i) The list of purposes the pursuit of which could be regarded as illegitimate and coming within the realm of the definition of torture.
(ii) The necessity, if any, for the act to be committed in connection with an armed conflict.
(iii) The requirement, if any, that the act be inflicted by or at the instigation of or with the consent or acquiescence of a public official or other person acting in an official capacity.

485. The Trial Chamber is satisfied that the following purposes have become part of customary international law: (a) obtaining information or a confession, (b) punishing, intimidating or coercing the victim or a third person. There are some doubts as to whether other purposes have come to be recognized under customary international law. . . .

486. There is no requirement under customary international law that the conduct must be solely perpetrated for one of the prohibited purposes. As was stated by the Trial Chamber in the *Delalic* case, the prohibited purpose must simply be part of the motivation behind the conduct and need not be the predominating or sole purpose.

487. Secondly, . . . [if] torture is charged as a violation of the laws or customs of war . . . , the Trial Chamber will have to be satisfied that the act was closely related to the hostilities. If, on the other hand, torture is charged as a crime against humanity . . . the Trial Chamber will have to be convinced beyond reasonable doubt that there existed an armed conflict at the relevant time and place.

488. Thirdly, the Torture Convention requires that the pain or suffering be inflicted by or at the instigation of or with the consent or acquiescence of a public official or other person acting in an official capacity. . . .

491. . . . [In contrast, the offenses provided for in Article 4 of Additional Protocol II can be] committed by any individual, regardless of his official status. . . . The Commentary to Additional Protocol II dealing specifically with the offences mentioned in Article 4 (2)(a), namely, violence to the life health, or physical or mental well being of persons in particular murder and cruel treatment such as torture, states:

> The most widespread form of torture is practiced by public officials for the purpose of obtaining confessions, but torture is not only condemned as a judicial institution; *the act of torture is reprehensible in itself, regardless of its perpetrator*, and cannot be justified in any circumstances.

493. A violation of one of the relevant articles of the [ICTY] Statute will engage the

perpetrator's individual criminal responsibility. In this context, the participation of the state becomes secondary and, generally, peripheral. With or without the involvement of the state, the crime committed remains of the same nature and bears the same consequences. . . .

497. On the basis of what has been said, the Trial Chamber holds that, in the field of international humanitarian law, the elements of the offence of torture, under customary international law are as follows:

(i) The infliction, by an act or omission, of severe pain or suffering, whether physical or mental.
(ii) The act of omission must be intentional.
(iii) The act or omission must aim at obtaining information or a confession, or at punishing, intimidating or coercing the victim or a third person, or at discriminating, on any ground, against the victim or a third person. . . .

Questions

1. Do you agree with the ICTY that the Convention against Torture (CAT) is not applicable to armed conflicts?
2. Should the CAT be set aside if an international agreement grants individuals more protection against torture?
3. Why does the ICTY find fault with the CAT's requirement that torture must have a certain type of purpose? Is it because the CAT's list is not exhaustive? Is it because the list includes "discrimination"?
4. Does the ICTY's definition unduly broaden the concept of torture by holding that the prohibited purpose need not be the "predominating or sole purpose" of the conduct?
5. Does it make sense that war crime tribunals should limit their jurisdiction to cases of torture that are "closely related" to armed conflicts?
6. Do you agree with the ICTY's judgment that the war crime of torture does not require that the pain or suffering "be inflicted by or at the instigation of or with the consent or acquiescence of a public official"?

Following the 9/11 attacks, the Bush administration greatly feared a second round of al-Qaeda attacks on the United States. Preventing such attacks became the administration's highest priority, which placed a huge premium on the value of intelligence concerning al-Qaeda's structure, operations, and plans for future terrorist attacks. The detainees who ended up in the custody of U.S. military forces after the invasion of Afghanistan were one obvious source of information, but many of these detainees were foot soldiers of the Taliban who knew little or nothing of any ongoing plots by al-Qaeda operatives. However, the possibility of an intelligence coup brightened considerably when U.S. and Pakistani forces captured Abu Zubaydah in a raid on safe houses in Faisalabad, Pakistan, on March 28, 2002. At the time, the Bush administration thought Zubaydah was al-Qaeda's chief of operations, someone who not only was familiar with al-Qaeda's membership but also would have considerable knowledge of al-Qaeda's future terrorist plots against the United States. Severely wounded at the time of his capture, Zubaydah spent some time in a Pakistani hospital before being transferred to a secret detention site in Thailand.

The FBI began Zubaydah's interrogation in Thailand, having some success using standard noncoercive techniques, but the Bush administration was convinced that Zubaydah was holding back information. To overcome Zubaydah's perceived resistance, the Bush administration transferred him to the custody of the CIA, which had developed a set of "enhanced interrogation techniques" (EITs) from Survival, Evasion, Resistance, and Escape (SERE), a military program that in part trained U.S. military personnel to endure abusive interrogations if captured. The CIA contemplated using the following ten EITs in Zubaydah's interrogation: (1) attention grasp (grasping the subject by his collar with both hands; (2) walling (bouncing the subject off of a flexible wall); (3) facial hold (holding the subject's head immobile with both hands); (4) insult slap (subject is slapped with an open palm across the face); (5) cramped confinement (subject is placed in a large box without any light for eighteen hours or a small box for two hours); (6) wall standing (subject is made to lean against a wall at such an angle that his fingers must support all of his body weight); (7) stress positions (for example, subject is made to kneel on the floor leaning backward at a forty-five-degree angle); (8) sleep deprivation (forcing subject to stay awake for no more than eleven days at a time; (9) cramped confinement with an insect (placing an insect into either the large or small confinement box while falsely informing the subject that the insect stings); and (10) waterboarding (pouring water over a subject's mouth and nose while he is strapped to an inclined board with his feet elevated).

Given the harsh nature of these EITs, it is not surprising that CIA officials wanted assurance from the Bush administration that their use was authorized and not in violation of the federal torture statute. The Office of Legal Counsel (OLC) in the Department of Justice, which provides authoritative legal advice to the president and all other executive agencies, gave the CIA verbal assurances in July 2002 and confirmed its assessment with two official memoranda dated August 1, 2002. The first memo addressed the general "standards of conduct for interrogation"; the second applied these standards to the circumstances of Zubaydah's interrogation, finding that the above ten EITs were authorized and not in violation of the federal torture statute. Jay Bybee, the head of OLC, signed both of these memos, often referred to as the "torture memos," but they were primarily the work of one of his deputies, John Yoo, a law professor on leave from the University of Berkeley. The following excerpt is from the general memo that interpreted the federal torture statute. This memo argued that the statute (1) required a specific intent to inflict severe pain; (2) defined "severe" pain in terms of death, organ failure, or serious impairment of bodily functions; (3) limited "severe mental pain or suffering" to "prolonged" mental harms; and last, (4) could not intrude upon the president's commander-in-chief power. Before reading the following excerpt, please review the federal torture statute (**reading 5.3**).

5.5 Memorandum for Alberto Gonzales, Counsel to the President

Re: Standards of Conduct for Interrogation under 18 U.S.C. §§2340–2340A

[A. Specific Intent] To violate Section 2340A, the statute requires that severe pain and suffering must be inflicted with specific intent. . . .[22]

. . . [B]ecause Section 2340A requires that a defendant act with the specific intent to inflict severe pain, the infliction of such pain must be the defendant's precise objective. If the statute had required only general intent, it would be sufficient to establish guilt by showing that the defendant "possessed knowledge with respect to the *actus reus* of the crime." If the defendant acted knowing that severe pain or suffering was reasonably likely to result from his actions, but no more, he would have acted only with general intent. . . .

As a theoretical matter, therefore, knowledge alone that a particular result is certain to occur does not constitute specific intent. . . . "Put differently, the law distinguishes actions taken 'because of' a given end from actions taken 'in spite of their unintended but foreseen consequences.'" Thus, even if the defendant knows that severe pain will result from his actions, if causing such harm is not his objective, he lacks the requisite specific intent even though the defendant did not act in good faith. Instead, a defendant is guilty of torture only if he acts with the express purpose of inflicting severe pain or suffering on a person within his custody or physical control. . . .

Further, a showing that an individual acted with a good faith belief that his conduct would not produce the result that the law prohibits negates specific intent. Where a defendant acts in good faith, he acts with an honest belief that he has not engaged in the proscribed conduct. . . .

Although a defendant theoretically could hold an unreasonable belief that his acts would not constitute the actions prohibited by the statute, even though they would as a certainty produce the prohibited effects, as a matter of practice in the federal criminal justice system it is highly unlikely that a jury would acquit in such a situation. Where a defendant holds an unreasonable belief, he will confront the problem of proving to the jury that he actually held that belief. . . . As a matter of proof, therefore, a good faith defense will prove more compelling when a reasonable basis exists for the defendant's belief.

[B. Severe Pain or Suffering] The key statutory phrase in the definition of torture is the statement that acts amount to torture if they cause "severe physical or mental pain or suffering." In examining the meaning of a statute, the text must be the starting point. Section 2340 makes plain that the infliction of pain or suffering per se, whether it is physical or mental, is insufficient to amount to torture. Instead, the text provides that the pain or suffering must be "severe." The statute does not, however, define the term "severe." In the absence of such a definition, we construe a statutory term in accordance with its ordinary or natural meaning. . . . Thus, the adjective "severe" conveys that the pain or suffering must be of such a high level of intensity that the pain is difficult for the subject to endure.

Congress's use of the phrase "severe pain" elsewhere in the United States Code can shed more light on its meaning. Significantly, the phrase "severe pain' appears in statutes defining an emergency medical condition for the purpose of providing health benefits. These statutes define an emergency condition as one "manifesting itself by acute symptoms of sufficient severity (including severe pain) such that a prudent lay person, who possesses an average knowledge of health and medicine, could reasonably expect the absence of immediate medical attention to result in—placing the health of the individual . . . (i) in serious jeopardy, (ii) serious impairment to bodily functions, or (iii) serious dysfunction of any bodily organ or part." Although these statutes address a substantially different subject from Section 2340, they are nonetheless helpful for understanding what constitutes severe physical pain. They treat severe pain as an indicator of ailments that are likely to result in permanent and serious physical damage in the absence of immediate medical treatment. Such damage must rise to the level of death, organ failure, or the permanent impairment of a significant bodily function. These statutes suggest that "severe pain," as used in Section 2340, must rise to a similarly high level—the level that would ordinarily be associated with a sufficiently serious physical condition or injury such as death, organ failure, or serious impairment of body functions—in order to constitute torture.

[C. Severe Mental Pain or Suffering.] . . . In order to prove "severe mental pain or suffering," the statute requires proof of "prolonged mental harm" that was caused by or resulted from one of four enumerated acts. . . .

. . . ["Prolonged"] adds a temporal dimension to the harm to the individual, namely, that the harm must be one that is endured over some period of time. Put another way, the acts giving rise to the harm must cause some lasting, though not necessarily permanent, damage. For example, the mental strain experienced by an individual during a lengthy and intense interrogation—such as one that state or local police might conduct upon a criminal suspect—would not violate Section 2340(2). On the other hand, the development of a mental disorder such as posttraumatic stress disorder, which can last months or even years, or even chronic depression, which also can last for a considerable period of time if untreated, might satisfy the prolonged harm requirement. . . .

Not only must the mental harm be prolonged to amount to severe mental pain and suffering, but also it must be caused by or result from one of the acts listed in the statute. In absence of a catchall provision, the most natural reading of the predicate acts . . . is that Congress intended it to be exhaustive. . . . We conclude that torture within the meaning of the statute requires the specific intent to cause prolonged mental harm by one of the acts listed in Section 2340(2).

. . . It could be argued that a defendant needs to have specific intent only to commit the predicate acts that give rise to prolonged mental harm. Under that view, so long as the defendant specifically intended to, for example, threaten a victim with imminent death, he would have had sufficient *mens rea* for a conviction. According to this view, it would be further necessary for a conviction to show only that the victim factually suffered prolonged mental harm, rather than that the defendant intended to cause it. We believe that this approach is contrary to the text of the statute. The statute requires that the defendant specifically intend to inflict severe mental pain or suffering. Because the statute requires this mental state with respect to the infliction of severe mental pain, and because it expressly defines severe mental pain in terms of prolonged mental harm, that mental state must be present with respect to prolonged mental harm. To read the statute otherwise would read the phrase "the prolonged mental harm cause by or resulting from" out of the definition of "severe mental pain or suffering."

A defendant could negate a showing of specific intent to cause severe mental pain or suffering by showing that he had acted in good faith that his conduct would not amount to the acts prohibited by the statute. Thus, if a defendant has a good faith belief that his actions will not result in prolonged mental harm, he lacks the mental state necessary for his action to constitute torture. A defendant could show that he acted in good faith by taking such steps as surveying professional literature, consulting with experts, or reviewing evidence gained from past experience. All of these steps would show that he has drawn on the relevant body of knowledge concerning the result proscribed . . . [by] the statute, namely prolonged mental harm. Because the presence of good faith would negate the specific intent element of torture, it is a complete defense to such a charge. . . .

. . . In short, reading the definition of torture as a whole, it is plain that the term encompasses only extreme acts. . . .

[D. Cruel, Inhuman or Degrading Treatment or Punishment] CAT also distinguishes between torture and other acts of cruel, inhuman, or degrading treatment or punishment. . . . CAT thus establishes a category of acts that are not to be committed and that states must endeavor to prevent, but that states need not criminalize, leaving those acts without the stigma of criminal penalties. CAT reserves criminal penalties and the stigma attached to those penalties for torture alone. In so doing, CAT makes clear that torture is at the farthest end of impermissible actions, and that it is distinct and separate from the lower level of "cruel, inhuman, or degrading treatment or punishment." . . .

[E. President's Commander-in-Chief Power] Even if an interrogation method arguably were to violate Section 2340A, the statute would be unconstitutional if it impermissibly encroached on the President's constitutional power to conduct a military campaign. As Commander-in-Chief, the President has the constitutional authority to order interrogations of enemy combatants to gain intelligence information concerning the military plans of the enemy. The demands of the Commander-in-Chief power are especially pronounced in the middle of a war in which the nation has already suffered a direct attack. In such a case, the information gained from interrogations may prevent future attacks by foreign enemies. Any effort to apply Section 2340A in a manner that interferes with the President's direction of such core war matters as the detention and interrogation of enemy combatants thus would be unconstitutional. . . .

[In short,] . . . Congress may no more regulate the President's ability to detain and interrogate enemy combatants than it may regulate his ability to direct troop movements on the battlefield. Accordingly, we would construe Section 2340A to avoid this constitutional difficulty, and conclude that it does not apply to the President's detention and interrogation of enemy combatants pursuant to his Commander-in-Chief authority. . . .

Questions

1. According to Yoo, would a CIA interrogator who knowingly inflicted "severe physical pain and suffering" on a detainee be guilty of torture if his "precise objective" was to obtain information from the detainee, not to inflict pain or suffering? Why or why not?
2. Is Yoo arguing that juries in the federal criminal justice system would likely find "specific intent" if the CIA interrogator knew that "severe pain and suffering" would be the result of his actions? Would such an action by a jury be warranted? If the substance of Yoo's memo is correct, would the jury's action be illegal?
3. What could a CIA interrogator do beforehand to establish that he or she did have a "reasonable basis" for believing that the EITs would not cause "severe physical or mental pain or suffering"?
4. Yoo claims that he is construing "severe pain or suffering" in accordance with its "ordinary or natural meaning" but then argues that pain is not "severe" unless it is comparable to the pain associated with death, organ failure, or serious impairment of a bodily function. Is that how the term "severe pain" is ordinarily used?
5. For his definition of "severe pain," Yoo also relies on federal statutes limiting emergency health benefits to cases involving "acute symptoms of sufficient severity," such that "a prudent lay person" could expect that the lack of immediate medical attention would result in placing the health of the individual "in serious jeopardy," cause a "serious impairment to bodily functions," or produce a "serious dysfunction of any bodily organ or part." Does it make sense to clarify the meaning of "severe pain" in a torture statute based on a statute governing when the federal government must legally provide emergency health benefits? Why or why not?
6. Yoo argues not only that "severe mental pain or suffering" requires a "prolonged mental harm" produced by one of the four predicate acts listed in the statute but also that the CIA interrogator must "specifically intend" the "prolonged mental harm." Does this mean that a CIA interrogator can threaten a detainee with imminent death but escape criminal prosecution on the ground he or she sincerely wished the detainee a quick recovery from any depression resulting from the threat? What could the interrogator do prior to the interrogation to reduce the likelihood of criminal liability?
7. Do any of the ten EITs that the OLC approved on August 1, 2002, constitute "cruel, inhuman, or degrading

treatment or punishment"? Did the Bush administration fulfill its duty under international law to prevent such "treatment or punishment"?

8. If the president directly ordered a CIA interrogator to engage in torture during an armed conflict, is Yoo correct that any criminal prosecution under the federal torture statute would be unconstitutional? Is it comparable to Congress ordering "troop movements on the battlefield"?

Following Zubaydah's interrogation in August 2002, Abd al-Rahim al-Nashiri, the organizer of the 2000 bombing of the USS *Cole*, was captured in Dubai in October 2002, and Khalid Sheikh Mohammad (KSM), the mastermind of the 9/11 attacks, was captured in Karachi, Pakistan, in March 2003. Both were quickly transferred to secret CIA detention centers where they were subjected to harsh EITs: for example, in one month, KSM endured 183 sessions of waterboarding, while a CIA interrogator threatened a naked and hooded al-Nashiri with a revving drill. During this same time frame, harsh interrogation techniques began to be used by military interrogators, first at Guantanamo Bay Naval Base (GBNB) and later at various detention centers in Afghanistan and Iraq, including the infamous Abu Ghraib prison. At this later site, detainee abuse was captured in photos that were published for the world to see in May 2004. The following month the OLC "torture memos" were leaked to the press, and soon thereafter the new head of the OLC, Jack Goldsmith, withdrew the memos on the ground that they were "sloppily reasoned, overbroad, and incautious."[23] A new OLC opinion written by Daniel Levin was issued on December 30, 2004. It questioned some of the claims made by Yoo in the earlier memo, but in the end it clearly stated that Yoo's conclusions would not be "different under the standards set forth in this memorandum."[24] In other words, EITs used on CIA or military detainees would not constitute torture if they stayed within the scope of the ten EITs the OLC had approved for Zubaydah's interrogation.

In response to the growing detainees abuse scandal, Congress enacted, over the strenuous objections of the Bush administration, the Detainee Treatment Act of 2005 (DTA) on December 30, 2005. The DTA prohibited, as defined by "the Fifth, Eighth, and Fourteenth Amendments to the Constitution," any "cruel, inhuman or degrading treatment or punishment" of any individual "in the custody or under the physical control of the United States"; required that all interrogations conducted by the U.S. military personnel be subject to the U.S. Army Field Manual; and granted criminal and civil immunity to all government agents and U.S. military personnel for using interrogation techniques that were "officially authorized" and deemed "lawful" at the time they were conducted so long as a "person of ordinary sense and understanding would not know the practices were unlawful."[25] Two months later, in February 2006, five special rapporteurs of the United Nations Commission on Human Rights published a report on the treatment of detainees at GBNB prior to 2006. The report was based on interviews of former detainees, their families and lawyers, and U.S. officials. The report concluded that the United States from 2002 until 2006 had violated the detainees' rights to physical and mental health and that, in some cases, the treatment of detainees constituted torture. The United States issued a formal reply to the report. The following reading includes excerpts from both the UN report and the reply by the U.S. government.

5.6 UN Commission on Human Rights, "Situation of Detainees at Guantánamo Bay," February 17, 2006

46. Beginning in 2001, the Administration of the United States, while officially reiterating its adherence to the absolute prohibition of torture, has put in place a number of policies that effectively weaken the prohibition.[26] A concrete example is the memorandum of 1 August 2002 from Jay S. Bybee . . . , which attempts to significantly narrow the definition of torture and claims that the necessity of self-defense can justify violation of the law prohibiting torture. . . .

47. . . .[S]everal subsequent internal Department of Justice memoranda have sought to widen the boundaries of what is permissible in terms of "counter-resistance techniques." On 16 April 2003, a memorandum was issued [by secretary of defense Donald Rumsfeld], authorizing 24 specific techniques. Its introduction states that "US Armed Forces shall continue to treat detainees humanely and, to the extent appropriate and consistent with military necessity, in a manner consistent with the principles of the Geneva Conventions." This formulation is ambiguous in that it implies that military necessity may override the principles of the Geneva Conventions. In this context, the Special Rapporteur also notes that in its reply to the questionnaire the United States exclusively uses the term "torture" and makes no reference to "cruel, inhuman and degrading treatment and punishment."

48. The debate in the Senate on 5 October 2005 is telling. Senator McCain, describing the confusion that exists regarding authorized and unauthorized interrogation techniques said: "What this also means is that confusion about the rules becomes rampant again. We have so many differing legal standards and loopholes that our lawyers and generals are confused. Just imagine our troops serving in the field." . . .

49. Following the ambiguous interpretations of what constitutes torture and ill-treatment . . . , the following interrogation techniques, which clearly went beyond earlier practice (as contained in Army Field Manual FM 34-52), were approved by the Secretary of Defense on 2 December 2002:

- "The use of stress positions (like standing) for a maximum of four hours;
- Detention in isolation up to 30 days;
- The detainee may have a hood placed over his head during transportation and questioning;
- Deprivation of light and auditory stimuli;
- Removal of all comfort items;
- Forced grooming (shaving of facial hair, etc.);
- Removal of clothing;
- Interrogation for up to 20 hours; and
- Using detainees' individual phobias (such as fear of dogs) to induce stress."

50. After having rescinded the above memorandum on 15 January 2003, the Secretary of Defense on 16 April 2003 authorized the following techniques:

- B. Incentive/Removal of Incentive, i.e., comfort items;
- S. Change of Scenery Down might include exposure to extreme temperatures and deprivation of light and auditory stimuli;
- U. Environmental Manipulation: Altering the environment to create moderate discomfort (e.g., adjusting temperature or introducing an unpleasant smell);
- V. Sleep Adjustment: Adjusting the sleeping times of the detainee (e.g., reversing sleep cycles from night to day). This technique is not sleep deprivation;
- X. Isolation: Isolating the detainee from other detainees while still complying with basic standards of treatment.

51. These techniques meet four of the five elements in the Convention definition of torture (the acts in question were perpetrated

by government officials; they had a clear purpose, i.e., gathering intelligence, extracting information; the acts were committed intentionally; and the victims were in a position of powerlessness). However, to meet the Convention definition of torture, severe pain or suffering, physical or mental, must be inflicted. Treatment aimed at humiliating victims may amount to degrading treatment or punishment, even without intensive pain or suffering. It is difficult to assess *in abstracto* whether this is the case with regard to acts such as the removal of clothes. However, stripping detainees naked, particularly in the presence of women and taking into account cultural sensitivities, can in individual cases cause extreme psychological pressure and can amount to degrading treatment, or even torture. The same holds true for the use of dogs, especially if it is clear that an individual phobia exists. Exposure to extreme temperatures, if prolonged, can conceivably cause severe suffering.

52. On the interviews conducted with former detainees, the Special Rapporteur concludes that some of the techniques, in particular the use of dogs, exposure to extreme temperatures, sleep deprivation for several consecutive days and prolonged isolation were perceived as causing severe suffering. He also stresses that the simultaneous use of these techniques is even more likely to amount to torture. The Parliamentary Assembly of the Council of Europe also concluded that many detainees had been subjected to ill-treatment amounting to torture, which occurred systematically and with the knowledge and complicity of the United States Government. The same has been found by Lord Hope of Craighead, a member of the United Kingdom's House of Lords, who stated that "some of [the practices authorized for use in Guantanamo Bay by the U.S. authorities] would shock the conscience if they were to be authorized for use in our own country." . . .

U.S. REPLY

It is particularly unfortunate that the Special Rapporteurs rejected the invitation to visit Guantanamo.[27] As a result, their Report does not reflect the direct, personal knowledge that this visit would have provided. Rather, the Report is presented as a set of conclusions—it selectively includes only those factual assertions needed to support those conclusions and ignores other facts that would undermine those conclusions. We categorically object to most of the Report's content and conclusions as largely without merit and not based in the facts.

We also underscore that the United States is a nation of laws governed by a constitutional democracy, with an independent judiciary and free press. The issues addressed in the Report are being fully and publicly debated and litigated in the United States. To preserve the objectivity and authority of their own Report, the Special Rapporteurs should have reviewed and presented objective and comprehensive material on all sides of an issue before stating their own conclusions. Instead, in the absence of any meaningful investigation, the Special Rapporteurs reached their own conclusions espoused by second- and third-hand accounts of Guantanamo and then presented an advocate's brief in support of them. In the process they have asserted the existence of *jus cogens* or non-derogable norms without citation of binding authority in support, and have relied on international human rights instruments, declarations, standards, and general comments of treaty bodies without serious analysis of whether the instruments by their terms apply extraterritorially; whether the United States is a State Party—or has filed reservations or understandings—to the instrument; whether the instrument, declaration, standard or general comment is legally binding or not; or whether the provisions cited have the meaning ascribed to them in the Report. This is not the basis on which international human right mechanisms should act. . . .

[Regarding torture, the UN report claims that U.S.] [i]nterrogation "techniques meet four of the five elements in the Convention definition of torture."

This statement is wholly misleading. The four elements described in the report are:

- acts conducted by government officials;
- act had a clear purpose (for example, to gather intelligence);
- acts were committed intentionally; and
- victims were in a position of powerless.

These four factors would apply to thousands of wholly benign acts regarding the treatment of any detainee anywhere in the world, including the use of incentives ranging from extra recreational time or access to extra sweets or reading materials. Saying that four of five elements of torture are satisfied creates the misleading impression that U.S. conduct is somehow abusive or nefarious. . . .

Questions

1. Is the UN report accurate when it claims that the legal standards governing U.S. interrogations were "ambiguous"? What, for example, is a "Change of Scenery Down"?
2. Do any of the interrogation techniques listed in Rumsfeld's December 2, 2002, memo cause you concern? Which ones? Why?
3. Do you agree with the UN report that removal of clothing, particularly in the presence of women, can cause "extreme psychological pressure" that might constitute "torture"?
4. What about exploiting a detainee's fear of dogs? Could that be "torture"? In your experience, can extreme temperatures cause "severe suffering"?
5. Would sleep deprivation at some point constitute "torture"? What about prolonged "isolation"?
6. Do any of these interrogation techniques "shock the conscience," as Lord Hope claims?
7. Is the U.S. reply to the UN report convincing? Is the UN report one-sided?
8. Is the UN report flawed because it does not cite "binding authority" for the illegality of torture?
9. Was the UN report misleading when it concluded that four of the five elements of torture were satisfied? Why or why not?

In a major address on terrorism, President Bush publicly disclosed on September 6, 2006, that the Central Intelligence Agency (CIA) had detained and interrogated a number of high-value terrorists at secret sites around the world. He defended the program vigorously, claiming that the interrogations, which had relied on "an alternative set of procedures," had "saved innocent lives by helping us stop new attacks—here in the United States and across the world." Bush conceded that these "alternative procedures" were "tough," but he also claimed "they were safe, and lawful, and necessary." In particular, Bush insisted that the "United States does not torture. It's against our laws, and it's against our values. I have not authorized it—and I will not authorize it." Despite the effectiveness of the CIA's interrogation program, Bush indicated that he was shutting it down. He acknowledged that some "may ask" why now. He said there were two basic reasons: first, the CIA had completed its questioning of these fourteen high-value terrorists, and for this reason, he was submitting legislation to Congress to create a system of military commissions that would try high-level terrorists for their "war crimes"; and second, the Supreme Court in *Hamdan v. Rumsfeld* (2006) had held that Common Article 3, which prohibits "outrages upon personal dignity" and "humiliating and degrading treatment," applies to the United States' war against al-Qaeda, which meant that U.S. military and intelligence personnel "could now be at risk of prosecution under the

War Crimes Act—simply for doing their jobs in a thorough and professional way." According to President Bush, "This is unacceptable," so he was calling on Congress to enact legislation that would "list the specific, recognizable offenses that would be considered crimes under the War Crimes Act."[28]

Congress quickly responded to Bush's requests by enacting the Military Commissions Act of 2006 (MCA), which President Bush signed on October 17, 2006. The MCA not only set up a system of military commissions to try the high-value detainees who had been transferred to GBNB but also revised the War Crimes Act by narrowing the criteria of what constitutes a "war crime." While previously any "violation" of Common Article 3 was potentially a "war crime," the MCA restricted the term to only "grave breaches" of this provision and listed the types of conduct that would qualify as a "grave breach." "Torture" and "cruel or inhuman treatment" were included on the list of "grave breaches," but the MCA defined these terms narrowly: "torture" was "an act specifically intended to inflict severe physical or mental pain or suffering."

In contrast, "cruel and inhuman treatment" was defined as "an act intended to inflict severe or serious physical or mental pain or suffering." "Severe" or "serious" pain, in turn, were defined further as a "bodily injury" that involves "(i) a substantial risk of death; (ii) extreme physical pain; (iii) a burn or physical disfigurement of a serious nature (other than cuts, abrasions or bruises); or (iv) significant loss or impairment of the function of a bodily member, organ, or mental faculty." Since "torture" required "severe" pain, while "cruel and inhuman treatment" required only "serious" pain, it would seem that an act would constitute "torture" only if it involved a "bodily injury" that, at a minimum, risked death or caused "extreme" pain, "serious" disfigurement, or "significant loss or impairment" of a "bodily member, organ, or mental faculty."[29] With these narrow definitions of "torture" and "cruel and inhuman treatment," along with the fact that the MCA did not criminalize "degrading" treatment or punishment, the CIA was arguably free to continue to use EITs for the interrogations of high-value terrorists with little or no fear of criminal liability. The use of such EITs might be unlawful under the Detainee Treatment Act of 2005, but they were not likely war crimes under Congress's new definitions of the above terms of the War Crimes Act.

Despite these narrow definitions of "torture" and "cruel and inhuman treatment," the CIA's use of EITs ended in 2007, and the CIA no longer had any detainees in its custody after April 2008. Notwithstanding these developments, President Barack Obama, just two days after his inauguration, on January 22, 2009, issued an executive order that required all detainees be treated "humanely"; banned all forms of "torture," "cruel treatment," "outrages upon personal dignity," and "humiliating and degrading treatment"; limited all U.S. interrogation techniques, including those of the CIA, to the ones authorized by the army field manual; prohibited the CIA from operating any detention facility in the future; and provided the International Committee of the Red Cross with timely access to any individual detained by the United States during an armed conflict.[30]

Although Obama's executive order left little room for doubt that EITs were unlawful, a number of former detainees sought judicial relief in the form of compensation for the injuries they had suffered at the hands of the CIA. One such individual was Khaled el-Masri, a German citizen who had been detained in Macedonia after border guards mistook him for an al-Qaeda operative who happened to have a similar name. After locking him in a hotel room for twenty-three days, Macedonian officials transferred him to CIA custody, at which point he was stripped, beaten, shackled, hooded, allegedly sodomized, and flown to Afghanistan, where he was detained in solitary confinement for four months. When his identity as a German citizen was finally confirmed, the CIA flew him to Albania and left him by the side of a road to make his own way back to Germany. El-Masri first sued the CIA in U.S. courts, but his case was dismissed based on the state secrets privilege.[31] He then successfully sued Macedonia in the European Court of Human Rights (ECHR), which unanimously held that Macedonia had violated a number of articles of the European Convention on Human Rights, including the prohibition against torture contained in Article 3. In the court's opinion, the Macedonian government had violated Article 3 by imprisoning el-Masri at the hotel, by cooperating with CIA officials in abusing him at the airport, and by participating in the removal of el-Masri from Macedonia to a place where there was a substantial likelihood that he would be tortured.

5.7 *El-Masri v. Macedonia*, ECHR, Grand Chamber, 39630/09, December 13, 2012

200. As to the applicant's treatment in the hotel, the Court observes that he was under constant guard by agents of the Macedonian security forces, interrogated in a foreign language of which he had a limited command, threatened with a gun and consistently refused access to anyone other than his interrogators.[32] Such treatment led the applicant to protest by way of a hunger strike for ten days.

201. The Government did not provide any justification for such treatment.

202. It is true that while he was kept in the hotel, no physical force was used against the applicant. However, the Court reiterates that Article 3 does not refer exclusively to the infliction of physical pain but also of mental suffering, which is caused by creating a state of anguish and stress by means other than bodily assault. There is no doubt that the applicant's solitary incarceration in the hotel intimidated him on account of his apprehension as to what would happen to him next and must have caused him emotional and psychological distress. . . .

204. In view of the foregoing, the Court considers that the treatment to which the applicant was subjected while in the hotel amounted on various counts to inhuman and degrading treatment in breach of Article 3 of the Convention. . . .

205. The Court observes that on 23 January 2004 the applicant, handcuffed and blindfolded, was taken from the hotel and driven to Skopje Airport. Placed in a room, he was beaten severely by several disguised men dressed in black. He was stripped and sodomized with an object. He was placed in an adult nappy and dressed in a dark blue short-sleeved tracksuit. Shackled and hooded, and subjected to total sensory deprivation, the applicant was forcibly marched to a CIA aircraft . . . , which was surrounded by Macedonian security agents who formed a cordon around the plane. When on the plane, he was thrown to the floor, chained down and forcibly tranquillized. . . .

206. The Court must firstly assess whether the treatment suffered by the applicant at Skopje Airport at the hands of the special CIA rendition team is imputable to . . . [Macedonia]. In this connection it emphasizes that the acts complained of were carried out in the presence of [Macedonian] officials . . . and within its jurisdiction. . . .

207. . . . The Government failed to submit any arguments providing a basis for an explanation or justification of the degree of force used at Skopje Airport. Accordingly, the physical force used against the applicant at the airport was excessive and unjustified in the circumstances.

208. Furthermore, the Court observes that it has already found that the procedure of forcible undressing by the police may amount to such an invasive and potentially debasing measure that it should not be applied without a compelling reason. No such argument has been adduced to show that the measure applied against the applicant, who was already in a particularly helpless situation, was necessary.

209. Nor was any explanation given to justify the use of physical restraints on the applicant. The same concerns the use of hooding. . . .

210. The forcible administration of a suppository while the applicant was held on the ground without any explanation was not based on any medical considerations. Furthermore, the manner in which the applicant was subjected to that procedure caused serious physical pain and suffering.

211. The Court notes that the above-mentioned measures were used in combination and with premeditation, the aim being to cause severe pain or suffering in order to obtain information, inflict punishment or intimidate the applicant. In the Court's view, such treatment amounted to torture in breach of Article 3 of the Convention. . . .

215. . . . [Last, the] Court must examine whether any responsibility may be attributed to . . . [Macedonia] for having transferred the applicant into the custody of the US authorities. . . .

218. . . . [The] Court attaches importance to the reports and relevant international and foreign jurisprudence, and—given the specific circumstances of the present case—to media articles . . . , which constitute reliable sources reporting practices that have been resorted to or tolerated by the U.S. authorities and that are manifestly contrary to the principles of the Convention. The Court has already found some of these reports "worrying" and expressed its grave concerns about the interrogation methods used by the U.S. authorities on persons suspected of involvement in international terrorism and detained in the naval base in Guantanamo Bay and in Bagram (Afghanistan). This material was in the public domain before the applicant's actual transfer into the custody of the U.S. authorities. It is capable of proving that there were serious reasons to believe that if the applicant was to be transferred into U.S. custody under the "rendition" program, he would be exposed to a real risk of being subjected to treatment contrary to Article 3. Consequently, it must be concluded that the Macedonian authorities knew or ought to have known, at the relevant time, that there was a real risk that the applicant would be subjected to treatment contrary to Article 3 of the Convention. . . .

221. Having regard to the manner in which the applicant was transferred into the custody of the U.S. authorities, the Court considers that he was subjected to "extraordinary rendition," that is, an "extrajudicial transfer of persons from one jurisdiction or State to another, for the purposes of detention and interrogation outside the normal legal system, where there was a real risk of torture or cruel, inhuman or degrading treatment."

222. Accordingly, . . . [Macedonia] has violated Article 3 of the Convention on this account.

Questions

1. Do you agree with the ECHR that el-Masri, given his emotional and psychological distress, was subjected to "inhuman and degrading treatment" while he was detained at the hotel? If you agree, what aspect of his detention at the hotel violates Article 3? If you don't, what type of abuse would

be necessary before you would find a violation of Article 3?
2. Do you agree with the ECHR that el-Masri was tortured at the Skopje Airport? Why or why not?
3. To what extent does the ECHR base its finding of torture on the fact that Macedonia provided no justification for the way the CIA rendition team treated el-Masri? Should this factor have a bearing on whether el-Masri was tortured? Is it a controlling factor, such that "degrading" treatment will qualify as "torture" if it is "excessive" and the state has no justification for it?
4. Would you agree with the ECHR's forceful conclusion that U.S. authorities were engaged in interrogation techniques that were "manifestly" contrary to Article 3 of the convention?
5. Should the ECHR have relied on media accounts to justify its conclusion that Macedonian officials knew or should have known that there was a "real risk" that el-Masri would be tortured or subjected to cruel, inhuman, or degrading treatment if they permitted the CIA rendition team to move el-Masri from Macedonia to Afghanistan?

The Senate Select Committee on Intelligence (SSCI) issued a five-hundred-page executive summary of its much larger classified report on the CIA's interrogation and detention program on December 14, 2014. Overall, the executive summary was a scathing indictment of the CIA's program, which had detained at least 119 individuals from 2002 until 2008, of whom at least 39 were subjected to EITs (including three who were waterboarded), and at least 26 were wrongfully held. The SSCI claimed that the CIA's program was not an effective means of acquiring intelligence; that the program had not been necessary to prevent terrorist attacks or save lives; that the CIA's justification for the use of EITs was based on inaccurate claims about their effectiveness; that the CIA interrogations were far more brutal and the conditions of confinement harsher than how the CIA represented them to policymakers; that the CIA impeded congressional and White House oversight of the program; that the CIA actively misled the American public about the effectiveness of the program; that the CIA used EITs not approved by the Department of Justice or CIA headquarters; and that the CIA program damaged the United States' standing and reputation in the world.[33] A minority of the committee, led by vice chairman Saxby Chambliss, issued a critique of the committee's executive summary, and the CIA published its own rebuttal, both documents claiming that the CIA program had indeed saved lives.[34]

In 2015, President Obama signed the National Defense Authorization Act, which included an amendment, sponsored by Senator John McCain, that restricted all U.S. interrogation techniques to those identified in the army field manual, thereby making it impossible for any future president to reauthorize the CIA's use of EITs by revising Obama's 2009 executive order.[35] However, during the 2016 campaign for the presidency, the new law did not stop candidate Donald Trump from reigniting the torture debate by insisting that he would "bring back" waterboarding and other harsh interrogation techniques because "torture works" and "political correctness" was preventing the country from defending itself.[36] A poll taken just before the election showed that 48 percent of Americans thought torture was acceptable in some circumstances.[37] Once Trump was in office, his lawyers in January 2017 drafted a new executive order on interrogation techniques, but the president never signed it. Members of Congress said they fully expected the administration to comply with the law; Secretary of Defense James Mattis advised Trump that "beer and cigarettes" work much better than torture; and, finally, CIA director Mike Pompeo testified at his confirmation hearings that he would refuse to obey any White House order to torture detainees. In an interview, Trump responded, "If they don't wanna do [it] that's fine. If they do wanna do [it], then I will work for that end."[38] Trump's somewhat lukewarm response raised the question whether he actually thought that torture "saves lives" or whether his rhetoric about torture was simply a means to rally his base.

The debate about the legality and effectiveness of torture cooled during the months that followed, as the Trump administration turned to substantive policy issues, but it resurfaced in March 2018 when Trump nominated Gina Haspel to become director of the CIA. Haspel, an undercover CIA officer for three decades, ran the agency's black prison site in Thailand in 2002. She took command soon after Abu Zubaydah was waterboarded and prior to Abd al-Rahim al-Nashiri's interrogation, which also included waterboarding. In 2005, as the chief of staff to Jose Rodriguez, the CIA's director of [covert] operations, Haspel drafted the order to destroy 92 videotapes of CIA interrogations of both al-Nashiri and Abu Zubaydah, which Rodriguez then signed. She did so despite a court order at the time requiring the agency to produce all relevant records related to its treatment of detainees abroad and a request by the 9/11 Commission for all CIA transcripts and recordings of CIA interrogations.[39] Obviously, Haspel's nomination shows that Trump does not believe that involvement in the CIA's coercive interrogation program should be a bar to professional advancement. In fact, it may suggest the opposite: that he believes such involvement is solid evidence that Haspel has what it takes to do the job.

In any case, Haspel's confirmation hearings will likely be contentious and difficult. Of the 51 Republican senators, John McCain (R-AZ) has said that Haspel must explain "the nature and extent" of her involvement in the CIA's enhanced interrogation program, while Rand Paul (R-KY) has already indicated he would do "everything" he could "to block" her nomination, arguing that her confirmation would send a "terrible" message to the world. "I don't want the message to be that . . . since torture's OK with Americans, it's going to be fine to torture Americans when they're captured, and I think that is the message that it sends."[40] Supporters of Haspel might claim that international terrorist groups, such as ISIS and al-Qaeda, will torture U.S. prisoners regardless of U.S. interrogation policy. However, it is worth bearing in mind that Paul's primary argument against torture is not a legal one, but one based on prudence: "If we do it to them, they'll do it to us." That fact raises an important question: Should the upcoming debate about Haspel's qualifications for the office of director of the CIA also include some focus on whether her conduct involving the CIA interrogation program was illegal, possibly constituting contempt of court, violating the federal torture statute, and, lastly, defying fundamental principles of international law? If so, how large a role should the last factor play in measuring her suitability for the office she is seeking? None whatsoever? Minimal? Substantial?

Considering her qualifications from this point of view is one way to reflect on the status that international law does have, or should have, in American legal thinking.

NOTES

1. Napoleon Bonaparte, letter to Louis Alexandre Berthier, November 11, 1798, in *Correspondence Napoleon*, ed. Henri Plon (1861), vol. 5, no. 3605, p. 128.

2. "General Orders No. 100: The Lieber Code," April 24, 1863, Yale Law School, Lillian Goldman Law Library, http://avalon.law.yale.edu, Article 16.

3. "General Orders No. 100," Articles 27 and 28.

4. "General Orders No. 100," Articles 81–85.

5. "Laws of War: Laws and Customs of War on Land (Hague IV); Annex to the Convention," Yale Law School, Lillian Goldman Law Library, http://avalon.law.yale.edu, Article 4.

6. See United Nations, "Universal Declaration of Human Rights," December 10, 1948, http://www.un.org, Article 5.

7. "Conventions (III) Relative to the Treatment of Prisoners of War, Geneva," August 12, 1949, Article 13, International Committee of the Red Cross (ICRC), https://ihl-databases.icrc.org.

8. "Conventions (III)," Common Article 3.

9. "European Convention on Human Rights," October 1, 1994, European Court of Human Rights, http://www.echr.coe.int.

10. European Court of Human Rights, "Case of Ireland v. The United Kingdom," January 18, 1978, http://hudoc.echr.coe.int.

11. "International Covenant on Civil and Political Rights," December 16, 1966, United Nations Human Rights Office of the High Commissioner, http://www.ohchr.org.

12. Additional Protocol I, Article 75, in "Protocols Additional to the Geneva Conventions of 12 August 1949," International Committee of the Red Cross (ICRC), https://www.icrc.org.

13. Additional Protocol II, Article 4, in "Protocols Additional."

14. "Convention against Torture and Other Cruel, Inhuman or Degrading Treatment or Punishment," December 10, 1904, United Nations Human Rights Office of the High Commissioner, http://www.ohchr.org.

15. For these and additional reservations the United States had to the Convention against Torture, see "Chapter IV: Human Rights; 9: Convention against Torture and Other Cruel, Inhuman or Degrading Treatment or Punishment; Declarations and Reservations: United States of America," December 10, 1984, United Nations Treaty Collection, https://treaties.un.org.

16. Federal Torture Statute, 18 U.S.C. 113C (1994). It should be noted that Congress provided victims of torture a civil remedy in the Torture Victims Protection Act of 1991. This remedy, however, was only available if the victim had exhausted all "adequate and available remedies in the place in which the conduct giving rise to the claim occurred," and in addition, the law imposed a statute of limitations of ten years. See 28 U.S.C. 1350 note.

17. *Askoy v. Turkey*, 21987/93 (1996), ECHR (December 18, 1996).

18. *Aydin v. Turkey*, 57/1996/676/866, ECHR (September 25, 1997).

19. *Selmouni v. France*, 25803/94, ECHR (July 28, 1999).

20. *Public Committee against Torture in Israel v. Israel*, H.C. 5100/94 (Israel 1999), BTSELEM: The Israeli Information Center for Human Rights in the Occupied Territories, https://www.btselem.org.

21. *Prosecutor v. Delalic*, IT-96-21-T, Trial Judgment (November 16, 1998).

22. Yoo's general memorandum is "Memorandum for Alberto R. Gonzales, Council to the President," August 1, 2002, National Security Archive, George Washington University, http://

nsarchive.gwu.edu. The second memo that focuses on Zubaydah's interrogation is "Memorandum for John Rizzo, Acting General Counsel of the Central Intelligence Agency: Interrogation of al Qaeda Operative," August 1, 2002, Federation of American Scientists, https://fas.org.

23. Jack Goldsmith, *The Terror Presidency: Law and Judgment in the Bush Administration* (New York: Norton, 2007), 10.

24. Daniel Levin, acting assistant attorney general, memorandum to James B. Comey, deputy attorney general, "Legal Standards Applicable under 18 U.S.C. 2340-2340A," December 30, 2004, Torture Database, https://www.thetorturedatabase.org.

25. "Detainee Treatment Act of 2005," Office of the Director of National Intelligence, https://www.dni.gov.

26. UN Commission on Human Rights, "Economic, Social and Cultural Rights; Civil and Political Rights: Situation of Detainees at Guantánamo Bay," February 17, 2006UNHCR refworld, http://www.refworld.org.

27. "Reply of the Government of the United States of America to the Report of the Five UNCHR Special Rapporteurs on Detainees in Guantanamo Bay, Cuba," March 10, 2006, U.S. Department of State, https://www.state.gov.

28. George W. Bush, "Address on the Creation of Military Commission to Try Suspected Terrorists," September 6, 2006, in "Selected Speeches of President George W. Bush, 2001–2008," 409–22, White House Archives, https://georgewbush-whitehouse.archives.gov.

29. Military Commissions Act of 2006, Public Law 109-366, 120 Stat. 2633, October 17, 2006, Section 6 (b), Library of Congress, https://www.loc.gov.

30. Barack Obama, "Executive Order 13491—Ensuring Lawful Interrogations," 74 Fed. Reg. 4893, January 22, 2009, American Presidency Project, http://www.presidency.ucsb.edu.

31. *El-Masri v. United States*, 479 F.3d 296 (4th Cir. 2007).

32. ECHR, Grand Chamber, "Case of El-Masri v. The Former Yugoslav Republic of Macedonia," 39630/09, December 13, 2012, http://hudoc.echr.coe.int. See also ECHR, Former Fourth Section, "Case of Al-Nashiri v. Poland," 28762/11, Final Version, February 2, 2015, http://hudoc.echr.coe.int.

33. Senate Select Committee on Intelligence, "Committee Study of the Central Intelligence Agency's Detention and Interrogation Program (SSCI Study)," executive summary, December 13, 2014, United States Senator for California Dianne Feinstein, https://www.feinstein.senate.gov.

34. "Committee Study of the Central Intelligence Agency's Detention and Interrogation Program: Minority Views," June 20, 2014, United States Senator for California Dianne Feinstein, https://www.feinstein.senate.gov; and "SSCI Study: CIA Comments on the Senate Select Committee on Intelligence Report on the Rendition, Detention, and Interrogation Program," June 27, 2013, released December 8, 2014, CIA, https://www.cia.gov.

35. See Public Law 114-92, Title X, Subtitle D—Counterterrorism, Section 1045, November 25, 2015.

36. Jenna Johnson, "Donald Trump on Waterboarding: 'Torture Works,'" *Washington Post*, February 17, 2016, https://www.washingtonpost.com/news/post-politics/wp/2016/02/17/donald-trump-on-waterboarding-torture-works/?utm_term=.8b5f74c00432.

37. Alec Tyson, "Americans Divided in Views of Use of Torture in U.S. Anti-terror Efforts," Pew Research Center, January 26, 2017, http://www.pewresearch.org/fact-tank/2017/01/26/americans-divided-in-views-of-use-of-torture-in-u-s-anti-terror-efforts/.

38. Brian Bennett, "If Trump Revives the Use of Torture and Black Sites, He Will Reopen a Debate over What the U.S. Stands For," *Los Angeles Times*, January 26, 2017, http://www.latimes.com.

39. Mark Mazzetti, "U.S. Says C.I.A. Destroyed 92 Tapes of Interrogations," *New York Times*, March 2, 2009, https://www.nytimes.com/2009/03/03/washington/03web-intel.html. See also Annabelle Timsit, "What Happened at the Thailand 'Black Site' Run by Trump's CIA

Pick," *Atlantic*, March 14, 2018, https://www.theatlantic.com/international/archive/2018/03/gina-haspel-black-site-torture-cia/555539.

40. David Smith, "Rand Paul to Oppose Gina Haspel as CIA Director over Her 'Gleeful Joy' at Torture," *Guardian*, March 14, 2018, https://www.theguardian.com/us-news/2018/mar/14/rand-paul-gina-haspel-cia-director-torture-gleeful-joy.

6

Military Commissions

★ ★ ★

Military tribunals are very old. For example, according to Polybius, military tribunes during the Roman Republic held court-martials for those caught sleeping while on picket duty, and the guilty were immediately beaten to death.[1] Typically such military tribunals exercised jurisdiction only over soldiers, but exceptions to this rule developed as history evolved, resulting in military trials of civilians. However, during the seventeenth century, a tradition arose in Great Britain that civilians were legally entitled to be tried in civilian courts by juries of their peers. Even though this tradition was not always honored, the Continental Congress generally respected it. During the American Revolution, the Congress enacted a military code composed of sixty-nine articles of war that subjected officers and soldiers in the Continental Army to a "general court-martial" for serious offenses.[2] For this reason, when John Andre, a British Army officer, was tried for spying in 1780, General Washington convened a special board of inquiry. Andre was neither a civilian nor a member of the Continental Army. At the end of his trial, the board recommended that Andre should be considered a spy and that "agreeable to the law and usage of nations," he should be sentenced to death. He was hanged on October 2, 1780.

The framers of the Constitution endorsed the position that juries should typically try civilian crimes. For example, Article III, which defined the civilian judicial powers of the United States, explicitly stated that "[t]he Trial of all Crimes, except in Cases of Impeachment; shall be by Jury" and that no one should be convicted of treason "unless on the Testimony of two Witnesses to the same overt Act, or on Confession in open Court." However, Article I granted Congress the power to "make Rules for the Government and Regulation of the land and naval Forces" and to "provide for organizing, arming and disciplining, the Militia, and for governing such Part of them as may be employed in the Service of the United States." Consistent with this language in Article I, the Fifth Amendment stated that "no person shall be held to answer for a capital, or otherwise infamous crime, unless on a presentment or indictment of a Grand Jury, except in cases arising in the land or naval forces, or in the Militia, when in actual service in time of War or public danger." Within this constitutional framework, Congress enacted a new version of the Articles of War in 1806, which remained in force until Congress revised them in 1921. Members of the U.S. military have therefore always been subject to trial by court-martial for serious offenses, without the benefit of a jury trial or indictment by a grand jury.

A controversial use of a military tribunal that did not qualify as a court-martial occurred during the First Seminole War in 1818. General Andrew Jackson attacked the Seminole Indian tribe, forcing the Spanish to cede Florida to the United States in 1819. During this conflict, Jackson convened a special military tribunal to try two British citizens who allegedly had provided assistance to the Seminoles: Alexander Arbuthnot and Robert Ambister. It was not at all clear how a U.S. military tribunal could have jurisdiction over civilian nationals of a country with which the United States was not at war. Moreover, although the military tribunal recommended a commutation of the death sentences imposed on the two men, Jackson rejected this advice. Both men were executed. While Britain and Spain objected to the legality of the trial and executions, Congress refused to censure the future president, although it did find fault with the nature of the proceedings.

During the Mexican-American War (1846–1848), the U.S. Army occupied much of Mexico. Confronted by various forms of criminal activity engaged in by soldiers and civilians on both sides of the conflict, General Winfield Scott had a problem because the jurisdiction of the court-martial system was confined to members of the U.S. armed forces. Scott's solution was to issue General Order 20, which created a system of "military commissions" that were authorized to try ordinary crimes in the occupied territories and "boards of inquiry" to punish those who violated the laws of war. Scott's new term of "military commissions" quickly took root in American military law. By the American Civil War, the term "boards of inquiry" had been abandoned and the jurisdiction of "military commissions" had broadened to include (1) ordinary crimes during military occupations, such as the U.S. occupation of Mexico; (2) ordinary crimes if martial law had been declared, as was the case during the American Civil War; and (3) offenses against the laws of war. Obviously, with this broader scope of jurisdiction, it sometimes became unclear during the Civil War whether a particular commission was functioning as a court of military occupation, a court of martial law, a war crimes court, or some sort of hybrid of two or three of them.

During the Civil War, in March 1863, Congress enacted a statute that authorized President Lincoln to suspend the writ of habeas corpus but required the president to provide federal circuit and district courts with the names of the detainees locked up in military prisons. If the local grand jury indicted any of these detainees, then the criminal case proceeded in civilian court; if the grand jury declined to indict, then the judge could compel the conditional release of the detainee. Moreover, if the requisite list of detainees was not provided to the court within twenty days of the arrest, the judge could also order release unless the local grand jury indicted the detainee in question. Based on this statutory authority, Lincoln suspended the writ throughout much of the Union in

September 1863. The following year, in October 1864, General Alvin P. Hovey, commander of the military district of Indiana, arrested Lambdin P. Milligan, a twenty-year resident of the state, and charged him before a military commission with the following charges: (1) conspiracy against the government of the United States; (2) affording aid and comfort to the rebels; (3) inciting insurrection; (4) disloyal practices; and (5) violations of the laws of war. The commission found Milligan guilty and sentenced him to death. Milligan petitioned the federal circuit court of Indiana for a writ of habeas corpus, arguing that the military commission had no jurisdiction to try him because he was not a resident of any state in rebellion and therefore he had a right to a jury trial.[3]

The divided Circuit Court certified three questions to the Supreme Court, but the key issue was whether the military commission had jurisdiction to try Milligan. While Milligan's appeal was pending, John Wilkes Booth assassinated President Lincoln on April 14, 1865, at Ford's Theater in Washington, D.C. As Booth fled south, Union soldiers shot and killed him in Maryland on April 26. In the meantime, the authorities quickly arrested eight other individuals and charged them with conspiracy to murder Lincoln, including Mary Surratt, who owned a boardinghouse where the conspirators met, and Samuel Mudd, a Maryland physician who had set Booth's broken leg during his flight south. President Andrew Johnson decided to try the defendants by military commission, rather than by the civil courts of the District of Columbia, even though the latter courts were open and functioning. On June 30, the military commission found all eight defendants guilty and sentenced three to life imprisonment and four to death by hanging, including Surratt, the first woman ever executed by the federal government.

The Supreme Court considered *Ex parte Milligan* in the aftermath of the trial of Lincoln's assassins and handed down its decision on April 3, 1866. The decision was unanimous in favor of the conclusion that the military commission that tried Milligan did not have jurisdiction to do so. Five of the justices, speaking through Justice David Davis, rested their argument on the Constitution, holding that Congress could not constitutionally authorize a military commission to try Milligan since Indiana was not under invasion and the courts in that state were open and functioning. Four of the justices, speaking through Chief Justice Salmon P. Chase, relied upon statutory grounds. Congress could authorize the use of military commissions to try residents of Northern states, even if civilian courts were open, but it had not done so in this case. Although neither Davis's nor Chase's opinion referred to the trial of Lincoln's assassins, it seems clear that the court must have been aware that its decision in *Milligan* had obvious implications for the awfulness of that proceeding.

6.1 *Ex parte Milligan*, 71 U.S. 2 (1866)

Mr. Justice DAVIS delivered the opinion of the court.

During the late wicked Rebellion, the temper of the times did not allow that calmness in deliberation and discussion so necessary to a correct conclusion of a purely judicial question. Then, considerations of safety were mingled with the exercise of power; and feelings and interests prevailed which are happily terminated. Now that the public safety is assured, this question, as well as all others, can be discussed and decided without passion or the admixture of any element not required to form a legal judgment. We approach the investigation of this case, fully sensible of the magnitude of the inquiry and the necessity of full and cautious deliberation. . . .

The controlling question in the case is this: Upon the *facts* stated in Milligan's petition, and the exhibits filed, had the military commission mentioned in it *jurisdiction*, legally, to try and sentence him? Milligan, not a resident of one of the rebellious states or a prisoner of war, but a citizen of Indiana for twenty years past and never in the military or naval service, is, while at his home, arrested by the military power of the United States, imprisoned, and, on certain criminal charges preferred against him, tried, convicted, and sentenced to be hanged by a military commission, organized under the direction of the military commander of the military district of Indiana. Had this tribunal the legal power and authority to try and punish this man?

No graver question was ever considered by this court, nor one which more nearly concerns the rights of the whole people; for it is the birthright of every American citizen when charged with crime, to be tried and punished according to law. . . . If there was law to justify this military trial, it is not our province to interfere; if there was not, it is our duty to declare the nullity of the whole proceedings. . . .

Have any of the rights guaranteed by the Constitution been violated in the case of Milligan? and if so, what are they?

Every trial involves the exercise of judicial power; and from what source did the military commission that tried him derive their authority? Certainly no part of the judicial power of the country was conferred on them; because the Constitution expressly vests it "in one supreme court and such inferior courts as the Congress may from time to time ordain and establish," and it is not pretended that the commission was a court ordained and established by Congress. They cannot justify on the mandate of the President; because he is controlled by law, and has his appropriate sphere of duty, which is to execute, not to make, the laws; and there is "no unwritten criminal code to which resort can be had as a source of jurisdiction."

But it is said that the jurisdiction is complete under the "laws and usages of war."

It can serve no useful purpose to inquire what those laws and usages are, whence they originated, where found, and on whom they operate; they can never be applied to citizens in states which have upheld the authority of the government, and where the courts are open and their process unobstructed. This court has judicial knowledge that in Indiana the Federal authority was always unopposed, and its courts always open to hear criminal accusations and redress grievances; and no usage of war could sanction a military trial there for any offence whatever of a citizen in civil life, in nowise connected with the military service. Congress could grant no such power; and to the honor of our national legislature be it said, it has never been provoked by the state of the country even to attempt its exercise. One of the plainest constitutional provisions was, therefore, infringed when Milligan was tried by a court not ordained and established by Congress, and not composed of judges appointed during good behavior. . . .

It is claimed that martial law covers with its broad mantle the proceedings of this military commission. The proposition is this: that in a time of war the commander of an armed force (if in his opinion the exigencies of the country demand it, and of which he is to judge), has the power, within the lines of his military district, to suspend all civil rights and their remedies, and subject citizens as well as soldiers to the rule of his will; and in the exercise of his lawful authority cannot be restrained, except by his superior officer or the President of the United States. . . .

The statement of this proposition shows its importance; for, if true, republican government is a failure, and there is an end of liberty regulated by law. . . . Civil liberty and this kind of martial law cannot endure together; the antagonism is irreconcilable; and, in the conflict, one or the other must perish. . . .

[Nonetheless, it] . . . is essential to the safety of every government that, in a great crisis, like the one we have just passed through, there should be a power somewhere of suspending the writ of habeas corpus. . . . The Constitution goes no further. It does not say after a writ of habeas corpus is denied a citizen, that he shall be tried otherwise than by the course of the common law. . . .

It follows, from what has been said on this subject, that there are occasions when martial rule can be properly applied. If, in foreign invasion or civil war, the courts are actually closed, and it is impossible to administer criminal justice according to law, then, on the theatre of active military operations, where war really prevails, there is a necessity to furnish a substitute for the civil authority, thus overthrown, to preserve the safety of the army and society; and as no power is left but the military, it is allowed to govern by martial rule until the laws can have their free course. As necessity creates the rule, so it limits its duration; for, if this government is continued after the courts are reinstated, it is a gross usurpation of power. Martial rule can never exist where the courts are open, and in the proper and unobstructed exercise of their jurisdiction. It is also confined to the locality of actual war. Because, during the late Rebellion it could have been enforced in Virginia, where the national authority was overturned and the courts driven out, it does not follow that it should obtain in Indiana, where that authority was never disputed, and justice was always administered. And so in the case of a foreign invasion, martial rule may become a necessity in one state, when, in another, it would be "mere lawless violence.". . .

The CHIEF JUSTICE delivered the following opinion.

[The majority] opinion . . . asserts not only that the military commission held in Indiana was not authorized by Congress, but that it was not in the power of Congress to authorize it. . . .

We cannot agree to this. . . .

We think that Congress had power, though not exercised, to authorize the military commission which was held in Indiana. . . .

Congress has the power not only to raise and support and govern armies but to declare war. It has, therefore, the power to provide by law for carrying on war. This power necessarily extends to all legislation essential to the prosecution of war with vigor and success. . . . We by no means assert that Congress can establish and apply the laws of war where no war had been declared or exists.

Where peace exists the laws of peace must prevail. What we do maintain is, that when the nation is involved in war, and some portions of the country are invaded, and all are exposed to invasion, it is within the power of Congress to determine in what states or districts such great and imminent public danger exists as justifies the authorization of military tribunals for the trial of crimes and offences against the discipline or security of the army or against the public safety. In Indiana, for example, at the time of the arrest of Milligan and his co-conspirators, it is established by the papers in the record, that the state was a military district, was the theatre of military operations, had been actually invaded, and was constantly threatened with invasion. It appears, also, that a powerful secret association, composed of citizens and others, existed within the state, under military organization, conspiring against the draft, and plotting insurrection, the liberation of the prisoners of war at various depots, the seizure of the state and national arsenals, armed cooperation with the enemy, and war against the national government.

We cannot doubt that, in such a time of public danger, Congress had power, under the Constitution, to provide for the organization of a military commission, and for trial by that commission of persons engaged in this conspiracy. The fact that the Federal courts were open was regarded by Congress as a sufficient reason for not exercising the power; but that fact could not deprive Congress of the right to exercise it. Those courts might be open and undisturbed in the execution of their functions, and yet wholly incompetent to avert threatened danger, or to punish, with adequate promptitude and certainty, the guilty conspirators. . . .

Questions

1. Does Justice Davis's remark about "the temper of the times" suggest that the court would have come to a different conclusion if it had heard Milligan's case during the Civil War? Does your answer undermine to some extent Justice Davis's opinion? How?
2. Davis underlines the fact that Milligan was "not a resident of one of the rebellious states," was not "a prisoner of war," had never been "in the military or naval service," was "a citizen of Indiana" who was arrested "at his home." Which of these facts is the key premise of Davis's argument that the military commission did not have jurisdiction to try Milligan?
3. According to Davis, why can't the authority of the military commission be based on the fact that Congress authorized President Lincoln to suspend the writ of habeas corpus?
4. Does Davis too quickly dismiss the suggestion that the authority of the military commission is derived from international law through the "laws and usages of war"? Even if the federal courts in Indiana were open, why is it that the "law of war" could not sanction a military trial of a civilian who was purposefully and actively obstructing the war effort?
5. Was Davis right to reject the view that the lawfulness of Milligan's military commission depended on whether there was a state of martial law in Indiana? Was he correct that, if there was such a state of marital law, then "republican government is a failure"? Is this an overstatement? Why?
6. Despite Davis's attitude toward "martial law," he argues that "every government" should somewhere have the power "of suspending the writ of habeas corpus." Why is Davis supportive of the one power but hostile to the other?
7. Chief Justice Chase objects to Davis's claim that martial law can only be lawful in times of actual invasion when the civilian courts are closed. Which justice has the better argument? Should Congress have the power to proclaim martial law if invasion is not underway but merely threatened?
8. Chase argues that Congress's war power includes the authority to set up military commissions to try civilians if invasion is threatened because the civilian courts might be "wholly incompetent to avert threatened danger, or to punish, with adequate promptitude and certainty, the guilty conspirators." Does he have a point? Why should military commissions not be used to "avert threatened danger" if they can lawfully be used to redress danger after it has arisen?

During the Civil War, over two thousand military commissions tried an assortment of ordinary criminals and violators of the laws of war, but most of these trials took place in border states where martial law was declared or in occupied Southern states, thereby producing some confusion regarding whether specific commissions were martial law courts, military occupation courts, or law-of-war courts.[4] Military commissions were also used in the wars with Native American Indians, including the Dakota War of 1862, which resulted in the trial and execution of thirty-eight Indians for violations of the laws of war.

In addition, during the Philippine-American War (1900–1901), military commissions, conducting themselves generally in accordance with court-martial rules and procedures, tried nearly eight hundred Philippine nationals for law-of-war violations.[5] During these conflicts, military commissions that tried enemies who allegedly violated the laws of war gradually became a definite and distinct type of military commission—one not to be confused with a military commission authorized under military occupation or martial law. Violators of the laws of war were perceived to be a separate group of culpable individuals because they had violated the legitimate and valid norms of international law. This attitude was reflected in the Treaty of Versailles, which brought World War I to an end in 1919. Article 228 of the treaty recognized the right of the allies to try Germans accused of violating the laws of war before their domestic military tribunals and to punish such individuals if they were found guilty.[6] This article enshrined in an international treaty the principle that state parties could lawfully use domestic military tribunals to try and punish violators of the laws of war.

Despite these provisions of the Treaty of Versailles, only France and Belgium chose to prosecute Germans for war crimes, but their efforts were stymied because Germany, in violation of its treaty obligations, refused to hand over suspected war criminals for trial. Instead, Germany offered to try suspected German war criminals in German courts: the so-called Leipzig trials. However, only a handful of Germans were tried at Leipzig; only a few were convicted; and only a couple served light sentences (less than one year's imprisonment). Nevertheless, the Leipzig trials reaffirmed the principle that violators of the laws of war were individually responsible for their conduct, thereby buttressing the Versailles principle that a state party to a conflict can try alleged enemy war criminals before domestic military tribunals.

In 1942, in the middle of World War II, the United States endorsed the Versailles principle by prosecuting eight German soldiers who traveled to the United States by submarine, landed on beaches, buried their military uniforms, and entered the country illegally, presumably for the purpose of committing espionage. Under the authority of a proclamation issued by President Roosevelt, the German soldiers, including one who had dual U.S.-German citizenship, were tried in Washington, D.C., before a military commission for "spying," "attempting to give intelligence to the enemy," "violating the law of war," and "conspiring" to commit the first three offenses. In their petition for a writ of habeas corpus, the Germans argued that the military commission did not have jurisdiction to try them, but the Supreme Court rejected this argument in a per curiam opinion, and six of the eight German nationals were executed eight days later. In a somewhat untimely fashion, the court did not issue a full opinion justifying its decision in *Ex parte Quirin* until three months later. The following excerpt focuses on why the court concluded that a military commission did have jurisdiction to try these defendants, in contrast to the court's earlier decision in *Ex parte Milligan*.

6.2 *Ex parte Quirin*, 317 U.S. 1 (1942)

MR. CHIEF JUSTICE STONE delivered the opinion of the Court.

. . . Article 15 [of the Articles of War] declares that "the provisions of these articles conferring jurisdiction upon courts-martial shall not be construed as depriving military commissions . . . or other military tribunals of concurrent jurisdiction in respect of offenders or offenses that by statute or by the law of war may be triable by such military commissions . . . or other military tribunals." . . .

From the very beginning of its history this Court has recognized and applied the law of war as including that part of the law of nations which prescribes, for the conduct of war, the status, rights and duties of enemy nations as well as of enemy individuals. By . . . Article 15, Congress has explicitly provided, so far as it may constitutionally do so, that military tribunals shall have jurisdiction to try offenders or offenses against the law of war in appropriate cases. . . .

. . . It is [therefore] unnecessary for present purposes to determine to what extent the President as Commander in Chief has constitutional power to create military commissions without the support of Congressional legislation. . . . We are concerned only with the question whether it is within the constitutional power of the National Government to place petitioners upon trial before a military commission for the offenses with which they are charged. We must therefore first inquire whether any of the acts charged is an offense against the law of war cognizable before a military tribunal, and if so whether the Constitution prohibits the trial. We may assume that there are acts regarded in other countries, or by some writers on international law, as offenses against the law of war which would not be triable by military tribunal here, either because they are not recognized by our courts as violations of the law of war or because they are of that class of offenses constitutionally triable only by jury. . . .

By universal agreement and practice, the law of war draws a distinction between the armed forces and the peaceful populations of belligerent nations and also between those who are lawful and unlawful combatants. Lawful combatants are subject to capture and detention as prisoners of war by opposing military forces. Unlawful combatants are likewise subject to capture and detention, but in addition they are subject to trial and punishment by military tribunals for acts which render their belligerency unlawful. The spy who secretly and without uniform passes the military lines of a belligerent in time of war, seeking to gather military information and communicate it to the enemy, or an enemy combatant who without uniform comes secretly through the lines for the purpose of waging war by destruction of life or property, are familiar examples of belligerents who are generally deemed not to be entitled to the status of prisoners of war, but to be offenders against the law of war subject to trial and punishment by military tribunals. . . .

Citizenship in the United States of an enemy belligerent does not relieve him from the consequences of a belligerency which is unlawful because in violation of the law of war. . . .

But petitioners insist that even if the offenses with which they are charged are offenses against the law of war, their trial is subject to the requirement of the Fifth Amendment that no person shall be held to answer for a capital or otherwise infamous crime unless on a presentment or indictment of a grand jury, and that such trials . . . must be by jury in a civil court. . . .

Presentment by a grand jury and trial by a jury . . . [are] procedures unknown to military tribunals, which are not courts in the sense of the judiciary Article [III] and which . . . are usually called upon to function under conditions precluding resort to such procedures. . . .

Petitioners . . . stress the pronouncement of the Court in the *Milligan* case that the law of war "can never be applied to citizens in states which have upheld the authority of the government, and where the courts are open and their process unobstructed." Elsewhere in the opinion, the Court was at pains to point out that Milligan, a citizen twenty years resident in Indiana, who had never been a resident of any of the states in rebellion, was not an enemy belligerent either entitled to the status of a prisoner of war or subject to the penalties imposed upon unlawful belligerents. We construe the Court's statement as to the inapplicability of the law of war to Milligan's case as having particular reference to the facts before it. From them the Court concluded that Milligan, not being part of or associated with the armed forces of the enemy, was a non-belligerent, not subject to the law of war save as—in circumstances found not there to be present, and not involved here—martial law might be constitutionally established. . . .

Questions

1. Is Chief Justice Harlan F. Stone's interpretation of Article 15 defensible? Even if it says that it does not "deprive" military commissions of concurrent jurisdiction, does this mean the article affirmatively authorizes such jurisdiction?
2. Should Chief Justice Stone have addressed the issue whether President Roosevelt could authorize military commissions without the support of congressional legislation?
3. According to Chief Justice Stone, one reason an offense against the law of war would not be triable by military commission in the United States is because the offense is one of the "class of offenses constitutionally triable only by jury." In your view, what type of offense would be a violation of the law of war yet constitutionally require a jury trial? Do any of the charges in *Milligan* or *Quirin* satisfy these criteria?
4. In your view, is Chief Justice Stone correct that the spy and the saboteur, if they pass through military lines and are out of uniform, are violating the law of war in ways that can be tried by military commissions? Why these offenses and not others?
5. Would Article III, Section 3 of the Constitution require that a U.S. citizen charged with treason be tried in a civilian court? If so, has Chief Justice Stone convinced you that a U.S. citizen can be tried by a military commission if he is a spy or saboteur during wartime?
6. To what extent is Chief Justice Stone claiming that Fifth and Sixth Amendment rights are inapplicable to military commissions because they are not "courts" in the sense of Article III of the Constitution? If they are not "courts" in this sense, then in what sense are they "courts"? If they are not "courts," how can they lawfully try any criminal offense?
7. Chief Justice Stone emphasizes that Milligan was not "part of or associated with the armed forces of the enemy" and therefore "was a non-belligerent." What if Stone had instead focused on the fact that in 1942 there was no actual invasion of the United States and the federal civilian courts were open and functioning in Washington, D.C.?

The Supreme Court's opinion in *Ex parte Quirin* was important because it directly or indirectly addressed three fundamental questions pertaining to military commissions: (1) Who can be tried by a military commission? (2) What procedures and standards must a military commission follow? (3) What offenses are within the jurisdiction of military commissions? The second question was important because the procedures used in World War II commissions no longer resembled those of a court-martial. In 1921 Congress had extensively revised the court-martial system, elevating evidentiary and procedural standards to ensure that members of the U.S. armed forces were, if charged with a crime, treated fairly in accordance with basic principles of due process. No such effort was made to standardize or improve the procedural and evidentiary safeguards of military commissions. In the *Quirin* case, President Roosevelt's proclamation creating the military commission granted it "power to make such rules for the conduct of the proceeding, consistent with the powers of military commissions under the Articles of War, as it shall deem necessary for a full and fair trial of the matters before it. Such evidence shall be admitted as would, in the opinion of the President of the Commission, have probative value to a reasonable man."[7] In addition, the proclamation directed the commission to transmit any judgment or sentence to Roosevelt "for my action thereon." The upshot was that the commission would have extensive latitude in determining its own procedural and evidentiary rules, subject only to review by the president.

The procedural and evidentiary shortcomings of military commissions were arguably evident in the 1945 trial of Tomoyuki Yamashita, the Japanese general in charge of the defense of the Philippines. The charge against Yamashita was not that he had engaged in any wartime atrocities or even that he knew about them but rather that he should have stopped them because he should have known about them. The evidence used to convict Yamashita of this alleged war crime was largely based on hearsay evidence that would not have been admitted into a court-martial. In a 6–2 decision, the Supreme Court (1) upheld the jurisdiction of the military commission on the ground that Yamashita violated the law of war by not fulfilling his duty to control the troops under his command; and (2) ruled that the Articles of War restricting the use of hearsay evidence in court-martials were not applicable to war crime trials of enemy combatants by military commissions. Although two justices dissented, arguing that the charge was not a violation of the law of war and that the trial was woefully inadequate in terms of due process, the majority's decision endorsed the view that trials of war criminals by military commissions did not have to satisfy court-martial standards of justice and fairness.[8]

Following World War II, the Nuremberg International Military Tribunal and the International Military Tribunal for the Far East, both international courts of justice, tried major Nazi and Japanese war criminals, but a number of allied countries, including the United States, France, Poland, Norway, China, and Greece, convened their own domestic military tribunals to try thousands of enemy combatants for war crimes.[9] Obviously, the quality of evidentiary standards and procedural norms of these military tribunals varied enormously among this diverse group of countries. In part to introduce a degree of uniformity and to elevate existing standards of justice, a number of the articles of the Third Geneva Convention established basic requirements for military trials of prisoners of war. For example, Article 102 announced that a "prisoner of war can be validly sentenced only if the sentence has been pronounced by the same courts according to the same procedure as in the case of members of the armed forces of the Detaining Power."[10] This provision, in effect, required the United States in the future to try enemy prisoners of war (POWs) for war crimes by court-martial, rather than by military commission. Moreover, Article 105 established specific "rights and means of defense," including the assistance of a "qualified advocate or counsel" of the defendant's choice, the right to call witnesses, and the services of a competent interpreter.[11]

In addition, Common Article 3 of the Geneva Conventions, the article of the convention applicable to armed conflicts "not of an international character," prohibited "the passing of sentences and the carrying out of executions without previous judgment pronounced by a regularly constituted court, affording all the judicial guarantees which are recognized as indispensable by civilized peoples."[12] As Common Article 3 has evolved into customary international law, its significance has increased substantially as it has become applicable to all types of conflicts, not just to those "not of an international character." Therefore, even if an alleged war criminal is not a POW, the United States could try such an individual by military commission only if it was "a regularly constituted court" that provided the defendant with "all the judicial guarantees which are recognized as indispensable by civilized peoples."

Additional Protocol I, adopted on June 8, 1977, was an international treaty that amended the Geneva Conventions by making its provisions more concrete and specific. Article 75 addressed "fundamental guarantees" possessed by all detainees in international conflicts, including what type of courts may lawfully pass judgment on those accused of crime and what judicial procedures must be followed. Although the United States has never ratified Additional Protocol I, a 1986 Department of Defense memo deemed much of the protocol customary international law (including the entirety of Article 75), thereby making the article, like Common Article 3, applicable to all types of armed conflict.[13] In the following year, a high-ranking State Department official confirmed the status of Article 75 in a speech at American University,[14] and, after the 9/11 attacks, William H. Taft, IV, the State Department's legal advisor, defended the same conclusion in 2003.[15]

6.3 Article 75 of Additional Protocol I (AP I) (1977)

4. No sentence may be passed and no penalty may be executed on a person guilty of a penal offense related to the armed conflict except pursuant to a conviction pronounced by an impartial and regularly constituted court respecting the generally recognized principles of regular judicial procedure, which include the following:[16]

a. the procedure shall provide for an accused to be informed without delay of the particulars of the offence alleged against him and shall afford the accused before and during his trial all necessary rights and means of defense;
b. no one shall be convicted of an offence except on the basis of individual penal responsibility;
c. no one shall be accused or convicted of a criminal offence on account of any act or omission which did not constitute a criminal offence under the national or international law to which he was subject at the time when it was committed; nor shall a heavier penalty be imposed than that which was applicable at the time when the criminal offence was committed; if, after the commission of the offence, provision is made by law for the imposition of a lighter penalty, the offender shall benefit thereby;
d. anyone charged with an offence is presumed innocent until proved guilty according to law;
e. anyone charged with an offence shall have the right to be tried in his presence;
f. no one shall be compelled to testify against himself or to confess guilt;
g. anyone charged with an offence shall have the right to examine, or have examined,

the witnesses against him and to obtain the attendance and examination of witnesses on his behalf under the same conditions as witnesses against him;

h. no one shall be prosecuted or punished by the same Party for an offence in respect of which a final judgment acquitting or convicting that person has been previously pronounced under the same law and judicial procedure;

i. anyone prosecuted for an offence shall have the right to have the judgment pronounced publicly; and

j. a convicted person shall be advised on conviction of his judicial and other remedies and of the time-limits within which they may be exercised. . . .

Questions

1. In your view, are U.S. military commissions "impartial" and "regularly constituted courts," or are they ad hoc military tribunals created in specific circumstances and biased in favor of the prosecution?
2. Do military commissions respect "recognized principles of regular judicial procedure"? Are these principles the ones that are used in civilian courts? If so, what is the purpose of a military commission? Why not try all war crimes in civilian courts? Would a civilian trial place jurors at risk? Would a military commission be better able to protect witnesses?
3. Paragraph (4)(a) requires that the accused be afforded "all necessary rights and means of defense." What rights and means are "necessary"? Would they include a right to counsel? A right to interview the prosecution's witnesses? A right to review the prosecution's evidence before trial?
4. If a criminal offense must be a violation of national or international law to which the accused was subject at the time of the crime, does this mean that the United States cannot prosecute someone for an act that is a war crime under U.S. law but did not violate the law of the nation where the conduct occurred or international law?
5. Paragraph (4)(g) grants the accused the right to obtain the attendance of witnesses on his behalf "under the same conditions as witnesses against him." Does this provision mean that the state must supply air travel for an accused's foreign witnesses if the prosecution has any foreign witnesses?
6. Does Article 75 establish such high standards of due process that it is unlikely states will comply with them? Which provisions, in particular, set the bar too high?

Despite Article 75 of AP I, President George W. Bush issued a military order on November 13, 2001, that authorized the use of military commissions to try noncitizens who were members of al-Qaeda, who engaged in international terrorism against the United States, or who "harbored" al-Qaeda members or international terrorists. Modeled on President Roosevelt's 1942 military order, Bush issued this order based on his Article II constitutional powers and powers granted to him by Congress. The order had a number of important provisions. First, the order granted military commissions the jurisdiction to try "any and all offenses triable by military commission," without any limitation or restriction. Second, the order found that it was "not practicable" for the military commissions to follow "the principles of law and the rules of evidence generally recognized in the trial of criminal cases in the United States district courts." Instead, the presiding officer or the majority of the members of the commission was empowered to admit into evidence any testimony or document that had "probative value to a reasonable person." Third, the order required the protection of classified information from disclosure during trial, implying that the defendant could be excluded from the proceedings, if necessary. Fourth, conviction and sentencing required not unanimity but only the concurrence of two-thirds of the members of the commission. Fifth, convictions and sentences were not subject to judicial review but were instead reviewed by the president or the secretary of defense. Sixth, anyone subject to the order could not seek any "remedy or maintain any proceeding" in any court of the United States, any foreign court, or any international tribunal.[17]

Secretary of Defense Donald Rumsfeld issued a series of orders and instructions that implemented President Bush's underlying military order. On July 3, 2003, President Bush determined that six detainees held at Guantanamo Bay Naval Base were subject to his military order, which meant they were triable by military commission. In 2004, charges were filed against four of these detainees, including Salim Ahmed Hamdan, a Yemeni national and allegedly Osama bin Laden's personal driver and bodyguard. Hamdan was charged with conspiracy to commit the following war crimes: attacking civilians, murder by an unprivileged belligerent, and terrorism. He challenged the legality of the military commission system authorized by Bush's military order in the federal district court of the District of Columbia, arguing that conspiracy was not a violation of the law of war and that the procedures of the military commission violated basic tenets of military and international law, including the defendant's right to see and hear all the evidence against him.

While Hamdan challenged President Bush's system of military commissions, the International Committee of the Red Cross (ICRC) published a study of customary international humanitarian law (customary law of war) that it had begun in 1996. This study was important, according to the ICRC, because most armed conflicts today are "non-international," and customary international humanitarian law governs these conflicts more so than treaty law. One of the many topics covered by this study is "Fair Trial Guarantees," which is of course directly relevant to whether President Bush's system of military commissions was consistent with international law. According to the ICRC, since the "Fair Trial Guarantees" constituted customary international law, they were applicable to both international and noninternational armed conflicts.

6.4 ICRC, Rule 100: "Fair Trial Guarantees" (2005)

Several trials held after the Second World War, but before the adoption of the Geneva Convention in 1949, found the defendants guilty of denying fair trial to prisoners of war or civilians.[18] The right to fair trial is provided for in all four Geneva Conventions and in Additional Protocols I and II. Depriving a protected person of a fair and regular trial is a grave breach under the Third and Fourth Geneva Conventions and under Additional Protocol I. Common Article 3 of the Geneva Conventions prohibits the sentencing of persons or the carrying out of executions without previous judgment pronounced by a regularly constituted court. Depriving a person of the right to a fair trial is listed as a war crime in the Statutes of the International Criminal Court, of the International Criminal

Tribunals for the former Yugoslavia and for Rwanda and of the Special Court for Sierra Leone. . . .

Pursuant to Common Article 3 of the Geneva Conventions, only a "regularly constituted court" may pass judgment on an accused person. The Third Geneva Convention requires that courts judging prisoners of war offer the essential guarantees of "independence" and "impartiality." . . .

. . . A court is regularly constituted if it has been established and organized in accordance with the laws and procedures already in force in a country. . . .

. . . In order to be independent, a court must be able to perform its functions independently of any other branch of the government, especially the executive. In order to be impartial, the judges composing the court must not harbor preconceptions about the matter before them, nor act in a way that promotes the interests of one side. In addition to this requirement of subjective impartiality, regional human rights bodies have pointed out that a court must also be impartial from an objective viewpoint, i.e., it must offer sufficient guarantees to exclude any legitimate doubt about its impartiality. . . .

Necessary rights and means of defense . . .

(i) *Right to defend oneself or to be assisted by a lawyer of one's own choice. . . .*
(ii) *Right to free legal assistance if the interest of justice so require. . . .*
(iii) *Right to sufficient time and facilities to prepare the defense. . . .*
(iv) *Right of the accused to communicate freely with counsel. . . .*

Additional Protocols I and II provide that accused persons have the right to be tried in their presence. . . .

. . . Both the UN Human Rights Committee and the Inter-American Commission on Human Rights have indicated that the prohibition against compelling accused persons to testify against themselves or to confess guilt can never be dispensed with.

The UN Human Rights Committee has underlined that "the law should require that evidence provided by means of such methods or any other form of compulsion is wholly unacceptable." The UN Convention against Torture provides that statements which have been made as a result of torture may not be invoked as evidence in any proceeding. This view is confirmed in national and international case-law. . . .

Questions

1. Should depriving a war criminal of a fair trial itself constitute a war crime? Should it be considered a "grave breach" of the Geneva Conventions—the most serious type of war crime?
2. According to the ICRC's definition of a "regularly constituted court," does a U.S. military commission qualify? Why or why not?
3. What if the laws and procedures for establishing military commissions in the United States are "already in force" but commissions themselves have been established only sporadically since the Civil War? Would they still be "regularly constituted"?
4. Could the system of military commissions created by President Bush be "independent" if all convictions and sentences were subject only to the review of the secretary of defense and the president?
5. Can a military commission trying a member of al-Qaeda be "impartial" if it is composed of professional military officers who might be called upon to actively prosecute the war against al-Qaeda?
6. Could a military commission ever be impartial "from an objective viewpoint"? Is such a requirement valid?
7. Are military tribunals inherently neither "independent" nor "impartial"?

8. How should a defendant's right to a lawyer of his choice be balanced against the government's right to protect classified information? What if the government thinks that a defendant's lawyer is a clear security risk?
9. Should there be any exceptions to the rule that accused persons have a right to be present throughout their trial? What kind of problems could this rule pose for the protection of sources and methods of gaining foreign intelligence information?
10. Even if evidence obtained by torture should be excluded from any trial, is the rule against the use of all coercion compatible with the type of force typically used by the military to capture and detain international terrorists?

Hamdan's case challenging the legality of President' Bush's system of military commissions finally arrived at the Supreme Court in 2006. In a 5–3 decision, Justice John P. Stevens, writing for the majority (Justices Anthony Kennedy, David Souter, Ruth Bader Ginsburg, and Stephen Breyer) concluded that the military order violated Article 36 of the Uniform Code of Military Justice (UCMJ), the code of military justice that Congress enacted into law following World War II. Article 36 granted the president authority to issue regulations for military commissions that shall, "as far as he considers practicable," follow the procedures and principles used in criminal trials of the federal district court. But such regulations had to be "uniform insofar as practicable" with the trial procedures of courts-martial, and in no case could they be "contrary to or inconsistent" with rules and procedures of the UCMJ. In short, military commissions had to follow the rules of the Manual for Courts-Martial unless they were "impracticable," but the Bush administration had not provided any explanations for why the existing deviations from these rules were needed. For this reason, the majority concluded that Bush's military order violated Common Article 3 of the Geneva Convention since a military commission could not qualify as a "regularly constituted court" unless some practical need explained why its procedures differed from those of a court-martial.

Justice Stevens, writing only for a plurality of the justices (the same as above but without Justice Kennedy), also argued that the military commission lacked jurisdiction because conspiracy was not a crime triable by a law-of-war military commission. Stevens concedes that the common law of war—without any statute or treaty—might render a certain offense triable by military commission, but the precedent had to be "plain and unambiguous." In Stevens's opinion, no such precedent existed for trying conspiracy by military commissions. Another problem with the commissions, according to Stevens and the plurality, was that the specific procedures of the military commissions violated Article 75 of Additional Protocol I, which was "indisputably part of the customary international law." For example, Article 75 required that a defendant must have the right to attend his trial, absent disruptive conduct, and must have access to all the evidence that the government is using to convict him. Both of these rights were not protected by the specific procedures governing Bush's military commissions, and for that reason, they were unlawful. Relatively short excerpts from the concurrence of Justices Breyer and the dissents of Justices Clarence Thomas and Samuel Alito are also included in the next reading.

6.5 *Hamdan v. Rumsfeld*, 548 U.S. 557 (2006)

JUSTICE STEVENS [excerpt from the majority opinion] . . .

Together, the UCMJ, the AUMF, and the DTA at most acknowledge a general Presidential authority to convene military commissions in circumstances where justified under the "Constitution and laws," including the law of war. Absent a more specific congressional authorization, the task of this Court is, as it was in *Quirin*, to decide whether Hamdan's military commission is so justified. It is to that inquiry we now turn. . . .

. . . [The principle that procedures of military commissions must be uniform with the principles of courts-martial] is not an inflexible one; it does not preclude all departures from the procedures for use by courts-martial. But any departure must be tailored to the exigency that necessitates it. That understanding is reflected in Article 36 of the UCMJ, which provides:

a. The procedure, including modes of proof, in cases before courts-martial, courts of inquiry, military commissions, and other military tribunals may be prescribed by the President by regulations which shall, so far as he considers practicable, apply the principles of law and the rules of evidence generally recognized in the trial of criminal cases in the United States district courts, but which may not be contrary to or inconsistent with this chapter [of the UCMJ].
b. All rules and regulations made under this article shall be uniform insofar as practicable and shall be reported to Congress.

Article 36 places two restrictions on the President's power to promulgate rules of procedure for courts-martial and military commissions alike. First, no procedural rule he adopts may be "contrary to or inconsistent with" the UCMJ—however practical it may seem. Second, the rules adopted must be "uniform insofar as practicable." That is, the rules applied to military commissions must be the same as those applied to courts-martial unless such uniformity proves impracticable.

Hamdan argues that Commission Order No. 1 violates both of these restrictions; he maintains that the procedures described in the Commission Order are inconsistent with the UCMJ and that the Government has offered no explanation for their deviation from the procedures governing courts-martial, which are set forth in the Manual for Courts-Martial. Among the inconsistencies Hamdan identifies is that between § 6 of the Commission order, which permits exclusion of the accused from proceedings and denial of his access to evidence in certain circumstances, and the UCMJ's requirement that "[a]ll . . . proceedings" other than votes and deliberations by courts-martial "shall be made a part of the record and shall be in the presence of the accused." Hamdan also observes that the Commission Order dispenses with virtually all evidentiary rules applicable to courts-martial. . . .

. . . [Accordingly,] Commission Order No. 1 . . . necessarily violates Article 36(b). . . .

The Court of Appeals thought, and the Government asserts, that Common Article 3 does not apply to Hamdan because the conflict with al-Qaeda, being "'international in scope,'" does not qualify as a "'conflict not of an international character.'" That reasoning is erroneous. The term "conflict not of an international character" is used here in contradistinction to a conflict between nations. . . .

Common Article 3, then, is applicable here and . . . requires that Hamdan be tried by a "regularly constituted court affording all the judicial guarantees which are recognized as indispensable by civilized peoples." . . .

. . . At a minimum, a military commission "can be 'regularly constituted' by the standards of our military justice system only if some practical need explains deviations from court-martial practice." As we have explained, no such need has been demonstrated here. . . .

JUSTICE STEVENS [excerpt from the plurality opinion] . . .

The charge against Hamdan . . . alleges a conspiracy extending over a number of years, from 1996 to November 2001. All but two months of that more than 5-year-long period preceded the attacks of September 11, 2001, and the enactment of the AUMF—the Act of Congress on which the Government relies for exercise of its war powers and thus for its authority to convene military commissions. Neither the agreement with Osama bin Laden and others to commit war crimes, nor a single overt act, is alleged to have occurred in a theater of war or on any specified date after September 11, 2001. None of the overt acts that Hamdan is alleged to have committed violates the law of war.

These facts alone cast doubt on the legality of the charge and, hence, the commission; as Winthrop makes plain, the offense alleged must have been committed both in a theater of war and *during*, not before, the relevant conflict. But the deficiencies in the time and place allegations also underscore—indeed are symptomatic of—the most serious defect of this charge: The offense it alleges is not triable by law-of-war military commission. . . .

The Government . . . points out that the Nazi saboteurs in *Quirin* were charged with conspiracy. . . .

That the defendants in *Quirin* were charged with conspiracy is not persuasive, since the Court declined to address whether the offense actually qualified as a violation of the law of war—let alone one triable by military commission. . . .

Finally, international sources confirm that the crime charged here is not a recognized violation of the law of war. As observed above, none of the major treaties governing the law of war identifies conspiracy as a violation thereof. And the only "conspiracy" crimes that have been recognized by international war crimes tribunals . . . are conspiracy to commit genocide and common plan to wage aggressive war, which is a crime against the peace and requires for its commission actual participation in a "concrete plan to wage war." . . .

The charge's shortcomings are not merely formal, but are indicative of a broader inability on the Executive's part here to satisfy the most basic precondition—at least in the absence of specific congressional authorization—for establishment of military commissions: military necessity. Hamdan's tribunal was appointed not by a military commander in the field of battle, but by a retired major general stationed away from any active hostilities. Hamdan is charged not with an overt act for which he was caught redhanded in a theater of war and which military efficiency demands be tried expeditiously, but with an *agreement* the inception of which long predated the attacks of September 11, 2001, and the AUMF. That may well be a crime, but it is not an offense that "by the law of war may be tried by military commissio[n]." . . .

Inextricably intertwined with the question of regular constitution is the evaluation of the procedures governing the tribunal and whether they afford "all the judicial guarantees which are recognized as indispensable by civilized peoples." Like the phrase "regularly constituted court," this phrase is not defined in the text of the Geneva Conventions. But it must be understood to incorporate at least the barest of those trial protections that have been recognized by customary international law. Many of these are described in Article 75 of Protocol I to the Geneva Conventions of 1949, adopted in 1977 (Protocol I). Although the United States declined to ratify Protocol I, its objections were not to Article 75 thereof. Indeed, it appears that the Government "regard[s] the provisions of Article 75 as an articulation of safeguards to which all persons in the hands of an enemy are entitled." Among the rights set forth in Article 75 is the "right to be tried in [one's] presence." . . .

JUSTICE BREYER concurring [joined by JUSTICES KENNEDY, SOUTER, and GINSBURG] . . .

. . . The Court's conclusion ultimately rests upon a single ground: Congress has not issued the Executive a "blank check." Indeed, Congress has denied the President the legislative authority to create military commissions of the kind at issue here. Nothing prevents the President from returning to Congress to seek the authority he believes necessary. . . .

JUSTICE THOMAS dissenting [joined by Justices Antonin Scalia and Samuel Alito] . . .

Ultimately, the plurality's determination that Hamdan has not been charged with an offense triable before a military commission rests not upon any historical example or authority, but upon the plurality's raw judgment of the "inability on the Executive's part here to satisfy the most basic precondition . . . for establishment of military commissions: military necessity." This judgment starkly confirms that the plurality has appointed itself the ultimate arbiter of what is quintessentially a policy and military judgment, namely, the appropriate military measures to take against those who "aided the terrorist attacks that occurred on September 11, 2001." . . .

Today a plurality of this Court would hold that conspiracy to massacre innocent civilians does not violate the laws of war. This determination is unsustainable. . . . [A]ccording to the plurality, when our Armed Forces capture those who are plotting terrorist atrocities like the bombing of the Khobar Towers, the bombing of the U.S.S. *Cole*, and the attacks of September 11—even if their plots are advanced to the very brink of fulfillment—our military cannot charge those criminals with any offense against the laws of war. Instead, our troops must catch the terrorists "redhanded," in the midst of *the attack itself*, in order to bring them to justice. Not only is this conclusion fundamentally inconsistent with the cardinal principal of the law of war, namely protecting non-combatants, but it would sorely hamper the President's ability to confront and defeat a new and deadly enemy. . . .

Nothing in the text of Article 36(b) supports the Court's sweeping conclusion that it represents an unprecedented congressional effort to change the nature of military commissions from common-law war courts to tribunals that must presumptively function like courts-martial. . . . To the contrary, the UCMJ expressly recognizes that different tribunals will be constituted in different manners and employ different procedures. . . .

Even if Article 36(b) could be construed to require procedural uniformity among the various tribunals contemplated by the UCMJ, . . . [t]he Court provides no explanation why the President's determination that employing court-martial procedures in the military commissions established pursuant to Military Commission Order No. 1 would hamper our war effort is in any way inadequate to satisfy its newly minted "practicability" requirement. On the contrary, this determination is precisely the kind for which the "Judiciary has neither aptitude, facilities nor responsibility and which has long been held to belong in the domain of political power not subject to judicial intrusion or inquiry." . . .

JUSTICE ALITO dissenting [joined by JUSTICES SCALIA and THOMAS] . . .

I see no basis for the Court's holding that a military commission cannot be regarded as "a regularly constituted court" unless it is similar in structure and composition to a regular military court or unless there is an "evident practical need" for the divergence. There is no reason why a court that differs in structure or composition from an ordinary military court must be viewed as having been improperly constituted. Tribunals that vary significantly in structure, composition, and procedures may all be "regularly" or "properly" constituted. Consider, for example, a municipal court, a state trial court of general jurisdiction, an Article I federal trial court, a federal district court, and an international court, such as the International Criminal Tribunal for the Former Yugoslavia. Although these courts are "differently constituted" and differ substantially in many other respects, they are all "regularly constituted." . . .

. . . [If] some of the procedures that may be used in military commission proceedings are improper, the appropriate remedy is to proscribe the use of those particular procedures, not to outlaw the commissions. I see no justification for striking down the entire commission structure simply because it is possible that petitioner's trial might involve the use of some procedure that is improper. . . .

Questions

1. According to Justice Stevens's majority opinion, is the law of war controlling in this case because it is valid customary international law or because Congress has declared it to be so?
2. Justice Stevens claims that the rule requiring the procedures of military commissions be the same as those of courts-martial is not "inflexible," but is he consistent?
3. How does Justice Stevens justify his conclusion that a military commission is a "regularly constituted court" only if there is some "practical need" for its procedures to be different from those of a court-martial? What is a "practical need"? Who should decide whether one exists?
4. Why do you think Justice Kennedy refused to endorse the reasoning in Justice Stevens's plurality opinion?
5. Do you agree with Justice Stevens that conspiracy is not a violation of the law of war? How does Justice Thomas attack this position?
6. If conspiracy to commit genocide or wage aggressive war is triable by a military commission, according to Justice Stevens, why is conspiracy to murder civilians not triable? In your view, would a conspiracy to commit genocide or aggressive war be triable by a military commission only if the genocide or aggressive war in fact occurred? Is that what Justice Stevens is claiming?
7. In your view, does Justice Stevens think that Article 75 of Additional Protocol I is judicially enforceable?
8. Why is it significant that Justice Breyer underlines the fact that Congress can change Article 36 of the UCMJ?
9. Is Justice Thomas correct that the majority is intruding itself into policy and military judgments?
10. Justice Thomas claims that Justice Stevens would permit a trial by a military commission only if the defendant was caught "redhanded," that is, in the "midst of an attack." Is this a fair characterization? Why or why not?
11. Is Justice Thomas correct that judges should defer to the president's determination that court-martial procedures were not "practicable" in war crime trials of international terrorists?
12. Is Justice Alito correct that there can be many different types of "regularly constituted courts"? Even if he is right, is a military commission necessarily a "regularly constituted court" for that reason?

Congress responded to the Supreme Court's decision in *Hamdan* by quickly enacting the Military Commissions Act (MCA) of 2006. This law significantly revised President Bush's system of military commissions based in part on what the court's majority had held in *Hamdan*. For example, the MCA made it clear that not all the trial procedures of courts-martial applied to the new system of military commissions, including the right to a speedy trial and specific rights related to compulsory self-incrimination. Second, the law identified military commissions authorized by it as "regularly constituted courts" for purposes of Common Article 3 of the Geneva Conventions. Third, it permitted defendants to retain their own civilian counsel but required that such counsel be U.S. citizens and have a security clearance at the level secret or higher. Fourth, it prohibited the admissibility of any statement obtained by torture, but some coerced statements could be admitted if the statement was reliable and probative and its admission would best serve the interests of justice. Fifth, it permitted the admissibility of hearsay evidence if it was reliable, probative, and not unduly prejudicial so long as the opposing side was fully informed regarding how the evidence was obtained. Sixth, it required that classified information not be disclosed. Seventh, it permitted a defendant to appeal a conviction or sentence by a military commission to a Court of Military Commission Review, then to the U.S. Court of Appeals for the D.C. Circuit, and finally, to the U.S. Supreme Court. Last, the MCA included a list of specific offenses that could be tried by military commissions, a list that included "inchoate conspiracy" (which does not require the commission of the underlying offense but only an agreement to commit the unlawful act and an overt act in furtherance of the conspiracy) and "providing material support to terrorism." As noted by four justices in *Hamdan*, "inchoate conspiracy" was not generally considered a violation of the laws of war, a conclusion that presumably also applied to the offense of providing material support.[19]

In 2009, the new Obama administration revised the Bush administration's MCA of 2006.[20] Some of the changes were cosmetic; others were more substantive, but a key factor was that the 2009 MCA included the same substantive list of offenses triable by military commission that was in the 2006 version, including "inchoate conspiracy" and "providing material support to terrorism." These two charges had become standard in cases brought before the Bush/Obama system of military commissions. For example, following Hamdan's victory at the Supreme Court in 2006, a military commission convicted him of providing material support in 2008. In the same year, another military commission convicted Ali Al Bahlul, an al-Qaeda propagandist, of conspiracy, providing material support, and solicitation. Both defendants appealed, arguing that their convictions violated the ex post facto clause since their alleged unlawful conduct occurred prior to the enactment of the MCA of 2006.

The full court of appeals for the D.C. Circuit eventually considered this argument in an en banc decision in *Al Bahlul v. United States (Al Bahlul I)*. The court unanimously held that Bahlul's convictions for providing material support and solicitation had to be overturned because they violated the ex post facto clause. The rationale for this conclusion was that such charges had rarely, if ever, been tried by U.S. military commissions in American history and therefore the charges could not be considered violations of the "law of war" before Congress identified them as such in 2006. However, six of the seven judges came to the opposite conclusion regarding the charge of conspiracy. Even though conspiracy was not understood to be a violation of the international "law of war," U.S. military commissions had tried such cases a number of times in American history, thereby lending support to the proposition that it was a violation of the military common law of the United States. According to the court, the most "significant precedent" was the trial by military commission of President Lincoln's assassins. Even though these assassins did not just conspire to kill Lincoln but in fact assassinated him, the court held that the term "law of war" in American law could reasonably be understood to prohibit conspiracies to commit war crimes.

For this reason, Bahlul's conspiracy conviction did not violate the ex post facto clause since his conduct was arguably unlawful at the time he engaged in it.[21]

The en banc court in *Al Bahlul I* confined itself to ruling on the ex post facto objection to Bahlul's conviction and did not consider (1) whether Congress had the Article I power to transform conspiracy into a war crime triable by military commission, or (2) whether the creation of such a war crime intruded upon the Article III powers of the federal judiciary. These issues were addressed in a second round of litigation referred to as *Al Bahlul II*. In June 2015, a 2–1 panel of D.C. Circuit judges held that Congress did not have the constitutional authority to create the war crime of conspiracy since international law did not recognize such an offense.[22] However, the full D.C. Circuit in September 2015 vacated the panel's decision in *Al Bahlul II* and granted the government's request for a rehearing en banc. The D.C. Circuit handed down its second en banc decision in the *Al Bahlul* litigation on October 20, 2016. A 6–3 majority held (1) that even if conspiracy was not a violation of the international law of war, Congress did have an Article I power to establish it as an offense triable by military commission; and (2) that trying such an offense before a military commission did not intrude upon the Article III powers of the federal judiciary. The majority was not united in its reasoning, but two judges joined Judge Brett Kavanaugh's plurality opinion. The three judges in dissent issued a joint opinion. The following reading includes excerpts from Judge Kavanaugh's concurrence and the joint dissent. The excerpts highlight sharply contrasting positions on whether Congress has the authority to create new types of war crimes not recognized by international law in the ongoing conflict with al-Qaeda and associated forces.

6.6 *Al Bahlul v. United States (Al Bahlul II)*, 840 F.3d 757 (D.C. Cir. 2016) (en banc)

JUDGE KAVANAUGH . . . concurring . . .

This case therefore raises one central legal question: Under the U.S. Constitution, may Congress establish military commissions to try unlawful enemy combatants for the offense of conspiracy to commit war crimes, even if conspiracy is not an offense under the international law of war? The answer is yes. . . .

First, the text and original understanding of Article I demonstrate that international law does not impose a limit on Congress's authority to make offenses triable by military commissions.

The premise of Bahlul's Article I argument is that Congress's *sole* source of constitutional authority to make offenses triable by military commission is the Define and Punish Clause of Article I [that grants Congress the power to "define and punish . . . offenses against the Law of Nations]." . . .

. . . [T]he premise of Bahlul's Article I argument is flawed. . . . Congress's Article I authority to establish military commissions . . . does not derive exclusively from that clause.

Rather, the war power clauses of Article I, Section 8—including the Declare War Clause and the Captures Clause, together with the Necessary and Proper Clause—supply Congress with ample authority to establish military commissions and make offenses triable by military commission. And the Declare War Clause and the other war powers clauses in Article I do not refer to international law or otherwise impose international law as a constraint on Congress's authority to make offenses triable by military commission. . . .

Second, the overall structure of the Constitution reinforces the conclusion that international law does not impose a limit on Congress's authority to make offenses triable by military commission.

. . . The Framers assigned the national government—in particular, Congress and the President—the authority to make wartime decisions on behalf of the United States. . . .

What matters most for present purposes is that the Framers certainly did not purport to afford foreign nations (acting through international law of war or otherwise) any constitutional authority over the wartime decisions of the United States, such as the determination of which war crimes may be prosecuted by U.S. military commissions. It would be a historical anomaly to conclude that "We the People of the United States" gave foreign or international bodies the power to constrain U.S. war-making authority in that way. Yet that would be the necessary consequence of the argument put forward by Bahlul and the joint dissent. They would incorporate international law into the U.S. Constitution as a *judicially enforceable constraint* on the wartime decisions of the Congress and the President. *As a matter of U.S. constitutional law,* Congress and the President would be subject to the dictates of the international community, a community that at any given time may be unsupportive of or even hostile to U.S. national security interests. . . .

Third, . . . landmark Supreme Court precedent likewise supports the conclusion that Congress's authority to establish offenses triable by military commission is not confined by international law.

The Supreme Court's leading constitutional decision regarding military commissions is *Ex Parte Quirin*. In its decision, the Court emphasized that U.S. military commissions have long been authorized by Congress, and the Court noted in particular that military commissions have long tried the offense of spying. But spying was not and has never been an offense under the international law of war. The Court nonetheless relied on and approved of trying spying offenses by military commission. [Accordingly,] . . . Congress has authority under Article I to make offenses triable by military commission even if those offenses are not crimes under the international law of war. . . .

Fourth, . . . the historical practice of the Legislative and Executive Branches matters. . . .

. . . From the earliest days of the Republic, Congress has gone beyond international law in specifying the offenses that may be tried by military commission. Beginning in 1776, the Continental Congress codified the offense of spying—a non-international-law offense—as a crime triable by military tribunal. Likewise, in September 1776, Congress authorized trial by military tribunal for another non-international-law offense: aiding the enemy. . . .

Fifth, in addition to the historical practice in Congress, the historical practice in the Executive Branch demonstrates that international law is not a constraint on which offenses may be tried by military commission. . . .

The two most important military commission precedents in U.S. history—the trials of the Lincoln conspirators and the Nazi saboteurs—were trials for the offense of conspiracy. . . .

Bahlul also contends that Article III of the U.S. Constitution confines U.S. military commissions to international law of war offenses.

. . . Based solely on the text of Article III, Bahlul might have a point. But the Supreme Court has long recognized an exception to Article III for military commissions to try enemy war crimes. . . .

In this context, if historical practice demonstrates that an offense is triable by U.S. military commission, that history resolves the Article III issue. As explained [above] . . . , the history of U.S. military commissions trying non-international-law-of-war offenses is extensive and dates from the beginning of the Republic. That historical practice therefore amply demonstrates that Article III is not a barrier to U.S. military commission trials of non-international-law-of-war offenses, including the offense of conspiracy to commit war crimes. . . .

. . . [W]hat if an offense is neither an international law of war offense nor historically rooted in U.S. military commission practice? Consider a hypothetical new statute that makes cyber-attacks by enemy forces a war crime triable by military commission. *Quirin* stated that Article III does "not restrict whatever authority was conferred by the Constitution to try offenses against the law of war by military commission," and does not bar "the practice of trying, before military tribunals without a jury, offenses committed by enemy belligerents against the law of war." Perhaps that language suggests that Article III permits what Article I authorizes with respect to which enemy war crimes may be tried by U.S. military commission. But we need not answer that hypothetical in this case and need not define with precision the outer limits of the Constitution in this context, other than to say that international law is not such a limit. Wherever one might ultimately draw the outer boundaries of Congress authority to establish offenses triable by military commission, the [U.S.] historically rooted offense of conspiracy to commit war crimes is well within those limits. . . .

ROGERS, TATEL, and PILLARD Circuit Judges, dissenting . . .

. . . The prosecution of Bahlul in a law-of-war military commission for inchoate conspiracy infringes the judiciary's power to preside over the trial of all crimes, as set forth in Article III of the Constitution. History and precedent have established a narrow, atextual exception to Article III under which the military may try enemy belligerents for offenses against the international "laws of war," but inchoate conspiracy is not such an offense. . . .

The principal decision that governs here is *Ex parte Quirin*. . . .

Focusing on the first charge alone [violation of the law of war], . . . the Court proceeded to consider whether the defendants had been charged with a violation of the international rules governing armed conflicts. It ultimately concluded that they had been, expressing its belief that passing behind enemy lines in civilian dress with the purpose of committing hostile acts was then an offense under international law. . . .

. . . [W]e, as a lower court, should be hesitant to stretch the exception . . . in the ways the government suggests. For one thing, a Supreme Court plurality has already described *Quirin* as "the high-water mark of military power to try enemy combatants for war crimes." . . .

Given the foregoing principles, the Article III inquiry in this case turns on whether conspiracy to commit war crimes is an offense under the international laws of war. As the government candidly and rightly concedes, it is not. . . .

Significantly for the issue before us, international law has adopted conspiracy as a standalone offense in only two circumstances. First, it has recognized conspiracy to commit genocide as a crime against humanity. Second, it has acknowledged conspiracy to wage aggressive war as a crime against peace. Outside of these two contexts, however, the crime of conspiracy has gained no traction in international law. Those exceptions are plainly not at issue here, for al Bahlul was charged with neither. . . .

. . . [T]he government insists that *Quirin* itself demonstrates that the atextual Article III exception for military trials of "law of war" offenses extends to purely domestic war crimes [such as conspiracy]. In support, it claims that "spying and the kindred offense of sabotage"—the offenses the Court examined in *Quirin*—were not, and have never been, offenses against the international laws of war. In its view, this shows that the "law of war" to which the Court referred in carving out an Article III exception includes purely domestic offenses.

The greatest flaw in the government's argument is that the Court expressly identified the "law of war" as a branch of international law. . . . Had the Court thought that the term actually encompassed a domestic "common law of war," it likely would have said as much. . . .

But the government's argument suffers from yet another major flaw—the Supreme Court's analysis makes clear that it viewed "spying and the kindred offense of sabotage" as offenses against the international laws of war. . . .

. . . [A]though it is true that *Quirin*, *Yamashita*, and *Hamdan* looked to the war power in discussing congressional authority to *establish* military commissions, they consistently looked to the Define and Punish Clause alone in addressing Congress's authority to confer *jurisdiction over particular offenses*. For instance, in *Yamashita*, the Court explained that "the [military] commission derives its *existence* from the war powers, but that its jurisdiction over specific offenses come from Congress's 'exercise of the power conferred upon it by Article I, § 8, cl. 10 of the Constitution to "define and punish . . . offenses against the Law of Nation . . ." of which the law of war is a part.'" . . .

There is no . . . robust history of trying inchoate conspiracy before [U.S.] law-of-war military commissions. The government has identified only a handful of at best ambiguous examples, and none in which a conviction was for inchoate conspiracy by a law-of-war commission that was affirmed by the Judicial Branch. The examples are unpersuasive in themselves and insufficient to establish a longstanding historical practice that would justify a more expansive understanding of the law-of-war military commission exception to Article III.

First, the government places substantial reliance on Civil War era historical practice, but that practice does not support its case. For instance, although the charges against the Lincoln assassins referred to conspiracy, the specification listed the elements of the completed offense—"traitorously" murdering President Lincoln. . . . As such, it appears that conspiracy was at most a theory of liability on which to hold each of the partners to account for the assassination completed by Booth alone. . . .

. . . [A]lthough the government and four of our colleagues contend that Congress's longstanding practice of making spying and aiding the enemy triable by military tribunal "strongly support the conclusion that international law is not a constitutional constraint on Congress's authority to make particular crimes triable by military commission," it seems that, if anything, Congress's consistent practice to codify those two offenses—and those two offenses alone—undermines that conclusion. Had Congress, over the last two hundred years, actually believed itself free to punish by military tribunal whatever wartime conduct it deemed necessary, it would be rather surprising that it codified [for trial by military commission] only two offenses, both of which were subject to military trial at the time the Constitution was adopted. Thus, while these two offenses may fall within an Article III exception based on longstanding historical practice, we find them uninformative regarding Congress's general authority to make purely domestic crimes punishable by military commission. . . .

. . . [In] Judge [Kavanaugh]'s . . . view, the Constitution cannot possibly give the international community—through the development of international law—the ability to limit Congress's exercise of its war powers. It is not international law, however, that constrains Congress's authority here—it is Article III. . . . The international-law constraint that *Quirin* recognized and that we would apply here functions not as a independent constraint on the political branches' powers to wage war, but rather as an essential demarcation between military and civilian jurisdiction. Without it, "the line between civilian and military jurisdiction would become elusive—if not altogether illusory." . . .

The idea that international law has a role to play in our constitutional framework is also not as surprising as one might think. The Framers of the Constitution well understood that our country's newly forged sovereignty brought with it both rights and obligations.

John Jay, the first Chief Justice of the United States, explained in 1793 that the United States "had, by taking a place among the nations of the earth, become amenable to the laws of nations." Embracing the law of nations and adhering to its principles, he further explained, was the new nation's "duty" and in its own "interest." . . .

. . . [I]f international law does not mark the boundaries between civilian and military jurisdiction, what does? On this, our colleagues are silent. Based on the principles articulated by the government and embraced in Judge Kavanaugh's opinion, however, it would seem that Congress and the President could vest military commissions with authority to try enemy belligerents for almost any crime so long as it related in some way to "hostilities." Especially in this new era of "war" against difficult-to-identify enemies on difficult-to-identify "battlefields," such positions would appear to leave few, if any, enforceable limits on the political branches' authority to avoid Article III courts and prosecute individuals in military commissions. Thus, allowing military commissions to take cognizance of inchoate conspiracy charges might seem to some a small and harmless encroachment on the judiciary's domain, it could very well open the door to much broader intrusions. . . .

Questions

1. Does Judge Kavanaugh too quickly assume that Congress's war powers include not only the power to establish military commissions but also the power to create new offenses or war crimes that are triable by military commission? Would such a power mean that Congress could change the laws of war? What's the dissent's view?
2. If Congress can use its Article I war powers to establish military commissions to try new war crime offenses, can it use its other Article I powers—such as its power to tax, coin money, or regulate interstate commerce—to establish military commissions to try new offenses in these policy areas? Why or why not?
3. To what extent would a denial of Congress's authority to try crimes that are not international war crimes by military commission subject "the People of the United States" to the "dictates of the international community"?
4. Is the trial of Lincoln's assassins a good precedent for the conspiracy trial of Bahlul? Why or why not? What about the *Quirin* case?
5. Judge Kavanaugh refrains from defining the "outer limits" of Congress's power to expand the jurisdiction of military commissions, but he does say that language from *Quirin* "suggests that Article III permits what Article I authorizes." What does he mean by this statement?
6. According to the dissent, if inchoate conspiracy to commit genocide or to wage aggressive war is deemed a violation of international law, why can't other forms of conspiracy be so recognized? Is it because the substantive crimes of genocide and aggressive war are of a different magnitude from other crimes, such as a conspiracy to kill civilians, one of the charges against Bahlul? Are such distinctions useful? Justifiable?
7. The dissent seems to have no objection if the offenses of "spying" and "aiding the enemy" (and perhaps "espionage") are subject to trial by military commissions because they are "established" historical exceptions to the jurisdiction of civilian Article III courts. But if these exceptions are acceptable, why should it be unconstitutional for a new exception to evolve or be established by statute? Why only two, but not three or four? Is this the kind of slippery slope that would endanger the equal and independent status of the third branch of the federal government?
8. The dissent asks, "[I]f international law does not mark the boundaries between civilian and military jurisdiction, what does?" How would you answer this question?

On October 10, 2017, the Supreme Court, without comment, denied Bahlul's petition for a writ certiorari, leaving undisturbed the D.C. Circuit Court's holding that, even if conspiracy was not a violation of the law of war, Congress had the Article I power to convert it into an offense triable by a military commission without intruding upon the Article III powers of the federal judiciary.[23] The denial of the petition was a clear win for the government. However, despite the fact that the federal courts have upheld the lawfulness of the system of military commissions established by Congress in 2006 and reformed in 2009, what this system has actually accomplished over the last ten-plus years is spotty at best. A quick overview would include the conviction of David Hicks in 2007, but this conviction was overturned in 2015 on the ground that it violated the ex post facto clause. Charges against Binyam Ahmed Mohamed were dropped, and he was returned to the United Kingdom in 2009. Salim Ahmed Hamdan was convicted and transferred to Yemen in 2008, but the D.C. Circuit overturned his conviction in 2012. Ibrahim Ahmed Mahmoud al Qosi pleaded guilty in 2010, but twelve years of his fourteen-year sentence were suspended and he was transferred back to Sudan in 2012. Noor Uthman Muhammed pleaded guilty in 2011, but he was transferred to Sudan in 2013. After Omar Ahmed Khadr pleaded guilty in exchange for an eight-year sentence, he was transferred to Canada, where he was released in 2015. There are currently a half-dozen active military commission cases, including the prosecutions of Khalid Shaikh Mohammad (KSM), the so-called mastermind of the 9/11 attacks; Ramzi bin al Shibh, the alleged twentieth hijacker; and Abd al-Rahim al-Nashiri, the organizer of the bombing of the USS *Cole*, but these cases have been bogged down in pretrial hearings for years. With this kind of track record, an obvious question is whether military commissions are in fact contributing to the war effort against al-Qaeda and associated forces or whether we would be better off without them.[24]

Against this background, Sayfullo Saipov, an Uzbek immigrant inspired by ISIS ideology, used a rental truck on Tuesday, October 31, 2017, to run down eleven people on a west Manhattan bike path, killing eight. At a cabinet meeting the next day, President Trump characterized the U.S. criminal justice system as a "joke" and a "laughingstock" because it did not deal with terrorists as harshly as it should. Calling for the death penalty for Saipov, he added, "We also have to come up with punishment that's far quicker and far greater than the punishment these animals are getting right now. They'll go through court for years. And at the end, they'll be—who knows what happens. We need quick justice and we need strong justice—much quicker and much stronger than we have right now."[25] For these reasons, Trump said he would support transferring Saipov to Guantanamo Bay and trying him before a military commission, but federal officials in New York City instead charged Saipov in civilian court. On Thursday of that week, Trump tweeted that he would "love to send the NYC terrorist to Guantanamo but statistically that process takes much longer than going through the Federal system."[26] Perhaps overnight someone had informed President Trump of the lackluster record of the U.S. military commission system, but that does not explain why Trump thinks the federal justice system is a "joke" and a "laughingstock" or why, by advocating the death penalty for Saipov, he gratuitously gave the defendant a ready-made issue to appeal if and when he is convicted and sentenced. In January 2018, Saipov's lawyers indicated he would plead guilty and accept a life sentence without parole if the death penalty was set aside, but prosecutors instead asked the judge for a firm trial date because the victims "have a strong desire for closure."[27]

While Saipov's case moved forward in the federal district court in New York, dark clouds gathered around the U.S. military commission system. The problem had initially arisen in October 2017 when all the experienced defense lawyers for al-Nashiri, the defendant charged with the 2000 bombing of the USS *Cole*, quit because they believed the military was monitoring their attorney-client communications. In November, Colonel Vance Spath, the presiding judge in the case, held Brigadier General John Baker, chief counsel for military commissions defense lawyers, in contempt of court for refusing to order the defense lawyers, who were civilian Pentagon employees, to return to their duties. Baker was held in confinement for several days until Harvey Rishikof, the convening authority of military commissions who had general supervisory authority over the system (including authority over charges, plea negotiations, and the selection of members or "jurors" of the commissions), ordered his release and suggested that the military should build a "clean" facility to ensure that no governmental monitoring was occurring. Soon thereafter, Rishikof's office also rejected, on procedural grounds, the charges prosecutors had recommended in the 2002 bombings in Bali, Inodonesia.[28]

A couple of months after these events, on February 3, 2018, Secretary of Defense James Mattis fired Rishikof, even though he had appointed him to his post less than a year before, in April 2017. On February 16, presumably because the defendants lacked experienced counsel, Colonel Spath suspended the case against al-Nashiri indefinitely.[29] Ammar al-Baluchi, one of the defendants in the 9/11 case, along with KSM, then filed a motion to dismiss the charges because Mattis's removal of Rishikof constituted an exercise of "unlawful command influence" over the convening authority. On February 27, Colonel James Pohl, the presiding judge in the 9/11 case, ordered Mattis to explain why he had fired Rishikof. In a March 19 affidavit, Mattis claimed he did it because of Rishikof's poor "management/corporate decision-making, professional judgment, and temperament," citing as one example Rishikof's attempt to obtain, outside regular channels, aerial imagery of the Guantanamo Bay Naval Base, and not because of Rishikof's "judicial or quasi-judicial acts." The next day Rishikof filed his own affidavit stating that he was unaware of any criticisms of his management style, but he noted that some of his decisions and recommendations concerning "conspiracy charges, capital charges, [and] guilty pleas in the 9/11 and USS *Cole* cases" were not popular with everyone.[30] In addition, Rishikof disclosed to Judge Pohl that he "was considering plea deals" in the 9/11 case and warned that his firing might undermine the ability of any future convening authority "to give fair, impartial, independent, and sound advice while understanding that any decision regarding a case could result in immediate termination of employment, suspension of credentials [such as national security clearances], and being escorted from the facility without advance discussion or notice."[31]

Rishikof's affidavit suggests that he was not fired because of his management style, but because Mattis, and perhaps President Trump, did not like him negotiating plea deals with terrorists facing the death penalty. Of course, the political price for such plea deals would be high because many Americans sympathize with the wishes of the families of the victims of these attacks. And it would be political officials, such as President Trump, who would have to pay the political price of these deals, not former high-level bureaucrats, such as Rishikof. However, that such a price might have to be paid is arguably the only way that the military commissions system can have the "independence" and the "impartiality" demanded by the "due process" clause of the Fifth Amendment and required by the standards of international law. As documented in **reading 6.4**, the ICRC argues that international customary law requires that war crimes be tried by "regularly constituted courts," which means they have to be "independent"—that is, they must have the ability to perform their "function independently of any other branch of government, especially the executive," and they have to be "impartial"—that is, "the court must not harbor preconceptions about the matter before them, nor act in a way that promotes the interests of one side."

The above events pose a number of questions: first, in your judgment, would Rishikof's firing qualify as "unlawful command influence"? To answer this question, is it appropriate to consider whether any new convening authority, to keep his or her job, will now likely take into account the wishes and preferences of superior officials, both military and civilian? Second, if you think there is evidence of "unlawful command influence," to what degree would your evaluation of it depend on domestic versus international law—that is, on the "due process" clause of the Fifth Amendment versus the ICRC's "Fair Trial Guarantees" sanctioned by customary international law? Finally, if the degree of "unlawful command influence" violates either "due process" or the requirements of international law, is there any way to "fix" the current system of military commissions, keeping in mind that the defendants entered U.S. military custody approximately fifteen years ago? Is the only viable remedy to close down the military commissions system and transfer all the defendants into the United States for trial in Article III civilian courts? Would such an option be politically popular? Should it matter? These questions will not disappear anytime soon, regardless of how Judge Pohl rules on al-Baluchi's motion to dismiss.

NOTES

1. Polybius, "Night Watches" and "The Tribunes' Court," in *Histories*, book 6, Perseus Digital Library, http://www.perseus.tufts.edu.

2. "The American Revolution, 1763–1783: Creating a Continental Army; The Continental Congress Establishes Articles of War," June 30, 1775, Library of Congress, https://www.loc.gov.

3. In May 1863, a military commission in Ohio convicted Clement Vallandigham, a member of the U.S. House of Representatives, of uttering disloyal sentiments and hindering the prosecution of the war and sentenced him to two years of imprisonment. Lincoln commuted the sentence and banished Vallandigham to the Confederacy, but he eventually ended up in Canada. Vallandigham's lawyers appealed the military commission's decision to the Supreme

Court, arguing that the commission did not have jurisdiction to try a civilian. In February 1864, the Supreme Court unanimously decided that it could not review Vallandigham's case since it did not have jurisdiction to hear appeals from military tribunals. See *Ex parte Vallandigham*, 68 U.S. 243 (1864).

4. Mark Neely, *The Fate of Liberty: Abraham Lincoln and the Civil Liberties* (New York: Oxford University Press, 1991).

5. Gary D. Solis, *The Law of Armed Conflict*, 2nd ed. (Cambridge: Cambridge University Press, 2016), 787.

6. Articles 227 and 228 are contained in part 7, Penalties of the Treaty of Versailles. "The Versailles Treaty," June 28, 1919, Yale Law School, Lillian Goldman Law Library, http://avalon.law.yale.edu.

7. Franklin D. Roosevelt, "Order Establishing a Military Commission to Try Eight Capture German Saboteurs," July 2, 1942, American Presidency Project, http://www.presidency.ucsb.edu.

8. *In re: Yamashita*, 327 U.S. 1 (1946).

9. See Solis, *Law of Armed Conflict*, 789.

10. "Convention (III) Relative to the Treatment of Prisoners of War," August 12, 1949, International Committee of the Red Cross (ICRC), https://ihl-databases.icrc.org.

11. "Convention (III)."

12. "Convention (III)."

13. W. Hays Parks, "1977 Protocols Additional to the Geneva Conventions: Customary International Law Implications," memorandum to Mr. John H. McNeill, assistant general counsel (international), OSD, May 9, 1986, Library of Congress, https://www.loc.gov.

14. Michael J. Matheson, "Remarks: The United States Position on the Relation of Customary International Law to the 1977 Protocols Additional to the 1949 Geneva Conventions," *American University Journal of International Law and Policy* 2 (1987): 427, http://digitalcommons.wcl.american.edu.

15. William H. Taft, IV, "The Law of Armed Conflict after 9/11: Some Salient Features," *Yale Journal of International Law* 28 (2003): 322, http://digitalcommons.law.yale.edu.

16. "Protocol Additional to the Geneva Conventions of 12 August 1949, and Relating to the Protection of Victims of International Armed Conflicts (Protocol I)," June 8, 1977, International Committee of the Red Cross (ICRC), https://ihl-databases.icrc.org. A set of rights comparable to those outlined in Article 75 of Additional Protocol I is contained in Article 14 of the International Covenant on Civil and Political Rights (ICCPR). The article entered into force March 23, 1976, and is available at "International Covenant on Civil and Political Rights," United Nations Human Rights Office of the High Commissioner, http://www.ohchr.org.

17. George W. Bush, "Detention, Treatment and Trial of Certain Non-Citizens in the War Against Terrorism," military order, November 13, 2001, 66 Fed. Reg. 57, 831-57836 (November 16, 2001), Federation of American Scientists, https://fas.org.

18. Jean-Marie Henckaerts and Louise Doswald-Beck, *Customary International Humanitarian Laws*, 2 vols. (Cambridge: Cambridge University Press, 2005), International Committee of the Red Cross (ICRC), https://ihl-databases.icrc.org.

19. Military Commissions Act of 2006, Public Law 109-366, October 17, 2006, Library of Congress, https://www.loc.gov.

20. Military Commission Act of 2009, Title VIII of the National Defense Authorization Act of 2010, Public Law 111-84, October 28, 2009, Office of Military Commissions, http://www.mc.mil.

21. *Al Bahlul v. United States (Al Bahlul I)*, 767 F.3d 1 (D.C. Cir. 2014) (en banc).

22. *Al Bahlul v. United States (Al Bahlul II)*, 792 F.3d 1 (D.C. Cir. 2015).

23. See "Bahlul v. United States: Petition for Certiorari Denied on October 10, 2017," *SCOTUS blog*, http://www.scotusblog.com.

24. For additional facts concerning the operations of the current system of military commissions, see the web page of the Office of Military Commissions at http://www.mc.mil.

25. Christina Wilkie and Marty Steinberg, "Trump Doubles Down that Alleged NYC Terrorist Should Get 'DEATH PENALTY!' That May Hurt Prosecution," CNBC, November 2, 2017, https://www.cnbc.com.

26. Wilkie and Steinberg, "Trump Doubles Down."

27. Benjamin Weiser, "Bike Path Terrorism Suspect Seeks Plea Deal to Avoid Death Penalty," *New York Times,* January 17, 2018, https://www.nytimes.com/2018/01/17/nyregion/saipov-bike-path-terrorist-death-penalty.html.

28. Charlie Savage, "Fired Pentagon Official Was Exploring Plea Deals for 9/11 Suspects at Guantanamo," *New York Times,* February 10, 2018, https://www.nytimes.com/2018/02/10/us/politics/guantanamo-sept-11-rishikof.html.

29. Charlie Savage, "Frustrated Military Tribunal Judge Indefinitely Halts *Cole* Bombing Case," *New York Times*, February 16, 2018, https://www.nytimes.com/2018/02/16/us/politics/guantanamo-cole.html.

30. See Stephen Szrom, "Summary: Declarations Regarding the Removal of Military Commission Convening Authority Rishikof," *Lawfare* (blog), March 23, 2018, https://www.lawfareblog.com/summary-declarations-regarding-removal-military-commission-convening-authority-rishikof.

31. Carol Rosenberg, "Fired War Court Overseer Says He Was Exploring Plea Deals in 9/11, USS *Cole* Cases," *Miami Herald*, March 22, 2018, http://www.miamiherald.com/news/nation-world/world/americas/guantanamo/article206477629.html.

7

Covert Action

★ ★ ★

Spying has been called the world's second oldest profession.[1] Homer's *Odyssey* and the Old Testament of the Bible support the truth of this characterization. Odysseus disguises himself to enter the city of Troy, and God himself ordered Moses to send spies into Canaan to find out the condition of the land and if the people who lived there were strong or weak, few or many.[2] But spying or espionage must be distinguished from "special operations" or "covert actions," both of which are twentieth-century terms that imply activity—often secret—to influence conditions or events. In other words, while spying refers to the collection of information, "covert action" has a more activist dimension. That does not mean covert action and spying are unrelated; often they are combined together in a symbiotic way. The spy first gathers information but then immediately acts on that information to achieve his or her objective. Examples would include the Greeks' use of the Trojan horse and the Old Testament tale of Samson and Delilah. Philistine leaders recruit Delilah to find out Samson's source of strength. Three times Samson misleads Delilah about his secret, but she continues to nag him, telling him that he would confide in her if he truly loved her. Samson gives up his secret, and Delilah shaves his head while he is sleeping. The Philistines then seize Samson and gouge out his eyes.[3] Delilah was not a mere spy; she was also a covert agent. She gathered information and then acted on behalf of the Philistines to change the political and military context of her time and place.

From these perhaps apocryphal beginnings, spying and covert action have had a flourishing history, far too large and varied to be summarized here. However, a few notable examples from American history will show that the new republic practiced "covert action" long before this particular term was coined after World War II. During the American Revolution, Benjamin Franklin, head of the American Commission in Paris, engaged in secret propaganda missions designed to foster French support for the American cause and secretly funneled French aid to the American revolutionaries. His efforts were so successful that the CIA in 1997 dedicated a conference room in his honor as a premier practitioner of the art of covert action.[4] During the American Civil War, with very limited success, the Confederacy relied on covert agents in Canada to foment rebellion and discontent in the northwestern states. During World War I, the United States and other allied countries ran operations aimed at aggravating and widening the ethnic divisions of the Austro-Hungarian Empire, while Germany launched a sabotage campaign in the United States to curtail the production and shipment of war materials.[5]

Although the above examples of "special operations" during wartime are historically important, covert action did not become a distinctive and centralized form of U.S. warfare until Franklin Roosevelt created the Office of Strategic Services (OSS) during World War II. At its height, the OSS had nearly twenty-four thousand personnel operating in both the European and Asian theaters. The mission of the OSS was twofold: to collect and analyze intelligence, but also to conduct and coordinate special military operations involving misinformation, propaganda, espionage, sabotage, the training and supply of resistance movements, and paramilitary operations. Some of these operations were "clandestine" in nature, which meant the OSS made every effort to keep the operation secret. Others were "covert" in that the OSS did its utmost to hide its sponsorship of the operation. Accordingly, an OSS covert action could be conducted in plain sight, without any effort to keep it hidden from the enemy or the general public, or it could be more clandestine in character. It would qualify as a "covert action" only if priority was given to preserving "plausible deniability" on the part of the OSS, that is, only if its sponsorship was hidden. Maintaining plausible deniability was especially important if the covert action involved unpopular, disreputable, or illegal conduct or if the covert action would become ineffective if the sponsor became known. For example, the OSS ran many black propaganda operations involving the spread of false rumors about German political leaders and military officials, rumors that were effective only if OSS sponsorship remained hidden.

President Harry Truman disbanded the OSS in October 1945, perhaps assuming that such covert and paramilitary capabilities would not be needed in peacetime. However, in January 1946 he created the Central Intelligence Group (CIG), which was to (1) "collect, evaluate, and disseminate intelligence" relating to the national security; (2) "plan for the coordination" of intelligence agencies; (3) perform "other services" that could be efficiently accomplished centrally; and (4) fulfill "such other functions" as the president and National Intelligence Authority may direct.[6] The following year in July, Congress enacted the National Security Act of 1947, which not only restructured the U.S. military but also created the National Security Council and the Central Intelligence Agency (CIA), the country's first peacetime, nonmilitary intelligence agency. Section 102(d) of the act assigned to the director of the CIA the following responsibilities:

> (1) to advise the National Security Council in matters concerning such intelligence activities of the Government departments and agencies as relate to national security;

(2) to make recommendations to the National Security Council for the coordination of such intelligence activities of the departments and agencies of the Government as relate to the national security;
(3) to correlate and evaluate intelligence relating to the national security, and provide for the appropriate dissemination of such intelligence within the Government using where appropriate existing agencies and facilities: PROVIDED, That the Agency shall have no police, subpoena, law-enforcement powers, or international security functions: PROVIDED FURTHER, That the departments and other agencies of the Government shall continue to collect, evaluate, correlate, and disseminate departmental intelligence: AND PROVIDED FURTHER, That the Director of Central Intelligence shall be responsible for protecting intelligence sources and methods from unauthorized disclosure;
(4) to perform, for the benefit of the existing intelligence agencies, such additional services of common concern as the National Security Council determines can be more efficiently accomplished centrally;
(5) to perform such other functions and duties related to intelligence affecting the national security as the National Security Council may from time to time direct.[7]

Some of these functions were comparable to those assigned to the CIG, but the latter two were quite vague in character. It was not clear whether Congress intended to authorize covert actions by one or both of these provisions.

The legislative record was murky. After a close examination of all the relevant transcripts, hearings, and legislative reports from 1947, the Select Committee to Study Governmental Operations with Respect to Intelligence Activities (the Church Committee) concluded in 1976 that there was insufficient evidence to answer the question. In the end, the report leans in the direction that Congress did not intend to authorize covert action, but it concedes there is no conclusive evidence either way.[8] In this context, it is noteworthy that Lawrence R. Houston, general counsel of the CIA, wrote a memorandum on September 25, 1947, arguing that any interpretation of the National Security Act of 1947 that authorized the CIA to conduct covert operations would be an "unwarranted extension" of the fourth and fifth functions assigned to the agency.

7.1 Lawrence R. Houston's Memorandum, September 25, 1947

1. A review of the National Security Act reveals two provisions [paragraphs 4 and 5 above] which might be construed as authority for CIA to engage in black propaganda or the type of activity known during the war as S.O. [Special Operations], which included ranger and commando raids, behind-the-lines sabotage, and support of guerilla warfare.[9] . . . Taken out of context and without knowledge of its history, these Sections could bear almost unlimited interpretation, provided the service performed could be shown to be of benefit to an intelligence agency or related to national intelligence.
2. Thus, black propaganda, primarily designed for subversion, confusion and political effect, can be shown incidentally to benefit positive intelligence as a means of checking reliability of informants, effectiveness of penetration, and so forth. Even certain forms of S.O. work could be held to benefit intelligence by establishment of W/T [wireless telegraph] teams in accessible

areas and by opening penetration points in confusion following sabotage or riot. In our opinion, however, either activity would be an unwarranted extension of the functions authorized in Sections 102 (d) (4) and (5). This is based on our understanding of the intent of Congress at the time these provisions were enacted.

3. A review of debates indicates that Congress was primarily interested in an agency for coordinating intelligence and originally did not propose any overseas collection activities for CIA. The strong move to provide specifically for such collection overseas was defeated, and, as a compromise, Section 102 (d) (4) and (5) were enacted, which permitted the National Security Council to determine the extent of the collection work to be performed by CIA. We do not believe that there was any thought in the minds of Congress that the Central Intelligence Agency under this authority would take positive action for subversion and sabotage. . . .
4. Aside from the discussions of normal departmental expenses for CIA as a whole, approval was given to the unvouchered funds requested by the Director of Central Intelligence mainly for the specific purposes of conducting clandestine intelligence operations outside the United States. We believe that there was no intent to use either the vouchered or unvouchered funds for M.O. [morale operations (propaganda)] or S.O. work. Either of these activities would require establishment of a new branch of office, employment of considerable personnel, the procurement of huge quantities of all types of goods and materials, and large sums for expenses of administrative support and incidentals. We believe this would be an [un]authorized use of the funds made available to CIA. It is our conclusion, therefore, that neither M.O. nor S.O. should be undertaken by CIA without previously informing Congress and obtaining its approval of the functions and the expenditure of funds for those purposes.
5. There is, however, one function now being properly performed by CIA which is so closely related to the matters discussed above as to be mentioned in connection therewith. An important by-product of the clandestine intelligence function is the acquisition of extensive information on plans in Western Europe for establishment of resistance movements in the event of further extension of Communist control. These plans include training of agents and W/Ts, organizing groups, providing outside contacts, and every other form of resistance. It is on such groups that M.O. and, particularly, S.O. would depend for most efficient function.
6. It is felt that this body of information might be the basis for consideration by the National Security Council, or a sub-committee thereof, in order to form a basic policy of cooperation with planned or actual resistance movements and to assign the implementation of such policy to the proper agency or body. If such implementation were then assigned to CIA, it would, we feel, still be necessary to go to Congress for authority and funds. . . .

Questions

1. Does Houston too quickly assume that history and context supports the conclusion that the National Security Act of 1947 did not grant the CIA authority to engage in covert actions when the CIA was in fact historically linked to the OSS through the CIG? Is it relevant that Houston himself was OSS's deputy chief of the Middle East theater during World War II? Is it possible that Houston intended his memo to keep most policymakers in the dark about the CIA's covert work?
2. Houston concedes that paragraphs 4 and 5 "could bear almost unlimited interpretation." Why would Congress use such broad language if it wanted to confine the CIA to a relatively narrow role of coordinating intelligence?
3. Why does Houston focus on the "incidental benefits" that covert operations may have on intelligence gathering

when covert operations are themselves arguably "intelligence activities" because they invariably collect information?

4. Does Houston contradict himself by saying that the CIA could engage in M.O. and S.O. work if it gets funding and Congress's approval? Does he mean that Congress would have to amend the National Security Act to broaden the CIA's authorities? Does he mean that appropriated funds would constitute legal authority for CIA covert actions even if the CIA was not statutorily authorized to engage in such activities?
5. Houston says that clandestine intelligence collection in Western Europe is a proper CIA function that produces extensive information on resistance movements that would oppose Communist expansion. Does his insight suggest that Congress did mean to confer covert action authority on the CIA when it referred to "other functions" in paragraph 5? In other words, is clandestine intelligence collection so closely linked to training and organizing resistance movements that it makes obvious sense to assign both functions to the same government entity?

Despite Houston's position that Congress did not intend to authorize CIA covert actions, there is some evidence that legislators in 1947 avoided explicit language so as not to tip off potential adversaries. For example, Representative Carter Manasco (D-AL) hesitated to say anything about the act for fear he might divulge something "that would give aid and comfort to any potential enemy we have." A related point is that members of Congress did not want to offend world public opinion.[10] The Senate had just ratified the UN Charter in 1945. Article 2 of the charter proclaimed the "sovereign equality of all its Members," mandated that all members settle their international disputes "by peaceful means" in a way that did not endanger international peace and security, and, finally, obliged all members to refrain from "the threat or the use of force against the territorial integrity or political independence of any state."[11] Against this background of international law, any explicit authorization of CIA covert action would have raised the question whether Congress was violating the spirit if not the letter of the UN Charter.

At the same time, the Truman administration could not ignore what was happening in Europe. In 1946, Winston Churchill had declared that an "Iron Curtain" divided Western and Eastern Europe, with the USSR not only dominating the communist governments of the eastern half but also doing what it could to subvert the democracies of the West. Worried that Greece and Turkey might fall next, President Truman in March 1947 ushered in the Cold War with his announcement that the United States would "support free peoples who are resisting attempted subjugation by armed minorities or by outside pressures,"[12] clearly referring to the expansionist tendencies of the USSR. A few months later, billions of dollars of economic aid were made available to European countries by way of the Marshall Plan.

In November 1947, two months after Houston wrote his memorandum, the National Security Council (NSC) instructed the CIA director to engage in covert psychological operations that would counteract and frustrate Soviet designs on Greece, Turkey, and other West European countries. Six months later, CIA covert action authority against the USSR was expanded to include sabotage, assistance to guerilla groups operating in hostile countries, support for refugee groups intent on liberating their home countries, and logistical training for anti-communists operating in countries threatened with subversion. In addition, the NSC, relying specifically on Section 102(d)(5) of the 1947 act, ordered the CIA to create an Office of Special Projects (OSP), one independent of all other "components" of the agency whose special mission would be covert operations.[13] In short, whether Congress intended the National Security Act of 1947 to authorize the CIA to engage in covert action, such authority quickly but secretly became the reality within a year of its enactment in the context of the perceived expansionist tendencies of the USSR.

A year later Congress enacted the Central Intelligence Agency Act of 1949. Although this law did not formally broaden the legal authorities of the CIA beyond the five listed in the 1947 act, it did include administrative provisions that exempted the CIA from normal reporting requirements regarding the receipt of unvouchered funds, the acquisition of material, the hiring of personnel, and the accounting for expended funds. Accordingly, by 1949 some members of Congress were aware that the CIA was playing a major clandestine role for the U.S. government and that this role included covert action. Certainly, relevant committees of Congress were fully informed, including the House and Senate Armed Services Committee, but it is possible that some members of Congress thought the administrative measures of the 1949 act were necessary for the CIA's clandestine intelligence-gathering mission.[14]

In any case, by 1949 doubts regarding the CIA's covert action authority had largely disappeared in the national security agencies of the executive branch. If Roosevelt could create the OSS during World War II, it seemed straightforward that Truman could authorize the CIA's covert action authority in the context of the Cold War under Article II of the Constitution, as long as Congress would provide some means of funding the secret operations. The 1949 act fulfilled this need.

During the same year that Congress enacted the Central Intelligence Agency Act, the International Court of Justice (ICJ) decided a case relating to Article 2's prohibition of the "use of force" by any state against the "territorial integrity" or "political independence" of any other state. The dispute was between Great Britain and Albania. On October 22, 1946, two British ships hit mines lying in the territorial waters of Albania in the Corfu Channel. Both ships were severely damaged, and eighty-six British officers and men were killed or injured. The British informed Albania that it intended to sweep the channel for mines, but the communist government of Albania refused to give its consent. Despite Albania's opposition, the British initiated "Operation Retail" on November 12 and 13 and swept the entire channel for mines. After reviewing the facts and the law, the ICJ held that Albania was culpable for the October 22 incident but that Britain had violated Albania's sovereignty by sweeping mines in its territorial waters. The case was the ICJ's first attempt to clarify the meaning of Article 2 of the UN Charter.

7.2 Corfu Channel Case, Judgment of April 9, 1949, ICJ Reports 1949

The United Kingdom Government does not dispute that "Operation Retail" was carried out against the clearly expressed wish of the Albanian Government.[15] It recognizes that . . . it could not be justified as the exercise of a right of innocent passage, and lastly that, in principle, international law does not allow a State to assemble a large number of warships in the territorial waters of another State and to carry out minesweeping in those waters. The United Kingdom Government states that the operation was one of extreme urgency, and that it considered itself entitled to carry it out without anybody's consent.

The United Kingdom Government put forward two reasons in justification. First, the Agreement of November 22, 1945, signed by the Governments of the United Kingdom, France, the Soviet Union, and the United States of America, authorizing regional mine clearance organizations, such as the Mediterranean Zone Board, to divide the sectors in their respective zones amongst the States concerned for sweeping. Relying on the circumstances that the Corfu Channel was in the sector allotted to Greece by the Mediterranean Zone Board on November 5th, i.e., before the signing of the above-mentioned [November 22nd] Agreement, the United Kingdom Government put forward a permission given by the Hellenic Government to resweep the navigable channel.

The Court does not consider this argument convincing.

It must be noted that, as the United Kingdom Government admits, the need for resweeping the Channel was not under consideration in November 1945; for previous sweeps in 1944 and 1945 were considered as having effected complete safety. As a consequence, the allocation of the sector in question to Greece, and therefore, the permission of the Hellenic Government which is relied on, were both of them merely nominal. It is also to be remarked that Albania was not consulted regarding the allocation to Greece of the sector in question, despite the fact that the Channel passed through Albanian territorial waters.

But, in fact, the explosions of October 22, 1946, in a channel declared safe for navigation, and one which the United Kingdom Government, more than any other government, had reason to consider safe, raised quite a different problem from that of a routine sweep carried out under the orders of the mineclearance organizations. These explosions were suspicious; they raised a question of responsibility.

Accordingly, this was the ground on which the United Kingdom Government chose to establish its main line of defense. According to that Government, the *corpora delicti* must be secured as quickly as possible, for fear they should be taken away, without leaving traces, by the authors of the minelaying or by the Albanian authorities. This justification took two distinct forms in the United Kingdom Government's arguments. It was presented first as a new and special application of the theory of intervention, by means of which the State intervening would secure possession of evidence in the territory of another State, in order to submit it to an international tribunal and thus facilitate its task.

The Court cannot accept such a line of defense. The Court can only regard the alleged right of intervention as the manifestation of a policy of force, such as has, in the past, given rise to most serious abuses and such as cannot, whatever be the defects in international organization, find a place in international law. Intervention is perhaps still less admissible in the particular form it would take here; for, from the nature of things, it would be reserved for the most powerful States, and might easily lead to perverting the administration of international justice itself.

The United Kingdom . . . has further classified "Operation Retail" among methods of self-protection or self-help. The Court cannot accept this defense either. Between independent States, respect for territorial sovereignty is an essential foundation of international relations. The Court recognizes that the Albanian Government's complete failure to carry out its duties after the explosions, and the dilatory nature of its diplomatic notes, are extenuating circumstances for the action of the United Kingdom Government. But to ensure respect for international law, of which it is the organ, the Court must declare that the action of the British Navy constituted a violation of Albanian sovereignty. . . .

Questions

1. Should Albania's culpability for knowing about the minefield, but not informing the British, have a bearing on whether Great Britain violated its sovereignty by sweeping the channel?
2. Was this a case of "extreme urgency," and should such urgency be enough to justify a violation of Albania's sovereignty?
3. Given the fact that Britain had received permission from Greece to sweep the channel on November 5, 1945, could it legally do so on November 12 and 13, 1946? Why does the ICJ call this permission "nominal"? Is it relevant that Albania had no minesweepers to clear the mines in the channel?
4. Britain's main defense was that it had to intrude upon Albania's sovereignty over its territorial waters to preserve evidence regarding who was responsible for laying the minefield in the first place. Why didn't the ICJ accept this defense? Do you agree with the court that such a defense might "pervert" the administration of international justice?
5. Britain's last claim was that "Operation Retail" was a method of "self-help." Why did the ICJ find this justification unpersuasive? Is this defense the same as self-defense? Why or why not?

The relevance of the ICJ's decision in the Corfu Channel case to the legality of the CIA's covert actions in European countries during the post–World War II period is not at all clear. First, it must be emphasized that this case involved British military ships engaged in an overt military activity in the territorial waters of another country without its consent. In contrast, CIA covert actions in foreign countries usually do not include U.S. military personnel, and the CIA may or may not have the consent of the host country or a faction thereof. In any case, the CIA by 1949 was actively involved in Eastern Europe, organizing and supplying resistance movements in Ukraine, Poland, and Czechoslovakia. Moreover, in the Italian general election of April 1948, the CIA is reported to have spent $10 million to defeat the Communists and ensure the victory of the Christian Democrats, the first of many CIA efforts to influence Italian elections. A comparable effort was made to undermine communist influence over the Italian and French trade associations.[16] Perhaps such interference in the domestic elections and labor groups would not violate the "territorial integrity" of the French or Italian state, but did they "threaten" or "protect" the "political independence" of Italy and France in the context of communist expansionism?

Whether the ICJ would have deemed some of these CIA covert actions violations of international law in the immediate post–World War II period, the pace and size of such operations picked up quickly in the early 1950s. The CIA office in charge of covert action expanded from 302 personnel in 1949 to 2,812 in 1952, while its budget increased from $4.7 million in 1949 to $82 million in 1952.[17] Major operations during the 1950s and 1960s include the 1953 overthrow of Mohammed Mossadegh, the prime minister of Iran, and the installation of the Shah of Iran, a strong ally of the United States until the Islamic Revolution in 1979; the 1954 coup d'etat against the administration of Jacob Arbenz, the president of Guatemala; the 1961 Bay of Pigs operation involving 1,500 Cuban exiles invading Cuba in a futile effort to bring down the regime of Fidel Castro; involvement in the 1961 assassinations of Rafael Trujillo, dictator of the Dominican Republic, and Patrice Lumumba, prime minister of the Congo; the 1964 military coup against the civilian government of Brazil; the 1965 overthrow of Sukarno in Indonesia; and the Phoenix Program, which consisted of capturing, interrogating, and assassinating Viet Cong officials and sympathizers during the Vietnam War.

The period from 1949 until 1970 was something of a "golden age" for CIA covert action. There was very little oversight by Congress, and the American public was largely unaware of what the CIA was doing around the world. Although there were rumors and speculation, the CIA worked hard to maintain "plausible deniability" concerning the above operations. And though the above list includes setbacks and failures, such as the Bay of Pigs fiasco, the CIA by 1970 had become the primary means by which the United States covertly shaped and influenced foreign events and trends. Whether these covert actions were consistent with international law or basic principles of American political morality is a separate question. The General Assembly of the United Nations indirectly addressed this issue in Resolution 2625, adopted on October 24, 1970. The focus of the resolution was on the principles of international law that governed friendly relations and cooperation among states in accordance with the UN Charter. Although technically not binding on member states, the resolution is relevant evidence regarding the substance or emergence of customary international law.

7.3 General Assembly Resolution 2625

Having considered the principles of international law relating to friendly relations and co-operation among States,[18]

1. [The General Assembly] Solemnly proclaims the following principles: . . .

Every State has the duty to refrain in its international relations from the threat or use of force against the territorial integrity or political independence of any State, or in any other manner inconsistent with the purposes of the United Nations. Such a threat or use of force constitutes a violation of international law and the Charter of the United Nations and shall never be employed as a means of settling international issues. . . .

Every State has the duty to refrain from organizing or encouraging the organization of irregular forces or armed bands including mercenaries, for incursion into the territory of another State.

Every State has the duty to refrain from organizing, instigating, assisting or participating in acts of civil strife or terrorist acts in another State or acquiescing in organized activities within its territory directed towards the commission of such acts, when the acts referred to in the present paragraph involve a threat or use of force. . . .

No State or group of States has the right to intervene, directly or indirectly, for any reason whatever, in the internal or external affairs of any other State. Consequently, armed intervention and all other forms of interference or attempted threats against the personality of the State or against its political, economic and cultural elements, are in violation of international law.

No State may use or encourage the use of economic, political or any other type of measure to coerce another State in order to obtain from it the subordination of the exercise of its sovereign rights and to secure from it advantage of any kind. Also, no State shall organize, assist, foment, finance, incite, or tolerate subversive, terrorist or armed activities directed towards the violent overthrow of the regime of another State, or interfere in civil strife in another State. . . .

By virtue of the principle of equal rights and self-determination of peoples enshrined in the Charter of the United Nations, all peoples have the right freely to determine, without external interference, their political status and to pursue their economic, social, and cultural development, and every State has the duty to respect this right in accordance with the provisions of the Charter. . . .

Questions

1. Can you imagine a CIA covert operation that would not constitute a "threat" to the "political independence" of a state? What if a small faction of the state cooperated with the CIA's operation? Would that be enough to render it legitimate in terms of Resolution 2625?
2. According to the resolution, states not only have a duty to refrain from the "threat or use of force" against the "territorial integrity" or "political independence" of any state but also have a duty to refrain from any "threat" of force that would be "inconsistent with the purposes of the United Nations." Is there any kind of "threat" or "use" of force that would be consistent with the purposes of the UN?
3. If it is a violation of customary international law to organize or encourage irregular forces or armed bands for incursion into the territory of another state or to organize, instigate, assist, or participate "in acts of civil strife," are all CIA attempts at coups d'etat violations of international law?
4. Contrary to the resolution, can you imagine a situation where a state may lawfully intervene "directly or indirectly" in the "internal or external affairs" of another state?
5. According to the resolution, no state can use "economic" or "political" measures "to coerce" the exercise of another state's "sovereign rights." Would this provision prohibit the use of economic sanctions? What kind of "coercion" does this provision prohibit?
6. Is the principle of "equal rights and self-determination" enshrined in the UN Charter a utopian dream? How would you make it a workable reality?

In 1970, socialist Salvador Allende was elected president of Chile. Alarmed by this development, the Nixon administration authorized the CIA to organize a military coup that would bring down the Allende regime. The coup took place in 1973, and it resulted in a military junta led by General Augusto Pinochet. During the same time frame, the Watergate affair and the Vietnam War seriously eroded American trust in their political institutions and leaders. In addition, the 1975–1976 revelations of the Church Committee also shocked the American people. The Federal Bureau of Investigation, the National Security Agency, and the CIA had been deeply involved with illegal activities, including illegal wiretapping, surveillance of American citizens and domestic political groups, opening the mail of U.S. residents, spreading disinformation about civil rights leaders, and human experimentation with LSD and other psychedelic drugs. The Church Committee also confirmed that the CIA had been involved with political assassinations in foreign countries and published a staff report that went into painful detail concerning the CIA's role in the military coup in Chile.[19]

One aspect of the history of CIA covert action uncovered by the Church Committee was that many such operations were implemented with little or no supervision or approval by anyone outside the CIA. The president and Congress could "plausibly deny" knowledge of an operation, thereby to some extent absolving them of political and legal responsibility. In 1974, Congress addressed this problem with the Hughes-Ryan Amendment, which prohibited the expenditure of appropriated funds by or on behalf of the CIA for any operation, other than an intelligence-gathering operation,

> unless and until the President finds that each such operation is important to the national security of the United States and reports, in a timely fashion, a description and scope of such operation to the appropriate committees of the Congress, including the Committee on Foreign Relations of the United States Senate and the Committee on Foreign Affairs of the United States House of Representatives.[20]

In effect, the Hughes-Ryan Amendment set up procedural mechanisms (both the presidential finding and the timely notice to Congress) that would increase both executive branch supervision and congressional oversight of the CIA's covert action program.

With the Intelligence Oversight Act of 1980, Congress streamlined congressional oversight by requiring only the House and Senate Intelligence Committees to be kept "fully and currently informed of all intelligence activities for which the United States is responsible." However, the law extended this duty to keep the intelligence committees informed from the president to the heads of all the intelligence agencies and defined the phrase "significant anticipated intelligence activity" to include all CIA covert actions. The implication was that the Director of the CIA was obliged to give the intelligence committees prior notice of all covert actions, at least when they were "anticipated." The law made only one exception to this rule. The president could limit prior notice to the so-called Gang of Eight—the Speaker of the House and House minority leader; Senate majority and minority leaders; and the chair and ranking member of the two intelligence committees—when it was necessary "to meet extraordinary circumstances affecting vital interest of the United States." Finally, the law imposed on the "heads" of all intelligence entities a duty to report to the intelligence committees "in a timely fashion" any illegal intelligence activity that they became aware of in the course of their duties.[21]

The Reagan administration more or less ignored these provisions of the 1980 Oversight Act during the Iran-Contra affair of the 1980s. The affair consisted of two major CIA covert action programs that were financially linked together. First, the administration authorized the CIA to provide military training and support to the Contras, an insurgent group fighting the left-wing Sandinista regime of Nicaragua, as well as to engage in separate independent operations against the Sandinistas, such as the mining of Nicaraguan harbors and the bombing of

Nicaraguan ports. The second major piece of the Iran-Contra affair was a secret program of selling arms to Iran to gain the release of American hostages held in Lebanon. As news reports about the administration's support for the Contras surfaced in 1982 and 1983, Congress tightened restrictions on aid to the Contras by enacting the 1984 Boland Amendment, which prohibited any U.S. "agency or entity" involved with "intelligence activities" from providing support for any "military or paramilitary operations in Nicaragua by any nation, group, organization, movement, or individual."[22] In response to the amendment, the Reagan administration shifted control of the Contra covert operation from the CIA to the National Security Council (NSC), relying on the questionable assumption that the NSC was not an "entity" involved with "intelligence activities."

Two years later, in 1986, a Beirut newspaper reported that the United States had, with the help of Israel, secretly sold arms to Iran, in violation of a U.S. arms embargo on Iran and a law that generally prohibited transfers of weapons to countries, such as Iran, that supported international terrorism. The president could authorize a transfer of weapons to such a country only if he signed a finding that the transfer was necessary for national security and only if notice of the finding was sent to Congress. Reagan failed to provide such notice, and news reports soon revealed that the proceeds of the arms sales to Iran, along with other funds, had been given to the Contras, arguably in violation of the 1984 Boland Amendment.

Both the Senate and the House of Representatives established committees to investigate the Iran-Contra affair in early 1987. The two committees held joint hearings and issued a joint majority report in November 1987. Eighteen senators and members of the House signed the joint majority report, which was harshly critical of the Reagan administration's covert action policy, concluding that it exhibited a "disdain for the law" and a failure to respect Congress's legitimate oversight role. However, two Republican senators and six Republican members of the House, including Dick Cheney (R-WY), the ranking Republican on the House committee and future vice president during the George W. Bush administration, refused to accept the majority's conclusions. The minority report conceded that the Reagan administration had made "mistakes of judgment" but "nothing more," in particular no violations of law or the Constitution. In fact, according to the minority report, the underlying problem of the Iran-Contra affair was not an abuse of executive powers but rather "an aggrandizing theory of Congress' foreign policy powers," along with a refusal by Congress to recognize that it was the president who was the country's constitutionally sanctioned "foreign policy leader." These two reports illuminate sharply contrasting reactions to the Iran-Contra affair and the role covert action should play in U.S. democracy.

7.4 Report of the Congressional Committees Investigating the Iran-Contra Affair

The very premise of democracy is that "we the people" are entitled to make our own choice on fundamental policies.[23] But freedom of choice is illusory if policies are kept, not only from the public, but from its elected representatives. . . .

1. *Covert Operations.* Covert operations should be conducted in accordance with strict rules of accountability and oversight. In the mid-1970s, in response to disclosures of abuses within the intelligence community, the Government enacted a series of safeguards. Each covert action was to be approved personally by the President, funded by Congressional appropriations, and Congress was to be informed.

In the Iran-Contra Affair, these rules were violated. The President, according to [Admiral John] Poindexter, was never informed of the diversion [of funds to the Contras]. The President says he knew nothing of the covert action to support the Contras, or the companies funded by non-appropriated monies set up by [Colonel Oliver] North to carry out that support. Congress was not notified of either the Iran or the Contra operations.

Covert actions should be consistent with publicly defined U.S. foreign policy goals. Because covert operations are secret by definition, they are of course not openly debated or publicly approved. So long as the policies which they further are known, and so long as they are conducted in accordance with law, covert operations are acceptable. Here, however, the Contra covert operation was carried out in violation of the country's public policy as expressed in the Boland Amendment; and the Iran covert operation was carried out in violation of the country's stated policy against selling arms to Iran or making concessions to terrorists. These were not covert actions, they were covert policies; and covert policies are incompatible with democracy.

Finally, covert operations are intended to be kept from foreign powers, not from the Congress and responsible Executive agencies within the United States Government itself. As Clair George, CIA Director of Operations, testified: "to think that because we deal in lies, and overseas we may lie and we may do other such things, that therefore that gives you some permission, some right or some particular reason to operate that way with your fellow employees, I would not only disagree with that, I would say it would be the destruction of a secret service in a democracy." In the Iran-Contra Affair, secrecy was used to justify lies to Congress, the Attorney General, other Cabinet officers, and the CIA. It was used not as a shield against our adversaries, but as a weapon against our own democratic institutions. . . .

2. *Disdain for Law.* In the Iran-Contra Affair, officials viewed the law not as setting boundaries for their actions, but raising impediments to their goals. When the goals and the law collided, the law gave way:

The covert program of support for the Contras evaded the Constitution's most significant check on Executive power: the President can spend funds on a program only if he can convince Congress to appropriate the money.

When Congress enacted the Boland Amendment, cutting off funds for the war in Nicaragua, Administration officials raised funds for the Contras from other sources—foreign governments, the Iran arms sales, and private individuals. . . . Conducting the covert program in Nicaragua with funding from the sale of U.S. Government property and contributions raised by Government officials was a flagrant violation of the Appropriations Clause of the Constitution.

In addition, the covert program of support for the Contras was an evasion of the letter and spirit of the Boland Amendment. The President made it clear that while he opposed restrictions on military or paramilitary assistance to the Contras, he recognized that compliance with the law was not optional. "[W]hat I might personally wish or what our Government might wish still would not justify us violating the law of the land," he said in 1983.

A year later, members of the NSC staff were devising ways to continue support and direction of Contra activities during the period of the Boland Amendment. What was previously done by the CIA—and now prohibited by the Boland Amendment—would be done instead by the NSC staff.

The President set the stage by welcoming a huge donation for the Contras from a foreign Government—a contribution clearly intended to keep the Contras in the field while U.S. aid was barred. The NSC staff thereafter solicited other foreign Governments for military aid, facilitated the efforts of U.S.

fundraisers to provide lethal assistance to the Contras, and ultimately developed and directed a private network that conducted, in North's words, a "full service covert operation" in support of the Contras.

This could not have been more contrary to the intent of the Boland Amendment.

Numerous other laws were disregarded:

- North's full-service covert operation was a "significant anticipated intelligence activity" required to be disclosed to the Intelligence Committees of Congress. . . . No such disclosure was made.
- By Executive Order, a covert operation requires a personal determination by the President before it can be conducted by an agency other than the CIA. It requires a written Finding before any agency can carry it out. In the case of North's full-service covert operation in support of the Contras, there was no such personal determination and no such Finding. In fact, the President disclaims any knowledge of this covert action.
- False statement to Congress are felonies if made with knowledge and intent. Several Administration officials gave statements denying NSC staff activities in support of the Contras which North later described in his testimony as "false," and "misleading, evasive, and wrong."
- The application of proceeds from U.S. arms sales for the benefit of the Contra war effort violated the Boland ban on U.S. military aid to the Contras, and constituted a misappropriation of Government funds derived from the transfer of U.S. property.
- The U.S. Government's approval of the pre-Finding 1985 sales by Israel of arms to the Government of Iran was inconsistent with the Government's obligations under the Arms Export Control Act.
- The testimony to Congress in November 1986 that the U.S. Government had no contemporaneous knowledge of the Israeli shipments, and the shredding of documents relating to the shipments while a Congressional inquiry into those shipments was pending, obstructed Congressional investigations.
- The Administration did not make, and clearly intended never to make, disclosure to the Intelligence Committees of the Finding—later destroyed—approving the November 1985 HAWK shipment [of missiles], nor did it disclose the covert action to which the Finding related.

The Committees make no determination as to whether any particular individual involved in the Iran-Contra Affair acted with criminal intent or was guilty of any crime. That is a matter for the Independent Counsel and the courts. But the Committees reject any notion that worthy ends justify violations of law by Government officials; and the Committees condemn without reservation the making of false statements to Congress and the withholding, shredding, and alteration of documents relevant to a pending inquiry.

Administration officials have, if anything, an even greater responsibility than private citizens to comply with the law. There is no place in Government for law breakers.

3. *Congress and the President.* The Constitution of the United States gives important powers to both the President and the Congress in the making of foreign policy. The President is the principal architect of foreign policy in consultation with the Congress. The policies of the United States cannot succeed unless the President and the Congress work together.

Yet, in the Iran-Contra Affair, Administration officials holding no elected office repeatedly evidenced disrespect for Congress' efforts to perform its Constitutional oversight role in foreign policy [by not keeping Congress informed and by making false statements to Congress]. . . .

- Poindexter testified, referring to his efforts to keep the covert action in support of the Contras from Congress: "I simply did not want any outside interference."
- North testified: "I didn't want to tell Congress anything about this covert action." . . .
- And numerous other officials made false statements to, and misled, the Congress.

Several witnesses at the hearings stated or implied that foreign policy should be left solely to the President to do as he chooses, arguing that shared powers have no place in a dangerous world. But the theory of our Constitution is the opposite; policies formed through consultation and the democratic process are better and wiser than those formed without it. Circumvention of Congress is self-defeating, for no foreign policy can succeed without the bipartisan support of Congress.

In a system of shared powers, decision-making requires mutual respect between the branches of government. . . .

MINORITY REPORT, CONGRESSIONAL COMMITTEES INVESTIGATING THE IRAN-CONTRA AFFAIR

The bottom line . . . is that the mistakes of the Iran-Contra Affair were just that—mistakes in judgment, and nothing more. There was no constitutional crisis, no systematic disrespect for the "rule of law," no grand conspiracy, and no Administration-wide dishonesty or coverup. In fact, the evidence will not support any of the more hysterical conclusions the Committees' Report tries to reach. . . .

The excesses of the Committees' Report are reflections of something far more profound. Deeper than the specifics of the Iran-Contra Affair lies an underlying and festering institutional wound these Committees have been unwilling to face. In order to support rhetorical overstatement about democracy and the rule of law, the Committees have rested their case upon an aggrandizing theory of Congress' foreign policy powers that is itself part of the problem. . . .

The country's future security depends upon a modus vivendi in which each branch recognizes the other's legitimate and constitutionally sanctioned sphere of activity. Congress must recognize that an effective foreign policy requires, and the Constitution mandates, the President to be the country's foreign policy leader. . . . No President can ignore Congress and be successful over the long term. Congress must realize, however, that the power of the purse does not make it supreme. . . .

Finally, the Committees' Report tries—almost as an overarching thesis—to portray the Administration as if it were behaving with wanton disregard for the law. In our view, every single one of the Committees' legal interpretations is open to serious questions. On some issues—particularly the ones involving the statutes governing covert operations—we believe the law to be clearly on the Administration's side. . . . What the Committees' Report has done with the legal questions, however, is to issue a one-sided legal brief that pretends the Administration did not even have worthwhile arguments to make. As if that were not enough, the Report tries to build upon these one-sided assertions to present a politicized picture of an Administration that behaved with contempt for the law. If nothing else would lead readers to view the report with extreme skepticism, the adversarial tone of the legal discussion should settle the matter. . . .

AFTERWORD: SUMMARY OF LEGAL CONCLUSIONS

[I.] Nicaragua

The main period under review during these investigations was October 1984 through October 1986. During this period, various versions of the Boland Amendment restricted the expenditure of appropriated funds available to agencies or entities involved in intelligence activities from being spent directly or indirectly to support military or paramilitary operations in Nicaragua. . . .

(1) The Constitution protects the power of the President, either acting himself or through agents of his choice, to engage in whatever diplomatic communications with other countries he may wish. It also protects the ability of the President and his agents to persuade U.S. citizens to engage voluntarily in otherwise legal activity to serve what they consider to be the national interest. That includes trying to persuade other countries to contribute their own funds for causes both countries support. To whatever extent the Boland Amendments tried to prohibit such activity, they were clearly unconstitutional.

(2) If the Constitution prohibits Congress from restricting a particular Presidential

action directly, it cannot use the appropriations power to achieve the same unconstitutional effect. Congress does have the power under the Constitution, however, to use appropriations riders to prohibit the entire U.S. Government from spending any money, including salaries, to provide covert or overt military support to the Contras. Thus, the Clark Amendment prohibiting all U.S. support for the Angolan Resistance in 1976 was constitutional. Some members of Congress may have thought they were enacting a prohibition as broad as the Clark Amendment. The specific language of the Boland Amendment was considerably more restricted, however, in two respects.

(a) By limiting the coverage to agencies or entities involved in intelligence activities, Congress chose to use language borrowed directly from the Intelligence Oversight Act of 1980. In the course of settling on that language in 1980, Congress deliberately decided to exclude the National Security Council (NSC) from its coverage. At no time afterward did Congress indicate an intention to change the language's coverage. The NSC therefore was excluded from the Boland Amendment and its activities were therefore legal under this statute.

(b) The Boland prohibitions also were limited to spending that directly or indirectly supported military or paramilitary operations in Nicaragua. Under this language, a wide range of intelligence-gathering and political support activities were still permitted, and were carried out with the full knowledge of the House and Senate Intelligence Committees. . . .

[II.] Iran

The Administration was also in substantial compliance with the laws governing covert actions throughout the Iran arms initiative.

(1) It is possible to make a respectable legal argument to the effect that the 1985 Israeli arms transfers to Iran technically violated the terms of the Arms Export Control Act (AECA) or Foreign Assistance Act (FAA), assuming the arms Israel transferred were received from the United States under one or the other of these statutes. However:

(a) Covert transfers under the National Security Act . . . were understood to be alternatives to transfers under the AECA and FAA that met both of these latter acts' essential purposes by including provisions for Presidential approval and Congressional notification.

(b) The requirement for U.S. agreement before a country can retransfer arms obtained from the United States is meant to insure that retransfers conform to U.S. national interests. In this case, the Israeli retransfers occurred with Presidential approval indicating that they did so conform.

(c) The Israeli retransfer and subsequent replenishment [by the United States] made the deal essentially equivalent to a direct U.S. sale, with Israel playing a role fundamentally equivalent to that of a middleman. Since the United States could obviously have engaged in a direct transfer, and did so in 1986, whatever violation may have occurred was, at most, a minor and inadvertent technicality.

(2) A verbal approval for covert transactions meets the requirements of the Hughes-Ryan Amendment and National Security Act. Verbal approval ought to be reduced to writing as a matter of sound policy, but they are not illegal.

(3) Similarly, the President has the constitutional and statutory authority to withhold notifying Congress of covert activities under very rare conditions. President Reagan's decision to withhold notification was essentially equivalent to President Carter's decisions in 1979–1980 to withhold notice for between 3 and 6 months in parallel Iran hostage operations. We do not agree with President Reagan's decision to withhold notification for as long as he did. The decision was legal, however, and we think the Constitution mandates that it should remain so. If a President withholds notification for too long and then cannot adequately justify the decision to Congress, that President can expect to pay a stiff political price, as President Reagan has certainly found out. . . .

Questions

1. Is it believable that President Reagan was not told that the proceeds of the arms sales to Iran were being used to fund the Contras? If it is believable, how does this fact bear upon the legitimacy of covert action in a democracy?
2. The majority report argues that covert actions should be consistent with the public policy of the United States. What is the rationale for this requirement if an operation is "covert" for the purpose of hiding U.S. sponsorship? Do you support or oppose this requirement?
3. What do you make of the report's distinction between "covert actions" and "covert policies"? Are the latter really "incompatible" with democracy? Why?
4. Do you agree with the majority report's assessment that raising funds for the Contras from foreign governments, the arms sales to Iran, and private individuals was a "flagrant" violation of the appropriations clause of the Constitution? Did it violate the letter of the Boland Amendment? The "spirit" of the amendment?
5. If the NSC, rather than the CIA, raised nonappropriated funds for the Contras, would it nonetheless constitute a "covert" action that must be disclosed to the congressional intelligence committees?
6. The majority report argues that covert actions will be "better and wiser" if they are formed through "consultation and the democratic process." Do you agree?
7. The minority report claims that the majority report is a "one-sided legal brief" that presents a "politicized picture" of the Reagan administration. Is there any validity to this claim?
8. In what sense does the minority report claim that the Boland Amendment is unconstitutional?
9. The minority report concedes that Congress can use the appropriations power to prohibit the entire U.S. government from supporting the Contras but argues that it cannot use this power to limit the president's options more narrowly, for example, by prohibiting certain executive agencies and departments from supplying military support or training to the Contras. Does this distinction make any sense?

The Iran-Contra Affair was controversial not only in terms of domestic constitutional and statutory law but also in terms of international law. The primary question was whether the CIA's military and paramilitary support for the Contras against the Sandinista regime of Nicaragua, along with certain independent actions that the CIA took against the Sandinista regime (such as mining Nicaraguan harbors and bombing the country's ports, oil storage facilities, and naval bases), was in violation of international law. In 1984, Nicaragua sued the United States in the International Court of Justice (ICJ), the primary judicial institution within the United Nations, claiming that the U.S. program of covert action constituted an act of aggression in violation of Article 2(4) of the UN Charter and customary international law. Although the United States had not consented to the jurisdiction of the ICJ in disputes under the charter, the ICJ reviewed Nicaragua's claims under customary international law and concluded that the covert actions of the United States violated the international norms governing the "threat" or "use" of force. Even if U.S. covert actions against Nicaragua fell short of "acts of war," they were nonetheless violations of international law.

7.5 *Nicaragua v. United States* (1986) I.C.J. 14

227. . . . What is . . . [a violation of customary international law, as embodied in Article 2, paragraph 4 of the UN Charter] . . . is recourse to either the threat or the use of force against the territorial integrity or political independence of any State.[24] For the most part, the complaints by Nicaragua are of the actual use of force against it by the United States. Of the acts which the Court has found imputable to the Government of the United States, the following are relevant in this respect:

- the laying of mines in Nicaraguan internal or territorial waters . . . ;
- certain attacks on Nicaraguan ports, oil installations and a naval base. . . .

These activities constitute infringements of the principle of the prohibition of the use of force . . . unless they are justified by circumstances which exclude their unlawfulness. . . .

228. . . . As to the claim that United States activities in relation to the *contras* constitute a breach of the customary international law principle of the non-use of force, the Court finds that, subject to the question whether the action of the United States might be justified as an exercise of the right of self-defense, the United States has committed a prima facie violation of that principle by its assistance to the *contras* in Nicaragua by "organizing or encouraging the organization of irregular forces or armed bands . . . for incursion into the territory of another State." . . . [Assistance] of this kind is contrary to the principle of the prohibition of the use of force when the acts of civil strife referred to "involve a threat or use of force." In the view of the Court, while the arming and training of the *contras* can certainly be said to involve the threat or use of force against Nicaragua, this is not necessarily so in respect of all the assistance given by the United States Government. In particular, the Court considers that the mere supply of funds to the *contras*, while undoubtedly an act of intervention in the internal affairs of Nicaragua . . . does not in itself amount to a use of force.

229. The Court must thus consider whether . . . the acts in question of the United States are justified by the exercise of its right of collective self-defense. . . . For the Court to conclude that the United States was lawfully exercising its right of collective self-defense, it must first find that Nicaragua engaged in an armed attack against El Salvador, Honduras or Costa Rica. . . . [The Court concludes that Nicaragua's alleged provision of arms to the opposition in El Salvador and its alleged incursions into the territories of Honduras and Costa Rica did not qualify as armed attacks.]

232. The exercise of the right of collective self-defense presupposes that an armed attack has occurred; and it is evident that it is the victim State, being the most directly aware of that fact, which is likely to draw general attention to its plight. It is also evident that if the victim State wishes another State to come to its help in the exercise of the right of collective self-defense, it will normally make an express request to that effect. Thus, in the present instance, the Court is entitled to take account, in judging the asserted justification of the exercise of collective self-defense by the United States, of the actual conduct of El Salvador, Honduras, and Costa Rica at the relevant time, as indicative of a belief by the State in question that it was the victim of an armed attack by Nicaragua, and of the making of a request by the victim State to the United States for help in the exercise of collective self-defense. . . . [The Court concludes that none of the three states requested help from the United States before the United States mined Nicaragua's ports and attacked its facilities.]

235. . . . [Also, at] no time . . . has the United States Government . . . [filed] the report which is required by Article 51 of the United Nations Charter in respect of measures which a State believes itself bound to take when it exercises the right of individual or collective self-defense. . . . This fact is all the more noteworthy because in the Security Council, the United States has itself taken the view that

failure to observe the requirement to make a report contradicted a State's claim to be acting on the basis of collective self-defense. . . .

237. . . . [Additional factors that the Court must consider are the canons of necessity and proportionality, which] may constitute an additional ground of wrongfulness. On the question of necessity, the Court observes . . . [that the actions of the United States] were only taken . . . several months after the major offensive of the armed opposition against the Government of El Salvador had been completely repulsed (January 1981), and the actions of the opposition considerably reduced in consequence. Thus it was possible to eliminate the main danger to the Salvadorian Government without the United States embarking on activities in and against Nicaragua. Accordingly, it cannot be held that these activities were undertaken in the light of necessity. . . . [Regarding proportionality, the Court also observed that, whatever] uncertainty may exist as to the exact scale of the aid received by the Salvadorian armed opposition from Nicaragua, it is clear that . . . [mining Nicaragua's ports and attacking its facilities] could not have been proportionate to that aid. Finally on this point, the Court must also observe that the reaction of the United States in the context of what it regarded as self-defense was continued long after the period in which any presumed armed attack by Nicaragua could reasonably be contemplated.

238. Accordingly, the Court concludes that the plea of collective self-defense against an alleged armed attack on El Salvador, Honduras, or Costa Rica, . . . cannot be upheld; and accordingly that the United States has violated the principle prohibiting recourse to the threat or use of force . . . and by its assistance to the contras to the extent that this assistance "involve[s] a threat or use of force." . . .

Questions

1. Is the ICJ correct that the CIA covert assistance to the Contras was in fact equivalent to a "threat" or "use" of force in violation of Article 2?
2. Do you agree with the ICJ that a country can invoke individual or collective self-defense only if an armed attack "has occurred"? Does this rule preclude the legitimacy of using covert action to respond to an imminent attack? What about a probable attack that is not imminent?
3. Why did the ICJ conclude that the CIA violated the international law's prohibition of the use of force by arming, training, and encouraging the Contras but then find that Nicaragua's support for the opposition forces in El Salvador did not constitute an armed attack that would justify collective self-defense? What is the difference between the two cases?
4. The ICJ seems to endorse the rule that a victim state must publicly request help before another state can use paramilitary action against the attacking state. Do you agree with this rule? What if the victim state wants the military assistance to be provided covertly? Why is that option not acceptable?
5. Even if an armed attack "has occurred," the ICJ argues, the victim state or helping state can only respond in accordance with the "canons of necessity and proportionality." What do these two additional requirements mean, and how are they applicable to CIA paramilitary covert actions?

In response to the Reagan administration's failures to comply with the provisions of the Intelligence Oversight Act of 1980, Congress enacted a number of reforms in the Intelligence Authorization Act, Fiscal Year 1991. First, the law preserved the existing duty imposed on the president and the heads of intelligence agencies to keep the congressional intelligence committees "fully and currently informed" of all intelligence activities, including all covert actions approved by the president. Second, to approve a covert action, the president must "determine" that the action in question is necessary to support identifiable foreign policy objectives of the United States and is important to the national security of the United States. Third, this determination must be set forth in a *written* "finding," but in case of an emergency, the president has forty-eight hours to submit it. Fourth, a "finding" could not authorize any covert action that already had occurred; it had to specify each government agency or entity that was participating in the covert action, as well as any third party, such as a foreign government or other foreign entity; and it could not authorize any action that violated "the Constitution or any statute of the United States."[25]

The 1991 law maintained the president's right not to keep the congressional committees "fully and currently informed" if it was "essential to limit access to the finding to meet extraordinary circumstances affecting vital interests of the United States." In such a situation, the president had to report the "finding" to the so-called Gang of Eight, "fully [but not currently] inform the congressional intelligence committees in a timely fashion," and "provide a statement of the reasons for not giving prior notice." Moreover, 180 days after the president has provided such a statement of reasons to the congressional intelligence committees, he must provide all members of the intelligence committees with access to the finding or supply the Gang of Eight with a "statement of reasons" why it was "essential" to continue to "limit access to the finding to meet extraordinary circumstances affecting vital interests of the United States."[26]

The 1991 act also included a statutory definition of "covert action." This definition was Congress's attempt to delineate precisely as practicable what activities of the CIA and other governmental agencies were subject to the reporting requirements of the act. An activity qualified as a "covert action" only if it was meant "to influence political, economic, or military conditions abroad" and only if it was "intended that the role of the United States Government will not be apparent or acknowledged publicly." However, even if a government activity met these two criteria, the 1991 act specifically excluded certain types of activities from the definition of covert action, including "intelligence" and "counterintelligence" activities, "traditional diplomatic or military activities or routine support to such activities," and "traditional law enforcement activities."

Of these exceptions, the scope of "traditional military activities" has become more controversial in the post-9/11 world because U.S. Special Forces, in its "shadow war" with al-Qaeda, the Taliban, and associated forces, have assumed new and diverse roles, including extensive intelligence gathering and analysis. The concern is that such activities are shoehorned into a category of "traditional military activity," one known as the "operational preparation of the environment." Intelligence gathering by U.S. Special Forces could "prepare the environment" for active military operations that might happen years in the future. If intelligence-gathering operations were for this purpose, the military has no obligation to report them to the congressional intelligence committees because they are arguably excluded from the definition of "covert action."

A different set of problems arises if U.S. Special Forces merge with CIA teams engaged in covert paramilitary action against terrorists. Soon after the 9/11 attacks, President George W. Bush signed a covert action "finding" authorizing the CIA to kill or capture high-level al-Qaeda terrorists wherever they may be located. These killings were not considered unlawful "assassinations" because the United States was in an armed conflict with al-Qaeda and the terrorists identified for targeting were considered legitimate enemy combatants, even if they were unlawful combatants. Many of these "targeted killings" were conducted by CIA drone strikes, but the CIA also relied on "kill or capture" missions that were heavily manned by U.S. Special Forces. The most famous mission of this type was the May 2, 2011, raid to "kill or capture" Osama bin Laden. After months of intensive intelligence gathering, the CIA determined that it was likely bin Laden was hiding in a large compound located in the city of Abbottabad, Pakistan. The mission to "kill or capture" bin Laden—Operation Neptune Spear—was formally a "covert action" with the CIA in charge, but in reality it was a SEAL Team 6 operation. Two helicopters with twenty-four SEALs flew approximately 150 miles from Jalalabad, Afghanistan, to Abbottabad, found bin Laden on the top floor in a bedroom of his house, killed him, and returned to Afghanistan with the body. The SEALs were on the ground in Abbottabad for no more than forty minutes.

The bin Laden "kill or capture" raid raised a number of significant legal issues, such as whether the SEALs lost their combatant immunity since they were participating in a CIA covert action. In other words, if Pakistani authorities captured any of the SEALs, could they lawfully be charged under Pakistani criminal law? Fortunately, Pakistani authorities did not capture any of the SEALs on the bin Laden raid, but this question regarding their combatant status could arise in future CIA covert operations.

A second issue was whether the bin Laden raid violated Pakistan's sovereignty. Pakistan had granted the United States permission to conduct air strikes, including drone strikes, in the so-called tribal areas adjacent to the Afghan border, but the bin Laden raid placed U.S. military personnel on the ground deep inside the sovereign territory of Pakistan. Moreover, the U.S. could have easily asked Pakistan to arrest bin Laden unilaterally, to cooperate in a joint venture for this purpose, or to consent to a U.S. operation. The Obama administration did none of these things because it feared that Pakistan's premier intelligence agency—the Inter-Services Intelligence (ISI)—would tip off bin Laden. So forewarned, bin Laden would have quickly disappeared.

Given this risk, the lawyers in the Obama administration invoked the controversial doctrine that the United States could lawfully infringe Pakistan's sovereignty because bin Laden was an "active and imminent" threat to Americans, thereby activating the right of national self-defense, and because Pakistan was "unable or unwilling" to alleviate this threat emanating from its soil. A number of Western countries have accepted this exception to the principle of national sovereignty, but it was highly controversial whether the United States could invoke it without even asking Pakistani authorities whether they were "willing" to assist in the operation. Evidently, according to Obama's lawyers, the risk of a tip-off outweighed the need for positive evidence of unwillingness.[27] In a speech he delivered on September 16, 2011, four months after the bin Laden raid, John Brennan, Obama's chief counterterrorism advisor, explicitly stated that the administration reserved "the right to take unilateral action if or when other governments are unwilling or unable to take the necessary actions themselves."[28] The Obama administration later issued a formal report that elaborated on the exception.

7.6 Report on the Legal and Policy Frameworks Guiding the United States' Use of Military Force and Related National Security Operations, December 2016

Under international law, a State may use force on the territory of another State in self-defense only if it is necessary to do so in order to address the threat giving rise to the right to use force in the first instance.[29] States therefore must consider whether actions in self-defense that would impinge on another State's sovereignty are necessary, which entails assessing whether the territorial State is able and willing to mitigate the threat emanating from its territory and, if not, whether it would be possible to secure the territorial State's consent before using force on its territory against a non-State actor.

In some cases, international law does not require a State to obtain the consent of the State on whose territory force will be used against a non-State armed group. Under international law, States may defend themselves, in accordance with the inherent right of individual and collective self-defense, when they face actual or imminent armed attacks by a non-State armed group and the use of force is necessary because the government of the State where the threat is located is unable or unwilling to prevent the use of its territory by the non-State actor for such attacks. In particular, there will be cases in which there is a reasonable and objective basis for concluding that the territorial State is unable or unwilling to confront effectively a non-State actor in its territory so that it is necessary to act in self-defense against the non-State actor in that State's territory without its consent.

As the Executive Branch has said previously, this "unable or unwilling" standard, in the circumstances here, is "an important application of the requirement that a State, when relying on self-defense for its use of force in another State's territory, may resort to force only if it is necessary to do so—that is, if measures short of force have been exhausted or are inadequate to address the threat posed by the non-State actor emanating from the territory of another State." Through this legal basis for action, customary international law recognizes that a State may defend itself against a non-State actor that is able to launch attacks from within another State's territory.

The unable or unwilling standard is not a license to wage war globally or to disregard the borders and territorial integrity of other States. Indeed, this legal standard does not dispense with the importance of respecting the sovereignty of other States. To the contrary, applying the standard ensures that the sovereignty of other States is respected. Specifically, applying the standard ensures that force is used on foreign territory without consent only in those exceptional circumstances in which a State cannot or will not take effective measures to confront a non-State actor that is using the State's territory as a base for attacks and related operations against other States. With respect to the "unable" prong of the standard, inability perhaps can be demonstrated most plainly where, for example, a State has lost or abandoned effective control over the portion of its territory where the armed group is operating. With respect to the "unwilling" prong of the standard, unwillingness might be demonstrated where, for example, a State is colluding with or harboring a terrorist organization operating from within its territory and refuses to address the threat posed by the group. . . .

Once a State has lawfully resorted to force in self-defense against a particular actor in response to an actual or imminent armed attack by that group, it is not necessary as a matter of international law to reassess whether an armed attack is occurring or imminent prior to every subsequent action taken against the group, provided that hostilities have not ended. In addition, in armed conflict with non-State actors that are prone to shifting operations from country to country, the United States does not view its ability to use military force against a non-State actor with which it is engaged in an ongoing armed conflict as limited to "hot" battlefields. This does not mean the United States can strike wherever it chooses: the use of force in self-defense in an ongoing armed conflict is limited by respect for States' sovereignty and the considerations discussed above, including the customary international law requirements of necessity and proportionality when force could implicate the rights of other States. . . .

Questions

1. In what sense was the "kill or capture" bin Laden raid a "necessity"? Was the raid "necessary" to prevent future attacks on the United States? Was it "necessary" because, in the context of an "armed conflict," bin Laden posed a "threat" that Pakistan was "unwilling" to deal with? Or was it a "necessary" punitive response to the 9/11 attacks?
2. Should the raid's purpose matter in terms of its legality under international law?
3. Was the bin Laden raid in response to an "actual" or "imminent" armed attack by a nonstate armed group?
4. Who should decide whether there is a "reasonable and objective basis for concluding that the territorial State is unable or unwilling" to alleviate the threat posed by a nonstate armed group?
5. Did the United States "exhaust" alternative measures to respond to the bin Laden threat? Were these measures "inadequate"?
6. How is the "unable or unwilling" standard not a "license" to wage war globally? To "disregard the borders and territorial integrity of other States"?
7. How does the "unable or unwilling" standard ensure that "the sovereignty of other States is respected"?

Whether or not the bin Laden raid violated Pakistan's sovereignty according to international law, Obama's lawyers claimed that it was authorized by U.S. domestic law—an argument they called their "trump card."[30] The raid was purportedly consistent with domestic law because, in the view of the administration, Congress had, in the Intelligence Authorization Act, Fiscal Year 1991, provided the president with statutory authority to approve covert actions that violated non-self-executing treaties or customary international law. One of Obama's lawyers, Caroline Krass, defended this position as the Senate considered whether to confirm her nomination as the general counsel of the CIA in late 2013 and early 2014. In her written answers to questions posed by the Senate Intelligence Committee, answers that would have been cleared by the administration, she implicitly suggested that any legal obligation to comply with certain forms of international law loses its binding character if and when the president approves a covert action under the 1991 act.

7.7 Caroline Krass's Written Answers to Questions Posed by the Senate Intelligence Committee, December 2013/January 2014

Question: Under what circumstances must covert action involving the use of force comply with treaties to which the United States is a party, including the United Nations Charter and the Geneva Conventions?[31]

Answer: The President may direct covert action to the extent authorized by Article II of the Constitution and through the process and within the limits imposed by Congress. Congress has regulated covert action through the National Security Act of 1947, as amended. Section 503(a)(5) of the Act explicitly provides that a covert action finding "may not authorize any action that would violate the Constitution or any statute of the United States." By this language, Congress did not prohibit the President from authorizing a covert action that would violate a non-self-executing treaty or customary international law. Such a covert action would, however, need to comply with treaty provisions implemented in a domestic statute. For example, the War Crimes Statute, 18 U.S.C. §2441, implements certain provisions in the Geneva Conventions. As a general matter, and including with respect to the use of force, the United States respects international law and complies with it to the extent possible in the execution of covert action activities.

Question: Do you consider the United Nations Charter and the Geneva Conventions self-executing treaties, such that they are legally binding upon actions carried out by the U.S. government, including covert actions?

Answer: I am not aware of any provisions in the U.N. Charter or the Geneva Conventions that are self-executing as a matter of U.S. domestic law. To my knowledge, all of the federal courts of appeals that have considered the question have found the provisions of the U.N. Charter or the Geneva Conventions at issue in the case to be non-self-executing. . . .

Question: Are there circumstances in which a use of force, or other action, by the U.S. government that would be unlawful if carried out overtly is lawful when carried out covertly? Please explain.

Answer: As matter of domestic law, I cannot think of any circumstances in which a use of force or other action by the U.S. government that would be unlawful if carried out overtly would be lawful when carried out covertly, but I have not studied this question. . . .

Question: If . . . the U.S. respects international law and complies with it to the extent possible in the execution of covert action activities, how does the U.S. decide when to abide by international law and when it does not apply?

Answer: When reviewing covert action activities, the CIA General Counsel works with senior lawyers from the other departments and agencies, including those at the Justice, State, and Defense Departments, both to ensure that the proposed covert action activity does not violate U.S. domestic law and to identify any potential violations of international law. This review also considers whether there is a domestic legal requirement to follow provisions of international law in the execution of covert action activities—for example, if there are any relevant treaty provisions or principles of customary international law that have been implemented in a domestic statute. If there is such a domestic legal requirement, that requirement must be complied with. As the question indicates, I earlier stated that, as a general matter, the United States respects international law and complies with it to the extent possible in the execution of covert action activities. . . .

Questions

1. Krass seems to be saying that the president's authority to direct covert actions "involving the use of force" is limited to what is authorized by Article II of the U.S. Constitution, unless Congress grants additional statutory

authority. Does this mean that the president can only initiate covert actions on his own authority that are "defensive" in character? Or is Krass implying that the president's Article II powers are broader in character? Which interpretation makes more sense?

2. Regarding the president's statutory authority to direct covert actions, does Krass imply that Congress has already, by the National Security Act of 1947, authorized the president to initiate covert actions that violate non-self-executing treaties or customary international law because it has only prohibited covert actions that violate "the Constitution or any statute of the United States"? If so, is this a convincing argument? Is nonprohibition equivalent to authorization?
3. Since Article VI of the Constitution identifies "all" treaties as the "supreme Law of the Land," would this mean that any covert action that violates a non-self-executing treaty is a violation of the Constitution? Would Krass agree?
4. Krass notes that the War Crimes Statute implements certain provisions of the Geneva Convention, but would these limitations on covert actions be applicable only in the context of armed conflicts? Would covert actions in peacetime, even if they involved the use of force, not be subject to the War Crimes Act?
5. Krass claims that the United States respects international law "to the extent possible in the execution of covert action activities," but can the United States engage in "covert action involving the use of force" without violating international law?
6. When Krass concludes that the UN Charter and the Geneva Conventions are not self-executing, is she implying they are not "judicially enforceable" or, given the nature of the question she is addressing, that they are not "legally binding" if and when the United States is conducting a covert action?
7. How do you understand Krass's claim that she is not aware of any action by the U.S. government "that would be unlawful if carried out overtly" but "lawful when carried out covertly"? How does her reference to "domestic" law relate to this question? Is she saying that covert actions cannot violate international law?
8. Can lawyers provide much of a check on covert actions involving force if, as Krass argues, the president is authorized by Congress to pursue covert actions that violate non-self-executing treaties and customary international law? If the president can lawfully violate international law, would the issue of whether to proceed with a covert action that involves the use of force be a policy question, one for policymakers, not lawyers?
9. Do foreign countries have the same right to engage in covert action that Krass claims the United States has, or is this one of the United States' "exceptional" rights?

Whether covert action authority is a license for the president to ignore non-self-executing treaties and customary international law, if and when the need arises, is still an open question. The bin Laden raid is not a clear precedent because the Obama administration did not rely on this "trump card" to justify its violation of Pakistan's sovereignty but instead relied on the controversial "unable or unwilling" exception. Nonetheless, this "open question" is not about to be resolved anytime soon. The shadowy conflict with al-Qaeda, the Taliban, and other associated radical Islamic groups all but ensures that CIA covert actions supported by special operations forces, such as SEAL Team 6, will continue to be used in the future, especially in the Middle East and North and East Africa. Large-scale commitments of U.S. troops in this part of the world are no longer politically palatable. They are likely to be ineffective, in terms of nation building, or counterproductive, in terms of promoting radical Islamic anti-Americanism in countries occupied by American troops.

However, it is unlikely that the United States will completely abandon these countries. Instead, for the foreseeable future, CIA covert action will be the means by which the United States provides training, political funding, and paramilitary support to groups that appear (at the time) to be aligned with U.S. values and interests, while at the same time eliminating persons who are perceived to be threats to American citizens and military personnel through a program of targeted killing (the subject of the next chapter). An example of the first type of covert action is the Obama administration's effort, begun in 2013, to support moderate Islamic groups fighting the regime of Bashar al-Assad in the Syrian civil war. It is true that the new administration of Donald Trump is not inclined to continue this program, possibly because Russian intervention has greatly strengthened Assad's military capability, but U.S. covert actions of this type will not likely disappear from the region.[32] An example of the second type of covert action was the SEAL team raid in Yemen in early February 2017 in which the CIA played a "key" but undefined role, perhaps one that, as in the bin Laden mission, brought the raid under the CIA's statutory "covert action" authority. The Yemen raid's apparent goal was to kill or capture Qassim al-Rimi, the head of al-Qaeda in the Arabian Peninsula. In the end, al-Rimi survived, perhaps because he was not even at the site of the raid, but killed in the firefight were one SEAL member, fourteen al-Qaeda fighters, and a number of civilians, including an eight-year-old girl, Nawr al-Awlaki, a U.S. citizen and the daughter of Anwar al-Awlaki (killed by a drone strike in 2011 and discussed in chapter 8).[33]

These examples confirm what history also suggests: CIA covert actions that involve large amounts of personnel, logistics, and finances or that are very risky, and, therefore, likely to be unsuccessful in a way that will draw media scrutiny, rarely remain "covert." The futility of keeping U.S. sponsorship of such covert actions secret suggests that perhaps the United States, at least at times, uses "covert action" authority to circumvent the norms of international law, rather than to maintain U.S. deniability. In part for this reason, such examples also highlight the tension between covert actions involving the use of force and international law. Can the United States supply moderate Islamic groups opposing Assad's regime with weapons and munitions without violating Syria's sovereignty (see **reading 7.5**)? Can the United States initiate "kill or capture" raids in Yemen without the consent of the Yemeni government without violating international law? These questions will continue to resurface so long as the policy of the United States relies heavily on covert actions involving the use of military force in unstable areas of the world, such as the Middle East and North and East Africa.

NOTES

1. Phillip Knightley, *The Second Oldest Profession: Spies and Spying in the Twentieth Century* (London: A. Deutsch, 1986).

2. Numbers 13:1–20.

3. Judges 16.

4. See P. K. Rose, "The Founding Fathers of American Intelligence," Central Intelligence Agency Library, March 16, 2007, last updated July 7, 2008, https://www.cia.gov.

5. Mark Stout, "Intelligence in World War I: 1914–1918," *Journal of U.S. Intelligence Studies* 20 (Spring/Summer 2014): 35–38, https://www.afio.com.

6. See "Final Report of the Select Committee to Study Governmental Operations with Respect to Intelligence Activities" (Church Committee), in book 1, *Foreign and Military Intelligence*, Senate Report No. 94-7555 (1976), p. 483, https://www.intelligence.senate.gov (hereafter "Church Comm. Report").

7. The National Security Act of 1947 has been amended several times over the last six decades. The original act is http://global.oup.com/us/companion.websites/9780195385168/resources/chapter10/nsa/nsa.pdf. The above quotation is from Section 102(d) of the original Act.

8. "Church Comm. Report," 491.

9. Lawrence R. Houston, general counsel of the CIA, memorandum to Roscoe H. Hillenkoetter, director of the CIA, "CIA Authority to Perform Propaganda and Commando Type Functions," September 25, 1947, Brooklyn College, http://www.brooklyn.cuny.edu.

10. "Church Comm. Report," 485.

11. "Charter of the United Nations; Chapter 1: Purposes and Principles," June 26, 1945, Article 2, United Nations, http://www.un.org.

12. "Address of the President to Congress, Recommending Assistance to Greece and Turkey," March 12, 1947, Harry S. Truman Presidential Library and Museum, https://www.trumanlibrary.org.

13. "Church Comm. Report," 490–91.

14. "Church Comm. Report," 495.

15. "Corfu Channel (*United Kingdom of Great Britain and Northern Ireland v. Albania*)," April 9, 1949, International Court of Justice, http://www.icj-cij.org.

16. Tim Weiner, *Legacy of Ashes* (New York: Anchor, 2007), 30, 40.

17. "Church Comm. Report," 31.

18. General Assembly Resolution 2625 (XXV), "Declaration on Principles of International Law concerning Friendly Relations and Co-operation among States in Accordance with the Charter of the United Nations," A/RES/25/2625, October 24, 1970, http://www.un-documents.net.

19. Church Committee, "Covert Action in Chile, 1963–1973," staff report, 1975, U.S. Senate Select Committee on Intelligence, https://www.intelligence.senate.gov.

20. Hughes-Ryan Amendment, Foreign Assistance Act of 1974, Pub. L. No. 93-559, §32 (1974).

21. See Intelligence Oversight Act of 1980, Public Law No. 96-450, October 14, 1980, Sections 407 and 501.

22. Boland Amendment, Public Law No. 98-473, §8066(a) (1984).

23. "Report of the Congressional Committees Investigating the Iran-Contra Affair," Senate Report No. 100-216 and House Report No. 100-433, November 17, 1987, Executive Summary, pp. 17–20; Minority Report, Internet Archive, https://archive.org/details/reportofcongress87unit.

24. The ICJ's opinion in *Nicaragua v. United States* is available at "ICJ, Nicaragua v. United States," June 27, 1986, International Committee of the Red Cross (ICRC), https://casebook.icrc.org.

25. Intelligence Authorization Act of 1991, Pub. L. No. 102-88, Section 602, §§ 501 and 503, "S.1325: Intelligence Authorization Act, Fiscal Year 1991," June 28, 1991, Congress.gov, https://www.congress.gov.

26. Intelligence Authorization Act of 1991.

27. See Charlie Savage, *Power Wars: The Relentless Rise of Presidential Authority and Secrecy*, rev. ed. (New York: Back Bay, 2017), 262–64; Ashley Deeks, "'Unwilling or Unable': Toward a Normative Framework for Extraterritorial Self-Defense," *Virginia Journal of International Law* 52 (2012): 483.

28. John Brennan, "Strengthening our Security by Adhering to Our Values and Law," Remarks at Harvard Law School, September 16, 2011, White House Archives, https://obamawhitehouse.archives.gov.

29. "Report on the Legal and Policy Frameworks Guiding the United States' Use of Military Force and Related National Security Operations," December 2016, White House Archives, https://obamawhitehouse.archives.gov.

30. Savage, *Power Wars*, 264–65.

31. Caroline Krass's written answers to questions posed by the Senate Intelligence Committee are available at Senate Committee on Intelligence, U.S. Senate, "Additional Prehearing Questions for Ms. Caroline D. Krass upon Her Nomination to Be the General Council of the Central Intelligence Agency," December 17, 2013, Federation of American Scientists, https://fas.org; and at "Questions for the Record: Caroline D. Krass; Responses to Post-Hearing Questions by Caroline Krass," December 17, 2013, Federation of American Scientists, https://fas.org.

32. Greg Jaffe and Adam Entous, "Trump Ends Covert CIA Program to Arm Anti-Assad Rebels in Syria, a Move Sought by Moscow," *Washington Post*, July 19, 2017.

33. Cynthia McFadden, William M. Arkin, and Tracy Connor, "Yemen Raid Had Secret Target: Al Qaeda Leader Qassim al-Rimi," NBC News, February 7, 2017, http://www.nbcnews.com.

8

Targeted Killing

★ ★ ★

A "targeted killing" is an intentional killing by a state of a specific enemy combatant or civilian who is taking a direct part in hostilities during an international or noninternational conflict. The target is chosen not just on the basis of his or her status as an enemy combatant but also on the basis of his or her identity or military value. For example, during World War II, U.S. naval intelligence decrypted Japanese military communications that revealed the specific time when Admiral Isoroku Yamamoto, the mastermind of the Pearl Harbor attack, would be flying from Rabaul to Balalae Airfield in the Solomon Islands on April 18, 1943. Acting under orders from President Franklin D. Roosevelt, Admiral Chester W. Nimitz dispatched eighteen P-38s to intercept and shoot down Yamamoto's plane for the specific purpose of killing him. Another World War II example of lawful targeted killing was the British attempt to kill German general Erwin Rommel at his headquarters in Libya during November 1941. The attempt was unsuccessful, but it was lawful since Rommel, like Yamamoto, was unquestionably an enemy combatant of high military value in what was indisputably an armed international conflict.

Targeted killings become more legally controversial to the degree that there is (a) doubt about the target's status as an enemy combatant; (b) doubt about whether the military value of the target outweighs the attack's risk to innocent civilian life; or (c) doubt about whether the conflict in question even qualifies as an international or noninternational conflict. This chapter will explore the legality of targeted killing in a variety of contexts but with a focus on the ongoing conflict between the United States and radical Islamic groups.

The controversy about targeted killing arises from the assumption that all human beings have a right to life during times of peace and all civilians not taking a direct part in hostilities retain this right even during wartime. The principle is enshrined in the due process clauses of the Fifth and Fourteenth Amendments to the U.S. Constitution: no person shall "be deprived of life, liberty, or property without due process of law." Neither the federal government nor a state can lawfully kill someone intentionally "without due process of law" unless it is necessary for self-defense or the defense of others. For example, a police officer may lawfully use lethal force but only if the assailant poses an imminent threat to life, whether to the life of the police officer or to the life of an innocent bystander. A comparable principle is enshrined in international law. Article 3 of the United Nation's Universal Declaration of Human Rights of 1948 proclaims that "everyone has the right to life, liberty and security of person"; Article 2 of the 1950 European Convention on Human Rights insists that "everyone's right to life shall be protected by law"; and last, Article 6 of the 1976 International Covenant on Civil and Political Rights (ICCPR) underlines the basic principle a third time by announcing that "every human being has the inherent right to life. This right shall be protected by law. No one shall be arbitrarily deprived of his life."

An example of a targeted-killing program that was arguably unlawful because it involved the intentional killing of civilians was the CIA's Phoenix Program during the Vietnam War. This classified program was an effort to stabilize rural areas of South Vietnam from 1965 to 1972 by destroying the political and military infrastructure of the Viet Cong. This southern insurgent movement was in alliance with North Vietnam to unite the country under the leadership of Ho Chi Minh. To dismantle the Viet Cong infrastructure, the CIA sponsored a network of provincial and local "intelligence committees" that put together lists of suspected Viet Cong members. These lists were then sent to tactical forces, including South Vietnamese police units, U.S. Navy SEAL teams, and U.S. Army special operations groups. These tactical units "neutralized" the individuals on the list by either arresting them for interrogation and detention or killing them outright. It is estimated that the Phoenix Program "neutralized" approximately eighty thousand persons, of whom more than twenty-five thousand were killed. Of course, many of the "neutralized" may have been Viet Cong combatants, but the program was arguably unlawful because many of its victims were civilian Viet Cong supporters or sympathizers.[1]

Since the Phoenix Program allegedly killed a significant number of civilians for the political purpose of destroying the political infrastructure of an insurgent group, critics of U.S. involvement in Vietnam referred to it as an "assassination" program. This characterization is noteworthy because, as discussed in chapter 3, the United States has considered "assassination" a violation of the laws of war since Abraham Lincoln promulgated the Lieber Code in 1863. During the 1970s, in the aftermath of the Watergate crisis and President Nixon's resignation, the Church Committee reignited the debate over the legitimacy of "assassination" by uncovering the CIA's involvement with several assassination plots, including plots against Fidel Castro of Cuba, Patrice Lumumba of the Congo, and Ngo Dinh Diem of South Vietnam.

Hoping to preempt any move by Congress to enact a federal statute prohibiting assassination during peacetime, President Gerald Ford issued Executive Order 11905 that banned political assassination on February 18, 1976. President Jimmy Carter affirmed the ban with Executive Order 12036 in 1978, and President Ronald Reagan followed suit with Executive Order 12333 in 1981.

Although this latter order has been revised a number of times, it has retained the following ban: "No person employed by or acting on behalf of the United States Government shall engage in, or conspire to engage in, assassination." Because the ban did not define the meaning of "assassination," Executive Order 12333 left many questions about what exactly it prohibited during conventional military operations, counterinsurgency operations, and peacetime counterterrorist operations. In 1989, W. Hays Parks, chief of the International Law Branch of the International Affairs Division of the Office of the Judge Advocate General of the Army, issued an official memo that defined "assassination" in the context of national and international law. In terms of how the executive branch of the U.S. government understands the scope of "lawful" targeted-killing operations in the above three contexts, in contrast to "unlawful" assassinations, this memo became a foundational document.

8.1 W. Hays Parks on Assassination (1989)

. . . Peacetime assassination, then, would seem to encompass the murder of a private individual or public figure for political purposes, and in some cases . . . also require that the act constitute a covert activity, particularly when the individual is a private citizen.[2] Assassination is unlawful killing, and would be prohibited by international law even if there was no executive order proscribing it.

. . . Assassination in wartime takes on a different meaning. . . . In wartime the role of the military includes the legalized killing (as opposed to murder) of the enemy, whether lawful combatants or unprivileged belligerents, and may include in either category civilians who take part in the hostilities.

The term assassination when applied to wartime military activities against enemy combatants or military objectives does not preclude acts of violence involving the element of surprise. Combatants are liable to attack at any time or place, regardless of their activity when attacked. Nor is a distinction made between combat and combat service support with regard to the right to be attacked as combatants; combatants are subject to attack if they are participating in hostilities through fire, maneuver, and assault; providing logistic, communications, administrative, or other support; or functioning as staff planners. . . . Nor does the prohibition on assassination limit means that otherwise are lawful; no distinction is made between an attack accomplished by aircraft, missile, naval gunfire, artillery, mortar, infantry assault, ambush, landmine or booby trap, a single shot by a sniper, a commando attack, or other, similar means. All are lawful means for attacking the enemy and the choice of one vis-à-vis another has no bearing on the legality of the attack. If the person attacked is a combatant, the use of a particular lawful means for attack (as opposed to another) cannot make an otherwise lawful attack either unlawful or assassination. . . .

The foregoing has endeavored to define assassination in the sense of what the term normally encompasses, as well as those lawful acts carried out by military forces in time of war that do not constitute assassination. The following is a discussion of assassination in the context of specific levels of conflict.

Conventional War. . . . [A]ssassination in the context of a conventional war consists of "outlawry of an enemy, or putting a price upon an enemy's head, as well as offering a reward for an enemy 'dead or alive.'" . . .

This prohibition [does not preclude] . . . the attack of enemy combatants with the intent to kill rather than capture so long as those who endeavor to surrender are availed that opportunity when circumstances permit. This is not always possible. The death of an enemy combatant who endeavors to surrender while caught in the center of a kill zone of an infantry ambush normally would not be [an assassination]. . . . Neither would the killing of an enemy soldier who, in the midst of an assault by his unit, has a change of heart and throws down his weapon, raises his hands, and dies in a hail of bullets put out by the defending unit repelling the enemy attack. The test is one of reasonableness.

Another unresolved issue concerns which civilians may be regarded as combatants, and therefore subject to lawful attack. While there is general agreement among the law of war experts that civilians who participate in hostilities may be regarded as combatants, there is no agreement as to the degree of participation necessary to make an individual civilian a combatant. No existing law of war treaty provides clarification or assistance. Historically, however, the decision as to level at which civilians may be regarded as combatants or "quasi-combatants" and thereby subject to attack generally has been a policy rather than legal matter. The technological revolution in warfare that has occurred over the past two centuries has resulted in a joining of limited segments of the civilian population with each nation's conduct of military operations and vital support activities.

Three points can be made in this respect. (A) Civilians who work within a military objective are at risk from attack during the times in which they are present within that objective, whether their injury or death is incidental to the attack of that military objective or results from their direct attack. Neither would be assassination. (B) The substitution of a civilian in a position or billet that normally would be occupied by a member of the military will not make that position immune from attack. (C) Finally, one rule of thumb with regard to the likelihood that an individual may be subject to lawful attack is his or her immunity from military service if continued service in his or her civilian position is of greater value to the nation's war effort than that person's service in the military. A prime example would be civilian scientists occupying key positions in a weapons program regarded as vital to a nation's national security or war aims. Thus, more than 90% of the World War II Project Manhattan personnel were civilians, and their participation in the U.S. atomic weapons program was of such importance as to have made them liable to legitimate attack. Similarly, the September 1944 Allied bombing raids on the German rocket sites at Peenemünde regarded the death of scientists involved in research and development of that facility to have been as important as destruction of the missiles themselves. Attack of these individuals would not constitute assassination.

Counterinsurgency. . . . The wearing of civilian attire does not make a guerrilla immune from lawful attack, and does not make a lawful attack on a guerrilla an act of assassination. As with the attack of civilians who have combatant responsibilities in conventional war, the difficulty lies in determining where the line should be drawn between guerrillas/combatants and the civilian population in order to provide maximum protection from intentional attack to innocent civilians. The law provides no precise answer to this problem. . . . [U]ltimately the issue is settled along policy rather than legal lines. If a member of a guerrilla organization falls above the line established by competent authority for combatants, a military operation to capture or kill an individual designated as a combatant would not be assassination.

Peacetime operations. . . . The Charter of the United Nations recognizes the inherent right of self defense and does not preclude unilateral action against an immediate threat. In general terms, the United States recognizes three forms of self defense:

- Against an actual use of force, or hostile act;
- Pre-emptive self defense against an imminent use of force; and
- Self defense against a continuing threat.

A national decision to employ military force in self defense against a legitimate terrorist threat would not be unlike the employment of force in response to a threat by conventional forces; only the nature of the threat has changed, rather than the international legal right of self defense. The terrorist organizations envisaged as appropriate to necessitate or warrant an armed response by U.S. military forces are well-financed, highly organized paramilitary structures engaged in the illegal use of force.

Summary. Assassination constitutes an act of murder that is prohibited by international law and Executive Order 12333. The purpose of Executive Order 12333 and its predecessors was to preclude unilateral actions by individual agents or agencies against selected foreign public officials, and to establish beyond any doubt that the United States does not condone assassination as an instrument of national policy. Its intent was not to limit lawful self defense options against legitimate threats to the national security of the United States or individual U.S. citizens. Acting consistent with the Charter of the United Nations, a decision by the President to employ clandestine, low visibility or overt military force would not constitute assassination if U.S. military forces were employed against the combatant forces of another nation, a guerrilla force, or a terrorist or other organization whose actions pose a threat to the security of the United States. . . .

Questions

1. Do you agree with Parks that a murder of a private individual for political purposes usually constitutes an assassination in peacetime only if the assassins act "covertly"? Does this mean that ISIS is not guilty of "assassination" when it beheads one of its victims for the purpose of publishing a film of the killing on social media? What if a "public official" kills someone for a political purpose? According to Parks, would that be an "assassination"? Why do you think Parks excludes such political murders from his definition?
2. In your opinion, why does Parks argue that "assassination" has a different meaning during wartime? Do you agree or disagree?
3. Is it Parks's view that an enemy combatant during wartime, no matter how far from the battlefield and regardless of what weapons were used, cannot by definition be "assassinated"? What if such a killing was done covertly for political purposes? Would you call it an "assassination"?
4. If an enemy combatant during wartime can be killed anytime and anywhere, why does Parks claim that, during a conventional war, "putting a price upon an enemy's head" would constitute an "assassination"? Why is it lawful to kill an enemy covertly but not to give those who are close to the target an incentive to do the job for you?
5. Is Parks correct that, during wartime, a state can target an enemy civilian scientist working in a vital weapons program far from any battlefield without engaging in "assassination"?
6. Are you comfortable with Parks's conclusion that in counterinsurgencies there is no legal line between guerrillas and civilians? What does he mean when he says that the issue is one of "policy"?
7. Parks argues that even in peacetime the United States can in self-defense use military force to target and kill any individual who is an "imminent" or "continuing" threat without violating the ban on "assassination." If he is correct, what does the ban actually prohibit?

A year before Parks finished his legal memo on the meaning of "assassination," British soldiers in the Special Air Service (SAS) shot three members of the Irish Republican Army (IRA) who were allegedly about to set off a car bomb at a guard ceremony in Gibraltar. The soldiers were told that any of the three suspects could set off the bomb by pressing a button on a hidden radio-control device and that the IRA members would likely detonate the bomb if the soldiers confronted them. With this information, the soldiers at close range shot two of the IRA members eight and five times, respectively, after they made "what appeared to the soldiers to be threatening movements." They were shot "as they fell to the ground but not when they were lying on the ground." Almost immediately after these shootings, the third IRA member was shot sixteen times at close range in a separate incident. He was shot "until he hit the ground and probably in the instance as or after he hit the ground."[3] It was subsequently discovered that the three IRA members were unarmed, none of them had any detonation device, and there was no bomb in the car.

Relatives of the dead IRA members filed a lawsuit, claiming that the killings violated Article 2 of the European Convention on Human Rights. The case eventually reached the European Court of Human Rights (ECHR), which handed down its decision in 1995. The court held that SAS soldiers did not violate Article 2 because, given the information that had been provided to them, they thought it was "absolutely necessary" to kill the IRA members to safeguard innocent lives. However, in a closely divided 10–9 decision, the court concluded that the antiterrorist operation "as a whole" was not "controlled and organized in a manner which respected the requirements of Article 2." The majority of the court focused partly on the fact that the IRA members could have been arrested at the border before entering Gibraltar, while the dissent doubted the wisdom of analyzing the shootings with the benefit of hindsight.

8.2 *McCann v. United Kingdom*, 21 E.H.R.R 97 (1995)

201. The question arises,[4] however, whether the anti-terrorist operation as a whole was controlled and organized in a manner which respected the requirements of Article 2 (art. 2) and whether the information and instructions given to the soldiers which, in effect, rendered inevitable the use of lethal force, took adequately into consideration the right to life of the three suspects. . . .

203. It may be questioned why the three suspects were not arrested at the border immediately on their arrival in Gibraltar and why . . . the decision was taken not to prevent them from entering Gibraltar if they were believed to be on a bombing mission. Having had advance warning of the terrorists' intentions it would certainly have been possible for the authorities to have mounted an arrest operation. . . . [T]he Security Services and the Spanish authorities had photographs of the three suspects, knew their names as well as their aliases and would have known what passports to look for.

204. On this issue, the Government submitted that at that moment there might not have been sufficient evidence to warrant the detention and trial of the suspects. Moreover, to release them, having alerted them to the authorities' state of awareness but leaving them or others free to try again, would obviously increase the risks. Nor could the authorities be sure that those three were the only terrorists they had to deal with or of the manner in which it was proposed to carry out the bombing.

205. The Court confines itself to observing in this respect that the danger to the population of Gibraltar—which is at the heart of the Government's submissions in this case—in not preventing their entry must be considered to outweigh the possible consequences of having insufficient evidence to warrant their detention and trial. In its view, either the authorities knew that there was no bomb in the car—which the Court has already discounted—or there was a serious miscalculation by those responsible for controlling the operation. As a result, the scene was set in which the fatal shooting, given the intelligence assessments which had been made, was a foreseeable possibility if not a likelihood. . . .

210. . . . [Moreover, in] the absence of sufficient allowances being made for alternative

possibilities, and the definite reporting of the existence of a car bomb which, according to the assessments that had been made, could be detonated at the press of a button, a series of working hypotheses were conveyed to . . . [the SAS soldiers] as certainties, thereby making the use of lethal force almost unavoidable.

211. However, the failure to make provision for a margin of error must also be considered in combination with the training of the soldiers to continue shooting once they opened fire until the suspect was dead. . . . Against this background, the authorities were bound by their obligation to respect the right to life of the suspects to exercise the greatest of care in evaluating the information at their disposal before transmitting it to soldiers whose use of firearms automatically involved shooting to kill. . . .

213. In sum, having regard to the decision not to prevent the suspects from traveling into Gibraltar, to the failure of the authorities to make sufficient allowances for the possibility that their intelligence assessments might, in some respects at least, be erroneous and to the automatic recourse to lethal force when the soldiers opened fire, the Court is not persuaded that the killing of the three terrorists constituted the use of force which was no more than absolutely necessary in defense of persons from unlawful violence within the meaning of Article 2 . . . of the Convention. . . .

Joint dissenting opinion . . .

8. . . . First, in undertaking any evaluation of the way in which the operation was organized and controlled, the Court should studiously resist the temptations offered by the benefit of hindsight. The authorities had at the time to plan and make decisions on the basis of incomplete information. . . . It would be wrong to conclude in retrospect that a particular course would, as things later transpired, have been better than one adopted at the time under the pressures of an ongoing anti-terrorist operation and that the latter course must therefore be regarded as culpably mistaken. It should not be so regarded unless it is established that in the circumstances as they were known at the time another course should have been preferred.

9. Secondly, the need for the authorities to act within the constraints of the law, while the suspects were operating in a state of mind in which members of the security forces were regarded as legitimate targets and incidental death or injury to civilians as of little consequence, would inevitably give the suspects a tactical advantage which should not be allowed to prevail. The consequences of the explosion of a large bomb in the center of Gibraltar might well be so devastating that the authorities could not responsibly risk giving the suspects the opportunity to set in train the detonation of such a bomb. Of course the obligation of the United Kingdom under Article 2 . . . of the Convention extended to the lives of the suspects as well as to the lives of all the many others, civilian and military, who were present in Gibraltar at the time. But, quite unlike those others, the purpose of the presence of the suspects in Gibraltar was the furtherance of a criminal enterprise which could be expected to have resulted in the loss of many innocent lives if it had been successful. They had chosen to place themselves in a situation where there was a grave danger that an irreconcilable conflict between the two duties might arise. . . .

11. As regards the particular criticisms of the conduct of the operation which are made in the judgment, foremost among them is the questioning of the decision not to prevent the three suspects from entering Gibraltar. . . .

The judgment does not, however, go on to say that it would have been practicable for the authorities to have arrested and detained the suspects at that stage. Rightly so, in our view, because at that stage there might not be sufficient evidence to warrant their detention and trial. To release them, after having alerted them to the state of readiness of the authorities, would be to increase the risk that they or other IRA members could successfully mount a renewed terrorist attack on Gibraltar. In the circumstances as then known, it was accordingly not "a serious miscalculation" for the authorities to defer the arrest rather than merely stop the suspects at the border and turn them back into Spain. . . .

Questions

1. According to W. Hays Parks's criteria, did the SAS soldiers "assassinate" the three IRA members? Would you agree with Parks's assessment? Why or why not?
2. Is the majority correct that killing the IRA members was not "absolutely necessary" since authorities could have arrested them at the border? If the authorities did not have enough evidence to arrest and try them, could the killing still be lawfully justifiable? How would the dissent answer this question?
3. If the primary British goal is to protect the innocent population, what are the advantages and disadvantages of arresting the IRA members at the border versus letting them into Gibraltar?
4. Since SAS soldiers are trained to kill their targets—not to wound them—was it proper for the authorities to request their assistance in the first place? Why or why not?
5. Is the dissenting opinion correct in faulting the majority for relying too much on the benefit of hindsight?
6. What does the dissenting opinion mean when it says that IRA members would be given a "tactical advantage" if the authorities were required to act within the constraints of law? Are the dissenting justices saying that this "tactical advantage . . . should not be allowed to prevail"? Does this "tactical advantage" justify the SAS soldiers acting in a way that would otherwise be unlawful?
7. If the majority is correct that the information and instructions given to the SAS soldiers "rendered inevitable the use of lethal force," were these shootings an example of "targeted killing"? If so, were they unlawful because the shootings occurred in Gibraltar at a time of peace? If the shootings had occurred in Northern Ireland, at a time when the British government was arguably in a state of armed conflict with the IRA, would the shootings have been lawful?

Comparable questions concerning targeted killing arose during the second intifada (2000–2005) when Palestinian groups initiated a series of attacks against targets in Israel, including civilian targets, such as shopping centers, restaurants, coffeehouses, and markets. Thousands of Israelis and Palestinians were killed and wounded. The Israeli government responded by instituting a "policy of targeted frustration." This policy consisted of Israeli security forces killing members of terrorist organizations who were "involved in the planning, launching, or execution of terrorist attacks against Israel." In the end, Israeli security forces killed nearly 300 members of terrorist organizations in Judea, Samaria, and the Gaza Strip, along with approximately 150 Palestinian civilians who were "proximate" to the location of the strikes, and wounded hundreds more. In 2002, the Public Committee against Torture in Israel challenged the legality of this policy of targeted killing in Israel's High Court of Justice.

After several hearings and arguments in the case, the High Court of Justice handed down its decision in *Public Committee against Torture in Israel v. Israel* in 2006. The High Court's opinion came to a number of significant conclusions relevant to the legality of Israel's policy of "targeted frustration." First, the conflict between Israel and the terrorist groups located inside the occupied territories was, in the court's opinion, an "international armed conflict" subject to the Geneva Conventions, the Additional Protocols, and international customary law. Second, because the terrorists did not comply with the "laws and customs of war," they were "unlawful" enemy combatants, not lawful enemy combatants. Third, since the terrorists were not lawful combatants, they were "civilians" who had a right to life and could not lawfully be targeted unless—"and for such time"—they take "a direct part in hostilities."

The High Court's main contribution was to elaborate and clarify when a civilian takes a "direct part in hostilities." In the court's view, a civilian takes a "direct" part in hostilities not only when "using weapons in an armed conflict, while gathering intelligence, or while preparing himself for the hostilities" but also when transporting combatants to the place of hostilities, preparing weapons for use in the conflict, or supervising military operations. The High Court was not willing to provide an exhaustive definition of what constitutes taking a "direct" part in hostilities, insisting that a case-by-case functional analysis of the civilian's role in the conflict was necessary. However, in its judgment, military planners and commanders were clearly taking a "direct" part in hostilities and could be subject to targeted killing, while those who sold food or medicine to unlawful combatants, provided logistical or financial support, or distributed propaganda were not taking a "direct" part in hostilities and could not lawfully be subject to targeted killing. Finally, the High Court held that a civilian could be lethally targeted only if the information substantiating the conclusion that the target was taking a "direct" part in hostilities was "thoroughly verified," leaving little or no doubt about the target's functional role in the conflict, and as an additional matter, a less harmful method of responding to the threat, such as arresting, interrogating, and trying the target, was not possible.[5]

Following the 9/11 attacks in 2001, the United States initiated its own program of targeted killing, first in Afghanistan and then in Iraq and other countries in the Middle East and Africa. The means used in these lethal operations varied, from hit teams composed of special forces troops to air strikes, such as the one that killed Abu Musab al-Zarqawi in Iraq in 2006. However, within a decade of 9/11, unmanned aerial vehicles (UAVs) armed with Hellfire missiles and laser-guided bombs, commonly referred to as "drones," had become the preferred method by which the U.S. military and the CIA eliminated specific terrorists. The advantages of using drones for the purpose of targeted killing were relatively obvious: (1) drones could stay aloft over the target for seventeen hours; (2) they send back real-time imagery of a possible target's movements to pilots and intelligence analysts on the ground thousands of miles away; and last, (3) they permitted the use of precision weapons at a time and place that would reduce the risk to innocent civilians. In short, drones increased the likelihood that the target would be killed, while at the same time they eliminated or reduced the risk of collateral damage, without placing U.S. personnel in harm's way.

Although the U.S. drone program has been shrouded in secrecy, it is generally believed that the first CIA drone strike, on November 3, 2002, killed Qaed Senyan al-Harithi, the al-Qaeda leader who was responsible for the bombing of the USS *Cole*. Eighteen months later, Nek Mohammed, a leader within the Pakistani Taliban, was killed by a drone strike in South Waziristan, one of the Federally Administered Tribal Areas in western Pakistan. On January 13, 2006, there was an attempted drone strike against Ayman al-Zawahiri, al-Qaeda's "number two," in northwestern Pakistan. Although Zawahiri was not present, eighteen people were killed, including women, children, and five senior al-Qaeda operatives. A drone strike eliminated Abu Laith al Libi, al-Qaeda's chief of operations, in North Waziristan on January 29, 2008.[6]

Also during 2008, the Bush administration approved the use of drones for "signature strikes," that is, strikes directed not at individual targets but rather at groups of "military-age males" in areas of known terrorist activity based on their "patterns of movement." The new policy permitted military forces to conduct drone strikes against al-Qaeda- or Taliban-based convoys of vehicles operating in the border region of Afghanistan and Pakistan if there was a low risk of civilian casualties.[7] Of course, since the presumption was that men in the convoy were members of al-Qaeda or the Taliban, an assessment of collateral damage was somewhat pro forma. Although not literally a form of targeted killing, the use of drones for "signature strikes" is a highly controversial dimension of the ongoing war against radical Islamic terrorist groups, especially since its use has spread from Afghanistan and Pakistan to Yemen and perhaps Somalia.

The pace of targeted drone attacks accelerated greatly under President Barack Obama, with more strikes occurring in the first year of his administration than during the entire presidency of George W. Bush, including one that killed Baitullah Mehsud, the leader of the Pakistan Taliban, on August 5, 2009. On March 25, 2010, in an address to the American Society of International Law, Harold Koh, the U.S. Department of State's legal advisor, defended the legality of Obama's armed conflict with al-Qaeda, the Taliban, and associated groups, including the drone-based targeted-killing program. The following excerpts from Koh's address include his brief remarks on the "targeting practices" of the Obama administration.

8.3 Harold Koh, "Targeting Practices" (2010)

. . . Recently, a number of legal objections have been raised against U.S. targeting practices.[8] While today is obviously not the occasion for a detailed legal opinion responding to each of these objections, let me briefly address four:

First, some have suggested that the *very act of targeting* a particular leader of an enemy force in an armed conflict must violate the laws of war. But individuals who are part of such an armed group are belligerents and, therefore, lawful targets under international law. During World War II, for example, American aviators tracked and shot down the airplane carrying the architect of the Japanese attack on Pearl Harbor, who was also the leader of enemy forces in the Battle of Midway. This was a lawful operation then, and would be if conducted today. Indeed, targeting particular individuals serves to narrow the focus when force is employed and to avoid broader harm to civilians and civilian objects.

Second, some have challenged *the very use of advanced weapons systems*, such as unmanned aerial vehicles, for lethal operations. But the rules that govern targeting do not turn on the type of weapon system used, and there is no prohibition under the laws of war on the use of technologically advanced weapons systems in armed conflict—such as pilotless aircraft or so-called smart bombs—so long as they are employed in conformity with applicable laws of war. Indeed, using such advanced technologies can ensure both that the best intelligence is available for planning operations, and that civilian casualties are minimized in carrying out such operations.

Third, some have argued that the use of lethal force against specific individuals fails to provide adequate process and thus constitutes *unlawful extrajudicial killing*. But a state that is engaged in an armed conflict or in legitimate self-defense is not required to provide targets with legal process before the state may use lethal force. Our procedures and practices for identifying lawful targets are extremely robust, and advanced technologies have helped to make our targeting even more precise. In my experience, the principles of distinction and proportionality that the United States applies are not just recited at meetings. They are implemented rigorously throughout the planning and execution of lethal operations to ensure that such operations are conducted in accordance with all applicable law.

Fourth and finally, some have argued that our targeting practices violate *domestic law*, in particular, the long-standing *domestic ban on assassinations*. But under domestic law, the use of lawful weapons systems—consistent with the applicable laws of war—for precision targeting of specific high-level belligerent leaders when acting in self-defense or during an armed conflict is not unlawful, and hence does not constitute "assassination."

Questions

1. Does Koh's first point suggest that the United States believes members of al-Qaeda and the Taliban are "belligerents" and therefore can be targeted on the basis of their status, not on the fact that they are taking a "direct part in hostilities"? Is Koh's approach consistent with what the Israeli High Court of Justice decided in *Public Committee against Torture in Israel v. Israel*?
2. Is Koh's second claim valid? Should the rules of armed conflict remain the same if lethal force is inflicted by sophisticated drones?
3. In his third claim, Koh argues that "legal process" is not required before the United States can use lethal force in an "armed conflict" or in "legitimate self-defense" but then insists that the "procedures and practices" that the United States uses for identifying lawful targets are "extremely robust" and that they are "implemented rigorously" to ensure that lethal operations are conducted in accordance with "all applicable law." If lethal operations are in fact governed by "all applicable law," how are they not subject to a "legal process"? What does Koh mean by "legal process"?
4. Finally, does Koh's fourth claim rely on a circular argument—an assassination is unlawful; killing belligerents in an armed conflict is lawful; and therefore killing belligerents in an armed conflict is not assassination? Are such arguments very convincing?

A few months after Koh's address, Philip Alston, the United Nations' special rapporteur on extrajudicial executions, published a study on the legality of targeted killing in three different contexts: (1) during a state of armed conflict; (2) outside the state of armed conflict; and (3) when one state engages in targeted killing in the territory of another state. In his study, Alston argued that both "international humanitarian law" (IHL), which is another name for the laws of armed conflict or *jus in bello*, and human rights law (HRL) are generally applicable. While IHL is controlling in circumstances involving armed hostilities, HRL is controlling in all other situations, including situations involving "law enforcement operations." In circumstances involving armed hostilities in an armed conflict, targeted killing, according to Alston, is lawful only if three conditions are met: (1) the target must be a "combatant" or a civilian who "directly participates in hostilities"; (2) the killing must be a "military necessity"; and last, (3) any harm inflicted on civilians (the collateral damage) must be proportionate to the anticipated military advantage gained by the attack.

In contrast, targeted killing outside a state of armed conflict is governed completed by HRL. In such circumstances, lethal force is lawful only if it is "strictly and directly" required to protect life. According to Alston, this standard means that a targeted killing is lawful only if there is no other way to alleviate the threat to life, whether by an arrest, a capture, or nonlethal incapacitation. Moreover, if the targeted killing involves one state killing a person in the territory of another state, then additional criteria must be met. The killing must not only meet the IHL standards if it occurs in the context of hostilities associated with an armed conflict or the HRL standards if it occurs outside of actual hostilities. Also, either the attacking state must have the "consent" of the second state or the targeted killing must be a justifiable "act of self defense" under Article 51 of the UN Charter. According to Alston, there are only two ways for a cross-border targeted killing to qualify as an act of self-defense: the state in which the targeted killing occurs must have attacked the state responsible for the targeted killing or the former state must be either "unwilling or unable" to prevent the attacks that are being launched from its territory on the state responsible for the targeted killing. Alston explicitly uses these three contexts of targeted killing to raise questions regarding Koh's defense of the Obama administration's use of targeted killing in the conflict with al-Qaeda, the Taliban, and associated forces.

8.4 Philip Alston's Report on Targeted Killing

22. The Legal Adviser to the Department of State [Harold Koh] recently outlined the Government's legal justifications for targeted killings.[9] They were said to be based on its asserted right to self-defense, as well as on IHL, on the basis that the US is "in an armed conflict with Al-Qaeda, as well as the Taliban and associated forces." While this statement is an important starting point, it does not address some of the most central legal issues including: the scope of the armed conflict in which the US asserts it is engaged, the criteria for individuals who may be targeted and killed, [and] the existence of any substantive or procedural safeguards to ensure the legality and accuracy of killings. . . .

[SCOPE OF ARMED CONFLICT]:

51. The test for the existence of an international armed conflict is clear under IHL: "Any difference arising between two States and leading to the intervention of armed forces" qualifies as armed conflict, regardless of its intensity, duration or scale. . . .

52. The tests for the existence of a non-international armed conflict are not as categorical as those for international armed conflict. . . . Under treaty and customary international law, the elements which would point to the existence of a non-international armed conflict against a non-state armed group are:

(i) The non-state armed group must be identifiable as such, based on criteria that are objective and verifiable. This is necessary for IHL to apply meaningfully, and so that States may comply with their obligation to distinguish between lawful targets and civilians. The criteria include:

- Minimal level of organization of the group such that armed forces are able to identify an adversary (GC Art. 3; AP II).
- Capability of the group to apply the Geneva Conventions (i.e., adequate command structure, and separation of military and political command) (GC Art. 3; AP II).
- Engagement of the group in collective, armed, anti-government action (GC Art. 3).
- For a conflict involving a State, the State uses its regular military forces against the group (GC Art. 3).
- Admission of the conflict against the group to the agenda of the UN Security Council or the General Assembly (GC Art. 3).

(ii) There must be a minimal threshold of intensity and duration. The threshold of violence is higher than required for the existence of an international armed conflict. To meet the minimum threshold, violence must be:

- "Beyond the level of intensity of internal disturbances and tensions, such as riots, isolated and sporadic acts of violence and other acts of a similar nature" (AP II).
- "[P]rotracted armed violence" among non-state armed groups or between a non-state armed group and a State;
- If an isolated incident, the incident itself should be of a high degree of intensity, with a high level of organization on the part of the non-state armed group;

(iii) The territorial confines can be:

- Restricted to the territory of a State and between the State's own armed forces and the non-state group (AP II); or
- A transnational conflict, i.e., one that crosses State borders (GC Art. 3). This does not mean, however, that there is no territorial nexus requirement.

53. Taken cumulatively, these factors make it problematic for the US to show that—outside the context of the armed conflicts in Afghanistan or Iraq—it is in a transnational non-international armed conflict against "al-Qaeda, the Taliban, and other associated forces" without further explanation of how those entities constitute a "party" under the IHL of non-international armed conflict, and whether and how any violence by any such group rises to the level necessary for an armed conflict to exist.

54. The focus, instead, appears to be on the "transnational" nature of the terrorist threat. Al-Qaeda and entities with various degrees of "association" with it are indeed known to have operated in numerous countries around the world including in Saudi Arabia, Indonesia, Pakistan, Germany, the United Kingdom and Spain, among others, where they have conducted terrorist attacks. Yet none of these States, with the possible exception of Pakistan, recognize themselves as being part of an armed conflict against al-Qaeda or its "associates" in their territory. Indeed, in each of those States, even when there have been terrorist attacks by al-Qaeda or other groups claiming affiliation with it, the duration and intensity of such attacks has not risen to the level of an armed conflict. Thus, while it is true that non-international armed conflict can exist across State borders, and indeed often does, that is only one of a number of cumulative factors that must be considered for the objective existence of an armed conflict.

55. With respect to the existence of a non-state group as a "party," al-Qaeda and other alleged "associated" groups are often only loosely linked, if at all. Sometimes they appear to be not even groups, but a few individuals who take "inspiration" from al-Qaeda. The idea that, instead, they are part of continuing hostilities that spread to new territories as new alliances form or are claimed may be superficially appealing but such "associates" cannot constitute a "party" as required by IHL—although they can be criminals, if their conduct violates US law, or the law of the State in which they are located.

56. To ignore these minimum requirements, as well as the object and purpose of IHL, would be to undermine IHL safeguards against the use of violence against groups that are not the

equivalent of an organized armed group capable of being a party to a conflict—whether because it lacks organization, the ability to engage in armed attacks, or because it does not have a connection or belligerent nexus to actual hostilities. It is also salutary to recognize that whatever rules the US seeks to invoke or apply to al-Qaeda and any "affiliates" could be invoked by other States to apply to other non-state armed groups. To expand the notion of non-international armed conflict to groups that are essentially drug cartels, criminal gangs or other groups that should be dealt with under the law enforcement framework would be to do deep damage to the IHL and human rights frameworks. . . .

[CRITERIA FOR INDIVIDUALS WHO MAY BE TARGETED AND KILLED]:

57. The greatest source of the lack of clarity with respect to targeted killings in the context of armed conflict is who qualifies as a lawful target, and where and when the person may be targeted.

58. In international armed conflict, combatants may be targeted at any time and any place (subject to the other requirements of IHL). Under the IHL applicable to non-international armed conflict, the rules are less clear. In non-international armed conflict, there is no such thing as a "combatant." Instead . . . States are permitted to directly attack only civilians who "directly participate in hostilities" (DPH). . . .

61. Some types of conduct have long been understood to constitute direct participation, such as civilians who shoot at State forces or commit acts of violence in the context of hostilities that would cause death or injury to civilians. Other conduct has traditionally been excluded from direct participation, even if it supports the general war effort; such conduct includes political advocacy, supplying food or shelter, or economic support and propaganda (all also protected under other human rights standards). Even if these activities ultimately impact hostilities, they are not considered "direct participation." But there is a middle ground, such as for the proverbial "farmer by day, fighter by night," that has remained unclear and subject to uncertainty.

62. In 2009, the . . . [International Committee of the Red Cross (ICRC)] issued its Interpretive Guidance on DPH, which provides a useful starting point for discussion. In non-international armed conflict, according to the ICRC Guidance, civilians who participate directly in hostilities and are members of an armed group who have a "continuous combat function" may be targeted at all times and in all places. . . .

65. . . . [The] ICRC's Guidance raises concern from a human rights perspective because of the "continuous combat function" (CCF) category of armed group members who may be targeted anywhere, at any time. In its general approach to DPH, the ICRC is correct to focus on function (the kind of act) rather than status (combatant vs. unprivileged belligerent), but the creation of CCF category is, de facto, a status determination that is questionable given the specific treaty language [AP I, Article 51(3)] that limits direct participation to "for such time" as opposed to "all the time."

66. Creation of the CCF category also raises the risk of erroneous targeting of someone who, for example, may have disengaged from their [continuous combat] function. If States are to accept this category, the onus will be on them to show that the evidentiary basis is strong. In addition, States must adhere to the careful distinction the ICRC draws between continuous combatants who may always be subject to direct attack and civilians who (i) engage in sporadic or episodic direct participation (and may only be attacked during their participation), or (ii) have a general war support function ("recruiters, trainers, financiers and propagandists") or form the political wing of an organized armed group (neither of which is a basis for attack). . . .

68. . . . [A]lthough the US has not made public its definition of DPH, it is clear that it is more expansive than that set out by the ICRC; in Afghanistan, the US has said that drug traffickers on the "battlefield" who have

links to the insurgency may be targeted and killed. This is not consistent with the traditionally understood concepts under IHL—drug trafficking is understood as criminal conduct, not an activity that would subject someone to a targeted killing. And generating profits that might be used to fund hostile actions does not constitute DPH. . . .

72. It is important to note that if a targeted killing violates IHL (by, for example, targeting civilians who were not "directly participating in hostilities"), then regardless of who conducts it—intelligence personnel or State armed forces—the author, as well as those who authorized it, can be prosecuted for war crimes. . . .

[PROCEDURAL SAFEGUARDS]:

77. Less-than-lethal measures are especially appropriate when a State has control over the area in which a military operation is taking place, when "armed forces operate against selected individuals in situations comparable to peacetime policing," and in the context of non-international armed conflict, in which rules are less clear. In these situations, States should use graduated force and, where possible, capture rather than kill. . . .

78. In addition, precautionary measures that States should take in armed conflict to reduce casualties include:

Provide effective advance warning to the civilian population, through leaflets, broadcast warnings, etc. in the areas in which targeted killings may take place. The warnings must be as specific as possible. Any such warning does not, however, discharge the obligation to distinguish between lawful targets and civilians. "Warnings are required for the benefit of civilians, but civilians are not obligated to comply with them. A decision to stay put—freely taken or due to limited options—in no way diminishes a civilian's legal protections."

The use of civilians as "shields" is strictly prohibited. But one side's unlawful use of civilian shields does not affect the other side's obligation to ensure that attacks do not kill civilians in excess of the military advantage of killing the targeted fighter. . . .

80. The . . . concern with drones is that because they make it easier to kill without risk to a State's forces, policymakers and commanders will be tempted to interpret the legal limitations on who can be killed, and under what circumstances, too expansively. States must ensure that the criteria they apply to determine who can be targeted and killed—i.e., who is a lawful combatant, or what constitutes "direct participation in hostilities" that would subject civilians to direct attack—do not differ based on the choice of weapon. . . .

84. Furthermore, because operators are based thousands of miles away from the battlefield, and undertake operations entirely through computer screens and remote audio feed, there is a risk of developing a "Playstation" mentality to killing. States must ensure that training programs for drone operators who have never been subjected to the risks and rigors of battle instill respect for IHL and adequate safeguards for compliance with it. . . .

Questions

1. Is Alston correct that it is "problematic" for the United States to legally justify its program of targeted killing outside Afghanistan and Iraq? Is he saying that al-Qaeda and the Taliban do constitute "parties" to an armed conflict inside these two states but that they do not constitute "parties" to an armed conflict outside of them? Why does he come to this conclusion? Is the implication that any U.S. drone attack outside Afghanistan and Iraq, such as in Pakistan, is illegal even if that country consents to the attack? Why or why not?
2. What does Alston mean when he claims there are no "combatants" in a noninternational armed conflict? Does

Koh agree? Does the Israeli High Court of Justice? Do you consider members of al-Qaeda, the Taliban, and associated forces as "combatants" or civilians who are "participating in hostilities"? Why does this distinction matter?

3. What is the significance of basing targeting decisions on DPH versus membership in an armed terrorist group, such as al-Qaeda, the Taliban, or an associated force? Why does the United States prefer the latter approach?
4. Alston argues that the ICRC's position on whether certain members of a nonstate terrorist group have a "continuous combat function (CCF)" raises concerns from a "human rights perspective." What are these concerns?
5. Is Alston persuasive when he argues that Taliban members who deal drugs in Afghanistan for the purpose of funding hostile actions against U.S. forces cannot lawfully be targeted? If he is not persuasive, what is wrong with his analysis?
6. Is Alston implying that some aspects of the U.S. targeted-killing program qualify as war crimes? If so, is he right?
7. Why does Alston think that "less-than-lethal measures" are more appropriate in noninternational conflicts? Do you agree? Why or why not?
8. Does Alston's claim that states should give "specific warnings" to civilians who live in areas subject to possible drone strikes have a potential downside? What is the trade-off?
9. What does Alston mean when he claims that drone-based targeted killing risks a "Playstation" approach to killing? Is he right? Is there any credible way to prevent such a mentality if drone-based attacks are used extensively in an armed conflict?

Although the Obama administration sharply increased the number of targeted drone strikes in 2009, there was considerable controversy whether the United States could use lethal force against an American citizen outside areas of active hostilities. This question became increasingly pressing as Anwar al-Awlaki, an American citizen born in New Mexico in 1971, evolved from a radical Islamic imam in 2002 (at which point he left the United States) into a recruiter, propagandist, and eventually, operational planner of terrorist attacks for Al-Qaeda in the Arabian Peninsula (AQAP). Matters came to head when it was discovered that al-Awlaki had, to some extent, inspired Malik Hasan's mass shooting at Fort Hood, Texas, on November 5, 2009, which killed thirteen people and injured dozens of others, and also had recruited and trained Umar Farouk Abdulmutallab, the so-called underwear bomber who had tried to bring down a Northwest Airlines flight over Detroit, Michigan, on Christmas Day 2009.

Shaken by how close this latter attack had come to success, the Obama administration asked the Department of Justice's Office of Legal Counsel (OLC), the highest legal authority in the executive branch of the federal government, to consider the legality of a lethal operation against al-Awlaki. Newspaper accounts soon thereafter reported that the Obama administration had placed al-Awlaki's name on a secret "kill list." The OLC completed on July 16, 2010, the classified legal memo addressing whether the United States could conduct a lethal operation against al-Awlaki. It argued that such a lethal operation would be consistent with U.S. domestic law and international law, even if the strike occurred in Yemen, far removed from active battlegrounds.[10] In August 2009, Awlaki's father filed a federal lawsuit, seeking an injunction prohibiting the Obama administration from killing his son, but the federal district court in December dismissed the case on two grounds. First, Awlaki's father lacked "standing" to bring the case because his son could surrender to U.S. authorities and initiate his own legal challenge to the lawfulness of including his name on the government's kill list. Second, the decision to kill a U.S. citizen in an armed conflict was a "political question," one constitutionally committed to the political branches of the federal government and, for that reason, judicially unreviewable.[11] Ten months after this ruling, on September 30, 2011, Awlaki was killed by a U.S. drone strike.

In February 2013, over two years after al-Awlaki's death, *Newsweek* published an unsigned and undated Department of Justice (DOJ) white paper on the lawfulness of lethal operations "outside the area of active hostilities" against U.S. citizens who are senior operational leaders of al-Qaeda or associated forces. Although the white paper draws heavily from the July 2010 OLC memo, it has a broader focus since it is not directed specifically at the facts and circumstances that purportedly made Awlaki's targeted killing lawful. The white paper gave the American public its first look at the legal reasoning underlying one dimension of the Obama administration's targeted-killing program.

8.5 DOJ White Paper on Targeted Killing of U.S. Citizens

This white paper sets forth a legal framework for considering the circumstances in which the U.S. government could use lethal force in a foreign country outside the area of active hostilities against a U.S. citizen who is a senior operational leader of al-Qa'ida or an associated force of al-Qa'ida—that is, an al-Qa'ida leader actively engaged in planning operations to kill Americans.[12] The paper does not attempt to determine the minimum requirements necessary to render such an operation lawful; nor does it assess what might be required to render a lethal operation against a U.S. citizen lawful in other circumstances, including an operation against enemy forces on a traditional battlefield or an operation against a U.S. citizen who is not a senior operational leader of such forces. Here the Department of Justice concludes only that where the following three conditions are met, a U.S. operation using lethal force in a foreign country against a U.S. citizen who is a senior operational leader of al-Qa'ida or an associated force would be lawful: (1) an informed, high-level official of the U.S. government has determined that the targeted individual poses an imminent threat of violent attack against the United States; (2) capture is infeasible, and the United States continues to monitor whether capture becomes feasible; and (3) the operation would be conducted in a manner consistent with applicable law of war principles. . . .

Claiming that for purposes of international law, an armed conflict generally exists only when there is "protracted armed violence between governmental authorities and organized armed groups," some commentators have suggested that the conflict between the United States and al-Qa'ida cannot lawfully extend to nationals outside Afghanistan in which the level of hostilities is less intense or prolonged than in Afghanistan itself. There is little judicial or other authoritative precedent that speaks directly to the question of the geographic scope of a non-international armed conflict in which one of the parties is a transnational, non-state actor and where the principal theater of operations is not within the territory of the nation that is a party to the conflict. Thus, in considering this potential issue, the Department looks to principles and statements from analogous contexts.

The Department has not found any authority for the proposition that when one of the parties to an armed conflict plans and executes operations from a base in a new nation, an operation to engage the enemy in that location can never be part of the original armed conflict, and thus subject to the laws of war governing that conflict, unless and until the hostilities become sufficiently intensive and protracted within that new location. That does not appear to be the rule of the historical practice, for instance, in a traditional international conflict. [For example,] . . . if a neutral state has been unable for any reason to prevent violations of its neutrality by the troops of one belligerent using its territory as a base of operations, the other belligerent has historically been justified in attacking those enemy forces in that state." . . . Particularly in a non-international armed conflict, where terrorist organizations may move their base of operations from one country to another, the determination of whether a particular operation would be part of an ongoing armed conflict would require consideration of the particular facts and circumstances in each case, including the fact that transnational non-state organizations such as al-Qa'ida may have no single site serving as their base of operations.

If an operation of the kind discussed in this paper were to occur in a location where al-Qa'ida or an associated force has a significant and organized presence and from which al-Qa'ida or an associated force, including its senior operational leaders, plan attacks against U.S. persons and interests, the operation would be part of the non-international armed conflict between the United States and al-Qa'ida that the Supreme Court recognized in *Hamdan*. Moreover, such an operation would be consistent with international legal principles of sovereignty and neutrality if it were conducted, for example, with the consent of the host nation's government or after a determination that the host nation is unable or unwilling to suppress the threat posed by the individual targeted. In such circumstances, targeting a U.S. citizen of the kind described in this paper would be authorized under the AUMF and the inherent right to national self-defense. Given this authority, the question becomes whether and what further restrictions may limit its exercise. . . .

The Department assumes that the rights afforded by Fifth Amendment's Due Process Clause [i.e., the state cannot take away a person's life without due process of law] . . . attach to a U.S. citizen even while he is abroad. . . .

The Due Process Clause would not prohibit a lethal operation of the sort contemplated here. In *Hamdi*, a plurality of the Supreme Court used the *Mathews v. Eldridge* balancing test to analyze the Fifth Amendment due process rights of a U.S. citizen who had been captured on the battlefield in Afghanistan and detained in the United States, and who wished to challenge the government's assertion that he was a part of enemy forces. The Court explained that "the process due in any given instance is determined by weighing 'the private interest that will be affected by the official action' against the Government's asserted interest, 'including the function involved' and the burdens the Government would face in providing greater process." The due process balancing analysis applied to determine the Fifth Amendment rights of a U.S. citizen with respect to law-of-war detention supplies the framework for assessing the process due a U.S. citizen who is a senior operational leader of an enemy force planning violent attacks against Americans before he is subjected to lethal targeting.

In the circumstances considered here, the interests on both sides would be weighty. An individual's interest in avoiding erroneous deprivation of his life is "uniquely compelling." No private interest is more substantial. At the same time, the government's interest in waging war, protecting its citizens, and removing the threat posed by members of enemy forces is also compelling. . . . [However,] "the realities of combat" render certain uses of force "necessary and appropriate," including force against U.S. citizens who have joined enemy forces in the armed conflict against the United States and whose activities pose an imminent threat of violent attack against the United States—and "due process analysis need not blink at those realities." These same realities must also be considered in assessing "the burdens the Government would face in providing greater process" to a member of enemy forces. . . .

Certain aspects of this legal framework require additional explication. *First*, the condition that an operational leader present an "imminent" threat of violent attack against the United States does not require the United States to have clear evidence that a specific attack on U.S. persons and interests will take place in the immediate future. Given the nature of, for example, the terrorist attacks on September 11, in which civilian airliners were hijacked to strike the World Trade Center and the Pentagon, this definition of imminence, which would require the United States to refrain from action until preparation for an attack are concluded, would not allow the United States sufficient time to defend itself. The defensive options available to the United States may be reduced or eliminated if al-Qa'ida operatives disappear and cannot be found when the time of their attack approaches. Consequently, with respect to al-Qa'ida leaders who are continually planning attacks, the United States is likely to have only a limited window of opportunity within which to defend Americans in a manner that has both a high likelihood of success and sufficiently reduces the probabilities of civilian causalities. Furthermore, a "terrorist 'war' does not consist of a massive attack across an international border, nor does it consist of one isolated incident that occurs and is then past. It is a drawn out, patient, sporadic pattern of attacks. It is very difficult to know when or where the next incident will occur." Delaying action against individuals continually planning to kill Americans until some theoretical end state of the planning for a particular plot would create an unacceptably high risk that the action would fail and that American casualties would result.

By its nature, therefore, the threat posed by al-Qa'ida and its associated forces demands a broader concept of imminence in judging when a person continually planning terror attacks presents an imminent threat, making the use of force appropriate. In this context, imminence must incorporate consideration of the relevant window of opportunity, the possibility of reducing collateral damage to civilians, and the likelihood of heading off future disastrous attacks on Americans. Thus, a decision maker determining whether an al-Qa'ida operational leader presents an imminent threat of violent attack against the United States must take into account that certain members of al-Qa'ida (including any potential target of lethal force) are continually plotting attacks against the United States; that al-Qa'ida would engage in such attacks regularly to the extent it were able to do so; that the U.S. government may not be aware of all al-Qa'ida plots as they are developing and thus cannot be confident that none is about to occur; and that, in light of these predicates, the nation may have a limited window of opportunity within which to strike in a manner that both has a high likelihood of success and reduces the probability of American casualties. . . .

Second, regarding the feasibility of capture, capture would not be feasible if it could not be physically effectuated during the relevant window of opportunity or if the relevant country were to decline to consent to a capture operation. Other factors such as undue risk to U.S. personnel conducting a potential capture operation also could be relevant. Feasibility would be a highly fact-specific and potentially time-sensitive inquiry.

Third, it is a premise here that any such lethal operation by the United States would comply with the four fundamental law-of-war principles governing the use of force: necessity, distinction, proportionality; and humanity (the avoidance of unnecessary suffering). . . .

. . . [The] Department notes that under the circumstances described in this paper, there exists no appropriate judicial forum to evaluate these [due process] constitutional considerations. It is well established that "[m]atters intimately related to foreign policy and national security are rarely proper subject for judicial intervention" because such matters "frequently turn on standards that defy judicial application," or "involve the exercise of a discretion demonstrably committed to the executive or legislature." Were a court to intervene here, it might be required inappropriately to issue an ex ante command to the President and officials responsible for operations with respect to their specific tactical judgment to mount a potential lethal operation against a senior operational leader of al-Qa'ida or its associated forces. And judicial enforcement of such orders would require the Court to supervise inherently predictive judgments by the President and his national security advisors as to when and how to use force against a member of an enemy force against which Congress has authorized the use of force. . . .

. . . [The] Department believes that use of lethal force addressed in this white paper would constitute a lawful killing under the public authority doctrine if conducted in a manner consistent with the fundamental law of war principles governing the use of force in a non-international conflict. Such an operation would not [be murder, and it would not] violate the assassination ban in Executive Order No. 12333. . . . A lawful killing in self-defense is not an assassination. In the Department's view, a lethal operation conducted against a U.S. citizen whose conduct poses an imminent threat of violent attack against the United States would be a legitimate act of national self-defense that would not violate the assassination ban. Similarly, the use of lethal force, consistent with the laws of war, against an individual who is a legitimate military target would be lawful and would not violate the assassination ban.

Questions

1. Philip Alston argues that targeted killing outside the area of active hostilities is generally illegal, while the DOJ's white paper claims that it is lawful, at least when targeting senior operational leaders of al-Qaeda. Which position is more defensible?
2. In your view, would a senior operational leader of al-Qaeda be a civilian who could be targeted only when "directly participating in hostilities," a civilian who could be targeted while exercising a "continuous combat function" (the ICRC's formulation), or a "combatant" who could be targeted at any time (the United States' perspective)?
3. The white paper concedes that a U.S. citizen who is a senior operational leader of al-Qaeda has a Fifth Amendment right not to be deprived of life without due process of law. Would a better argument be that such a person has renounced his U.S. citizenship by assuming a leadership role in an organization at war with the United States? Why do you suppose the DOJ does not make this argument?
4. The white paper applies a "balancing analysis" to the question whether a U.S. citizen could be subject to lethal targeting, one that the Supreme Court had relied on to decide whether a U.S. citizen could be detained as an "enemy combatant." Is this a proper application of the "balancing analysis"? Does the irrevocability of death require a different kind of analysis?
5. In its application of the "balancing analysis," does the government have its thumb on the scale by assuming that any senior operational leader of al-Qaeda is "continuously" planning attacks against the United States?
6. The white paper argues in favor of a "broader concept of imminence," such that a target can be considered an "imminent" threat based on whether there is a "window of opportunity" to kill the target, a low likelihood of collateral damage to civilians, and a reduction in the possibility of future attacks on Americans. Is this "broader concept of imminence" defensible? Would such a definition mean that U.S. citizens who are allegedly senior operational leaders of al-Qaeda or its associated forces could be killed whenever they become vulnerable to lethal targeting and could not be captured without risk to U.S. personnel?
7. The white paper argues that targeted killing is only lawful if capture is not feasible but then insists that capture is not feasible unless the host country consents. Why would the host country's consent to capture be necessary if the United States could kill the target if the host country was "unable or unwilling to suppress the threat posed by the individual targeted"? Why should killing face fewer hurdles than capturing?
8. Although the white paper recognizes the due process rights of a U.S. citizen abroad, it rejects any judicial role

in the determination of whether a U.S. citizen could be lawfully targeted on the ground that he or she is a senior operational leader of al-Qaeda. Is this position defensible because any judicial role in such a determination would require a court "to supervise inherently predictive judgments by the President"? What's wrong with judges supervising presidential predictive judgments?

Although the DOJ white paper argues that the U.S. government must, if it is feasible, capture, rather than kill, a U.S. citizen who is a senior operational leader of al-Qaeda, the targeted killing of Osama bin Laden on May 2, 2011, strongly suggests that no such rule applies to senior operational leaders of al-Qaeda who are not U.S. citizens. The killing of bin Laden was not done with a drone strike, but it was nonetheless a case of targeted killing. Two Black Hawk helicopters flew a twenty-three-member team of Navy SEALs from an air base in Jalalabad, Afghanistan, to bin Laden's secret compound in Abbottabad, Pakistan. The SEALs used explosives to gain access to the main residence of the compound, killing four members of bin Laden's entourage along the way. Three SEALs found bin Laden on an upper floor and shot him in the head and chest, killing him instantly. The killing was lawful because bin Laden did not surrender, but of course it is arguable that the SEALs did not give bin Laden a meaningful opportunity to surrender or that the SEALs could have incapacitated bin Laden with nonlethal measures. Accordingly, the killing of bin Laden underlines the subtlety of the difference between not giving a combatant a chance to surrender, which is legal, versus refusing to accept a surrender, which is illegal.

Three months after *Newsweek* published the DOJ's white paper on targeted killing of U.S. citizens, the Obama administration released a so-called fact sheet titled "U.S. Policy Standards and Procedures for the Use of Force in Counterterrorism Operations outside the United States and Areas of Active Hostilities." This "fact sheet" summarized a classified Presidential Policy Guidance (PPG) on targeted killing that Obama signed on May 22, 2013. The fact sheet clearly indicated that the PPG did not govern how the United States used lethal force in "areas of active hostilities" or how the Obama administration defined this phrase. Were "areas of active hostilities" confined to Afghanistan and Iraq, or did it also include ongoing hostilities in Yemen, Somalia, Libya, or Syria? This lack of clarity meant that the rules governing a large dimension of the Obama administration's targeted-killing program remained secret, including the degree to which "signature strikes" were used in "areas of hostile activities." Second, even though the fact sheet only contained "policy" standards, it nonetheless had a bearing on the important question of whether the Obama administration was targeting non-U.S. citizens outside "areas of active hostilities" differently from U.S. citizens.

8.6 "Fact Sheet" on Targeted Killing, May 22, 2013

. . . One constant is our commitment to conducting counterterrorism operations lawfully.[13] In addition, we consider the separate question of whether force should be used as a matter of policy. The most important policy consideration, particularly when the United

States contemplates using lethal force, is whether our actions protect American lives.

PREFERENCE FOR CAPTURE

. . . The policy of the United States is not to use lethal force when it is feasible to capture a terrorist suspect, because capturing a terrorist offers the best opportunity to gather meaningful intelligence and to mitigate and disrupt terrorist plots. Capture operations are conducted only against suspects who may lawfully be captured or otherwise taken into custody by the United States and only when the operation can be conducted in accordance with all applicable law and consistent with our obligations to other sovereign states. . . .

STANDARDS FOR THE USE OF LETHAL FORCE

Any decision to use force abroad—even when our adversaries are terrorists dedicated to killing American citizens—is a significant one. Lethal force will not be proposed or pursued as punishment or as a substitute for prosecuting a terrorist suspect in a civilian court or a military commission. Lethal force will be used only to prevent or stop attacks against U.S. persons, and even then, only when capture is not feasible and no other reasonable alternatives exist to address the threat effectively. In particular, lethal force will be used outside areas of active hostilities only when the following preconditions are met:

First, there must be a legal basis for using lethal force, whether it is against a senior operational leader of a terrorist organization or the forces that organization is using or intends to use to conduct terrorist attacks.

Second, the United States will use lethal force only against a target that poses a continuing, imminent threat to U.S. persons. It is simply not the case that all terrorists pose a continuing, imminent threat to U.S. persons; if a terrorist does not pose such a threat, the United States will not use lethal force.

Third, the following criteria must be met before lethal action may be taken:

1. Near certainty that the terrorist target is present;
2. Near certainty that non-combatants will not be injured or killed;
3. An assessment that capture is not feasible at the time of the operation;
4. An assessment that the relevant governmental authorities in the country where action is contemplated cannot or will not effectively address the threat to U.S. persons; and
5. An assessment that no other reasonable alternatives exist to effectively address the threat to U.S. persons.

Finally, whenever the United States uses force in foreign territories, international legal principles, including respect for sovereignty and the law of armed conflict, impose important constraints on the ability of the United States to act unilaterally—and on the way in which the United States can use force. The United States respects national sovereignty and international law. . . .

. . . If the United States considers an operation against a terrorist identified as a U.S. person, the Department of Justice will conduct an additional legal analysis to ensure that such action may be conducted against the individual consistent with the Constitution and laws of the United States.

. . . These new standards and procedures do not limit the President's authority to take action in extraordinary circumstances when doing so is both lawful and necessary to protect the United States or its allies. . . .

Questions

1. By labeling capture a "preference," does the "fact sheet" permit other policy factors to outweigh it? Would a capture operation always entail risk to U.S. personnel? In your view, would such risk outweigh the preference?

2. The fact sheet states that lethal force will be used only if capture is not feasible. Would the Navy SEALs have had no choice but to capture bin Laden if the fact sheet had been in force at the time he was killed?
3. The DOJ white paper confined the use of lethal force against U.S. citizens to those who were "senior operational leaders" of al-Qaeda or associated forces, while the fact sheet includes a "senior operational leader of a terrorist organization." Does this mean that the fact sheet authorizes the use of lethal force against noncitizen leaders of all terrorist groups that pose a threat to Americans? In 2013, two years after bin Laden was killed, did it make sense for the Obama administration to detach its targeted-killing program from the group responsible for the 9/11 attacks? Does the right of national self-defense justify such a position? Do all nations have an equal right to act in self-defense in this manner?
4. While the DOJ white paper permitted lethal operations against U.S. citizens only if they were "senior operational leaders" of al-Qaeda or associated forces, the fact sheet permits such operations to be used against "forces that [a terrorist] organization is using or intends to use to conduct terrorist attacks." Does this mean that the United States can kill noncitizen foot soldiers of terrorist groups in foreign countries even if they are outside "areas of active hostilities"?
5. The fact sheet requires "near certainty" that noncombatants will not be injured or killed before lethal force can be used. Is this a realistic standard? Does it encourage the assumption that all males of military age in the vicinity of the attack are in fact combatants? The fact sheet includes a footnote containing the following language: "[I]t is not the case that all military-aged males in the vicinity of a target are deemed to be combatants." What is the significance of this qualification? If gender, age, and proximity to a target are insufficient to "deem" someone a combatant, what additional factor would be enough? A military style of dress? A weapon? A distinctive pattern of movement? A nearby vehicle of a certain type?

The day after President Obama released the fact sheet, he defended the legality of his targeted-killing program in a speech he delivered at the National Defense University. He argued that the program was "legal" and "effective," but that did not mean, he cautioned, that it was "wise or moral in every instance." It was for this reason that his administration placed policy constraints on the use of drones beyond the constraints required by law. Obama focused on the policy constraint of requiring "near-certainty that no civilians will be killed or injured" by a strike. He called this constraint "critical" since there was a "wide gap" between U.S. assessments of civilian casualties from drone strikes and nongovernmental reports. Although Obama conceded that the "near-certainty" standard did not prevent all civilian casualties, drone attacks, in his view, were still necessary because doing nothing "would invite far more civilian casualties." Civilian victims of al-Qaeda attacks, including Muslim victims, Obama argued, "dwarfs any estimate of civilian casualties from drone strikes."[14]

Four months later, on September 18, 2013, Ben Emmerson, the UN's special rapporteur on the promotion and protection of human rights and fundamental freedoms while countering terrorism, issued an interim report to the UN General Assembly on the use of drones in counterterrorism operations. Emmerson's report addressed some of the same issues of international law that Philip Alston (**reading 8.4**) had addressed in 2010: a state could not engage in drone strikes in another state without that state's permission or the approval of the Security Council; there was no consensus on whether a threatened state could engage in drone strikes in another state if the latter state was "unable or unwilling" to neutralize the threat; and last, it was not clear whether the standard of an "imminent attack" required "clear evidence that a specific attack will be carried out in the immediate future." Emmerson's report highlighted two additional issues regarding drone attacks: first, the need for more transparency and accountability so the public could accurately assess the number of civilian casualties; second, the doubtful legality of U.S. drone attacks outside "areas of active hostilities," areas where, in his judgment, international human rights law was controlling, not the laws of war.

8.7 Ben Emmerson's Interim Report on Targeted Killing

41. The single greatest obstacle to an evaluation of the civilian impact of drone strikes is lack of transparency which makes it extremely difficult to assess claims of precision targeting objectively.[15] As the United Nations High Commissioner for Human Rights pointed out during an address to the Security Council on 18 August 2013, the current lack of transparency creates an accountability vacuum and affects the ability of victims to seek redress. . . .

45. . . . Put simply, there is an onus on any State using lethal force to account for civilian casualties. . . . [The] Special Rapporteur considers that the principle of transparency should apply to the preliminary fact-finding inquiries required in any case where there are grounds to believe that civilians may have been killed or injured. Subject to redactions on grounds of national security, a full explanation should be made public in each case. In the view of the Special Rapporteur, this obligation ought to be viewed as an inherent part of the State's legal obligations of accountability under international humanitarian law and international human rights law. . . .

46. In the United States, the involvement of CIA in lethal counter-terrorism operations in Pakistan and Yemen has created an almost insurmountable obstacle to transparency. This is because, just as all secret services, it operates on the basis of neither confirming nor denying its operations. Similarly, the conduct of covert targeting operations by United States special forces under the auspices of the Joint Special Operations Command is almost invariably classified. . . .

47. One consequence is that the United States has to date failed to reveal its own data on the level of civilian casualties inflicted through the use of remotely piloted aircraft in classified operations conducted in Pakistan and elsewhere, or any information on its methodology for evaluating this. The Special Rapporteur does not accept that consideration of national security justify withholding statistical and basic methodological data of this kind. . . .

59. The overwhelming majority of remotely piloted aircraft strikes have been conducted within conventional theatres of armed conflict. The United States, however, has publicly asserted a right under international law to use lethal force in counter-terrorism operations conducted outside areas of active hostilities. This gives rise to a number of issues on which there is either no clear international consensus, or United States policy appears to challenge established norms. . . .

60. International human rights law prohibits arbitrary killing. This prohibition is reflected in specific treaty obligations and forms part of customary international law. Outside situations of armed conflict, the use of deadly force by the State is lawful only if strictly necessary and proportionate, if aimed at preventing an immediate threat to life and

if there is no other means of preventing the threat from materializing. It follows that lethal remotely piloted aircraft attacks will rarely be lawful outside a situation of armed conflict, because only in the most exceptional of circumstances would it be permissible under international human rights law for killing to be the sole or primary objective of an operation. . . .

63. The classic formulation for deciding whether a state of non-international armed conflict has come into existence focuses on the intensity and protraction of the conflict and the degree of organization of the parties. In one view, these criteria are premised upon an assumption of territorial limitation. Intensity, for example, is a relative criterion that has traditionally been measured by analyzing the frequency and severity of armed attacks being conducted within a given area. Moreover, on a practical and operational level, it is necessary to define the geographical scope of the conflict in order to determine whether international humanitarian law principles of targeting apply to any particular operations. If it were otherwise, the law would permit attacks that result in proportionate civilian casualties in areas that are otherwise free of hostilities, a result that may be thought to undermine the very object and purpose of international humanitarian law. . . .

64. ICRC [International Committee of the Red Cross] has noted the absence of a clear international consensus on the issue. Its view, however, is that the existence of a non-international armed conflict must be determined by reference to each situation of violence on a case-by-case basis, and that international humanitarian law does not permit the targeting of persons directly participating in hostilities who are located in non-belligerent States, given that, otherwise, the whole world is potentially a battlefield. . . .

65. Those who advocate the United States position, on the other hand, argue that the geography of conflict has evolved, and that where a State is engaged in non-international armed conflict with a non-State armed group operating transnationally there is no traditional battlefield. They point to the absence of State practice or settled *opinio juris* to imply the existence of a legal rule confining non-international armed conflicts to a defined geographical area, arguing that the principle of territorial applicability described above is, in reality, *lex ferenda* [future law] rather than *lex lata* [current law]. . . .

Questions

1. Do you agree with Emmerson that the United States is not sufficiently transparent about the number of civilian casualties of its drone strikes? Is there any way to assess whether U.S. drone strikes are violating the laws of war unless there is an accurate estimate of the number of civilian casualties for each strike?
2. Is there a legitimate national security reason to keep information about civilian casualties of drone strikes classified? What is the reason? Is keeping such information classified itself a violation of international humanitarian law?
3. In your view, can the United States lawfully target individuals "outside areas of active hostilities"? Should such areas be subject to the laws of war or international human rights law? What difference would it make?
4. Why does Emmerson think that a targeted killing "outside areas of active hostilities" would be lawful only in very "rare" circumstances? In what circumstances would it be lawful?
5. Why does Emmerson argue that the United States' position that a noninternational armed conflict does not need a territorial limitation undermines "the very object and purpose of international humanitarian law"?
6. If the legal rule "confining non-international armed conflicts to a defined geographical area" is a "future law," should the United States respect it today?

In October 2013 Amnesty International released its report "'Will I Be Next?' US Drone Strikes in Pakistan," while Human Rights Watch published "'Between a Drone and Al-Qaeda': The Civilian Cost of US Targeted Killings in Yemen."[16] Both reports argued that the Obama administration's targeted-killing program violated the fundamental right to life. Based on data compiled by the Long War Journal, the New America Foundation, and the Bureau of Investigative Journalism, Amnesty International reported that the total number of U.S. drone strikes at the time was between 348 and 374, the total number killed was between 2,065 and 3,613, and the number of civilians killed was between 153 and 926, including 168 to 200 children.[17]

Although these statistics seemed to provide support for Obama's claim that his counterterrorism policies had "put al-Qaeda's core leadership on a path to defeat,"[18] the 2014 rise of the Islamic State of Iraq and Syria (ISIS, also known as ISIL and IS) cast a shadow on his assertion. Unlike al-Qaeda, which pursued its terror campaign unhindered by political responsibilities, ISIS was committed to controlling territory and resources, in both Iraq and Syria. In pursuit of this goal, ISIS declared a caliphate in June 2014, but that did not mean ISIS had abandoned its strategy of directing and inspiring terrorist attacks in the West. In September 2014, ISIS leader Abu Muhammad al-Adnani released a video directing jihadists around the world to kill Westerners, "especially the spiteful and filthy French," in "any manner or way however it may be."[19]

Adnani may have especially urged attacks against the French because in August 2014 France committed three thousand troops to counterterrorism operations in the Sahel region of Africa, especially in Mali, Chad, and Niger. Whether or not that was Adnani's motivation, soon after his video was published, major ISIS-inspired attacks followed in France. In January 2015, gunmen killed twelve people and injured eleven at the office of newspaper *Charlie Hebdo* in Paris. Later that year, in November, ISIS gunmen and suicide bombers attacked a concert hall, a stadium, and several restaurants and bars in Paris, killing 130 people and injuring hundreds more. On March 22, 2016, three suicide bombers killed thirty-two and injured more than three hundred in Brussels, Belgium. A few months later, on July 14, 2016, an ISIS-inspired terrorist used a rental truck to run over hundreds of people celebrating Bastille Day in Nice, France, killing eighty-six people and injuring dozens more.

French president Francois Holland responded to these attacks by declaring "France is at War" against "terrorism [and] jihadism,"[20] a declaration that seemed to move France closer to the U.S. position that it was engaged in a "global war" against "al-Qaeda and associated forces." Following the rise of ISIS in 2014, other European countries drifted in a similar direction by engaging in targeted killings of alleged terrorists. For example, on August 21, 2015, the United Kingdom killed two British citizens who had joined ISIS by a drone strike in Syria. Defending the lawfulness of the strike, Prime Minister David Cameron invoked the UK's "inherent right to self protection," claiming that the attack was "a new departure" but one that "was necessary and proportionate for the individual self-defense of the UK."[21] In a report issued in May 2016, Parliament's Joint Committee on Human Rights pushed back, asking for further clarification of a number of legal issues surrounding the drone strike, in particular whether human rights law or the law of war applied to situations "outside of armed conflict."[22]

On July 1, 2016, the Obama administration, in an effort to achieve more transparency regarding its counterterrorism operations, released a three-page summary of the number of combatant and noncombatant deaths resulting from U.S. government strikes against terrorist targets between January 20, 2009, and December 31, 2015. The summary claimed that the United States had conducted 473 strikes "outside areas of active hostilities," killing between 2,372 and 2,581 combatants and between 64 and 116 noncombatants.[23] By limiting itself to strikes "outside areas of active hostilities," the summary explicitly noted that it was excluding the number of strikes that had occurred in Afghanistan, Iraq, and Syria, thereby implying that a large dimension of the Obama administration's program of targeted killing remained shrouded in secrecy and the American public had little to no information regarding the number of civilian deaths that had occurred in these three countries as a result of Obama's targeted-killing program.

Moreover, the administration's estimate of civilian casualties "outside areas of active hostilities" (between 64 and 116) was significantly lower than nongovernmental estimates, which ranged at the time from two hundred to eight hundred civilian deaths.[24] Critics argued that the Obama administration should release casualty assessments for each drone strike, thereby allowing a more individualized assessment of the collateral damage of each attack, but government sources claimed that the publication of such information would risk compromising sources and methods of gathering intelligence. The larger question, however, was whether the Obama administration's targeted-killing program "outside areas of active hostilities" was consistent with international law. As noted above, vicious attacks by individuals affiliated or inspired by ISIS triggered a debate in Europe about the nature of the conflict with Islamic terrorism, but there is yet substantial European resistance to the U.S. position on the lawfulness of targeted killing "outside areas of active hostilities," a program of killing that, in the view of many Europeans, violates human rights law.[25]

In August 2016, as a result of a Freedom of Information lawsuit initiated by the American Civil Liberties Union, the Obama administration released a redacted version of the Presidential Policy Guidance (PPG), the essentials of which had been in the 2013 "Fact Sheet" (see **reading 8.6**).[26] At the time of the PPG's release, the 2016 presidential campaign was in full swing, with candidate Donald Trump advocating an expansion of targeted killing of Islamic terrorists, even vowing that he would "take out" their families—a clear violation of the law of war. Once in office, Trump ordered his national security staff to review Obama's PPG to see if any changes should be made. On September 21, 2017, the *New York Times* reported that Trump planned to replace the PPG with a new policy titled "Principles, Standards, and Procedures" (PSP). According to the *Times*, the new policy would relax two central principles of the Obama administration's approach to targeted killing. First, no longer would targeted killing outside "areas of active hostilities" be limited to high-level terrorists who pose a "continuing and imminent threat" to Americans. According to Trump's new policy, it will be acceptable and lawful to target terrorist "foot-soldiers," who have no special skills (such as bomb making) or any leadership function. Second, it will no longer be necessary for proposed drone attacks or raids to be vetted by high administration officials. Operational military officers will decide if targeted killings should proceed.[27]

Trump's PSP will apply to countries outside "areas of active hostilities." It will therefore not be applicable to Afghanistan, Syria, or Yemen, but it could be extended to any country not in active conflict if members of al-Qaeda, ISIS, the Taliban, or other "associated" groups are present, depending perhaps on whether the host country grants permission for the strike or raid. Such permission might be necessary under Trump's PSP because no longer would the targeted-killing program be confined to those who posed a "continuing and imminent threat" to Americans. If there is no such threat, then the right of self-defense is presumably inapplicable, and the consent of the host country would seem to be required. Moreover, since Trump's program of targeted killing is broader than Obama's, it is possible, if not likely, that it will increase the number of civilian deaths and casualties for the obvious reason that it is more difficult to distinguish between "foot-soldiers" and "civilians," as opposed to "civilians" and "high-level terrorists." However, Trump's PSP purportedly has kept the Obama requirement that, before a targeted killing could be initiated, there must be "near certainty" that no civilians will be killed.[28] How this requirement will be implemented is not clear if operational military officers have the authority to pull the trigger when there is a window of opportunity to kill a "foot-soldier" of al-Qaeda, ISIS, the Taliban, or any other "associated" group. As the criteria of targeted killing are weakened and the decision-making process becomes more decentralized and discretionary, it seems more likely, not less, that mistakes and misjudgments are bound to occur. For these reasons, Trump's new PSP has raised the temperature of the debate as to whether U.S. targeted-killing policy is consistent with the right to life, a right that is sanctioned by both domestic and international law. The PSP remains a secret classified document, which itself, arguably, might be a violation of international law (see **reading 8.7**). Is it consistent with international law for the United States, in the context of a transnational "armed conflict" with a dispersed group of nonstate actors, to target individuals with lethal force outside "areas of active hostilities" while refusing to disclose to the American public and the peoples of the world the criteria, principles, and standards by which it designates "enemy combatants" for termination?[29]

NOTES

1. See, generally, Andrew R. Finlayson, "A Retrospective on Counterinsurgency Operations," *Studies in Intelligence* 51, no. 2 (2007), https://www.cia.gov; Dale Andrade, *Ashes to Ashes: The Phoenix Program and the Vietnam War* (New York: Lexington, 1990); and Mark Moyar, *Phoenix and the Birds of Prey: Counterinsurgency and Counterterrorism in Vietnam* (Lincoln, NE: Bison, 2007).

2. W. Hays Parks, "Executive Order 12333 and Assassination," November 2, 1989, Center for Ethics and the Rule of Law, University of Pennsylvania Law School, https://www.law.upenn.edu.

3. See Findings of Fact, *McCann v. United Kingdom*, 21 E.H.R.R 97 (1996), para. 132, European Court of Human Rights (HUDOC), http://hudoc.echr.coe.int.

4. Findings of Fact, *McCann v. United Kingdom*. The court's parenthetical references to earlier paragraphs in the opinion have been deleted from this excerpt. Also, the spelling has been adapted to American standards.

5. *Public Committee against Torture v. Israel*, Supreme Court of Israel, sitting as the High Court of Justice, 2006 46 I.L.M 375, paragraphs 16, 25, 26, 30–40.

6. See "Drone Strikes in Pakistan: Interactive Timeline; 10 Years of Drone Strikes in Pakistan," Bureau of Investigative Journalism, June 18, 2014, https://www.thebureauinvestigates.com.

7. See Eric Schmitt and David Sanger, "Pakistan Shift Could Curtail Drone Strikes," *New York Times*, February 22, 2008.

8. Harold Koh, "The Obama Administration and International Law," Keynote Speech at the Annual Meeting of the American Society of International Law, March 25, 2010, https://2009-2017.state.gov/s/l/releases/remarks/139119.htm.

9. Philip Alston, "Report on Extrajudicial, Summary or Arbitrary Executions," Addendum: Study on Targeted Killings, U.N. Doc. A/HRC/14/24/Add.6 (May 28, 2010), United Nations Human Rights Office of the High Commissioner, http://www.ohchr.org.

10. David J. Barron, "Applicability of Federal Criminal Laws and the Constitution to Contemplated Lethal Operations against Shaykh Anwar al-Aulaki," July 16, 2010, National Security Archive, http://nsarchive.gwu.edu. A redacted version of this Office of Legal Counsel (OLC) memo was made public in 2014.

11. *Al-Aulaqi v. Obama*, 727 F. Supp. 2d 1 (2010).

12. "Department of Justice White Paper: Lawfulness of a Lethal Operation Directed against a U.S. Citizen Who Is a Senior Operational Leader of al-Qa'ida or an Associated Force," November 8, 2011, MSNBC, http://www.msnbc.com.

13. "Fact Sheet: U.S. Policy Standards and Procedures for the Use of Force in Counterterrorism Operations outside the United States and Areas of Active Hostilities," White House Office of the Press Secretary, May 23, 2013, https://www.whitehouse.gov. The Obama administration released a redacted form of the 2013 PPG in August 2016. See "Procedures for Approving Direct Action against Terrorist Targets Located outside the United States and Areas of Active Hostilities," May 22, 2013, American Civil Liberties Union, https://www.aclu.org.

14. President Obama, "Remarks by the President at the National Defense University," May 23, 2013, White House Office of the Press Secretary, https://www.whitehouse.gov.

15. Ben Emmerson, "Interim Report of the Special Rapporteur on the Promotion and Protection of Human Rights and Fundamental Freedoms while Countering Terrorism" (A/68/389), September 18, 2013, Lawfare, https://www.lawfareblog.com. Emmerson submitted his Final Report (A/HRC/25/59) with the same title on March 11, 2014 (see Official Document System of the United Nations, https://documents-dds-ny.un.org).

16. "'Will I Be Next?' US Drone Strikes in Pakistan," Amnesty International, October 21, 2013, http://www.amnestyusa.org; and "'Between a Drone and Al-Qaeda': The Civilian Cost of US Targeted Killings in Yemen," Human Rights Watch, October 22, 2013, https://www.hrw.org.

17. "Will I Be Next?," 13.

18. Barack Obama, State of the Union Address, January 28, 2014.

19. Yara Bayoumy, "ISIS Urges More Attacks on Western 'Disbelievers,'" *Independent*, September 22, 2014.

20. Jethro Mullen and Margot Haddad, "'France Is at War,' President Francois Hollande Says after ISIS Attack," CNN, November 16, 2016.

21. Patrick Wintour and Nicholas Watt, "UK Forces Kill British ISIS Fighters in Targeted Drone Strike on Syrian City," *Guardian*, September 7, 2015.

22. Joint Committee on Human Rights, "The Government's Policy on the Use of Drones for Targeted Killing," May 10, 2016, 50–52, http://www.publications.parliament.uk.

23. "Summary of Information regarding U.S. Counterterrorism Strikes outside Areas of Active Hostilities," Office of the Director of National Intelligence, July 1, 2016, https://www.dni.gov.

24. Charlie Savage and Scott Shane, "U.S. Reveals Death Toll from Airstrikes outside War Zones," *New York Times*, July 1, 2016, http://www.nytimes.com.

25. See Anthony Dworkin, "Europe's New Counter-Terror War," European Council on Foreign Relations, October 2016, http://www.ecfr.eu.

26. "Procedures for Approving Direct Action against Terrorist Targets Located outside the United States and Areas of Active Hostilities," American Civil Liberties Union, May 22, 2013, https://www.aclu.org.

27. Charlie Savage, "Trump Poised to Drop Some Limits on Drone Strikes and Commando Raids," *New York Times*, September 21, 2017, https://www.nytimes.com.

28. Ibid.

29. On December 21, 2017, the American Civil Liberties Union filed a Freedom of Information lawsuit against the Trump administration to force it to publish the PSP. The complaint is available at https://www.aclu.org/legal-document/aclu-v-dod-complaint.

9

Electronic Surveillance

★ ★ ★

Governments have been gathering foreign intelligence information about the capabilities and intentions of their enemies, adversaries, and even allies since the dawn of time. This practice is unlikely to change since such information is a prerequisite for the formulation of a viable foreign policy and an effective national defense. For centuries, the principal source of information of this type was human beings. Spies or undercover agents would convince their sources, by whatever means, to disclose what they knew about their country's technical capacities, strategies, and goals. The rise of electronic communications during the late nineteenth century, whether over a wire (the telegraph and the telephone) or by radio waves, opened up a new dimension of governmental surveillance. Technicians could eavesdrop on a foreign government's communications by tapping a wire or by intercepting radio signals, a form of collection called SIGINT (Signals Intelligence), without going through the bother of finding and exploiting a human source. As electronic communications became more pervasive in the twentieth and twenty-first centuries, the effectiveness of electronic surveillance as a means of gathering foreign intelligence information increased proportionately. The birth of the internet and its radical expansion in the 1990s created an international digitized world, one that involved not only communications between governments, corporations, nongovernmental organizations (NGOs), and individuals but also enormous databases of information about such entities and persons, including bank, travel, communication, and medical records. This digitized universe of information was a gold mine for governments seeking foreign intelligence information. It has ushered in what has been called a "golden age of surveillance."[1]

In the United States, electronic surveillance for national security purposes was first utilized during the Civil War, as both sides tapped telegraph wires to gather relevant information concerning military plans and movements. During World War I, Herbert O. Yardley was the head of the army's code-breaking unit that deciphered thousands of messages from enemy and friendly nations alike, and President Woodrow Wilson ordered the electronic monitoring of domestic groups that opposed the war. The entity that eventually became the Federal Bureau of Investigation (FBI) headed up this effort and over time extended it to all types of dissident "subversive" groups. One reason electronic surveillance expanded during the first half of the twentieth century was that the Supreme Court ruled in *Olmstead v. United States* (1928) that it did not constitute a "search" within the meaning of the Fourth Amendment if there was no physical intrusion into a person's home, office, or other protected area, which did not happen in this case because the wiretap was placed on the phone line at the street, not in the home.[2]

In 1934, Congress enacted the Federal Communications Act, which prohibited wiretapping by federal officers, but only if they "divulged" or "published" the intercepted conversation. The upshot was that federal law enforcement and intelligence officers could continue to wiretap without the need for any judicial warrant, although the evidence or information gathered from the tap could not be used as evidence in a courtroom or disclosed to anyone outside the responsible governmental agency. In 1940, President Franklin D. Roosevelt opined that electronic surveillance would be appropriate where "grave matters involving defense of the nation were involved" and advised the attorney general that he should "secure information by listening devices [directed at] the conversation or other communications of persons suspected of subversive activities against the Government of the United States, including suspected spies." However, Roosevelt added that such investigations should be kept "to a minimum" and that insofar as possible they should be directed at "aliens."[3] During World War II, the army collected copies of the international cables entering and leaving the United States. Following the war, this program continued under the code name "Shamrock," and President Harry Truman's attorney general authorized the FBI to use electronic surveillance whenever the "national interest" required it.[4]

In 1948, the United Nations General Assembly adopted the Universal Declaration of Human Rights, including Article 12, which proclaimed that "[n]o one shall be subjected to arbitrary interference with his privacy, family, home or correspondence."[5] The declaration was not a treaty and was therefore not legally binding on the parties, but at the same time it was a milestone in the evolution of human rights, and it exerted a profound influence on the development of international human rights law. Over time many of its provisions have become legally binding because they have been incorporated into other human rights treaties or because they have obtained the status of customary international law. An example of a human rights treaty that included a right to privacy is the 1953 European Convention on Human Rights, which established the European Court of Human Rights (ECHR). Article 8 of this treaty stated that "[e]veryone has the right to respect for his private and family life, his home and his correspondence."[6]

The Supreme Court revisited the constitutionality of electronic surveillance in *Katz v. United States* (1967), a case involving FBI agents attaching a listening device to the outside of a public telephone booth to obtain evidence that the defendant was transmitting wagering information by telephone in violation of a federal criminal statute. The court overruled *Olmstead* by holding that it was immaterial that the FBI did not physically intrude into the telephone booth. The defendant's rights were nonetheless violated, according to Justice Potter Stewart's majority opinion, because it was a mistake to understand the Fourth Amendment as a constitutional guarantee that protected only "physical areas" from government intrusion. As Stewart succinctly put it, "[T]he Fourth Amendment protects people, not places." In a concurring opinion, Justice John Harlan introduced a twofold test of what constitutes a "search": a person must have a subjective expectation of privacy and that expectation must be one that society recognizes as "reasonable." This test quickly became the orthodox understanding of what constituted a Fourth Amendment "search."[7]

Congress responded to *Katz* by enacting the Omnibus Crime and Control and Safe Streets Act of 1968. Title III of this statute regulated when electronic surveillance could be used in federal criminal investigations of designated federal offenses. In any federal prosecution of these offenses, a judicial warrant from a "neutral and detached" magistrate was required before electronic surveillance could be initiated. The magistrate could issue the warrant only if there was (1) "probable cause" to believe that an individual "is committing, has committed, or is about to commit" one of the designated offenses; (2) "probable cause" to believe that "particular communications" concerning the offense will be obtained through electronic surveillance; (3) "probable cause" to believe that any communications collected will be intercepted at "facilities" that are being used in connection with the specified offense; and (4) a finding that "normal investigative procedures" have failed to obtain the relevant evidence and are not likely to be successful in the future. In addition, Title III limited the surveillance to thirty days; imposed guidelines that prevented the collection of communications outside the warrant; required that all communications collected under an expired warrant be kept under seal; and mandated that the government inform the target of the electronic surveillance after the warrant had expired. Last, Title III granted a defendant who was trying to suppress evidence a right to examine the application materials for the warrant.[8]

Section 2511(3) of Title III stated that the statute did not limit "the constitutional power of the President to take such measures as he deems necessary to protect the Nation against actual or potential attack or other hostile acts of a foreign power, to obtain foreign intelligence information deemed essential to the security of the United States, or to protect national security information against foreign intelligence activities."[9] This provision clearly recognized the president's authority to use electronic surveillance to protect the nation from the hostile acts of foreign powers but left unanswered the question whether the president's Article II surveillance power extended to domestic groups that advocated revolution or opposed the Vietnam War. The Supreme Court addressed the issue of governmental surveillance of domestic groups in *United States v. United States District Court* (also known as the *Keith* case), which involved a federal prosecution of an alleged conspiracy by the White Panther Party to bomb a CIA office in Michigan. At the trial, the government wanted to use evidence collected by warrantless electronic surveillance to convict the defendants of conspiracy to destroy government property. Justice Lewis Powell delivered the opinion of the court excerpted below. No one doubted that such warrantless surveillance of a subversive domestic group was a "search," but was it a "reasonable" one permitted by the Fourth Amendment?

9.1 *United States v. United States District Court* (1972)

As the Fourth Amendment is not absolute in its terms, our task is to examine and balance the basic values at stake in this case: the duty of Government to protect the domestic security, and the potential danger posed by unreasonable surveillance to individual privacy and free expression.[10] If the legitimate need of Government to safeguard domestic security requires the use of electronic surveillance, the question is whether the needs of citizens for privacy and free expression may not be better protected by requiring a warrant before such surveillance is undertaken. . . .

It is true that there have been some exceptions to the warrant requirement. But those exceptions are few in number and carefully delineated; in general, they serve the legitimate needs of law enforcement officers to protect their own well-being and preserve evidence from destruction. . . .

The Government argues that the special circumstances applicable to domestic security surveillances necessitate a further exception to the warrant requirement. . . .

But we do not think a case has been made for the requested departure from Fourth Amendment standards. The circumstances described do not justify complete exemption of domestic security surveillance from prior judicial scrutiny. Official surveillance, whether its purpose be criminal investigation or ongoing intelligence gathering, risks infringement of constitutionally protected privacy of speech. Security surveillances are especially sensitive because of the inherent vagueness of the domestic security concept, the necessarily broad and continuing nature of intelligence gathering, and the temptation to utilize such surveillances to oversee political dissent. We recognize, as we have before, the constitutional basis of the President's domestic security role, but we think it must be exercised in a manner compatible with the Fourth Amendment. In this case we hold that this requires an appropriate warrant procedure.

We cannot accept the Government's argument that internal security matters are too subtle and complex for judicial evaluation. Courts regularly deal with the most difficult issues of our society. There is no reason to believe that federal judges will be insensitive to or uncomprehending of the issues involved in domestic security cases. Certainly courts can recognize that domestic security surveillance involves different considerations from the surveillance of "ordinary crime." If the threat is too subtle or complex for our senior law enforcement officers to convey its significance to a court, one may question whether there is probable cause for surveillance.

Nor do we believe prior judicial approval will fracture the secrecy essential to official intelligence gathering. The investigation of criminal activity has long involved imparting sensitive information to judicial officers who have respected the confidentialities involved. . . .

We emphasize, before concluding this opinion, the scope of our decision. As stated at the outset, this case involves only the domestic aspects of national security. We have not addressed, and express no opinion as to, the issues which may be involved with respect to activities of foreign powers or their agents. . . .

Questions

1. Exceptions to the warrant requirement include (1) searches that are incident to a lawful arrest; (2) stop and frisks; (3) automobile/vehicle exception; and

(4) hot pursuit cases. If these kinds of searches can take place without a warrant, why should electronic surveillance of a domestic seditious group be unconstitutional? According to the court, what is different about the latter kind of search?
2. Are "security surveillances" more "sensitive" than "criminal surveillances" because "domestic security" is a "vague" concept, because such surveillance is "broad" and "continuing," or because there is a temptation to use them "to oversee political dissent"? Are any of these reasons persuasive?
3. Is the government correct that internal security cases are too "subtle" and "complex" for judicial evaluation of "reasonableness"? Why or why not?
4. Does requiring a judicial warrant for electronic surveillance in a domestic security case inevitably risk disclosure of sensitive intelligence information? What if the executive officials plan to respond to the domestic threat by means other than criminal prosecution, such as by spreading false information about the group or by turning the group's leaders into government informants?
5. Was the court right not to express any opinion regarding the government's use of warrantless electronic surveillance against foreign powers or their agents?

Although the Supreme Court in *Keith* required a judicial warrant for electronic surveillance in domestic security cases, Justice Powell also indicated that domestic security cases were so different from ordinary criminal cases that Congress could, if it wished, establish standards and procedures for such cases that would be less rigorous and more flexible than Title III requirements. Also, following the court's decision in *Keith*, several federal courts of appeal considered whether the Supreme Court's ruling should be extended to cases involving foreign security threats. The consensus of these courts was that requiring a warrant in cases involving foreign intelligence gathering would undermine the president's ability to carry out his Article II foreign affairs responsibilities, but these courts also confined such warrantless surveillance to targets who were "foreign powers" or their "agents" and "collaborators" and to situations where the executive branch's "primary" purpose was to gather foreign intelligence information. If the government's "primary" purpose was criminal prosecution, then a judicial warrant would be required.[11]

At the international level, the right of privacy received the official support of the United Nations when the General Assembly adopted the International Covenant on Civil and Political Rights (ICCPR) on December 16, 1966, a formal treaty that took effect in 1976, following the Supreme Court's decision in the *Keith* case. Article 17 of the ICCPR read as follows:

> 1. No one shall be subjected to arbitrary or unlawful interference with his privacy, family, home, or correspondence. . . . 2. Everyone has the right to the protection of the law against such interference or attacks.[12]

Thirty-five countries ratified the ICCPR by 1976, but the United States did not ratify it until 1992. During the interim, following the revelations of the Church Committee concerning the abusive intelligence activities of the National Security Agency (NSA), the FBI, and the CIA, Congress enacted the Foreign Intelligence Surveillance Act (FISA) of 1978. Generally speaking, this statute regulated how and when the executive branch could gather foreign intelligence information inside the United States. Accordingly, while electronic surveillance of domestic security threats inside the United States remained subject to Title III constraints, electronic surveillance for the purpose of gathering foreign intelligence information inside the United States became subject to FISA.

Since the NSA is the principal intelligence agency of the U.S. government that gathers "foreign intelligence information" by "electronic surveillance," FISA's regulatory framework was directly applicable to it. FISA imposed controls on the NSA by defining several crucial terms, including "foreign intelligence information," "electronic surveillance," "foreign power," and "agent of a foreign power," and by requiring from one of the judges of a newly created court (the FISA court) that there was "probable cause" that the target of surveillance was either a "foreign power" or an "agent of a foreign power" before the NSA could initiate "electronic surveillance." To make this finding, the FISA judge would only consider the evidence presented by the government because it would be self-defeating to inform an "agent of a foreign power" that he or she was a possible target for surveillance. Any type of NSA surveillance that did not fit within FISA's definition of "electronic surveillance" was outside of FISA's statutory regulatory framework and subject only to the procedures and standards contained in executive orders issued by the president. The FISA court eventually grew to a size of eleven Article III judges, all with life tenure. The following excerpt reviews FISA's definitions of the key terms noted above.

9.2 Foreign Intelligence Surveillance Act of 1978

[**a. Definition of Foreign Intelligence (§ 101[e])**: Before a judge on the Foreign Intelligence Surveillance Court (FISC) could lawfully issue an order authorizing electronic surveillance, a high executive official must certify that the purpose of the surveillance is to collect "foreign intelligence information."[13] The definition varies depending on whether the surveillance target is or is not a "U.S. person," that is, a U.S. citizen or permanent resident.]

"Foreign Intelligence Information" means—

(1) information that relates to and, if concerning a United States person, is necessary to the ability of the United States to protect against—
   (A) actual or potential attack or other grave hostile acts of a foreign power or an agent of a foreign power;
   (B) sabotage or international terrorism by a foreign power or an agent of a foreign power; or
   (C) clandestine intelligence activities by an intelligence service or network of a foreign power or by an agent of a foreign power; or

(2) information with respect to a foreign power or foreign territory that relates to and, if concerning a United States person, is necessary to—
   (A) the national defense or the security of the United States; or
   (B) the conduct of the foreign affairs of the United States.

[**b. Definition of Electronic Surveillance (§ 101[f])**: There are four types of surveillance that are subject to FISA's standards and procedures. Any NSA surveillance that does not fit within one of these definitions is not subject to FISA, although it would be subject to any applicable executive orders or regulations.]

"Electronic surveillance" means—

(1) the acquisition by an electronic, mechanical, or other surveillance device of the contents of any wire or radio communi-

cation sent by or intended to be received by a particular, known United States person who is in the United States, if the contents are acquired by intentionally targeting that United States person, under circumstances in which a person has a reasonable expectation of privacy and a warrant would be required for law enforcement purposes;
(2) the acquisition by an electronic, mechanical, or other surveillance device of the contents of any wire communication to or from a person in the United States, without the consent of any party thereto, if such acquisition occurs in the United States;
(3) the intentional acquisition by an electronic, mechanical, or other surveillance device of the contents of any radio communication, under circumstances in which a person has a reasonable expectation of privacy and a warrant would be required for law enforcement purposes, and if both the sender and all intended recipients are located within the United States; or
(4) the installation or use of an electronic, mechanical, or other surveillance device in the United States for monitoring to acquire information, other than from a wire or radio communication, under circumstances in which a person has a reasonable expectation of privacy and a warrant would be required for law enforcement purposes.

[**c. Definition of a Foreign Power** (§ **101** [a]): FISA identifies six types of foreign powers and authorizes the attorney general to approve warrantless electronic surveillance of the first three types but requires an order from the FISA court to authorize electronic surveillance of the last three types of foreign powers.]

"Foreign power" means—
(1) a foreign government or any component thereof, whether or not recognized by the United States;
(2) a faction of a foreign nation or nations, not substantially composed of United States persons;
(3) an entity that is openly acknowledged by a foreign government or governments to be directed and controlled by such foreign government or governments;
(4) a group engaged in international terrorism or activities in preparation thereof;
(5) a foreign-based political organization, not substantially composed of United States persons; or
(6) an entity that is directed and controlled by a foreign government or governments.

[**d. Definition of an Agent of a Foreign Power** (**101**[**b**]): FISA's definition of an agent of a foreign power is bifurcated, depending on whether the target of the electronic surveillance is a "non-U.S. person" or a "U.S. person." It is important to understand that an "agent of a foreign power" need not be an agent of a foreign government but could be an "agent" of a foreign "faction," "entity," or "foreign-based political organization." Also, FISA prohibits any finding that a "U.S. person" is a "foreign power" or an "agent of a foreign power" based "solely upon the basis of activities protected by the first amendment of the Constitution of the United States." See §105(a)(3)(A). The FISA court can approve electronic surveillance of an "agent of a foreign power" for ninety days, three times longer than what is permissible under Title III, and to protect sources and methods of gathering foreign intelligence information, FISA has no requirement that the target be informed of the surveillance when the authorization expires.]

"Agent of a foreign power" means—
(1) any person other than a United States person who—
  (A) acts in the United States as an officer, member, or employee of a foreign power; or
  (B) acts for or on behalf of a foreign power which engages in clandestine intelligence activities in the United Sates contrary to the interests of the United States, when the circumstances of such person's presence in the United States indicate that such person may engage in such activities in the United States, or when such

person knowingly aid or abets any person in the conduct of such activities or knowingly conspires with any person to engage in such activities; or

(2) any person [including "U.S. persons"] who—

(A) knowingly engages in clandestine intelligence gathering activities for or on behalf of a foreign power, which activities involve or may involve a violation of the criminal statutes of the United States;

(B) pursuant to the direction of intelligence service or network of a foreign power, knowingly engages in any other clandestine intelligence activities for or on behalf of such foreign power, which activities involve or are about to involve a violation of the criminal statutes of the United States;

(C) knowingly engages in sabotage or international terrorism, or activities that are in preparation thereof, for or on behalf of a foreign power; or

(D) knowingly aid or abets any person in the conduct of activities described in subparagraph (A), (B), or (C) or knowingly conspires with any person to engage in activities described in subparagraph (A), (B), or (C).

Questions

1. Is it logical to define "foreign intelligence information" differently depending on whether the information is "concerning" a non-U.S. person rather than a U.S. person?
2. If the target of the electronic surveillance is a "non-U.S. person," information qualifies as "foreign intelligence information" if it "relates to" the "national defense or the security of the United States" or "the conduct of the foreign affairs of the United States." How broad is this category of "foreign intelligence information"? Can you identify a type of information that could not conceivably be collected by the NSA under this definition? If the target is a "U.S. person," in what way is the government's ability to collect "foreign intelligence information" under FISA more limited?
3. What types of electronic surveillance do not fall within FISA's definition of "electronic surveillance"? What if a U.S. citizen is outside the United States? What about a wire communication between someone inside the United States and someone abroad? What if the acquisition of a wire communication occurs outside the United States and the target is not a U.S. person? Would FISA apply if a U.S. person inside the United States telephoned someone in France by way of a satellite transmission? What if a wire communication between two non-U.S. persons outside the United States traveled across a wire located inside the United States? Would FISA have any bearing on the use of a listening device in a foreign country?
4. Why does FISA permit the attorney general to approve electronic surveillance of the first three types of "foreign powers" but require the approval of a FISA judge for the last three types?
5. How would you understand the terms "entity," "faction," and "foreign-based political organizations" as types of "foreign powers"?
6. What sort of evidence would constitute probable cause that a group is engaged in "activities in preparation" of international terrorism?
7. Are allied governments excluded from the category of "foreign powers"? What about international NGOs that are supportive of U.S. foreign policy?
8. Is it "reasonable" under the Fourth Amendment to treat nonresident aliens inside the United States differently from U.S. persons?
9. Are "clandestine intelligence activities" necessarily illegal? Can an alien lawfully gather information about U.S. foreign policy but nonetheless be subject to electronic surveillance because he or she is an agent of a for-

eign power? Would the surveillance be consistent with FISA if the alien "might" engage in clandestine intelligence activities?

10. If FISA surveillance can be approved on the ground that the target "may engage" in "clandestine intelligence activities" or "criminal conduct," how does Title III's standard of probable cause differ from FISA's? Which law permits authorization of surveillance based on "probable cause" of a "possibility"?

11. Should a U.S. person inside the United States be subject to potential FISA surveillance if he or she "aids," "abets," or "conspires" with a non-U.S. person who is engaged in lawful "clandestine intelligence activities" for the benefit of a U.S. ally?

In 1981 President Ronald Reagan issued Executive Order 12333, which was titled United States Intelligence Activities.[14] This executive order established guidelines for the collection of foreign intelligence information by U.S. intelligence agencies. Accordingly, all types of electronic surveillance conducted by the NSA that did not fall within FISA's definition of "electronic surveillance" were subject to the guidelines, rules, and standards of Executive Order 12333. The federal government's use of electronic surveillance was therefore subject to three different legal authorities: Title III governed electronic surveillance for the purpose of criminal investigations; FISA controlled certain types of electronic surveillance conducted for the purpose of gathering foreign intelligence information; and, last, Executive Order 12333 was the legal basis for the collection of foreign intelligence information by warrantless electronic surveillance that did not satisfy FISA's definition. Of these three "baskets" of electronic surveillance, the third was by far the largest, because it included the surveillance that the NSA engaged in outside the United States, the surveillance of all U.S. international radio communications, and the surveillance of all foreign-to-foreign communications that were transmitted across the wired communication networks located in the United States. In addition, when the NSA collects information under 12333, it can collect information by targeting specific individuals or entities or through "bulk" collection, which "vacuums up" substantive communications and data in a wholesale indiscriminate fashion and stores it in databases for later analysis. The NSA had little difficulty "vacuuming up" U.S. international communications if they were radio communications or if they traveled over a copper wire on the seabed floor, but once fiber-optic cables came into general use, the NSA could more easily tap them at the switches that linked the cable to a national communication network, rather than tapping the cable itself.

While each "basket" of surveillance was different in character, they all raised questions, in varying degrees, as to whether the United States was in compliance with either the Fourth Amendment or the international "right to privacy" recognized by the ICCPR and the Universal Declaration of Human Rights. However, the Fourth Amendment had little or no relevance to the lawfulness of NSA surveillance conducted under Executive Order 12333 outside the United States, especially if no U.S. person was targeted. The Supreme Court had ruled in *United States v. Verdugo-Urquidez* (1990) that nonresident aliens in foreign countries had no Fourth Amendment rights.[15] Whether NSA surveillance conducted under FISA or Executive Order 12333 was in compliance with the international right to privacy was an entirely separate question. In 1988, the United Nations Human Rights Committee (HRC) issued General Comment No. 16, which was titled "The Right to Respect of Privacy, Family, Home and Correspondence and Protection of Honor and Reputation." The Human Rights Committee is a body of independent experts (eighteen in number and elected to four-year terms by member states) that monitors implementation of the ICCPR by all state parties to the treaty. "General Comments" are the HRC's official interpretations of ICCPR's provisions. The following excerpt is from General Comment No. 16, which interprets Article 17 of the ICCPR (see p. 243 above).

9.3 UN Human Rights Committee, General Comment No. 16 (1988)

1. Article 17 provides for the right of every person to be protected against arbitrary or unlawful interference with his privacy, family, home or correspondence.[16] . . . In the view of the Committee this right is required to be guaranteed against all such interferences and attacks whether they emanate from State authorities or from natural or legal [corporate] persons. The obligations imposed by this article require the State to adopt legislative and other measures to give effect to the prohibition against such interferences and attacks as well as to the protection of this right. . . .

3. The term "unlawful" means that no interference can take place except in cases envisaged by the law. Interference authorized by States can only take place on the basis of law, which itself must comply with the provisions, aims and objectives of the Covenant.

4. The expression "arbitrary interference" is also relevant to the protection of the right provided for in article 17. In the Committee's view, the expression "arbitrary interference" can also extend to interference provided for under the law. The introduction of the concept of arbitrariness is intended to guarantee that even interference provide for by law should be in accordance with the provisions, aims and objectives of the Covenant and should be, in any event, reasonable in the particular circumstances. . . .

7. As all persons live in society, the protection of privacy is necessarily relative. However, the competent public authorities should only be able to call for such information relating to an individual's private life the knowledge of which is essential in the interests of society as understood under the Covenant. . . .

8. Even with regard to interferences that conform to the Covenant, relevant legislation must specify in detail the precise circumstances in which such interferences may be permitted. A decision to make use of such authorized interference must be made only by the authority designated under the law, and on a case-by-case basis. Compliance with article 17 requires that the integrity and confidentiality of correspondence should be guaranteed de jure and de facto. Correspondence should be delivered to the addressee without interception and without being opened or otherwise read. Surveillance, whether electronic or otherwise, interception of telephonic, telegraphic and other forms of communication, wire-tapping and recording of conversations should be prohibited. . . .

10. The gathering and holding of personal information on computers, data banks and other devices, whether by public authorities or private individuals or bodies, must be regulated by law. Effective measures have to be taken by States to ensure that information concerning a person's private life does not reach the hands of persons who are not authorized by law to receive, process and use it, and is never used for purposes incompatible with the Covenant. In order to have the most effective protection of his private life, every individual should have the right to ascertain in an intelligible form, whether, and

if so, what personal data is stored in automatic data files, and for what purposes. Every individual should also be able to ascertain which public authorities or private individuals or bodies control or may control their files. If such files contain incorrect personal data or have been collected or processed contrary to the provisions of the law, every individual should have the right to request rectification or elimination. . . .

Questions

1. Is the HRC correct that the international right to privacy is a guarantee that applies against both states and natural/legal persons?
2. According to the HRC, does Article 17 impose on states the obligation to protect an individual's privacy from unreasonable interference by natural/legal persons? What must the state do to fulfill this obligation? How would this duty relate to the recent disclosure that Facebook permitted third parties to have access to its data, such that the data of 87 million Americans ended up in the hands of Cambridge Analytica, a British political consulting firm that used it to help Donald Trump win the 2016 presidential election?
3. Is the HRC claiming that any state interference with the right to privacy is "lawful" only if it complies with the "provisions, aims and objectives of the Covenant"? Can this be the right interpretation if the preamble to the ICCPR states that its rights, including the right to privacy, are derived "from the inherent dignity of the human person"? How do you reconcile the imperatives of national security with human dignity?
4. The HRC also argues that state interference with the ICCPR's right to privacy can be "lawful" but violate Article 17 because it is "arbitrary." How is "arbitrariness" to be assessed? Paragraph 4 refers to "reasonableness," while paragraph 7 suggests that any interference is "arbitrary" if it is not "essential." Is there a difference between these two criteria? Which is valid?
5. In your opinion, is the NSA surveillance authorized by FISA (discussed above) both "lawful" and "non-arbitrary"? Is such surveillance "reasonable in the circumstances"? Is NSA surveillance under Executive Order 12333 "reasonable"? Are either consistent with human dignity?
6. Does FISA "specify in detail the precise circumstances" in which interference with Article 17's right to privacy is permissible?
7. Does the HRC prohibit all forms of wiretapping, or is it saying that it "should be prohibited"? Does it prohibit wiretapping by natural/legal persons, by the state, or by both?
8. Would the HRC's rule regarding "correspondence" be applicable to email?
9. Does FISA respect the HRC's requirement that every individual should have "the right to ascertain in an intelligible form, whether, and if so, what personal data is stored in automatic data files, and, for what purposes"?
10. Does FISA give the individual the right to know whether his or her personal information has been disseminated to other governmental agencies?

Since HRC's General Comment No. 16 was an interpretation of ICCPR, it had little or no bearing on U.S. surveillance practices until the Senate ratified the treaty in 1992. However, the Senate conditioned its ratification on a number of reservations, understandings, and declarations, including an explicit statement that Articles 1 through 27 of the treaty were not self-executing.[17] What this meant was that no individual was permitted to file a lawsuit alleging that the U.S. government was violating the rights contained in the ICCPR, including the right to privacy, unless Congress enacted appropriate implementation legislation. In short, although the Supremacy Clause of the U.S. Constitution implied that the ICCPR was "the supreme law of the land," no individual could file a lawsuit to enforce its provisions based solely upon the treaty.

Moreover, in its initial 1995 report to the HRC, the United States took the position that the ICCPR did not have extraterritorial application, which meant the ICCPR did not restrict how the federal government could engage in electronic surveillance *outside the United States* under Executive Order 12333. The United States defended its position based in part on its interpretation of Article 2, which said that each state party was obliged to respect ICCPR rights of "all individuals within its territory and subject to its jurisdiction."[18] The United States argued that this language meant no individual had rights under the ICCPR against the United States unless he or she was both "within" the territory of the United States and "subject" to its jurisdiction. The HRC disagreed, claiming the U.S. view was "contrary to the consistent interpretation of the Committee on this subject."[19] According to the HRC, the United States would violate the treaty if it did not respect the ICCPR rights of an alien "subject to its jurisdiction," even if the alien was outside the United States. The HRC's implication was that placing an alien outside the United States under electronic surveillance was subjecting that person to the "jurisdiction" of the United States, which was, of course, a highly debatable inference. After all, monitoring an alien's phone calls or emails abroad is somewhat "passive" in character. It was arguably not an exertion of either a state's de facto control or its legitimate authority over that individual, which would mean that any surveillance conducted by the NSA outside the United States under Executive Order 12333 did not have to comport with the ICCPR's right to privacy. However, there was no doubt that Article 17 of the ICCPR did limit how state members, including the United States, collected foreign intelligence information inside their own countries, especially in regard to their own citizens. Accordingly, at a minimum, HRC's General Comment No. 16 did raise the question whether FISA's provisions satisfied the standards of Article 17.

This issue of FISA's compliance with Comment No. 16 became more problematic because the Human Rights Committee (HRC) elevated the standards of Article 17 in *Toonen v. Australia* (1994), a case involving the criminalization of homosexual conduct. After quickly stating that adult consensual sexual activity was within the scope of privacy protected by Article 17, the HRC claimed that the prohibition could be consistent with the ICCPR only if it was "reasonable in the circumstances," that is, only if it were "proportional to the end sought" and "necessary in the circumstances of any given case." The committee then argued that the prohibition of homosexual conduct was not "proportional to the end sought" because there was no evidence that it prevented the spread of HIV/AIDS virus and that it was not "necessary" for the protection of morals since local authorities were not in fact enforcing the prohibition.[20] The implication of the committee's decision was that even lawful interference with privacy, such as surveillance conducted under FISA, violated Article 17 if it was neither "proportionate" nor "necessary."

The issue of whether FISA was consistent with Article 17 became more complicated after the 9/11 attacks because of two major developments. First, Congress revised FISA to permit the use of electronic surveillance if "a significant purpose" of the surveillance was to gather "foreign intelligence information." This slight change in language had important ramifications because the FISA court had formerly approved electronic surveillance only if collecting foreign intelligence information was the government's "primary purpose." The FISA court had enforced this requirement by building a "wall" between intelligence agents and law enforcement personnel, such that prosecutors were prohibited from directing and controlling FISA surveillance in cases involving overlapping criminal and intelligence investigations. To enforce the FISA court's "wall," the Department of Justice went so far as to prohibit communications between intelligence officials and law enforcement personnel unless they were "chaperoned" by high-level officials in the Justice Department.

Following the passage of the USA PATRIOT Act, the FISA court continued to enforce the "wall,"[21] but the government appealed the FISA court's decision to the Foreign Intelligence Surveillance Court of Review (FISCR), the first such appeal in the history of FISA. The FISCR concluded that FISA electronic surveillance was lawful, even if the government's "primary purpose" was criminal prosecution, so long as the government (1) "entertains a realistic option of dealing with the agent [of a foreign power] other than through criminal prosecution," for example, by stopping an ongoing conspiracy or by turning the agent into an informant; and (2) is investigating a "foreign intelligence crime," such as espionage or terrorism. In reaching this decision, the court of review held that broadening the scope of FISA electronic surveillance in this fashion did not violate the Fourth Amendment because the government had a "special need" to protect the nation from terrorists and espionage threats.

9.4 *In Re: Sealed Case*, 310 F.3d 717 (2002)

. . . [A]s the government points out, when it commences an electronic surveillance of a foreign agent, typically it will not have decided whether to prosecute the agent (whatever may be the subjective intent of the investigators or lawyers who initiate an investigation). So long as the government entertains a realistic option of dealing with the agent other than through criminal prosecution, it satisfies the significant purpose test. . . .

. . . It can be argued, however, that by providing that an application [for FISA surveillance] is to be granted if the government has only a "significant purpose" of gaining foreign intelligence information, the Patriot Act allows the government to have a primary objective of prosecuting an agent for a non-foreign intelligence crime. Yet we think that would be an anomalous reading of the [USA PATRIOT Act] amendment. For we see not the slightest indication that Congress meant to give that power to the Executive Branch. . . . That is not to deny that ordinary crimes might be inextricably intertwined with foreign intelligence crimes. For example, if a group of international terrorists were to engage in bank robberies in order to finance the manufacture of a bomb, evidence of the bank robbery should be treated just as evidence of the terrorist act itself. But the FISA process cannot be used as a device to investigate wholly unrelated ordinary crimes. . . .

The main purpose of ordinary criminal law is twofold: to punish the wrongdoer and to deter other persons from embarking on the same course. The government's concern with respect to foreign intelligence crimes, on the other hand, is overwhelmingly to stop or frustrate the immediate criminal activity. . . . Punishment of the terrorist or espionage agent is really a secondary objective; indeed, punishment of a terrorist is often a moot point [presumably because he or she died as a martyr.] . . .

The distinction between ordinary criminal prosecutions and extraordinary situations underlies the Supreme Court's approval of entirely warrantless and even suspicionless searches that are designed to serve the government's "special needs, beyond the normal need for law enforcement." Apprehending drunk drivers and securing the border constitute such unique interests beyond ordinary, general law enforcement.

A recent case, *City of Indianapolis v. Edmund*, is relied on by both the government and *amici*. In that case, the Court held that a highway checkpoint designed to catch drug dealers did not fit within its special needs exception because the government's "primary purpose" was merely "to uncover evidence of ordinary criminal wrongdoing." The Court rejected the government's argument that the "severe and intractable nature of the drug problem" was sufficient justification for such a dragnet seizure lacking any individualized suspicion. *Amici* particularly rely on the Court's statement that "the gravity of the threat alone cannot be dispositive of questions concerning what means law enforcement officers may employ to pursue a given purpose."

But by "purpose" the Court makes clear it was referring not to a subjective intent, which is not relevant in ordinary Fourth Amendment probable cause analysis, but rather to a programmatic purpose. The Court distinguished the prior check point cases *Martinez-Fuerte* (involving checkpoints less than 100 miles from the Mexican border) and *Sitz* (checkpoints to detect intoxicated motorists) on the ground that the former involved the government's "longstanding concern for the protection of the integrity of the border," and the latter was "aimed at reducing the immediate hazard posed by the presence of drunk drivers on the highways." The Court emphasized that it was decidedly not drawing a distinction between suspicionless seizures with a "non-law-enforcement purpose" and those designed for law enforcement. Rather, the Court distinguished general crime control programs and those that have another particular purpose, such as protection of citizens against special hazards or protection of our borders. The Court specifically acknowledged that an appropriately tailored road block could be used "to thwart an imminent terrorist attack." The nature of the "emergency," which is simply another word for threat, takes the matter out of the realm of ordinary crime control. . . .

FISA's general programmatic purpose, to protect the nation against terrorists and espionage threats directed by foreign powers, has from its outset been distinguishable from "ordinary crime control." After the events of September 11, 2001, . . . it is [also] hard to imagine greater emergencies facing Americans than those experienced on that date.

We acknowledge, however, that the constitutional question presented by this case—whether Congress's disapproval of the primary purpose text is consistent with the Fourth Amendment—has no definitive jurisprudential answer. The Supreme Court's special needs cases involve random stops (seizures) not electronic searches. In one sense, they can be thought of as a greater encroachment into personal privacy because they are not based on any particular suspicion. On the other hand, wiretapping is a good deal more intrusive than an automobile stop accompanied by questioning.

Although the Court in *City of Indianapolis* cautioned that the threat to society is not dispositive in determining whether a search or seizure is reasonable, it certainly remains a crucial factor. Our case may well involve the most serious threat our country faces. Even without taking into account the President's inherent constitutional authority to conduct warrantless foreign intelligence surveillance, we think the procedures and government showing required under FISA, if they do not meet the minimum Fourth Amendment warrant standards, certainly come close. We, therefore, believe firmly, applying the balancing test drawn from *Keith*, that FISA as amended is constitutional because the surveillances it authorizes are reasonable. . . .

Questions

1. Does the government always retain the option of not prosecuting an agent of a foreign power? If so, does this mean that collecting "foreign intelligence" information is always a "significant purpose" of FISA surveillance in cases involving a "foreign intelligence" crime?
2. What qualifies as a "foreign intelligence crime" as opposed to an "ordinary crime"? Should such crimes require a Title III warrant?
3. How easy would it be for the government to link an investigation of an "ordinary crime" by an agent of a foreign power with an investigation of a "foreign intelligence crime" so that the government can rely on FISA surveillance, even if its primary purpose is the criminal prosecution of the "ordinary crime"?
4. Is the FISCR correct that, in foreign intelligence crimes, the government's concern is not "to punish the wrongdoer and to deter other persons" but rather "overwhelmingly to stop or frustrate the immediate criminal activity"? If true, why are spies sentenced to long prison terms?
5. Is FISA surveillance in investigations of foreign intelligence crimes like a highway checkpoint that is designed to catch drug dealers (which the Supreme Court has deemed not to constitute a "special need"); is it like a checkpoint near the Mexican border or a checkpoint to detect intoxicated drivers (which do qualify as "special needs"); or is it not like any of these other types of searches?
6. Do foreign intelligence crimes pose a "special hazard" more so than serious ordinary crimes, such as murder, kidnapping, or rape?
7. Even if the Supreme Court said in *Keith* that the government could, without a judicial warrant, use "an appropriately tailored roadblock" to "thwart an imminent terrorist attack," does this concession have any bearing on the degree to which the government can use FISA electronic surveillance to prosecute all foreign intelligence crimes, not just imminent terrorist attacks?
8. If the president has "inherent constitutional authority to conduct warrantless foreign intelligence surveillance," can he ignore FISA standards and procedures completely? Why not?
9. In your view, if the government's primary purpose is criminal prosecution of a foreign intelligence crime, is FISA surveillance consistent with Article 17 of ICCPR? Is such surveillance "necessary"? If it is, is it "proportionate"?

The second major post-9/11 development regarding the use of electronic surveillance to collect foreign intelligence information was a secret President's Surveillance Program (PSP) that President George W. Bush established in October 2001. The PSP, also known as Stellar Wind, was based on Bush's Article II constitutional authority to gather foreign intelligence information. Few members of Congress knew anything about the program, at least initially. The program's purpose was to protect the United States from any additional terrorist attacks, but its legality was uncertain because it violated FISA by collecting foreign intelligence information from wire and radio communications (both telephone and internet) inside the United States without a FISA order.

The PSP had two different branches. First, it collected the substantive telephone and email communications of suspected terrorists abroad who communicated with anyone inside the United States, a targeted program that became known as the Terrorist Surveillance Program (TSP). With the cooperation of internet service providers and phone companies, the NSA obtained the relevant communications directly from the switches that linked U.S. phone and internet systems with the global communications network. The relevant communications were all those that were "to," "from," or "about" phone numbers or email addresses that were linked to international terrorists, although the program was narrowed in 2004 to members of al-Qaeda, the Taliban, and associated groups.

The second branch of the PSP consisted of the collection of the metadata of U.S. international and domestic telephone and internet communications. Communications metadata included not substantive communications but only data about communications, for example, the metadata of telephone communications would include the calling and called numbers, plus the date, time, and duration of the call. The program would not collect the names of subscribers or their addresses (though the NSA could gather this information independently from other public and private sources). The NSA collected this metadata directly from the internet and from the "call detail records" kept by the phone companies, such as AT&T, Verizon, and Sprint. In general, the metadata collection program indiscriminately, without any individual targeting, collected and stored in a database for five years as much communications metadata as the NSA could collect in bulk. If and when the NSA determined there was a "reasonable articulable suspicion" that a particular telephone number or email address was linked to a suspected terrorist, the NSA would check it against the database of communications metadata through a process known as "contact chaining" to discover if the suspected terrorist had communicated with anyone inside the United States. The NSA would then determine who the U.S.-based communicants of the terrorist were telephoning or emailing, and so on, up to three "hops" from the "seed" number of the suspected terrorist.

In March 2004, officials in the Department of Justice (DOJ) objected to certain features of the PSP, which led to a crisis in Attorney General John Ashcroft's hospital room after James Comey, acting attorney general, refused to certify that all aspects of PSP were lawful. The concern of senior DOJ officials was that certain features of the PSP could not be justified because they did not target terrorists associated with al-Qaeda, the Taliban, or associated forces. For that reason, surveillance of this kind could not reasonably be within Bush's Article II power to defend the country or the statutory authority provided by the 2001 Authorization for Use of Military Force (AUMF) to use military force against those responsible for the 9/11 attacks. For example, the PSP indiscriminately collected in bulk the metadata of internet communications inside the United States. This type of collection violated FISA and could not be justified based on Article II or the AUMF because most of the metadata collected was not linked in any way to al-Qaeda, the Taliban, or associated terrorist groups. In the end, facing a threat of resignation from a large number of DOJ officials unless changes were made to the PSP, Bush agreed to bring specific programs of the PSP under the rubric of FISA by seeking authorization for them from a FISA court judge.

On July 14, 2004, Colleen Kollar-Kotelly, the presiding judge of the FISA court, decided that the internet communications metadata program (metadata of email, social media websites, chat rooms, interactive games, etc.) could be authorized under FISA's pen register/trap-and-trace provisions, which traditionally had been used by the government to collect the communications metadata of agents of foreign powers inside the United States. Kollar-Kotelly's opinion addressed the important statutory issue as to whether the program only collected data that was "relevant" to an authorized investigation, a requirement of the statute, as well as the more general question whether the program was consistent with the Fourth Amendment. Although Judge Kollar-Kotelly held that the bulk collection of internet communications metadata collected "relevant" information and did not violate the Fourth Amendment, there was little doubt that the program in question, because of its secret nature, violated Article 17 of the ICCPR. The Bush administration had never fully informed Congress or the American people about the existence or scope of this program by 2004. In fact, a redacted copy of Judge Kollar-Kotelly's opinion was not publicly released until 2013, following the revelations of Edward Snowden. In the following excerpt, "xxxxxxx" indicates redacted words or phrases.

9.5 Judge Kollar-Kotelly's 2004 Opinion on Bulk Collection of Internet Communications Metadata

The Court is persuaded that, in the circumstances of this case, the scope of the proposed collection is consistent with the certification of relevance.[22] In so finding, the Court concludes that, under the circumstances of this case, the applicable relevance standard does not require a statistical "tight fit" between the volume of proposed collection and the much smaller proportion of information that will be directly relevant to xxxxxxxxxxxxx FBI investigations. In reaching this conclusion, the Court finds instructive Supreme Court precedents on when a search that is not predicated on individualized suspicion may nonetheless be reasonable under the Fourth Amendment.

The Supreme Court has recognized a "longstanding principle that neither a warrant nor probable cause, nor, indeed, any measure of individualized suspicion, is an indispensable component of reasonableness in every circumstance." Specifically, the Court has held that, "where a Fourth Amendment intrusion serves special governmental needs, beyond the normal need for law enforcement, it is necessary to balance that individual's privacy expectations against the Government's interests to determine whether it is impractical to require a warrant or individualized suspicion in the particular context."

This balancing analysis considers "the nature of the privacy interest allegedly compromised" and "the character of the intrusion" upon that interest. The privacy interest in the instant metadata is not of a stature protected by the Fourth Amendment. Moreover, the nature of the intrusion is mitigated by the restrictions on accessing and disseminating this information, under which only a small percentage of the data collected will be seen by any person.

The assessment of reasonableness under the Fourth Amendment also considers "the nature and immediacy of the government's concerns and the efficacy of the [program] in meeting them." In this case, the Government's concern is to identify and track xxxxxxxxxxxx operatives, and ultimately to thwart terrorist attacks. This concern clearly involves national security interests beyond the normal need for law enforcement and is at least as compelling as other governmental interests that have been held to justify searches in the absence of individualized suspicion [for example, drug testing of secondary school students engaged in extracurricular activities, highway checkpoints to identify drunk drivers, drug testing of Custom Service employees applying for promotion to sensitive positions, and drug and alcohol testing of railroad workers]. The Government's interest here has even greater "immediacy" in view of . . . intelligence reporting and assessment regarding ongoing plans for large scale attacks within the United States. . . .

In summary, the bulk collection proposed in this case is analogous to suspicionless searches or seizures that have been upheld under the Fourth Amendment in that the Government's need is compelling and immediate, the intrusion on individual privacy interests is limited, and bulk collection appears to be a reasonably effective means of detecting and monitoring xxxxxxxxxx related operatives and thereby obtaining information likely to be xxxxxx to ongoing FBI investigations. In these circumstances, the certification of relevance is consistent with the fact that only a very small proportion of the huge volume of information collected will be directly relevant to the FBI's xxxxxxxxxxxxxx investigations. . . .

The foregoing analysis has observed at various points that the Fourth Amendment does not apply to the proposed collection of meta data. This section explains the basis for that conclusion.

First, as a general matter, there is no reasonable expectation of privacy under the Fourth Amendment in the meta data to be collected. This conclusion follows directly from the reasoning of *Smith v. Maryland*, which concerned the use of a pen register on a home telephone line. In that case, the Supreme Court found that it was doubtful that telephone users had a subjective expectation of privacy in the numbers they dialed, and that in any case such an expectation "is not 'one that society is prepared to recognize as reasonable.'" The Court "consistently has held that a person has no legitimate expectation of privacy in information he voluntarily turns over to third parties," since he "assume[s] the risk" that the third party would reveal that information to the government. The Court found this principle applicable to dialed phone numbers, regardless of the automated means by which the call is placed and the "fortuity of whether or not the phone company in fact elects to make a quasi-permanent records of a particular number dialed."

The same analysis applies to the meta data involved in this application. Users of e-mail xxxxxxxxxxxxxxxxxxxxxx voluntarily expose addressing information for communications they send and receive to communications service providers. Having done so, they lack any legitimate expectation of privacy in such information for Fourth Amendment purposes. . . .

. . . However, since this application involves unusually broad collection and distinctive modes of analyzing information, the Court will explain why these special circumstances do not alter its conclusion that no Fourth Amendment search or seizure is involved.

First, regarding the breadth of the proposed surveillance, it is noteworthy that the application of the Fourth Amendment depends on the government's intruding into some individual's reasonable expectation of privacy. Whether a large number of persons are otherwise affected by the government's conduct is irrelevant. Fourth Amendment rights "are personal in nature, and cannot bestow vicarious protection on those who do not have a reasonable expectation of privacy in the place to be searched." . . . So long as no individual has a reasonable expectation of privacy in metadata, the large number of persons whose communications will be subjected to the proposed pen register/trap and trace surveillance is irrelevant to the issue of whether a Fourth Amendment search or seizure will occur. . . .

In this case, sophisticated analysis of archived meta data may yield more information about a person's Internet communications than what would at first be apparent. Nevertheless, such analysis would . . . involve merely a derivative use of information already obtained, rather than an independent governmental invasion of matters protected by the Fourth Amendment. Accordingly, the Court finds that the proposed collection and analysis does not involve a search or seizure under the Fourth Amendment. . . .

Questions

1. Judge Kollar-Kotelly argues the internet communication metadata is "relevant" on the ground that the Supreme Court has held that searches "not predicated on individualized suspicion may nonetheless be reasonable under the Fourth Amendment." Is this argument persuasive? How does the "reasonableness" of the government's conduct establish that the information collected is "relevant" to an investigation of international terrorism?
2. Why does Judge Kollar-Kotelly rely on the Supreme Court's "special needs" cases for her assessment of "relevance" when she ultimately concludes that internet communications metadata are "not of a stature protected by the Fourth Amendment"? Is it because, even if internet metadata is not protected by the Fourth Amendment, it is unclear whether the collection of it is authorized by the FISA pen register/trap-and-trace provision?
3. Does Judges Kollar-Kotelly's argument depend on the fact that a few of the email addresses stored in the NSA's database of internet communications metadata will at some point in the future be linked to email addresses associated with terrorists? Does this mean that she is equating email addresses that might "become relevant" to a terrorist investigation with email addresses that "are relevant" to a terrorist investigation?
4. Does Judge Kollar-Kotelly ignore the fact that *Smith v. Maryland* involved the use of a pen register on a targeted suspect, not the bulk collection of a large amount of internet communications metadata? In your view, is this difference significant?
5. Judge Kollar-Kotelly argues that the huge breadth of the NSA's collection program of internet communications metadata is irrelevant to whether there is a Fourth Amendment violation. Do you agree with her?
6. Do you agree with Judge Kollar-Kotelly that the NSA's "sophisticated analysis" of the internet communications metadata is not a search and seizure under the Fourth Amendment because it is "a derivative use of information already obtained"? Does this mean the government can analyze information any way it wishes if the initial collection of information is lawful, regardless if the analysis reveals intimate details of the lives of individual American citizens?
7. The government secretly discontinued the internet metadata bulk collection program in late 2011 because "its operational value" had declined. If the program became unnecessary in 2011, is it likely it would have been lawful and constitutional in 2004? Would it have been consistent with Article 17 of the ICCPR?

The bulk telephone communications metadata program was secretly shifted over to FISA in 2006. This program differed from the internet communications metadata program because the NSA was not obtaining this information from a wire but rather was receiving it from the voluntary cooperation of telephone companies that routinely kept "call detail records" for a period of years. The NSA therefore could not use FISA's pen register/trap-and-trace provision as a statutory foundation for the telephone metadata program. It relied instead on FISA's "business records" provision, also known as Section 215. This provision granted the government the authority to seek a FISA court order compelling the production of any "tangible thing" (which would include "business records") if there were "reasonable grounds" to believe they were "relevant" to an authorized investigation to obtain "foreign intelligence information not concerning a United States person or to protect against international terrorism or clandestine intelligence activities"—basically the same "relevance" standard that Judge Kollar-Kotelly addressed in her 2004 opinion.[23]

FISA Judge Malcolm Howard, on May 23, 2006, issued an order requiring all telephone companies to turn over metadata to the government on a daily basis, including both international and domestic metadata, but he did so without issuing an opinion justifying his decision. The order enabled the NSA to collect telephone metadata from all telephone companies, not just those that had voluntarily cooperated with it in the past, thereby increasing the size of the government's telephone metadata program. Without issuing any opinion, FISA judges reissued the telephone metadata order every ninety days until Edward Snowden's disclosures in June 2013 ignited an intense public debate concerning NSA surveillance. At that point, Judge Claire Eagan issued an opinion that upheld the lawfulness of the government's telephone metadata collection program based on reasoning that closely followed that of Judge Kollar-Kotelly's 2004 opinion.[24]

Six months later, Judge Richard J. Leon, a district court judge in Washington, D.C., issued an opinion that sharply disagreed with the view that the telephone metadata program was consistent with the Fourth Amendment. He rejected the assumption that *Smith v. Maryland* was the controlling precedent for the government's massive bulk collection program of telephone metadata, relying in part on the Supreme Court's 2012 ruling in *United States v. Jones*, a case involving the police's long-term use of a GPS device to monitor the location of a suspect's car. Although the court's majority opinion held that police violated the Fourth Amendment by physically attaching the GPS device to the car, thereby intruding upon the suspect's property, two concurring opinions by Justices Sonia Sotomayor and Samuel Alito suggested it was time to reconsider *Smith*'s assumption that no individual could have a reasonable expectation of privacy regarding information he or she voluntarily gave to third parties, such as the location of a car in plain view on public streets or the telephone metadata contained in the "business records" of phone companies.[25]

9.6 *Klayman v. Obama*, 957 F. Supp. 2d 1 (Dec. 2013)

. . . [T]he question in this case can more properly be styled as follows: When do present-day circumstances—the evolutions in the Government's surveillance capabilities, citizens' phone habits, and the relationship between the NSA and telecom companies—become so thoroughly unlike those considered by the Supreme Court thirty-four years ago that a precedent like *Smith* simply does not apply. . . .

First, the pen register in *Smith* was operational for only a matter of days between March 6, 1976 and March 19, 1976, and there is no indication from the Court's opinion that it expected the Government to retain those limited phone records once the case was over. . . . The NSA telephony metadata program, on the other hand, involves the creation and maintenance of a historical database containing *five years'* worth of data. And I might add, there is the very real prospect that the program will go on for as long as America is combatting terrorism, which realistically could be forever!

Second, the relationship between the police and the phone company in *Smith* is *noth-*

ing compared to the relationship that has apparently evolved over the last seven years between the Government and telecom companies. . . . In *Smith*, the Court considered a one-time, targeted request for data regarding an individual suspect in a criminal investigation, which in no way resembles the daily, all-encompassing, indiscriminate dump of phone metadata that the NSA now receives as part of its Bulk Telephony Metadata Program. It's one thing to say that people expect phone companies to occasionally provide information to law enforcement; it is quite another to suggest that our citizens expect all phone companies to operate what is effectively a joint intelligence-gathering operation with the Government.

Third, the almost-Orwellian technology that enable the Government to store and analyze the phone metadata of every telephone user in the United States is unlike anything that could have been conceived in 1979. In *Smith*, the Supreme Court was actually considering whether local police could collect one person's phone records for calls made after the pen register was installed and for the limited purpose of a small-scale investigation of harassing phone calls. The notion that the Government could collect similar data on hundreds of millions of people and retain that data for a five-year period, updating it with new data every day in perpetuity, was at best, in 1979, the stuff of science fiction. By comparison, the Government has at its disposal today the most advanced twenty-first century tools, allowing it to "store such records and efficiently mine them for information years into the future." . . .

Finally, *and most importantly*, not only is the Government's ability to collect, store, and analyze phone data greater now than it was in 1979, but the nature and quantity of the information contained in people's telephony metadata is much greater, as well. According to the 1979 U.S. census, in that year, 71,958,000 homes had telephones available, while 6,614,000 did not. In December 2012, there were a whopping 326,475,248 mobile subscriber connections in the United States, of which approximately 304 million were for phones and twenty-two million were for computers, tablets, and modems. The number of mobile subscribers in 2013 is more than *3,000 times* greater than the 91,600 subscriber connections in 1984 and more than *triple* the 97,035,925 subscribers in 2000. . . .

Admittedly, what metadata *is* has not changed over time. As in *Smith*, the *types* of information at issue in this case are relatively limited: phone numbers dialed, date, time, and the like. But the ubiquity of phones has dramatically altered the ubiquity the *quantity* of information that is now available and, *more importantly*, what that information can tell the Government about people's lives. . . . Records that once would have revealed a few scattered tiles of information about a person now reveal an entire mosaic—a vibrant and constantly updating picture of the person's life. . . .

Having found that a search occurred in this case, I next must "examin[e] the totality of the circumstances to determine whether [the] search is reasonable within the meaning of the Fourth Amendment." [A]s a general matter, warrantless searches are *per se* unreasonable under the Fourth Amendment.

The Supreme Court has recognized only a "few specifically established and well-delineated exceptions to that general rule, including one that applies when "special needs, beyond the normal need for law enforcement, make the warrant and probable-cause requirement impracticable." . . .

. . . Whether the program violates the Fourth Amendment will therefore turn on "the nature and immediacy of the government's concerns and the efficacy of the [search] in meeting them."

The Government asserts that the Bulk Telephony Metadata Program serves the "programmatic purpose" of "identifying unknown terrorist operatives and preventing terrorist attacks"—an interest that everyone, including this Court, agrees is "of the highest order of magnitude." . . .

Yet, turning to the efficacy prong, the Government does *not* cite a single instance in which analysis of the NSA's bulk metadata collection actually stopped an imminent attack, or otherwise aided the Government in achieving any objective that was time-sensitive in nature. . . . Given the limited record before me at this point in the litigation—most notably, the utter lack of evidence that a terrorist attack has ever been prevented because searching the NSA database was faster than other investigative tactics—I have serious doubts about the efficacy of the metadata collection program as a means of conducting time-sensitive investigations in cases involving imminent threats of terrorism. Thus, plaintiffs have a substantial likelihood of showing that their privacy interests outweigh the Government's interest in collecting and analyzing bulk telephony metadata and therefore the NSA's bulk collection program is indeed an unreasonable search under the Fourth Amendment. . . .[26]

Questions

1. If the bulk collection program of telephone metadata collects the same type of information the Supreme Court considered in *Smith v. Maryland*, how can Judge Leon claim this case is not the controlling precedent? Should a lower court judge set aside such a precedent or wait until the Supreme Court overturns the decision?
2. Do the phone companies "own" the telephone metadata records? Can individual subscribers have Fourth Amendment rights to information contained in records "owned" by someone else? How would Judge Leon respond?
3. Judge Leon points to the fact that the government keeps the telephone metadata for five years, but is that relevant to whether callers have a "reasonable expectation of privacy" regarding such information? If they do not have such an expectation at the time of collection, is it irrelevant how long the government keeps such information?
4. Even if telecommunication companies have joined the government in a "joint-intelligence operation," does this fact have any bearing on whether subscribers have a "reasonable expectation of privacy" regarding telephone metadata?
5. Even if the tools by which the government analyzes telephone metadata have improved over the last forty years, does that have a bearing on whether subscribers have a Fourth Amendment right that prevents the government from collecting such information in bulk?
6. Even if phones play a more important role in the lives of today's citizens than they did years ago, why would that fact have a bearing on whether the government could collect telephone metadata that is the same today as it was in 1979?
7. Should Judge Leon have deferred to the fifteen FISA judges that upheld the lawfulness of the bulk telephone metadata collection program thirty-five times from 2006 until December 2013 because, with their access to classified information, they have a better understanding of the program's benefits?
8. Even if the government cannot point to a single instance in which the bulk telephony metadata program actually prevented an "imminent attack," would the program still serve a "special need" if it, along with other sources and methods of gathering intelligence, might help to prevent terrorist attacks in the future?
9. Since the telephone metadata collection program was justified on the basis of FISA, would it be fair to conclude that it was consistent with Article 17 of the ICCPR after it became public in 2013?
10. Most members of Congress had opportunities to learn about the telephone metadata program when Section 215 was reauthorized in 2006, 2009, and 2011, even though many did not take

advantage of these briefings. Would the fact that more members of Congress knew about the program have a bearing on whether Section 215 authorized it? On whether the program was constitutional?

The last component of the PSP that made the transition to FISA was the TSP, a program that collected without a warrant substantive international phone and internet communications leaving or entering the United States. The shift had become necessary after the *New York Times* disclosed the existence of the TSP to the American public in December 2005.[27] Upset subscribers began to file lawsuits against the telecommunication companies that had cooperated in NSA's TSP program, which in turn persuaded these same companies to seek immunity from future lawsuits by refusing to turn over any additional communications unless there was a court order forcing them to do so. The telecommunication companies' concern was understandable because a federal district court judge in Michigan had ruled in 2006 that the TSP was likely illegal and ordered the government to shut it down.[28] However, the Bush administration in early 2007 succeeded in obtaining a court order compelling U.S. telecommunication companies to transfer to the NSA the communications of specified targets from FISA Judge Malcolm Howard, the same judge who had upheld the lawfulness of NSA's telephone metadata program in 2006. A key implication of Howard's decision was that he accepted the government's controversial argument that the switches linking the U.S. phone and internet network with international communication systems could be designated a "facility" within the meaning of FISA, even though this term traditionally had only referred to a specific target's phone numbers or email addresses, and that it was consistent with the Fourth Amendment for NSA officials, not judges, to make the determination that there was a "reasonable articulable suspicion" that a particular target abroad was associated with designated terrorist groups.[29] However, ninety days later, when Howard's order had to be renewed, his interpretations of FISA and the Fourth Amendment soon met with opposition from other FISA court judges.[30] Confronting this judicial roadblock, the Bush administration went to Congress for a legislative solution. Congress responded by enacting the temporary Protect America Act in August 2007 and the more permanent FISA Amendments Act (FAA) in July 2008.[31]

The key provision of the FAA was Section 702, which contained a fundamental trade-off. It protected privacy rights by requiring a FISA court order for any electronic surveillance that targeted a U.S. person abroad, a type of surveillance that the NSA had previously engaged in without a warrant under Executive Order 12333 if the point of collection was outside the United States. However, 702 also radically broadened the scope of NSA surveillance. It did so, first, by dropping the requirement that the target had to be associated with terrorist groups responsible for the 9/11 attacks. All that 702 required was reasonable grounds to believe that the target, while communicating with someone inside the United States, was himself or herself outside the United States. Accordingly, 702 could be used to collect all types of foreign intelligence information from communications entering and leaving the United States, including communications related to nuclear proliferation, international drug trafficking, other international criminal activity, foreign trade/investment policies, or the activities of international NGOs, such as Greenpeace, Amnesty International, or the Red Cross.

Second, Section 702 broadened the scope of NSA's collection of substantive communications by giving FISA judges the authority to compel "electronic communications service providers," such as Google, Yahoo, and Facebook, to turn over to the NSA stored communications of non-U.S. persons reasonably thought to be located outside the United States. Prior to this change in the law, the NSA had collected international communications from the telephone and internet "backbone" that were "to," "from," or "about" an NSA target located abroad in real time—a program referred to as Upstream. The new program, which was called PRISM, was limited to communications "to" and "from" a target, but it granted the NSA historical access to a huge volume of communications stored on the servers of internet communication providers. The importance of PRISM soon surpassed that of the older Upstream type of collection. As noted in the excerpt that follows, PRISM accounted for 91 percent of the internet communications that the NSA acquired each year under Section 702, leaving Upstream with only 9 percent of the total of collected internet communications.

It is important to note that under Section 702 a FISA judge did not make any "probable cause" determinations that a particular telephone number or email address was linked to one of the categories of foreign intelligence information sought by the executive branch. Instead, the judge's role was simply to certify that the category in question was indeed a legitimate type of "foreign intelligence information" and approve the procedures that the NSA used to ensure that the targets subject to 702 surveillance were indeed non-U.S. persons outside the United States. In addition, the FISA judge also approved the "minimization" standards that required the NSA to "minimize" the "acquisition" and the "retention" as well as prohibit the "dissemination" of "nonpublicly available information concerning unconsenting United States persons consistent with the need of the United States to obtain, produce, and disseminate foreign intelligence information."[32] However, over the years, the FISA court has significantly relaxed these "minimization" standards, permitting the NSA to share with other intelligence agencies, such as the FBI and the CIA, much of the "raw data" it collects, whether the collection is done under traditional FISA rules, Section 702, or Executive Order 12333.

As Section 702 broadened the scope of NSA surveillance through Upstream and PRISM, it dramatically expanded what the NSA calls the "incidental collection" of communications of U.S. persons inside the United States. This expansion happened because the NSA acquires both the foreign and the domestic end of any international communication it collects. That was 702's basic trade-off: the privacy rights of U.S. persons abroad were more protected, but the likelihood that the communications of U.S. persons inside the United States would be "incidentally" collected went up radically. Once these "incidental" communications were stored in government databases, government analysts could, in many instances, query the databases using U.S. person identifiers—a query that critics of the 702 program called "backdoor searches"—even if the purpose of the query was criminal law enforcement. Of course, it is not known how many of these U.S. international communications were already collected in bulk by the NSA outside the United States under Executive Order 12333. However, the 702 program was perhaps more useful to analyze the "incidental" communications of U.S. persons because the target of the collection was a non-U.S. person outside the United States who likely possessed "foreign intelligence information."

In April 2007, a FISA judge ruled that the substance of the PRISM program was consistent with the Fourth Amendment, a decision the FISA Court of Review upheld in August 2008.[33] However, in 2011, FISA Judge John D. Bates held that certain aspects of the Upstream program were constitutionally suspect. He had no problem with the Upstream's collection of telephone or internet communications if they were "to," "from," or "about" the target of the surveillance. "About" communications were those that contained the target's phone number or email address but was not "to" or "from" the target. However, Bates was concerned that Upstream collected not only single communication transactions (SCTs) but also multiple communication transactions (MCTs). These MCTs consisted of a number of SCTs. If one of the SCTs within an MCT was "to," "from," or "about" an NSA target's phone number or email address, the NSA would collect the entire MCT, including SCTs that were "wholly domestic communications" or international communications that were not "to," "from," or "about" an NSA target. Bates underlined the seriousness of the problem by pointing out that a study conducted by the NSA had concluded that tens of thousands of these two types of communications were being collected under Upstream, but also noted it was "technologically infeasible" for the NSA to collect only the discrete communications within an MCT that were "to," "from," or "about" an NSA target's phone number or email address.

In the end, Judge Bates concluded that the Upstream program was not consistent with the Fourth Amendment because it collected a substantial number of domestic and international communications that were completely unrelated to any NSA target. Deferring to an earlier decision by the FISA Court of Review, Judge Bates assumed there was a "foreign intelligence exception" to the warrant requirement and that the "reasonableness" of the NSA's collection of MCTs must be assessed based on the "totality of circumstances," balancing the needs of national security against the degree of intrusion into the privacy of U.S. persons. The following excerpt focuses on how Judge Bates applied this balancing test. It should be noted that a redacted version of Judge Bates's opinion did not become public until after Edward Snowden's revelations in 2013. Redacted portions of the opinion are marked with xxxxx's.

9.7 [Redacted], 2011 WL 10945618 (FISA Ct. Oct. 3, 2011)

. . . [I]t must [first] be noted that NSA's upstream collection makes up only a very small fraction of the agency's total collection pursuant to Section 702.[34] As explained above, the collection of telephone communications under Section 702 is not implicated at all by the government's recent disclosures regarding NSA's acquisition of MCTs. Nor do those disclosures affect NSA's collection of Internet communications directly from Internet service providers [the PRISM program] xxxxxxxxxxxxxxxxxxxxxxxxxxx, which accounts for approximately 91% of the Internet communications acquired by NSA each year under Section 702. And the government recently advised that NSA now has the capability, at the time of acquisition, to identify approximately 40% of its upstream collection as constituting discrete communications (non-MCTs) that are to, from, or about a targeted selector [i.e., a target's phone or email address]. Accordingly, only approximately 5.4% (40% of 9%) of NSA's aggregate collection of Internet communications (and an even smaller portion of the total collection) under Section 702 is at issue here. The national security interest at stake must be assessed bearing these numbers in mind. . . .

. . . [I]n terms of its size and its nature, the [privacy] intrusion resulting from NSA's acquisition of MCTs is substantial. The Court now understands that each year, NSA's upstream collection likely results in the acquisition of roughly two to ten thousand discrete wholly domestic communications that are neither to, from, nor about a targeted selector, as well as tens of thousands of other communications that are to or from a United States person or a person in the United States but that are neither to, from, nor about a targeted selector. In arguing that NSA's targeting and minimization procedures satisfy the Fourth Amendment notwithstanding the acquisition of MCTs, the government stresses that the number of protected communications acquired is relatively small in comparison to the total number of Internet communications obtained by NSA through its upstream collection. That is true enough, given the enormous volume of Internet transaction acquired by NSA through its upstream collection (approximately 26.5 million annually). But the number is small only in that relative sense. The Court recognizes that the ratio of non-target, Fourth Amendment-protected communications to the total number of communications must be considered in the Fourth Amendment balancing. But in conducting a review under the Constitution that requires consideration of the totality of the circumstances, the Court must also take into account the absolute number of non-target, protected communications that are acquired. In absolute terms, tens of thousands of non-target, protected communications annually is a *very* large number. . . .

The government stresses that the non-target communications of concern here . . . are acquired incidentally rather than purposefully. Insofar as NSA acquires entire MCTs because it lacks the technical means to limit collection only to the discrete portion or portions of each MCT that contain a reference to the targeted selector, the Court is satisfied that is the case. . . .

Here the quantity and nature of the information that is "incidentally" collected distinguishes this matter from the prior instances in which this Court and the [FISA] Court of Review have considered incidental acquisitions. As explained above, the quantity of incidentally acquired, non-target, protected communications being acquired by NSA through its upstream collection is, in absolute terms, very large, and the resulting intrusion is, in each instance, likewise very substantial. And with regard to the nature of the acquisition, the government acknowledged in a prior Section 702 docket that the term "incidental interception" is "most commonly understood to refer to an intercepted communication between a target using a facility [e.g., a specific phone or email address] subject to surveillance and a third party using a facility not subject to surveillance." . . . [H]ere, by contrast, the incidental acquisitions of concern are not direct communications between a non-target third party and the user of a targeted facility. Nor are they the communications of non-targets that refer directly to a targeted selector. Rather, the communications of concern here are acquired simply because they appear somewhere in the same *transaction* as a separate communication that is to, from, or about the targeted facility.

The distinction is significant and impacts the Fourth Amendment balancing. A discrete communication as to which the user of the targeted facility is a party or in which the targeted facility is mentioned is much more likely to contain foreign intelligence information than is a separate communications that is acquired simply because it happens to be within the same transaction as a communication involving a targeted facility. Hence, the national security need for acquiring, retaining, and disseminating the former category of communications is greater than the justification for acquiring, retaining, and disseminating the latter form of communication.

The [FISA] Court of Review and this Court have recognized that the procedures governing retention, use, and dissemination bear on the reasonableness under the Fourth Amendment of a program for collecting foreign intelligence information. As explained in the discussion of NSA's minimization procedures above, the measures proposed by NSA for handling MCTs tend to maximize, rather than minimize, the retention of non-target information, including information of or concerning United States persons. Instead of requiring the prompt review and proper disposition of non-target information (to the extent it is feasible to do so), NSA's proposed measures focus almost exclusively on those portions of an MCT that an analyst decides, after review, that he or she wishes to use. An analyst is not required to determine whether other portions of the MCT constitute discrete communications to or from a United States person or a person in the United States, or contain information concerning a United States person or person inside the United States, or, having made such a determination, to do anything about it. Only those MCTs that are immediately recognized as containing a wholly domestic discrete communication are purged, while other MCTs remain in NSA's repositories for five or more years, without being marked as MCTs. Nor, if an MCT contains a discrete communication of, or other information concerning, a United States person or person in the United States is the MCT marked as such. Accordingly, each analyst who retrieves an MCT and wishes to use a portion thereof is left to apply the proposed minimization measures alone, from beginning to end, and without the benefit of his colleagues' prior review and analysis. Given the limited review of MCTs that is required, and the difficulty of the task of identifying protected information within an MCT, the government's proposed measures seem to enhance, rather than reduce, the risk of error, overretention, and dissemination of non-target information, including information protected by the Fourth Amendment.

In sum, . . . [u]nder the totality of the circumstances, then, the Court is unable to find that the government's proposed application of NSA's targeting and minimization procedures to MCTs is consistent with the requirements of the Fourth Amendment. . . .

Questions

1. Is it surprising that Judge Bates and other FISA judges quickly accepted the conclusion that it was constitutional for the NSA to intercept inside the U.S. international wire communications "to" or "from" NSA targets who are outside the country? Should FISA judges decide whom to target for such surveillance? Does it matter that international radio communications have never required judicial approval of NSA targeting decisions? Should the same Fourth Amendment standards be applied to U.S. international wire and radio communications? Should it matter that the number of international wire communications has dramatically increased since FISA was enacted in 1978?
2. Do you agree that the collection of "about" communications under the Upstream program is consistent with the "reasonableness" requirement of the Fourth Amendment? Should Judge Bates have discussed this issue more in depth? Is it enough that an email contains the "selector" of an NSA target outside the United States to justify the collection? Would such a program be constitutional if it targeted only suspected terrorists outside the United States but not if it targeted anyone

outside the United States who might have "foreign intelligence information"? Do you know the email address of someone outside the United States who might have "foreign intelligence information"? If you do, what is the implication?

3. Judge Bates emphasized that only 5.4 percent of the internet communications collected by the NSA are MCTs, implicitly suggesting that this dimension of NSA surveillance did not contribute much to U.S. national security. But is this suggestion persuasive? If the NSA cannot at times technically separate MCTs from SCTs at the point of collection, how can it collect any SCTs without running the risk of collecting MCTs?
4. The government underlines the fact that the collection of MCTs leads to the acquisition of only a small number of constitutionally protected communications "relative" to the total number of internet communications that are collected, but Judge Bates focuses on the "absolute" number of constitutionally protected communications that are collected—tens of thousands. Which approach is preferable? Why?
5. Should it matter that the NSA does not "intentionally" collect constitutionally protected communications when it acquires an MCT? Certainly the government "foresees" that such collection is "inevitable," even if not "desired." Is that enough for a constitutional violation?
6. Judge Bates accepts the constitutionality of the NSA collecting the "incidental communications" of U.S. persons inside the United States when it collects communications "to," "from," or "about" NSA targeted selectors but rejects the constitutionality of the NSA collecting "wholly domestic communications" or international communications unrelated to any NSA target. What is the basis for this distinction? Is collection in both instances equally fortuitous, or is it more likely that someone who is in communication with an NSA target or who refers to an NSA target's selector has relevant "foreign intelligence information"? How much greater is the likelihood? Does the greater likelihood, if there is one, make the search "reasonable" under the Fourth Amendment?
7. Is Judge Bates correct that how the NSA handles MCTs after collection—that is, whether there is "prompt review" and "disposition of non-target information" and whether a reviewed MCT is "marked" as such—is relevant to whether the initial collection was "reasonable" under the Fourth Amendment? Can an argument be made that the "reasonableness" of a search is entirely dependent on the "totality of the circumstances" at the time of the search, not on circumstances that occur months or years later?
8. Judge Bates faults the NSA because its analysts only review those portions of an MCT that "he or she wishes to use." Which is the greater intrusion on privacy: to require NSA analysts to review communications that it should not have collected or to permit the NSA to keep nonrelevant communications for five years without reviewing them?
9. The Upstream program does not permit the NSA to use U.S. person identifiers to query the database, a query that critics of 702 call a "backdoor search." Does this fact have a bearing on whether the NSA's collection of MCTs is "reasonable" under the Fourth Amendment? Does Judge Bates place sufficient emphasis on this fact? Is it a part of the "totality of the circumstances"?

The government responded to Judge Bates's decision by reforming how the NSA handled MCTs in three ways. First, the NSA would "segregate" those MCTs "that are most likely to contain non-target information concerning

United States persons or persons in the United States" and permit only specially trained analysts to access this segregated database for the purpose of identifying "wholly domestic communications," which will be destroyed upon recognition. Second, any MCT in the "segregated" repository will not be moved or copied into databases that are generally accessible to NSA analysts unless they are "marked, tagged, or otherwise identified" as ones coming from the "segregated repository." In addition, analysts were not to use any discrete communications within an MCT that is not "to," "from," or "about" an NSA target's selector but rather "to" or "from" a U.S. person or a person inside the United States except to protect against "an immediate threat to human life." Third, the NSA would reduce the length of time it kept communications collected under the Upstream program from five to two years. In a decision handed down on November 30, 2011, Judge Bates concluded that these reforms rectified the Fourth Amendment deficiencies that he had identified in his October 3 opinion.[35] The reforms did little to nothing to reduce the number of MCTs the NSA collected that contained a "wholly domestic communication" or an international communication that was not "to," "from," or "about" an NSA target's selector, but they increased to an unknown degree the likelihood that the NSA would uncover these communications, dispose of some of them upon discovery, and use others for very limited purposes. It is not entirely clear why this increased likelihood would render the NSA's collection of private communications that were not "to," "from," or "about" NSA targets "reasonable" under the Fourth Amendment. Can you suggest a reason why it would render such collection "reasonable"?

A separate question was whether the expansive system of NSA surveillance authorized under Section 702 and other FISA provisions was in violation of the "proportionate" and "necessary" requirements of Article 17 of the ICCPR that the HRC had established in *Toonen v. Australia*. Even if the ICCPR had no extraterritorial application, it was highly debatable whether the NSA's post-9/11 system of surveillance, even if deemed lawful and constitutional by the FISA court and the FISA Court of Review, was "proportionate" to the national security threat or "necessary" for the collection of "foreign intelligence information." Obviously, with the enactment of 702, the scope and intensity of the NSA's surveillance system had grown far beyond the threat of terrorist attacks. Was this pervasive and intense system of surveillance "proportionate" to the foreign policy needs of the United States or "necessary" to counteract external threats?

This question gained global attention in June 2013 after Edward Snowden, a former CIA employee and contractor of the NSA, leaked a trove of documents revealing to the world a large number of the surveillance programs operated by the NSA, both internationally under the authority of Executive Order 12333 and domestically under the authority of FISA, including the bulk collection program of telephone metadata and the details of the Section 702 program discussed above. The revelations placed the NSA under a global spotlight as never before and highlighted the tension between the world composed of 195 sovereign nation-states represented in the United Nations and the interconnected world of the internet that enabled enormous quantities of communications and other data to continuously flow across national borders, much of it subject to surveillance by national intelligence agencies of technically advanced countries, including of course the NSA. In response to the global debate on surveillance inspired by Snowden's revelations, the United Nations General Assembly adopted a nonbinding resolution endorsing the right to privacy in the digital age in December 2013 and requested the UN high commissioner for human rights to submit a report on the subject.[36]

In response to the global outrage produced by Snowden's revelations, President Barack Obama issued Presidential Policy Directive—Signal Intelligence Activities (PPD-28) in January 2014. In this directive, Obama acknowledged that "all persons have legitimate privacy interests in the handling of their personal information" and recognized the "leadership role" that the United States played in upholding "universal human rights" and the "legitimate privacy and civil liberties concerns of U.S. citizens and citizens of other nations." For these reasons, the PPD-28 indicated that the United States would collect "nonpublicly available signals intelligence in bulk" only for the purpose of detecting and countering the following threats: (1) espionage; (2) terrorist threats; (3) the proliferation of weapons of mass destruction; (4) cybersecurity threats; (5) threats to U.S. or allied personnel; and (6) transnational criminal threats. Moreover, Obama continued, personal information about individuals, presumably including aliens outside the United States, would be retained and disseminated by U.S. intelligence agencies only if comparable information about U.S. persons is lawfully retained and disseminated, with the qualification that "intelligence must be retained for a sufficient period of time for the IC [intelligence community] to understand its relevance and use it to meet our national security needs."[37]

The PPD-28 was a significant change in executive policy, but any president could reverse it at any time, perhaps without public notification. Also, the limited purposes of collection outlined in the directive only pertained to "bulk collection," not to "targeted collection," such as that conducted under the 702 program of FISA. Last, the limitations on the retention and dissemination of personal information were rather vague, leaving NSA officials with considerable discretion to decide if information concerning "non-U.S. persons" was legitimate "foreign intelligence information." In short, it is not clear whether the new policy was enough to bring U.S. signals intelligence activities in conformity to Article 17 of the ICCPR, in particular the requirement that any intrusion into privacy must not be "arbitrary," that is, the intrusion must be "necessary" and "proportionate." Of course, the position of the United States was that the provisions of the ICCPR did not apply extraterritorially, meaning it had no application to how the NSA collected information about noncitizens outside the United States. The UN high commissioner addressed this issue in his report that he submitted to the UN General Assembly on June 30, 2014. The following excerpt focuses on the extraterritorial application of the ICCPR as well as the meaning of "necessary," "proportionate," and "lawful" surveillance for national security purposes.

9.8 UN High Commissioner's Report on Privacy in the Digital Age (2014)

25. In assessing the necessity of a [surveillance] measure, the Human Rights Committee . . . stressed that "the restrictions must not impair the essence of the right [. . .]; the relation between right and restriction, between norm and exception, must not be reversed."[38] The Committee further explained that "it is not sufficient that the restrictions serve the permissible purposes; they must also be necessary to protect them." Moreover, such measures must be proportionate: "the least intrusive instrument amongst those which might achieve the desired result." . . . Mass or "bulk" surveillance programs may thus be deemed to be arbitrary, even if they serve a legitimate aim and have been adopted on the basis of an accessible legal regime. In other words, it will not be enough that the measures are targeted to find certain needles in a haystack; the proper measure is the impact of the measures on the haystack, relative to the harm threatened; namely, whether the measure is necessary and proportionate.

26. . . . Mandatory third-party data retention—a recurring feature of surveillance regimes in many States, where Governments require telephone companies and Internet service providers to store metadata about their customers' communications and location for subsequent law enforcement and intelligence agency access—appears neither necessary nor proportionate.

27. One factor that must be considered in determining proportionality is what is done with bulk data and who may have access to them once collected. Many national frameworks lack "use limitations," instead allowing the collection of data for one legitimate aim, but subsequent use for others. The absence of effective use limitations has been exacerbated since 11 September 2001, with the line between criminal justice and protection of national security blurring significantly. The resulting sharing of data between law enforcement agencies, intelligence bodies, and other State organs risks violating article 17 of the Covenant, because surveillance measures that may be necessary and proportionate for one legitimate aim may not be so for the purposes of another. . . . [T]he expanding freedom to share that information among agencies and use it for purposes beyond those for which it was collected represents a substantial weakening of traditional data protections. . . .

28. . . . [Article 17 of the ICCPR] implies that any communications surveillance program must be conducted on the basis of a publicly accessible law, which in turn must comply with the State's own constitutional regime and international human rights law. "Accessibility" requires not only that the law is published, but that it is sufficiently precise to enable the affected person to regulate his or her conduct, with foresight of the consequences that a given action may entail. . . .

29. Consequently, secret rules and secret interpretations—even secret judicial interpretations—of law do not have the necessary qualities of "law." Neither do laws or rules that give the executive authorities, such as security and intelligence services, excessive discretion; the scope and manner of exercise of authoritative discretion granted must be indicated (in the law itself, or in binding, published guidelines) with reasonable clarity. A law that is accessible, but that does not have foreseeable effects, will not be adequate. . . .

30. The requirement of accessibility is also relevant when assessing the emerging practice of States to outsource surveillance tasks to others. There is credible information to suggest that some Governments systematically have routed data collection and analytical tasks through jurisdictions with weaker safeguards for privacy. Reportedly, some Governments have operated a transnational network of intelligence agencies through interlocking legal loopholes, involving the coordination of surveillance practice to outflank the protections provided by domestic

legal regimes. Such practice arguably fails the test of lawfulness because . . . it makes the operation of the surveillance regime unforeseeable for those affected by it. . . .

32. . . . [A] State party must respect and ensure the rights laid down in the Covenant to anyone within the power or effective control of that State Party, even if not situated within the territory of the State Party. This extends to persons within their "authority."

33. The Human Rights Committee has been guided by the principle, as expressed even in its earliest jurisprudence, that a State may not avoid its international human rights obligations by taking action outside its territory that it would be prohibited from taking "at home." . . . The notions of "power" and "effective control" are indicators of whether a State is exercising "jurisdiction" or governmental powers, the abuse of which human rights protections are intended to constrain. A State cannot avoid its human rights responsibilities simply by refraining from bringing those powers within the bounds of law. To conclude otherwise would not only undermine the universality and essence of the rights protected by international human rights law, but may also create structural incentives for States to outsource surveillance to each other.

34. It follows that digital surveillance therefore may engage a State's human rights obligations if that surveillance involves the States exercise of power or effective control in relation to digital communications infrastructure, wherever found, for example, through direct tapping or penetration of that infrastructure. Equally, where the State exercises regulatory jurisdiction over a third party that physically controls the data, that State also would have obligations under the Covenant. . . .

35. This conclusion is equally important in the light of ongoing discussion on whether "foreigners" and "citizens" should have equal access to privacy protections within national security surveillance oversight regimes. . . .

36. International human rights law is explicit with regard to the principle of non-discrimination. Article 26 of the International Covenant on Civil and Political Rights provides that "all persons are equal before the law and are entitled without any discrimination to the equal protection of the law" and, further, that "in this respect, the law shall prohibit any discrimination and guarantee to all persons equal and effective protection against discrimination on any ground such as race, color, sex, language, religion, political or other opinion, national or social origin, property, birth or other status." . . . In this regard, the Human Rights Committee has underscored the importance of "measures to ensure that any interference with the right to privacy complies with the principles of legality, proportionality and necessity regardless of the nationality or location of individuals whose communications are under direct surveillance." . . .

Questions

1. Do you agree with the high commissioner that a surveillance measure is consistent with the "necessary" and "proportionate" requirement of Article 17 only if it is the "least intrusive instrument" that yet achieves the desired result? What if the "least intrusive instrument" is more time consuming, less effective, or more expensive than a "more intrusive instrument"?
2. Is the high commissioner saying that all types of "bulk collection" of private data is in violation of Article 17 because it entails collecting data from innocent individuals, which is inherently "arbitrary"?
3. If a government can collect private information for national security purposes, why would it be "neither necessary nor proportionate" for the government to require telephone and internet service providers to retain the data for a period of time? Would it be less intrusive if the government collected this information as soon as the data was created? Why?

4. If the government can lawfully collect private information for one purpose, such as national security, why can it not also use it for another, such as law enforcement? If the intrusion of privacy occurs at the point of collection, why does it matter how the government uses information that is lawfully collected?
5. How can surveillance law for national security purposes be effective and at the same time "publicly accessible"? If the NSA's "sources and methods" for gathering foreign intelligence information are "publicly accessible" for everyone to know, wouldn't the targets of surveillance do whatever they could to avoid or circumvent NSA's techniques?
6. The NSA works closely with the intelligence agencies of Canada, the UK, Australia, and New Zealand (the so-called Five Eyes). Would it trouble you if the NSA shared information with these four intelligence agencies if they in return shared information with the NSA that it could not lawfully collect? If the shared information was collected lawfully in accordance with domestic law, is this type of coordination useful, or is it a way to circumvent domestic law?
7. Does the high commissioner argue that a person is "within" the jurisdiction of a state whenever the state is exercising "governmental powers," including the power of surveillance, over the individual? If so, is this a persuasive argument? Is it true that any other conclusion would "undermine the universality and essence" of human rights? Why?
8. What if the United States exercises "governmental powers," not over the target of surveillance, who is abroad and not a U.S. person, but over a private company inside the United States that has possession of private data regarding the target? Is such a target "within" the government's jurisdiction regardless of location? What is the high commissioner's position?
9. Is granting noncitizens outside the United States less privacy protections than citizens an illicit form of discrimination? Does it matter that Article 17 says "no one" shall be subject to arbitrary intrusions of privacy, not "no citizen" or "no resident"?

In a resolution adopted on November 19, 2014, the UN General Assembly "welcomed" the high commissioner's report on privacy, reaffirmed that "no one shall be subjected to arbitrary or unlawful interference" with his or her right to privacy, and noted not only that surveillance laws must be "publicly accessible, clear, precise, comprehensive and non-discriminatory" but also that every state party "must undertake the necessary steps to adopt laws or measures as may be necessary to give effect to the rights recognized in the Covenant."[39] It was in this context that Congress enacted the USA Freedom Act on June 2, 2015, which modified the NSA's telephone metadata collection program in several important ways.[40] The most dramatic change was the termination of the NSA's bulk collection program. In its place, the USA Freedom Act authorized the FISA court to issue an order requiring telecommunication companies to turn over to the NSA telephone metadata that were within two "hops" of a "specific selection term."

For reasons that are not clear, the act defines "specific selection term" in two different ways. If the government is seeking "call detail records" that the telecommunication companies created "before, on, or after" the date of the application of a FISA order and the purpose of the application is to protect against international terrorism, the "specific selection term" must identify a "person, account, or personal device." In contrast, if the government seeks such metadata "in any other manner," such as if the government is seeking "call detail records" that the telecommunication companies created "before, on, *and* after" the date of the FISA application, then the government can use a "specific selection term" that identifies not only a "person, account, or personal device" but also a "group, an entity, an association, a corporation, [or] a foreign power."[41]

The USA Freedom Act therefore ended the NSA's bulk collection of telephone metadata, that is, indiscriminate collection without the use of any identifiers, but it also authorized the NSA to use broader "specific selection terms" when it is seeking more data (when the data was created "before, on, *and* after" the date of the FISA application), rather than less data (when the data was created "before, on, *or* after" the date of the FISA application). Moreover, while the narrower form of collection is limited to investigations against international terrorism, the broader form of collection can be used for all types of authorized investigations, including of course international terrorism, and it is not subject to other restrictions that limit the scope of the narrower program. For example, there need not be a "reasonable articulable suspicion" that the "specific selection term" is associated with "a foreign power or agent of a foreign power"; the collection can continue for more than 180 days; and the rule limiting the collection to two "hops" from the "specific selection term" does not apply.[42] Accordingly, while the USA Freedom Act may protect in some ways the privacy rights of Americans, it nonetheless authorizes the NSA to collect a huge amount of telephone metadata. In fact, Charlie Savage reported in the *New York Times* on May 4, 2018, that the NSA collected 534 million "call detail records" in 2017, more than triple the number it collected in 2016, which once again raises the question whether the act is consistent with the Fourth Amendment and Article 17 of the ICCPR.

Later in 2015, the Court of Justice of the European Union (CJEU) decided a case that had a direct bearing on U.S. surveillance practices. The decision—*Schrems v. Data Protection Commissioner*—addressed the question whether Facebook Ireland could transfer the personal data of Europeans to its parent company in the United States. The issue implicated Directive 95/46/EC of the European Parliament, which permitted such transfers only if the third country's domestic laws provided an "adequate level of protection" to the data or if the transfer was in compliance with an international agreement. In 2000, the European Commission had ruled that the United States was in compliance with such an international agreement (the "Safe Harbor Privacy Principles"). However, in *Schrems* the CJEU, based largely on the Snowden revelations about the NSA's PRISM program, ruled that the "Safe Harbor Principles" did not provide sufficient protection for the data and, therefore, the transfer of the data from Ireland to the United States violated Directive 95/24/. The upshot of the CJEU's decision was that companies located in the EU could no longer transfer EU personal data to companies located in the United States, a result that would cost U.S. companies millions of dollars. The following excerpt from the CJEU's opinion focuses on why NSA's access to private data in the United States violated the privacy rights of Europeans.

9.9 *Schrems v. Data Protection Commissioner* (CJEU, Oct. 6, 2015, No. C-362-14 [Grand Chamber])

139. Article 25 of Directive 95/46 is based entirely on the principle that the transfer of personal data to a third country cannot take place unless that third country guarantees an adequate level of protection of such data.[43] The objective of that article is thus to ensure the continuity of the protection afforded by that directive where personal data is transferred to a third country. It is appropriate, in that regard, to bear in mind that that directive affords a high level of protection of citizens of the [European] Union with regard to the processing of their personal data. . . .

141. . . . [A] third country ensures an adequate level of protection only where, following a global assessment of the law and practice in the third country in question, it is able to establish that that third country offers a level of protection that is essentially equivalent to that afforded by directive [95/46], even though the manner in which that protection is implemented may differ from that generally encountered within the European Union. . . .

155. . . . [This case] proceeds on the basis of the following two findings of fact. First, personal data transferred by undertakings such as Facebook Ireland to their parent company established in the United States is then capable of being accessed by the NSA and by other United States security agencies in the course of a mass and indiscriminate surveillance and interception of such data. Indeed, in the wake of Edward Snowden's revelations, the evidence now available would admit of no other realistic conclusion. Second, citizens of the Union have no effective right to be heard on the question of the surveillance and interception of their data by the NSA and other United States security agencies.

157. . . . [A]ll companies involved in the PRISM program, which grant access to United States authorities to data stored and processed in the United States, appear to be certified under the safe harbor scheme. . . . [T]his has made the safe harbor scheme one of the conduits through which access is given to United States intelligence authorities to the collecting of personal data initially processed in the European Union. . . .

159. Those finding of fact demonstrate, in my view, that . . . [the Safe Harbor agreement] does not contain sufficient guarantees. . . .

163. . . . [Under the Safe Harbor agreement, privacy] may be limited: (a) to the extent necessary to meet national security, public interest, or law enforcement requirements; (b) by statute, government regulation, or case-law that create conflicting obligations or explicit authorizations, provided that, in exercising any such authorization, an organization can demonstrate that its non-compliance with the [Privacy] Principles is limited to the extent necessary to meet the overriding legitimate interests furthered by such authorization.

164. The problem arises essentially from the United States authorities' use of the derogations provided for in that provision. Because their wording is too general, the implementation of those derogations by the United States authorities is not limited to what is strictly necessary.

165. In addition to that too general wording is the fact that citizens of the [European] Union have no appropriate remedy against the processing of their personal data for purposes other than those for which it was initially collected and then transferred to the United States. . . .

184. . . . [O]nly the first objective [of national security] seems to be sufficiently precise to be regarded as an objective of general interest recognized by the European Union. . . .

185. It is now appropriate to ascertain the proportionality of the interference found. . . .

190. Such an interference must be an appropriate means of attaining the objective pur-

sued . . . and be necessary for the purpose of attaining the objective. . . .

198. I note, in that regard, that the access which the United States intelligence authorities may have to the personal data transferred covers, in a generalized manner, all persons and all means of electronic communication and all data transferred, including the content of the communications, without any differentiation, limitation or exception, according to the objective of general interest pursued.

199. Indeed, the access of the United States intelligence services to the data transferred covers, in a comprehensive manner, all persons using electronic communications services, without any requirement that the persons concerned represent a threat to national security.

200. Such mass, indiscriminate surveillance is inherently disproportionate and constitutes a unwarranted interference with the right . . . [to privacy]. . . .

208. It should . . . [also be noted that] there is no independent authority capable of verifying that the implementation of the derogations from the safe harbor principles is limited to what is strictly necessary. Yet we have seen that such control by an independent authority is, from the point of view of EU law, an essential component of the protection of individuals with regard to the processing of personal data. . . .

212. Furthermore, . . . there are no opportunities for citizens of the [European] Union to obtain access to or rectification or erasure of data, or administrative or judicial redress with regard to collection of and further processing of their personal data taking place under the United States surveillance programs.

213. It should be observed, last, that the United States rules on the protection of privacy may be applied differently to United States citizens and to foreign citizens. . . .

Questions

1. Is the CJEU requiring the United States to give a "high level" of protection to the personal data of Europeans without imposing the same burden on European states in terms of the personal data of U.S. persons? In other words, does this decision adopt a double standard, or does it imply that European states must reciprocate by providing adequate protection to U.S. personal data?
2. Is the CJEU claiming that PRISM is a program of "mass and indiscriminate surveillance"? If so, is the CJEU correct? How would the U.S. government respond?
3. Do U.S. persons have an "effective right to be heard" regarding U.S. personal data that is intercepted by European intelligence agencies? If not, should U.S. persons have such a right? If they should, what about a European "right to be heard" in the United States?
4. Is it defensible that the CJEU only finds "national security" to be an objective "precise enough" to be one of "general interest"? Is the court correct to ignore the objectives of "law enforcement" or the "public interest"? Is the CJEU implying that PRISM should not be used to collect general "foreign intelligence information" that is unrelated to terrorism or military threats? Is this a valid objection?
5. Does the Safe Harbor agreement basically say that PRISM is acceptable so long as it is authorized by statute? If so, is the CJEU correct that the language of the agreement is too general, permitting the United States to engage in surveillance that is not "strictly necessary" to meet "overriding legitimate interests"?
6. How should "necessity" and "proportionality" be related to each other? Is the CJEU saying that "proportionate" surveillance must also be "strictly necessary"? Is that a reasonable position?
7. To decide whether NSA's surveillance is "disproportionate," does the CJEU base

its evaluation on the fact the NSA "may have" access to all the personal data of every European resident stored in the United States or on what personal data the NSA actually accesses? Which is the more justifiable alternative?

8. Why does the CJEU ignore the role of the FISA court when it argues that there is no "independent authority capable of verifying that the implementation of the derogations from the safe harbor principles is limited to what is strictly necessary"? Is it because the FISA court functions in secret? Is it because the FISA court does not make individual "probable cause" decisions in the PRISM program? Is it because the FISA court in the past has only heard arguments from government attorneys? Do any of these factors justify why the CJEU ignored the role of the FISA court?
9. Should citizens of the EU, as the CJEU suggests, have access to the FISA court or other federal courts to challenge the legality of PRISM? If they did have such access, is it likely, as the CJEU also suggests, that the U.S. courts might apply different privacy rights to U.S. citizens and citizens of foreign countries? Would such an unequal application of privacy rights be justifiable? On what grounds?
10. Would the *Schrems* decision have any impact on NSA collection of private data outside the United States under Executive Order 12333? If not, is the decision somewhat symbolic? Or is it only a matter of time before NSA's surveillance practices outside of the United States become subject to the standards the CJEU announced in *Schrems*?

U.S. officials found the CJEU's *Schrems* decision to be hypocritical because, since Congress enacted FISA in 1979, few countries in the world have matched the degree to which the United States regulates surveillance for national security purposes. Nevertheless, if only for commercial reasons, the United States and the European Union quickly negotiated a new agreement (the EU-U.S. Privacy Shield) to regulate the transfer of personal data.[44] The new agreement did not change the PRISM program in any significant way, but it did require the United States to designate an "ombudsman" to review complaints filed by Europeans. Whether the Privacy Shield will satisfy the CJEU and other European courts is unknown, but the tension between national surveillance practices and the *Schrems* decision became more acute following a number of terrorist attacks in Europe from late 2015 to 2017, such as the Paris attacks in November 2015; the Brussels bombings in March 2016; the July 2016 truck attack on Bastille Day in Nice; the December 2016 Christmas market attack in Berlin; the March 2017 car attack on Westminster Bridge in London; and the August 2017 van attack on the La Rambla in Barcelona. In response, France in 2015 enacted what critics called the "Big Brother Act," which purportedly gave the state "extremely large and intrusive powers" with no judicial control,[45] and the United Kingdom enacted the Investigatory Powers Bill in November 2016, which arguably granted UK intelligence agencies and police "the most sweeping surveillance powers in the western world," while Germany passed a series of new surveillance laws in 2017.[46]

It was in this context that Joseph A. Cannataci, the UN's special rapporteur on the right to privacy, issued in 2017 a report that cited *Tele 2 Sverige*, a CJEU opinion handed down on December 21, 2016. In this opinion, CJEU reminded member states of their "duties to respect, promote, and protect the human right to privacy" but also noted "worrying trends," such as the merging of intelligence and law enforcement agencies, the gathering of personal data into one "bucket" that can be "used and reused for all kinds of known and unknown purposes," the analysis of personal data "without adequate authorization and supervision" by independent judges, and the lack of oversight of governmental surveillance activities at the international level. The report called for "a more privacy-friendly oversight of government surveillance," arguing that the United States in particular should do more to respect privacy as "a truly universal right," not one that "depends on the passport in your pocket," and align its surveillance policies with the human rights embedded in international law and endorsed by the CJEU.[47]

Cannataci's report forcefully illustrates the continuing tension between international law and the perceived security needs of national governments, including that of the United States, a tension that is not likely to dissipate anytime soon. During his 2016 campaign for the presidency, Donald Trump announced, "I want surveillance," and indicated that he would not let "political correctness" get in the way of his achieving this goal. When a reporter asked him if he supported "warrantless searches of Muslims," Trump replied, "The terrorist attacks in Europe were a sign that drastic measures were needed" and added that his surveillance policies would include "things that were frankly unthinkable a year ago."[48]

Trump's campaign rhetoric did not lead to substantive changes of surveillance policy during the first several months of his presidency, but a public debate on U.S. surveillance briefly flared up in late 2017 because Section 702 of FISA was set to expire. Although privacy advocates raised concerns based heavily on Edward Snowden revelations, Congress nonetheless in mid-January 2018 reauthorized the warrantless surveillance program for an additional six years. Although the vote was somewhat close in the Senate (65 to 34, with 60 votes needed to end the filibuster), the House voted 256 to 164 in favor of the program, and President Trump only lamented the fact that the reauthorization was not permanent, adding that we "cannot let our guard down in the face of foreign threats to our safety, our freedom, and our way of life."[49] His remark continued the tradition of defending the 702 program as a counterterrorism tool, which it was when President Bush created it under his Article II powers to direct the war against al-Qaeda and other international terrorist groups, but ignored the fact that for the past ten years the 702 program has functioned as a general program to collect foreign intelligence information. What specific types of foreign intelligence information are collected by this warrantless program is unknown because this crucial fact, one that is relevant to whether the program is consistent with both the Fourth Amendment and Article 17 of the ICCPR, remains classified.

A different privacy issue dealing with digital data arose in early 2018, one that is related in some ways to the CJEU's decision in *Schrems* (see **reading 9.9**) and the EU-U.S. Privacy Shield discussed earlier. In the past, foreign governments seeking data stored in the United States had to go through the Mutual Legal Assistance (MLA) process, which requires the Justice Department to obtain a judicial warrant under a probable cause standard that the data is linked to criminal activity in the country requesting the data. Obviously, this process is slow and cumbersome. In addition, in 2013, the Department of Justice submitted to Microsoft a warrant for emails it had stored in Ireland, but the company refused, arguing that the warrant's reach did not extend beyond the water's edge, even if the company had complete control over the data and the data was not protected by the Fourth Amendment because of the third-party doctrine. The case worked its way up to the Supreme Court, which heard oral argument on February 27, 2018, and is undecided at the time of this writing.[50] However, also during February, Senator Orrin Hatch (R-UT) introduced legislation (the CLOUD Act) that would regulate cross-border data access. In Hatch's words, the law would "help the United States and other countries resolve the problem of cross-border law enforcement data requests in the age of email and cloud computing."[51]

The key provision of the act authorized the president to negotiate executive agreements with foreign governments that would allow them to request the data of non-U.S. persons from U.S. service providers without going through the MLA if the United States, in reciprocal fashion, could request data stored in the foreign country. The president could finalize such an agreement only if the attorney general and the secretary of state certified that the foreign government had "robust substantive and procedural protections for privacy and civil liberties."[52] Once such an agreement was in place, the foreign government could request, without notification to either the U.S. government or the subject of the data, substantive internet communications from a U.S. service provider. Many human rights organizations, including Amnesty International and Human Rights Watch, opposed the bill, fearing that, even if foreign governments receive the requisite certification, they will not be able to resist the temptation to seek data either without probable cause or for reasons other than legitimate law enforcement. However, not all privacy advocates opposed the bill. Jennifer Daskal and Pete Swire argue that the status quo is "untenable" and that the CLOUD Act is better than any likely alternatives.[53] Despite this controversy about the privacy implications of the bill, the CLOUD Act never received a hearing or a markup by any committee in either the House or the Senate. Instead, Congress attached it to a $1.3 trillion omnibus spending bill and passed it on March 22, 2018, and Trump signed it into law the following day. One plausible effect of the law, although not indisputable, is that it will moot the Microsoft case discussed earlier. After all, if the CLOUD Act can lawfully permit a foreign government to seek data about a non-U.S. person from a U.S. provider inside the United States, then, *a fortiori*, a U.S. judicial warrant for data in the complete control of a service provider incorporated and located inside the United States would seem to be valid, regardless if the data is technically outside the United States.[54] On the other hand, only time will tell whether the CLOUD Act is a step forward or backward for the advancement of the right to privacy, whether in terms of the Fourth Amendment or Article 16 of the ICCPR.

NOTES

1. Peter Swire, "The FBI Doesn't Need More Access: We're Already in the Golden Age of Surveillance," Just Security, November 17, 2014, https://www.justsecurity.org.

2. *Olmstead v. United States*, 277 U.S. 438 (1928).
3. Quoted in "Foreign Intelligence Surveillance Act of 1978," House Intelligence Committee Report, No. 95-1283, p. 15, Federation of American Scientists, https://fas.org.
4. "Foreign Intelligence Surveillance Act," 16.
5. "Universal Declaration of Human Rights," United Nations, December 10, 1948, http://www.un.org.
6. European Convention on Human Rights, European Court of Human Rights, June 1, 2010, http://www.echr.coe.int.
7. See *Katz v. United States*, 389 U.S. 347 (1967).
8. See, generally, Pub. L. 90-351, Title III, §2518, Federal Communications Commission, https://www.fcc.gov.
9. Pub. L. 90-351, Title III, §2511(3).
10. *United States v. United States District Court*, 407 U.S. 297 (1972).
11. See *United States v. Brown*, 484 F.2d 418 (5th Cir. 1973); *United States v. Butenko*, 494 F.2d 593 (3rd Cir. 1974); *United States v. Buck*, 548 F.2d 871 (9th Cir. 1977); and *United States v. Truong Dinh Hung*, 629 F.2d 908 (4th Cir. 1980). The D.C. Circuit was the only court of appeal that required a judicial warrant for the gathering of foreign intelligence. See *Zweibon v. Mitchell*, 516 F.2d 594 (D.C. Cir. 1975).
12. "International Covenant on Civil and Political Rights," December 19, 1966, United Nations Treaty Collection, https://treaties.un.org.
13. Public Law 95-511 (October 25, 1978), Government Publishing Office, https://www.gpo.gov.
14. "Executive Order 12333: United States Intelligence Activities," National Archives, December 4, 1981, https://www.archives.gov.
15. *United States v. Verdugo-Urquidez*, 494 U.S. 259 (1990).
16. CCPR, General Comment No. 16, adopted at the thirty-second session of the Human Rights Committee, April 8, 1988, UNHCR refworld, http://www.refworld.org.
17. See "U.S. Reservations, Declarations, and Understandings, International Covenant on Civil and Political Rights," 138 Cong. Rec. S4781-01, daily ed., April 2, 1992, University of Minnesota Human Rights Library, http://hrlibrary.umn.edu.
18. See "International Covenant of Civil and Political Rights; Summary Record of the 1405th Meeting: United States of America," U.N. ESCOR Human Rights Comm., 53rd Sess., 1405th mtg, para. 20, U.N. Doc. CCPR/C/SR (1995), United Nations Human Rights Office of the High Commissioner, UN Treaty Body Database, http://tbinternet.ohchr.org. In later reports to HRC, the United States has continued to defend the position that the ICCPR has no extraterritorial application.
19. See "Concluding Observations of the Human Rights Committee: United States of America," U.N. Doc. CCPR/C/79/Add.50, A/50/40 (1995), para. 284, University of Minnesota Human Rights Library, http://hrlibrary.umn.edu. The HRC has not changed its position since 1995. See CCPR, General Comment No. 31, "The Nature of the General Legal Obligation Imposed on States Parties to the Covenant," adopted on March 29, 2004, UNHCR refworld, http://www.refworld.org; and "Concluding Observation on the Fourth Periodic Report of the United States of America," U.N. Doc. CCPR/C/USA/CO/4, April 23, 2014, para. 4, UNHCR refworld, http://www.refworld.org. In this report, the HRC claims that the UN International Court of Justice and state practice supports its position. For example, see "Legal Consequences of the Construction of a Wall in the Occupied Palestinian Territory" (Advisory Opinion), 2004 I.C.J. July 9, 2004, para. 109–11, International Court of Justice, http://www.icj-cij.org.
20. See *Toonen v. Australia*, Communication No. 488/1992. U.N. Doc CCPR/C50/D/488/1992 (1994), para. 8.1–8.7, University of Minnesota Human Rights Library, http://hrlibrary.umn.edu.
21. See *In re: all Matters Submitted to the Foreign Intelligence Surveillance Court*, 218 F. Supp. 2d 611 (decided May 17, 2002).

22. United States Foreign Intelligence Surveillance Court, Judge Kollar-Kotelly's PR/TT opinion, July 14, 2004, Office of the Director of National Intelligence, https://www.dni.gov.
23. 50 U.S.C. §1861(b)(2)(B).
24. *In re: Application of the Federal Bureau of Investigation for an Order Requiring Production of Tangible Things from [redacted]*, No. BR 13-109 (FISA Ct. Aug. 29, 2013), United States Foreign Intelligence Surveillance Court, http://www.fisc.uscourts.gov. See also *In re: Application of the Federal Bureau of Investigation for an Order Requiring Production of Tangible Things from [redacted]*, No. BR 13-158 (FISA Ct. Oct. 11, 2013), United States Foreign Intelligence Surveillance Court, http://www.fisc.uscourts.gov. For a comprehensive review of the statutory and constitutional issues regarding NSA's telephone metadata program, see Privacy and Civil Liberties Oversight Board, "Report on the Telephone Records Program Conducted under Section 215 of the USA Patriot Act and on the Operations of the Foreign Intelligence Surveillance Court," January 23, 2014, Privacy and Civil Liberties Oversight Board, https://www.pclob.gov.
25. *United States v. Jones*, 565 U.S. 400 (2012); 132 S. Ct. 945 (2012).
26. William H. Pauley, a federal district judge from New York, and Rosemary M. Collyer, a FISA court judge, explicitly criticized Judge Leon's constitutional analysis. See *ACLU v. Clapper*, 959 F. Supp. 2d 724 (Dec. 27, 2013) and *In re: Application of the Federal Bureau of Investigation for an Order Requiring the Production of Tangible Things*, No. BR 14-01 (FISA Ct. Mar. 20, 2014), United States Foreign Intelligence Surveillance Court, http://www.fisc.uscourts.gov. In August 2015, the D.C. Circuit court vacated the injunction Judge Leon issued to stop the government's bulk collection of telephone metadata on the ground that the plaintiffs lacked "standing" to file the lawsuit. See *Obama v. Klayman*, 800 F.3d 559 (D.C. Cir. 2015). The Second Circuit overturned Judge Pauley's holding on statutory grounds. See *ACLU v. Clapper*, F.3d 787 (2nd Cir. 2015).
27. See James Risen and Eric Lichtblau, "Bush Lets U.S. Spy on Callers without Courts," *New York Times*, December 16, 2005.
28. See *ACLU v. NSA*, 438 F. Supp. 2d 754 (2006). The decision was overturned on appeal on the ground that the plaintiffs lacked standing. See *ACLU v. NSA*, 493 F.3d 644 (6th Cir. 2007).
29. See United States Foreign Intelligence Surveillance Court, *In re: [redacted]*, No. [redacted] (FISA Ct. Jan. 10, 2007), Office of the Director of National Intelligence, https://www.dni.gov.
30. See United States Foreign Intelligence Surveillance Court, *In re: [redacted]*, No. [redacted] (FISA Ct. April 3, 2007), Office of the Director of National Intelligence, https://www.dni.gov.
31. FISA Amendments Act of 2008, Pub. Law. 110-261, July 10, 2008, Congress.gov, https://www.congress.gov. For a comprehensive discussion of the legality of the 702 program, see Privacy and Civil Liberties Oversight Board, "Report on the Surveillance Program Operated Pursuant to Section 702 of the Foreign Intelligence Surveillance Act," July 2, 2014, Privacy and Civil Liberties Oversight Board, https://www.pclob.gov.
32. See 50 U.S.C. §1881a(d)(1).
33. See *In re: Directives to Yahoo! Inc. Pursuant to Section 10B of the Foreign Intelligence Surveillance Act*, F.I.S.C.R., August 22, 2008, Federation of American Scientists, https://fas.org. Constitutional challenges to the Section 702 program filed in federal district court failed because U.S. persons did not have "standing" to file the lawsuit since they could not establish that the NSA obtained or will obtain their specific communications under the program. See *Clapper v. Amnesty International*, 568 U.S. 398 (2013).
34. For Judge Bates's opinion, see United States Foreign Intelligence Surveillance Court, "Memorandum Opinion," [Redacted], 2011 WL 10945618 (FISA Ct. Oct. 3, 2011), Office of the Director of National Intelligence, https://www.dni.gov.
35. See United States Foreign Intelligence Surveillance Court, "Memorandum Opinion," Bates Opinion and Order, part 1, *[Redacted]* (FISA Ct. Nov. 30, 2011), Office of the Director

of National Intelligence, https://www.dni.gov; and United States Foreign Intelligence Surveillance Court, "Top Secret/Comint/Orcon, Noforn," Bates Opinion and Order, part 2, November 2011, Office of the Director of National Intelligence, https://www.dni.gov.

36. A/RES/68/167, "The Right to Privacy in the Digital Age," December 18, 2013, United Nations Documents, http://undocs.org.

37. Barack Obama, "Presidential Policy Directive—Signal Intelligence Activities" (PPD-28), January 17, 2014, White House Archives, https://obamawhitehouse.archives.gov.

38. "The Right to Privacy in the Digital Age," A/HRC/27/37, June 30, 2014, United Nations Human Rights Office of the High Commissioner, http://www.ohchr.org.

39. UN General Resolution, "The Right to Privacy in the Digital Age," November 19, 2014, A/C.3/69/L.26/Rev.1, United Nations, http://www.un.org.

40. See USA Freedom Act, Public Law No. 114-23, June 2, 2015, Congress.gov, https://www.congress.gov.

41. See the Congressional Research Service's summary of the USA Freedom Act, at "H.R. 2048: USA FREEDOM Act of 2015," April 28, 2015, Congress.gov, https://www.congress.gov.

42. See the Congressional Research Service's summary of the USA Freedom Act.

43. "Opinion of Advocate General," Case 362/14, Maximillian Schrems v. Data Protection Commissioner, September 23, 2015, InfoCuria: Case-Law of the Court of Justice, http://curia.europa.eu.

44. See Privacy Shield Framework, "Welcome to the Privacy Shield," https://www.privacyshield.gov.

45. Kim Willsher, "France Approves 'Big Brother' Surveillance Powers Despite UN Concern," *Guardian*, July 24, 2015.

46. Ewen MacAskill, "Extreme Surveillance Becomes UK Law with Barely a Whimper," *Guardian*, November 19, 2016; Jefferson Chase, "Things to Know about Germany's Recent Surveillance Laws," *DW*, June 26, 2017, http://www.dw.com.

47. Joseph A. Cannataci, "Report of the Special Rapporteur on the Right to Privacy," A/HRC/34/60, February 24, 2017, pp. 14–22, 32–44, United Nations Human Rights Office of the High Commissioner, http://www.ohchr.org.

48. Timothy H. Edgar, *Beyond Snowden: Privacy, Mass Surveillance and the Struggle to Reform the NSA* (Washington, DC: Brookings Institution Press, 2017), 188–89.

49. Martin Matishak, "Trump Signs Surveillance Extension into Law," *Politico*, January 19, 2018, https://www.politico.com/story/2018/01/19/trump-surveillance-extension-351136.

50. *United States v. Microsoft*, October Term 2017, No. 17-2; the briefs filed in the case and commentary are available at http://www.scotusblog.com/case-files/cases/united-states-v-microsoft-corp.

51. Orrin Hatch, "The CLOUD Act: It's Time for Our Laws to Catch up with Our Technology," Press Release, February 26, 2018, https://www.hatch.senate.gov/public/index.cfm/2018/2/the-cloud-act-it-s-time-for-our-laws-to-catch-up-with-our-technology.

52. The Cloud Act, 115th Congress, 2nd Session, § 2523(b)(1), https://www.documentcloud.org/documents/4368041-CLOUD-Act-of-2018.html.

53. Jennifer Daskal and Peter Swire, "Privacy and Civil Liberties under the CLOUD Act: A Response," *Lawfare* (blog), March 21, 2018), https://www.lawfareblog.com/privacy-and-civil-liberties-under-cloud-act-response. Daskal and Swire's article is a response to a critical post by Neema Sing Guliani, American Civil Liberties Union legislative counsel, and Naureen Shah, Amnesty International. The exchange is an excellent introduction to the subject of cross-border data access and the CLOUD Act.

54. See Peter Swire and Jennifer Daskal, "What the CLOUD Act Means for Privacy Pros," *Daily Dashboard*, International Association of Privacy Professionals, March 26, 2018, https://iapp.org/news/a/what-the-cloud-act-means-for-privacy-pros.

10
Cyber War

★ ★ ★

How international and domestic law applies to cyberattacks is a work in progress. One obvious reason for the lack of consensus is that cyberspace is a relatively new field of human activity. The internet, which is the technical backbone of much of cyberspace, did not emerge until the early 1990s, and it did not begin to truly flourish as a global "network of networks" until the twenty-first century. It takes time for the law to adapt to a new technology, especially one that continues to evolve at such a rapid pace, linking devices, technologies, commercial enterprises, universities, nongovernmental organizations (NGOs), medical facilities, and public services into a vast interlocking system of ever-increasing complexity. Although the benefits of the internet are indisputable, the threats that lurk within cyberspace are many and diverse, which makes it more challenging, especially at the international level, for policymakers, experts, and lawyers to agree on what is the proper response to a specific type of threat. For example, cyber operations can kill or injure people, damage or destroy property, interfere with the sovereign affairs of a state, uncover national security secrets, tamper with financial records, steal intellectual property, interfere with communications, and so on. How should the law respond to these different types of threats? International law may be applicable to some, while domestic law may be the controlling authority for others. Sorting out these issues is a complex task that has yet to be resolved in any meaningful way.

One important distinction is between harmful cyber operations conducted by states or their proxies, by nonstate groups or individuals for illicit political purposes, and by private individuals for profit or other personal reasons. The domestic law of each state treats the vast majority of the third category as ordinary criminal offenses, such as computer fraud, identity theft, unlawful access to stored communications, and so on, all of which in the United States are prosecuted by the federal government.[1] It is conceivable that cyber operations falling into the second category could qualify as a national security threat if, for example, the nonstate group was a terrorist organization that had the cyber expertise to bring down a country's electrical grid or financial system. Whether such a cyber operation would qualify as an "armed attack" justifying an invocation of the law of armed conflict would depend on the specific circumstances. However, the most serious cyber threats, especially those that injure or kill human beings or cause damage to physical property, are typically initiated by states or their proxies. States use proxies as a way to hide their malicious conduct on the internet. As it is difficult to prove where an attack on the internet originated, using a proxy as a filter gives the state an easy way to deny responsibility for the harmful consequences of a cyber operation and thereby avoid any retaliation based on the law of armed conflict.

There are several challenges to reaching any consensus on issues regarding cybersecurity at the international level. Besides the political animosity and distrust that divide nation-states from one another, there is the reality that technical proficiency and capacity over the internet is radically unequal. States with a great deal of expertise, such as the United States, have an incentive to narrow the scope of international rules, thereby leaving them with more latitude and flexibility to pursue their national interests and agendas in cyberspace by, for example, collecting foreign intelligence information or shaping international public opinion. On the other hand, states with a great deal of expertise tend to be those with critical infrastructure heavily dependent on the internet and digitized information, making them more vulnerable to hostile attacks. Of course, the infrastructure of states with minimal expertise is also vulnerable to exploitation, control, or attack and therefore these states may want international law to give them the "information security" that they cannot achieve by technical means. However, over the last decade several undeveloped states, such as North Korea, have quickly developed the expertise necessary to engage in cyber operations on an asymmetric basis with major Western powers, including the United States. The technical dimension of cyberspace is therefore quite fluid, making it difficult to gauge what policy is in any state's interest.

A second major factor is the diversity of political regimes of internet-savvy countries. Countries in the West, such as the United States, are liberal representative democracies based on the rule of law and freedom of speech and the press. An internet that is truly international in character and committed to a "free flow of information" provides these countries with an effective means to spread their core values around the world. A system of international law that leaves much of the internet unregulated by law would empower these countries to spread their core ideology. In contrast, countries that are more authoritarian in nature, such as Russia, China, Iran, and North Korea, see the export of Western ideas of freedom and equality as a threat, not only to the individual regimes of such countries, but also to their cultural identities. Consequently, these countries envision a system of international law that would grant national sovereigns a great deal of authority over what is permitted to be transmitted across their computer infrastructure. In short, how international law will eventually regulate cyberspace depends to some extent on whether the internet will become a largely unregulated global network or a "balkanized" set of national networks regulated by national sovereigns with diverse political regimes.

At the international level, a discussion of issues related to cybersecurity began in 1998 at the United Nations in reaction to a resolution sponsored by Russia on "information and telecommunications technology in the context of international security." The resolution called for an "international computer security treaty" and "invited" all member states to inform the general secretary of their "general" appreciation of issues linked to "information security," their "definition" of what constitutes "unauthorized interference" with or "misuse of information and telecommunications systems," and their views on the advisability of developing "international principles that would enhance the security" of telecommunications systems and help to combat information terrorism and criminality."[2]

Although the General Assembly passed the resolution without vote, the proposal did not lead to any immediate substantive developments, primarily because the United States and European countries feared that such a treaty would limit freedom of information "under the guise of increasing information and telecommunications security." The United States did favor international cooperation to prevent cybercrime and cyberterrorism, but at the same time it remained committed to the "free flow of information" over the internet and opposed any new international restrictions on the internet beyond those already recognized by international law, including the law of armed conflict.[3]

Despite the standoff in the UN General Assembly between the United States and the Russian Federation in 1999, the General Assembly's First Committee on Disarmament and International Security established a Group of Governmental Experts (GGE) on "Developments in the Field of Information and Telecommunications in the Context of International Security." The purpose of the group was to study issues related to international cybersecurity, but it failed to reach any consensus on the issues. "The main stumbling block," according to a Russian delegate to the GGE, "was the question of whether international humanitarian law and international law sufficiently regulate the security aspects of international relations in cases of 'hostile' use of ICTs [Information and Communications Technologies] for politicomilitary purposes."[4] In other words, the fear was that the law of war did not provide sufficient protection against the hostile use of ICTs by technically advanced countries. However, Russia was able to overcome this "stumbling block" by obtaining a 2005 vote at the First Committee in favor of its approach to an international treaty on cybersecurity. The United States was the only country to vote against this draft resolution and Russia was able in 2006 to add a number of cosponsors, including China, Armenia, Belarus, Kazakhstan, Kyrgyzstan, Myanmar, Tajikistan, and Uzbekistan. On November 9, 2006, the First Committee submitted the following recommendation to the General Assembly, which the General Assembly adopted on December 6, 2006.

10.1 Developments in the Field of Information and Telecommunications in the Context of International Security (2006)

Noting that the dissemination and use of information technologies and means affect the interests of the entire international community and that optimum effectiveness is enhanced by broad international cooperation,[5]

Expressing its concern that these technologies and means can potentially be used for purposes that are inconsistent with the objectives of maintaining international stability and security and may adversely affect the integrity of the infrastructure of States to the detriment of their security in both civil and military fields,

Considering that it is necessary to prevent the use of information resources or technologies for criminal or terrorist purposes, . . .

Bearing in mind that the Secretary General . . . established in 2004 a group of governmental experts (GGE) [that could not reach any consensus on the issues]. . . .

1. *Calls upon* Member States to promote further at multilateral levels the consideration of existing and potential threats in the field of information security, as well as possible measures to limit the threats emerging in this field, consistent with the need to preserve the free flow of information;
2. *Considers* that the purpose of such measures could be served through the examination of relevant international concepts aimed at strengthening the security of global information and telecommunications systems;
3. *Invites* all Member States to continue to inform the Secretary-General of their views and assessments on the following questions:
   a. General appreciation of the issues of information security;
   b. Efforts taken at the national level to strengthen information security and promote international cooperation in this field;
   c. The content of the concepts mentioned in paragraph 2 above;
   d. Possible measures that could be taken by the international community to strengthen information security at the global level;
4. *Requests* the Secretary-General, with the assistance of a group of governmental experts, to be established in 2009 on the basis of equitable geographical distribution, to continue to study existing and potential threats in the sphere of information security and possible cooperative measures to address them, as well as the concepts referred to in paragraph 2 above, and to submit a report on the results of this study to the General Assembly at its sixty-fifth session [in 2010]. . . .

Questions

1. Is the Russian proposal a sensible one since the "dissemination and use of information technologies" does affect the "interests of the entire international community"? In deciding whether to support the Russian proposal, should a state consider its own interests, the interests of the international community, or some combination thereof?
2. Does the reference to what may "adversely affect the integrity of the infrastructure of States" suggest that fear of U.S. expertise in telecommunications and information technology is what is driving this resolution?
3. Has this Russian proposal gained support by recognizing the importance of cybercrime and cyberterrorism, as well as the "need to preserve the free flow of information" on the internet, all issues that were important to the United States and its allies? Would such concessions in 2006 be enough to convince you to support an international treaty on cybersecurity?
4. Does the resolution's repeated references to the language of paragraph 2 suggest that it is endorsing an international cybersecurity "treaty" even though this term is not mentioned explicitly?
5. Is it fair to imply that the proposal's emphasis on "information security," rather than "cyber security," is an implicit acknowledgment by Russia that its main concern is not crime, terrorism, or cyber war but rather its control over the information that travels across its borders through the internet?

6. Does the language of this resolution reveal the distrust that operates at the international level and the challenges of reaching international consensus?

Russia and its allies were placing their hopes on an international "information security" treaty evolving through the UN's GGE process, largely because the GGE delegates were appointed on the basis of "equitable geographical distribution" and instructed to consider "cooperative measures" at the international level and the principles identified in paragraph 2 of the 2006 UN Resolution. However, events can have a serious impact on the evolution of public policy, including international cybersecurity. The 2007 "distributed denial-of-service" (DDOS) attacks on nearly sixty Estonian websites, including newspapers, banks, and government sites, had a significant impact on international attitudes toward cybersecurity, especially in Eastern Europe. The attacks were launched by a botnet of eighty-five thousand computers that swamped and disabled the websites, forcing many to shut down, including commercial sites, causing serious economic disruptions to Estonia's economy. In part because the attacks occurred after Estonia removed the Bronze Soldier Soviet war memorial from Tallinn, Estonia's capital and largest city, the government of Estonia accused Russia of being responsible for the DDOS attacks and tried to invoke the right of collective self-defense under Article 5 of the North Atlantic Treaty Organization (NATO).

NATO declined Estonia's request for military aid on the ground that the DDOS attacks did not qualify as an "armed attack" because NATO had yet to define what constituted a "cyber armed attack." Andrus Ansip, Estonia's prime minister, objected to NATO's decision, claiming there was little to no difference between a blockade of a sovereign state's harbors or airports and a blockade of governmental, financial, and journalistic websites. The damage and injury inflicted by the latter could surpass that of the former. The government of Russia denied any responsibility for the Estonia attack even though some of the computers that participated in the attacks were owned and operated by Russian state institutions.[6]

The following year, in July–August 2008, Russia was implicated in another set of DDOS attacks on Georgia, the former Soviet Republic that was trying, at the time, to realign itself with the West, in part by joining NATO. In response, two of its largely Russian-speaking provinces—Abkhazia and South Ossetia—attempted to break away from Georgia. In support of this act of secession, Russian troops evicted Georgian troops from both provinces, an action that clearly constituted an "armed attack" against a sovereign state. An interesting aspect of the "armed conflict" was that "cyberattacks" against Georgian websites both preceded and accompanied the physical invasion of Georgia's territory. The DDOS attacks were mainly directed at governmental websites, presumably for the purpose of limiting Georgia's ability to communicate with the outside world, thereby sharply reducing the likelihood of any outside military aid. For this reason, the 2008 Georgian DDOS attacks were the first time "cyberattacks" appeared to be strategically integrated with a military operation that was indisputably an "armed attack." Researchers tracked the DDOS attacks to botnets that were "staged" in preparation for Russian air strikes against Georgia targets and operated by the Russian Business Network, a criminal gang based in St. Petersburg. Despite these coincidences, the Russian government denied any involvement in the DDOS attacks, although an official conceded that he could not exclude the possibility that individual Russians might be using the internet to express their opposition to Georgia's policies. Despite these outstanding uncertainties, the 2008 Georgia DDOS attacks, given their strategic role in a traditional military conflict, implicitly raised the question whether they were or were not an inherent part of an "armed conflict" and therefore subject to the laws of war.[7]

The Russian-implicated cyber operations of 2007 and 2008 highlighted a number of trends. First, at least in the eyes of the West, Russia no longer had "clean hands" in terms of cybersecurity, and that impression had an impact on Russia's goal of an international agreement on "information security." Second, the DDOS strikes underlined how quickly a country with limited resources could develop a cyber-strike capability. Third, it seemed that weaker powers might be able to use cyberattacks successfully in asymmetric conflicts, especially if they could exploit the challenges of attribution. Russia's use of "proxies" as a means to disrupt the cyber capabilities of its adversaries gave it considerable immunity from any armed response or serious countermeasure. All of these trends had an impact on how various countries and regional entities around the world evaluated their cyberspace vulnerabilities and potential offensive capabilities.

One regional entity that had no choice but to address the evolving situation was NATO, which conducted an internal assessment of its cybersecurity infrastructure and policies in 2007 and created the NATO Cooperative Cyber Defence Centre of Excellence (CCDCOE) in May 2008. This new cybersecurity NATO entity convened an international group of experts in 2009 to draft a manual on how international law, including the law of armed conflict, applied to cyber military operations. The following year, in June 2009, Secretary of Defense Robert Gates established United States Cyber Command (USCYBERCOM), whose mission was to "conduct full spectrum military cyberspace operations in order to enable actions in all domains, ensure U.S./Allied freedom of action in cyberspace and deny the same to our adversaries."[8] Meanwhile, the secretary general of the UN created the second UN Group of Governmental Experts (GGE), which consisted of representatives from fifteen countries, including China, France, Germany, Israel, the Russian Federation, Great Britain, and the United States. Unlike the first GGE, the second GGE reached "consensus" in its 2010 report on a number of points, including the following: first, existing "and potential threats in the sphere of information security are among the most serious challenges of the twenty-first century"; second, these threats "may cause substantial damage to economies and national and international security" and "emanate from a wide variety of sources, and manifest themselves in disruptive activities that target individuals, businesses, national infrastructure and Government's alike"; third, "often the origin of a disruption, the identity of the perpetrator or the motivation can be difficult to ascertain" such that the perpetrators "operate with substantial impunity from virtually anywhere"; fourth, the "motives for disruption vary widely, from simply demonstrating technical prowess, to the theft of money or information, or as an extension of

State conflict"; fifth, "there is increased reporting that States are developing ICTs as instruments of warfare and intelligence, and for political purposes"; sixth, noncriminal areas of transnational concern "include the risk of misperception resulting from a lack of shared understanding regarding international norms pertaining to State use of ICTs, which could affect management in the event of major incidents"; and last, existing "agreements include norms relevant to the use of ICTs by States" and given "the unique attributes of ICTs, additional norms could be developed over time."[9]

The second GGE report, although vague, strongly suggested that cybersecurity threats were serious, requiring the development of international norms, especially in terms of states using ICTs as "instruments of warfare and intelligence, and for political purposes." In this receptive environment, the Shanghai Cooperation Organisation (SCO), which China, Kazakhstan, Kyrgyzstan, Russia, Tajikistan, and Uzbekistan had established in 2003, submitted to the UN general secretary on September 12, 2011, a draft of an "International Code of Conduct for Information Security." The purpose of the proposal was "to further discuss the document within the framework of the United Nations so as to reach consensus on the international norms and rules standardizing the behavior of countries concerning information and cyberspace at an early date." The SCO described the proposal as the "first relatively comprehensive and systematic document in the world proposing the international rules on information and network security." The following excerpt focuses on the code's theme of national sovereignty and the right of the state to curb dissemination of harmful information.

10.2 SCO's International Code of Conduct for Information Security (2011)

Reaffirming that policy authority for Internet-related public issues is the sovereign right of States, which have rights and responsibilities for international Internet-related public policy issues,[10]

Recognizing . . . [that the] "[c]reation of a global culture of cyber security and taking stock of national efforts to protect critical information infrastructure,"

Stressing the need for enhanced efforts to close the digital divide by facilitating the transfer of information technology and capacity-building to developing countries in the areas of cybersecurity best practices and training . . . ,

Adopts the international code of conduct for information security as follows:

PURPOSE AND SCOPE

The purpose of the present code is to identify the rights and responsibilities of States in information space, promote their constructive and responsible behaviors. . . .

Adherence to the code is voluntary and open to all States.

CODE OF CONDUCT

Each State voluntarily subscribing to this code pledges:

a. To comply with the Charter of the United Nations and universally recognized norms governing international relations, which enshrine, inter alia, respect for the sovereignty, territorial integrity and political independence of all States, respect for human rights and fundamental freedoms, and respect for the diversity of history, culture and social systems of all countries;
b. Not to use ICTs, including networks, to carry out hostile activities or acts of aggression, pose threats to international

peace and security or proliferate information weapons or related technologies;

c. To cooperate in combating criminal and terrorist activities that use ICTs . . . and in curbing the dissemination of information that incites terrorism, secessionism or extremism or that undermines other countries' political, economic and social stability, as well as their spiritual and cultural environment; . . .

d. To reaffirm all the rights and responsibilities of States to protect, in accordance with relevant laws and regulations, their information space and critical information infrastructure from threats, disturbance, attack and sabotage;

e. To fully respect the rights and freedom in information space, including rights and freedom to search for, acquire and disseminate information on the premise of complying with relevant national laws and regulations;

f. To settle any dispute resulting from the application of the code through peaceful means and to refrain from the threat or use of force.

Questions

1. How are "sovereign right of states" over the internet to be reconciled with the internet's global and integrated character? What's the position of the "code of conduct"?
2. Do technically proficient countries, such as the United States, have an obligation to transfer "best practices" of cybersecurity to developing countries? What if such transfers would make it more difficult for the United States to gather "foreign intelligence information" or shape public opinion around the world?
3. What is the value of this code of conduct if it is "voluntary"? Does this mean the code is simply a set of moral admonitions in the area of cybersecurity? If they signed it, which countries of the world would actually feel obliged to respect such a pledge? The United States? China? Russia? North Korea?
4. One of the code's pledges is to respect the "diversity of history, culture and social systems of all countries." Is this a viable, worthwhile pledge? Are there certain "social systems" that are not worthy of respect? What about culture and history?
5. If a country pledges not "to carry out hostile activities or acts of aggression" on the internet, would it leave that country more vulnerable to these kinds of threats? Are offensive ICTs necessary for an effective defense?
6. As the code fully endorses the "freedom of searching for, acquiring and disseminating information" on the internet, but only up to the point permitted by "relevant national laws and regulations," does the exception swallow the rule? Why or why not?

At the time SCO submitted its code of conduct to the UN general secretary, a number of private security internet firms and journalists were unraveling the mysteries of Stuxnet—a multilevel clandestine cyberattack on the Iranian nuclear centrifuge program, a program essential to Iran's development of an independent nuclear industry and, in addition, nuclear weapons. Centrifuges are metal cylinders that spin to produce enriched uranium hexafluoride gas, separating the lighter U-235 isotope needed for atomic energy from the heavier U-238 isotopes. The Stuxnet attack began with a reconnaissance phase as early as 2005. At the time, unknown actors were able to place malware on the Iranian computer systems that recorded the data they needed to plan and shape the offensive attack. The attack would be successful only to the degree to which the data was accurate, up-to-date, and comprehensive. The first offensive attack began in 2007. It focused on the valves that permitted the gas to enter and leave the centrifuges. By manipulating the valves, the attack caused the pressures in the centrifuges to fluctuate and thereby partially solidifying the gas, which imbalanced the centrifuge, making it liable to detach itself from its moorings, destroying itself in the process, as well as other centrifuges in the vicinity. In June 2009, the cyberattack switched its focus from the centrifuge valves to the computer systems controlling the frequency converters that regulated how fast the centrifuges spun the hexafluoride gas. Acceleration and deceleration of the spin rate, over time, would cause the same result as the first attack: the centrifuges would become imbalanced and break apart. Throughout these two offensive attacks, Iranian technicians and officials did not know why their centrifuges were flying apart because Stuxnet was designed to send prerecorded data back to the control systems during the attacks. The prerecorded data showed no abnormalities in how the centrifuges were operating. Accordingly, Iranian technicians would find centrifuges destroyed but would not know what happened or why. Were the centrifuges faulty? Were they not properly installed and programmed? Was maintenance the issue? No one could be sure.[11]

The first inkling that something was seriously amiss in Iran's cyberspace appeared in June 2010. The story evolved slowly because it was so difficult for cybersecurity experts to figure out how the attack worked and because the subject matter was very technical, beyond the average human being's level of interest or comprehension. The major mystery, of course, was who was responsible for the physical destruction of nuclear centrifuges inside the sovereign state of Iran. Rumors were commonplace until the *New York Times* published an article on January 15, 2011, charging that Stuxnet was a joint sabotage operation between Israel and the United States to delay Iran's nuclear program. The sabotage program was successful, at least to the point that it destroyed approximately 984 centrifuges in 2009, delaying the Iranian nuclear program about three years. One computer security expert commented that Stuxnet was not about "sending a message" or "proving a concept" but rather "about destroying its targets with utmost determination in military style."[12] Despite this characterization, however, it could not be denied that Stuxnet was a targeted operation, focused only on Iranian computer systems that controlled the operations of nuclear centrifuges. No Iranian lives were lost and little or no incidental property damage was incurred. Of course, no U.S. or Israeli official has officially confirmed or denied the *New York Times* report, but the allegations contained in it have been widely accepted.

As the Stuxnet controversy continued to unfold in 2011, the SCO submitted to the UN general secretary in September a second code of conduct. This second code could be interpreted as a deliberate challenge to U.S. and Israeli cyber military operations. Were the United States and Israel "rogue" cyber nations willing to engage in cyberattacks that other countries were not permitted to engage in? Was the U.S. reluctance to negotiate an international treaty on "information security" or "cyber security" simply a way to preserve its flexibility regarding cyber operations that arguably did not qualify as an "armed attack" or an "act of war"? Can the United States draw the line between lawful cyber operations and illegal cyberattacks without any regard for international rules or standards? These kinds of questions ultimately persuaded the Obama administration to address the issue of offensive cyber operations in a speech delivered by Harold Koh, the State Department's legal advisor, at the USCYBERCOM Inter-Agency Legal Conference on September 18, 2012, at Fort Meade, Maryland. Koh's speech was fully cleared through an interagency process, which implied that the speech reflected the views of the U.S. government, not just those of the State Department or Koh personally. Koh's remarks are in response to what he calls "the most fundamental questions."

10.3 Harold Koh, "International Law in Cyberspace" (2012)

Question 1: Do established principles of international law apply to cyberspace?[13]

Answer 1: Yes, international law principles do apply in cyberspace. . . . Significantly, this view has not necessarily been universal in the international community. At least one country has questioned whether existing bodies of international law apply to the cutting edge issues presented by the internet. Some have also said that existing international law is not up to the task, and that we need entirely new treaties to impose a unique set of rules on cyberspace. But the United States has made clear our view that established principles of international law do apply in cyberspace.

Question 2: Is cyberspace a law-free zone, where anything goes?

Answer 2: Emphatically no. Cyberspace is not a "law-free" zone where anyone can conduct hostile activities without rules or restraint. Think of it this way. This is not the first time that technology has changed and international law has been asked to deal with those changes. In particular, because the tools of conflict are constantly evolving, one relevant body of law—international humanitarian law, or the law of armed conflict—affirmatively anticipates technological innovation and contemplates that its existing rules will apply to such innovation. To be sure, new technologies raise new issues and thus, new questions. Many of us in this room have struggled with such questions, and we will continue to do so over many years. But to those who say that established law is not up to the task, we must articulate and build consensus around how it applies and reassess from there whether and what additional understandings are needed. . . .

Question 3: Do cyber activities ever constitute a use of force?

Answer 3: Yes. Cyber activities may in certain circumstances constitute uses of force within the meaning of Article 2(4) of the UN Charter and customary international law. In analyzing whether a cyber operation would constitute a use of force, most commentators focus on whether the direct physical injury and property damage resulting from the cyber event looks like that which would be considered a use of force if produced by kinetic weapons. *Cyber activities that proximately result in death, injury, or significant destruction would likely be viewed as a use of force.* In assessing whether an event constituted a use of force in or through cyberspace, we must evaluate factors: including the context of the event, the actor perpetrating the action (recognizing challenging issues of attribution in cyberspace), the target and location, effects and intent, among other possible issues. Commonly cited examples of cyber activity that would constitute a use of force include, for example: (1) operations that trigger a nuclear plant meltdown; (2) operations that open a dam above a populated area causing destruction; or (3) operations that disable air traffic control resulting in airplane crashes. Only a moment's reflection makes you realize that this is common sense: if the physical consequences of a cyber attack work the kind of physical damage that dropping a bomb or firing a missile would, that cyber attack should equally be considered a use of force.

Question 4: May a State ever respond to a computer network attack by exercising a right of national self-defense?

Answer 4: Yes. A State's national right of self-defense, recognized in Article 51 of the UN Charter, may be triggered by computer network activities that amount to an armed attack or imminent threat thereof. As the United States affirmed in its 2011 International Strategy for Cyberspace, "when warranted, the United States will respond to hostile acts in cyberspace as we would to any other threat to our country."

Question 5: Do *jus in bello* rules apply to computer network attacks?

Answer 5: Yes. In the context of an armed conflict, the law of armed conflict applies to regulate the use of cyber tools in hostilities, just as it does other tools. The principles of necessity and proportionality limit uses of force in self-defense and would regulate what may constitute a lawful response under the circumstances. There is no legal requirement that the response to a cyber armed attack take the form of a cyber action, as long as the response meets the requirements of necessity and proportionality.

Question 6: Must attacks distinguish between military and nonmilitary objectives?

Answer 6: Yes. The *jus in bello* principle of distinction applies to computer network attacks undertaken in the context of an armed conflict. The principle of distinction applies to cyber activities that amount to an "attack"—as that term is understood in the law of war—in the context of an armed conflict. As in any form of armed conflict, the principle of distinction requires that the intended effect of the attack must be to harm a legitimate *military* target. We must distinguish military objectives—that is, objects that make an effective contribution to military action and whose destruction would offer a military advantage—from civilian objects, which under international law are generally protected from attack.

Question 7: Must attacks adhere to the principle of proportionality?

Answer 7: Yes. The *jus in bello* principle of proportionality applies to computer network attacks undertaken in the context of an armed conflict. The principle of proportionality prohibits attacks that may be expected to cause incidental loss to civilian life, injury to civilians, or damage to civilian objects that would be excessive in relation to the concrete and direct military advantage anticipated. Parties to an armed conflict must assess what the expected harm to civilians is likely to be, and weigh the risk of such collateral damage against the importance of the expected military advantage to be gained. In the cyber context, this rule requires parties to a conflict to assess: (1) the effects of cyber weapons on both military and civilian infrastructure and users, including shared physical infrastructure (such as a dam or a power grid) that would affect civilians; (2) the potential physical damage that a cyber attack may cause, such as death or injury that may result from effects on critical infrastructure; and (3) the potential effects of a cyber attack on civilian objects that are not military objectives, such as private, civilian computers that hold no military significance, but may be networked to computers that are military objectives. . . .

Question 9: In this analysis, what role does State sovereignty play?

Answer 9: States conducting activities in cyberspace must take into account the sovereignty of other States, including outside the context of armed conflict. The physical infrastructure that supports the internet and cyber activities is generally located in sovereign territory and subject to the jurisdiction of the territorial State. Because of the interconnected, interoperable nature of cyberspace, operations targeting networked information infrastructures in one country may create effects in another country. Whenever a State contemplates conducting activities in cyberspace, the sovereignty of other States needs to be considered. . . .

Let me [also] identify three particularly difficult questions that I don't intend to answer here today. Instead, my hope is to shed some light on some of the cutting-edge legal issues that we'll all be facing together over the next few years:

Unresolved Question 1: How can a use of force regime take into account all of the novel kinds of *effects* that States can produce through the click of a button?

As I said above, the United States has affirmed that established *jus ad bellum* rules do apply to uses of force in cyberspace. I have also noted some clear-cut cases where the physical effects of a hostile cyber action would be comparable to what a kinetic action could achieve: for example, a bomb might break a dam and flood a civilian population, but insertion of a line of malicious code from a distant computer might just as easily achieve that same result. As you all know, however, there are other types of cyber actions that do not have a clear kinetic parallel, which raise profound questions about exactly what we mean by "force." At the same time, the difficulty of reaching a definitive legal conclusion or consensus among States on when and under what circumstances a hostile cyber action would constitute an armed attack does not automatically suggest that we need an entirely new legal framework specific to cyberspace. Outside of the cyber-context, such ambiguities and differences of view have long existed among States.

To cite just one example of this, the United States has for a long time taken the position that the inherent right of self-defense potentially applies against *any* illegal use of force. In our view, there is no threshold for a use of deadly force to qualify as an "armed attack" that may warrant a forcible response. But that is not to say that any illegal use of force triggers the right to use any and all force in response—such responses must still be *necessary* and of course *proportionate*. We recognize, on the other hand, that some other countries and commentators have drawn a distinction between the "use of force" and an "armed attack," and view "armed attack"—triggering the right to self-defense—as a subset of uses of force, which passes a higher threshold of gravity. My point here is not to rehash old debates, but to illustrate that States have long had to sort through complicated *jus ad bellum* questions. In this respect, the existence of complicated cyber questions relating to *jus ad bellum* is not in itself a new development; it is just applying old questions to the latest developments in technology.

Unresolved Question 2: What do we do about "*dual-use* infrastructure" in cyberspace?

As you all know, information and communications infrastructure is often shared between State militaries and private, civilian communities. The law of war requires that civilian infrastructure not be used to seek to immunize military objectives from attack, including in the cyber realm. But how, exactly, are the *jus in bello* rules to be implemented in cyberspace? Parties to an armed conflict will need to assess the potential effects of a cyber attack on computers that are *not* military objectives, such as private, civilian computers that hold no military significance, but may be networked to computers that are valid military objectives. Parties will also need to consider the harm to the civilian uses of such infrastructure in performing the necessary proportionality review. Any number of factual scenarios could arise, however, which will require a careful, fact-intensive legal analysis in each situation.

That leads to my Final Question for this group: Why should U.S Government lawyers care about international law in cyberspace at all?

The Answer: Because compliance with international law frees us to do more, and do more legitimately, in cyberspace, in a way that more fully promotes our national interests. . . .

It is worth noting . . . a fundamental difference in philosophy about international law.

One way to think about law, whether domestic or international, is as a straitjacket, a pure constraint. This approach posits that nations have serious, legitimate interests, and legal regimes restrict their ability to carry them out. One consequence of this view is that, since law is just something that constrains, it should be resisted whenever possible. Resisting so-called "extensions" of the law to new areas often seems attractive: because, after all, the old laws weren't built for these new challenges anyway, some say, so we should tackle those challenges without the legal straitjacket, while leaving the old laws behind.

But that is *not* the United States Government's view of the law, domestic or international. We see law not as a straitjacket, but as one great university calls it when it confers its diplomas, a body of "wise restraints that make us free." International law is not purely constraint, it frees us and empowers us to do things we could never do without law's legitimacy. If we succeed in promoting a culture of compliance, we will reap the benefits. And if we earn a reputation for compliance, the actions we *do* take will earn enhanced legitimacy worldwide for their adherence to the rule of law.

These are not new themes, but I raise them here because . . . they resonate squarely with the strategy we have been pursuing in cyberspace over the past few years. Of course, the United States has impressive cyber-capabilities; it should be clear from the bulk of my discussion that adherence to established principles of law does not prevent us from using those capabilities to achieve important ends. But we also know that we will be safer, the more that we can rally other States to the view that these established principles *do* impose meaningful constraints, and that there is already an existing set of laws that protect our security in cyberspace. And the more widespread the understanding that cyberspace follows established rules—and that we live by them—the stronger we can be in pushing back against those who would seek to introduce brand new rules that may be contrary to our interests.

Questions

1. Koh defends the traditional U.S. position that existing international norms should be applied to cyberspace without introducing "brand new rules that may be contrary to our interests." Is his argument persuasive? Is it consistent with his acknowledgment that new internet technologies raise "new" issues and "new" questions?
2. In his speech, Koh does not mention the Stuxnet "attack" on the Iranian centrifuge program, but are the legal principles of the speech consistent with what we know of it? In your view, do any dimensions of Stuxnet violate the law of armed conflict?
3. Why, in Koh's view, is negotiating an international treaty not a viable means by which to "build consensus" on how international law applies to cybersecurity?
4. In his discussion of whether a cyberattack qualifies as a "use of force" in violation of Article 2(4) of the UN Charter, Koh highlights whether the "injury and property damage" of a cyber event "looks like" what would be caused by a traditional kinetic weapon, such as a bomb, in addition to other factors, such as "the context of the event," "the actor perpetrating the action," the "target and location," and the "effects and intent" of the operation. Is Koh saying that a cyberattack would not qualify as a "use of force," even if the damage is comparable to what a bomb would cause, if the "context," "target," and "location" was unusual in some sense or if the "intent" of the attacker was reasonable or the "effects" of the operation were relatively minor in character? Would these latter factors have some bearing on the legality of Stuxnet?
5. In response to his question 4, Koh clearly endorses the right to initiate a

cyberattack in self-defense and later amplifies his remarks by noting that the United States may lawfully initiate such an attack in response to any "illegal use of force," not just to a "use of force" that would qualify as an "armed attack" or "threat thereof." Could this right of self-defense justify the Stuxnet attack on the Iranian centrifuge program? Was the Iranian nuclear enrichment program an "illegal use of force"?

6. Koh adds that the right of self-defense against an illegal use of force can be lawfully exercised only if it is both "necessary" and "proportionate." Was Stuxnet "necessary" and "proportionate" if its goal was merely to delay the Iranian nuclear enrichment program? Could the delay have been accomplished in some other way? Could it have been accomplished with less damage to Iranian property?
7. In his response to question 6, Koh claims that the principle of distinction, which requires that the intended effect of an attack must be to harm a legitimate military target, applies to cyber activities that "amount to an 'attack'—as that term is understood in the law of war—in the context of an armed conflict." Accordingly, if Stuxnet was not an "armed attack," does this mean the principle of distinction did not apply, even if the operation was a violation of international law? An additional requirement is that, to qualify as an attack, the cyber operation must occur "in the context of an armed conflict"? Did an "armed conflict" exist between Iran and the United States while Stuxnet was in operation? If not, could Stuxnet only be justified as an act of self-defense? Is the latter a credible argument? If Stuxnet was not an armed attack, was it an "illegal use of force"? Why would that matter?
8. In his response to question 9, Koh claims that states contemplating cyber operations must "consider" the sovereignty of other states. What kind of requirement is this? Is it too vague? Does sovereignty demand more than "consideration"?
9. Koh claims that the U.S. government views international law not as a "straitjacket" but as a "body of 'wise restraints that make us free.'" Does this argument make any sense? Can a "restraint" make us "free"? Is compliance with traditional norms to resolve new questions of international law more supportive of the "rule of law" than the introduction of "brand new rules"? Or is the real concern that such "brand new rules" may be "contrary to our interests"?

Soon after Koh's important speech at the 2012 USCYBERCOM conference, the International Group of Experts sponsored in 2008 by the NATO Cooperative Cyber Defence Centre of Excellence (CCDCOE) published in 2013 the *Tallinn Manual on the International Law Applicable to Cyber Warfare*. Although the *Tallinn Manual*, the work of a group of private international law practitioners and scholars, was nonbinding and had no official status, it was an important document because it had the potential of shaping future debates, at both the national and international levels. Whether or not the *Tallinn Manual* plays such a future role, it is worth noting that there was considerable convergence between it and Koh's speech, at least at the level of general principle. The manual agreed with Koh that international law applied to cyberspace, that it was not a "law-free" zone, and that the law of armed conflict was applicable and binding. However, regarding more specific issues, the views of the manual and Koh diverged. For example, the manual relied on the International Court of Justice's opinion in the *Nicaragua* case (see **reading 7.5**) to conclude that a cyber operation against another state could constitute a "use of force" that violated international law, but not an "armed attack" that would justify a military response based on self-defense, while Koh claimed any "illegal use of force" would justify an armed response.[14]

Another significant divergence between the *Tallinn Manual* and the United States' position on cyber warfare concerned the principle of "distinction," which requires that the intended effect of an "attack" must be directed at a military target. But what qualifies as a "military target"? The manual endorsed the view that military objectives are only "those objects which by their nature, location, purpose or use make an effective contribution to military action and whose total or partial destruction, capture or neutralization, in the circumstances ruling at the time, offers a definite military advantage." In contrast, the United States defines "military target" to include targets that are not only "war-fighting and war-supporting" but also "war-sustaining." The latter category would arguably include civilian computer infrastructure that directly or indirectly aided the enemy's war effort. Since most of the world's computer infrastructure is owned privately and is significantly more vulnerable to cyberattacks than military infrastructure, the U.S. position significantly expands the scope of cyberattacks during armed conflicts.[15]

A related issue noted by Koh is that information and communications infrastructure is shared between state militaries and private civilian communities. How does this fact affect the proportionality analysis? A civilian computer system may not have any "war-sustaining" role but nonetheless be linked to a computer system of a legitimate military target. If an attack on the military target causes damage to the civilian computer system, must the military advantage of the attack outweigh the collateral damage to civilian infrastructure? First, it is important to note that Koh is claiming that effects on the civilian computer infrastructure that do not cause physical injury to persons or damage to property can be ignored. Such effects are simply not part of the collateral-damage assessment. Obviously, with such a rule, it is likely that civilian computer systems that are linked to legitimate military targets could suffer substantial detrimental consequences without loss of civilian life or property. The *Tallinn Manual* agreed that the consequences on civilian networks need to be subject to proportionality review only if they involve damage to persons or property but rejected the implication of Koh's position that an entire civilian network could be subject to direct attack, especially in terms of social networks that are used to transmit military information. The attacking state must take "precautions" that would provide social networks with a "degree of protection."[16]

Two general implications flow from this brief comparison of Koh's speech with the *Tallinn Manual*. First, it seems the United States favors international norms of law that would give it considerable flexibility in the use of cyber weapons: any "illegal use of force" would trigger the right of self-defense, so long as the response was "necessary" and "proportionate"; a civilian computer system could qualify as a legitimate military target if it was "war-sustaining"; and any effects on a civilian computer system linked to military systems could be ignored if they did not injure or damage civilian persons or property.

The June 2013 Snowden disclosures regarding the NSA's use of sophisticated internet technologies to gather "foreign intelligence information" around the world buttressed the perception that the United States and its Five Eyes partners (the UK, Canada, Australia, and New Zealand) were committed to exploiting their dominant position in cyberspace, in terms of both electronic espionage and cyber operations that do not qualify as a "use of force" or an "armed attack." Second, the fact that private experts sponsored by NATO's CCDCOE could not accept many of the specific conclusions and implications of Koh's speech reveals the challenges that exist in reaching consensus on how international law applies to cyber conflict.

Following the Stuxnet attack on the Iranian nuclear centrifuge program, the problem of "cyberattacks" became more pronounced as cyber weapons proliferated around the world and as states and cyber criminals began to strike at privately owned computer systems, whether for the purpose of espionage, intellectual theft, or political retribution. In 2012, Iran, presumably in retaliation for Stuxnet, injected the Shamoon virus into the computers of Saudi Aramco, thereby wiping out thirty thousand hard drives and disrupting the world's largest oil producer. In 2013, Thomas Donilon, President Obama's national security advisor, blew the whistle on China's aggressive attempts to steal "confidential business information and proprietary technologies through cyber intrusions."[17] Late in 2014, hackers under the control of North Korea destroyed three thousand computers and eight hundred servers and stole more than one hundred terabytes of data from Sony Pictures Entertainment. The cyberattack was in retaliation for the studio's planned release of *The Interview*, a film about a talk show host who gets entangled in a CIA plot to kill Kim Jong-un, North Korea's mercurial leader.[18]

In early 2015, the Shanghai Cooperation Organisation (SCO) resubmitted its proposal to the UN general secretary for a voluntary international "code of conduct" for information security. The proposal was nearly identical to the one the SCO submitted in 2011, but there was some modification of the language regarding freedom of speech on the internet. The 2015 proposal recognized that the rights of an individual in the offline environment must also be protected online, including the "right to seek, receive and impart information," but noted that the International Covenant on Civil and Political Rights acknowledged that these rights may be subject to "necessary" restrictions established by law, including restrictions that "respect the rights or reputations of others" and protect "national security," "public order," "public health," and "morals." In short, the 2015 SCO proposal for a voluntary code of conduct for information security clearly recognized the authority of states to regulate the "free flow of information" over the internet.[19]

Later that same year, in June, the Department of Defense (DOD) published its long-awaited *Law of War Manual*, a comprehensive analysis of the subject designed as a resource for DOD personnel, including "commanders, legal practitioners, and other military and civilian personnel." The manual included a chapter on "Cyber Operations," which recognized that "how the law of war applies to cyber operations is not well-settled, and aspects of the law in this area are likely to continue to develop, especially as new cyber capabilities are developed and States determine their views in response to such developments."[20] The following month, the UN's third Group of Governmental Experts (GGE) issued its report on "Developments in the Field of Information and Telecommunications in the Context of International Security" in July 2015. Building on the work of previous groups, the 2015 report claimed it had made important progress, in part by expanding "the discussion of norms" that regulate the use of ICTs (Information and Communications Technologies) in the context of "existing and emerging threats" in cyberspace. The following excerpt from the third GGE report focuses on the seriousness of emerging threats and the "norms, rules, and principles" that the international community should use to regulate them.

10.4 UN GGE 2015 Report

II. EXISTING AND EMERGING THREATS

3. ICTs provide immense opportunities for social and economic development and continue to grow in importance for the international community.[21] There are, however, disturbing trends in the global ICT environment, including a dramatic increase in incidents involving the malicious use of ICTs by State and non-State actors. These trends create risks for all States, and the misuse of ICTs may harm international peace and security.

4. A number of States are developing ICT capabilities for military purposes. The use of ICTs in future conflicts between States is becoming more likely.

5. The most harmful attacks using ICTs include those targeted against the critical infrastructure and associated information systems of a State. The risk of harmful ICT attacks against critical infrastructure is both real and serious.

6. The use of ICTs for terrorist purposes, beyond recruitment, financing, training and incitement, including for terrorist attacks against ICTs or ICT-dependent infrastructure, is an increasing possibility that, if left unaddressed, may threaten international peace and security.

7. The diversity of malicious non-State actors, including criminal groups and terrorists, their differing motives, the speed at which malicious ICT actions can occur and the difficulty of attributing the source of an ICT incident all increase risk. States are rightfully concerned about the danger of destabilizing misperceptions, the potential for conflict and the possibility of harm to their citizens, property and economy.

8. Different levels of capacity for ICT security among States can increase vulnerability in an interconnected world.

III. NORMS, RULES AND PRINCIPLES FOR THE RESPONSIBLE BEHAVIOR OF STATES

9. The ICT environment offers both opportunities and challenges to the international community in determining how norms, rules and principles can apply to State conduct of ICT-related activities. One objective is to identify further voluntary, non-binding norms for responsible State behavior and to strengthen common understanding to increase stability and security in the global ICT environment.

10. Voluntary, non-binding norms of responsible State behavior can reduce risks to international peace, security and stability. Accordingly, norms do not seek to limit or prohibit action that is otherwise consistent with international law. Norms reflect the expectations of the international community, set standards for responsible State behavior and allow the international community to assess the activities and intentions of States. Norms can help to prevent conflict in the ICT environment and contribute to its peaceful use to enable the full realization of ICTs to increase global social and economic development. . . .

13. [T]he present Group offers the following recommendations for consideration by States for voluntary, non-binding norms, rules or principles of responsible behavior of States aimed at promoting an open, secure, stable, accessible and peaceful ICT environment:

a. . . . States should cooperate in developing and applying measures to increase stability and security in the use of ICTs and to prevent ICT practices that are acknowledged to be harmful or that may pose threats to international peace and security;
b. In case of ICT incidents, States should consider all relevant information . . . ;
c. States should not knowingly allow their territory to be used for internationally wrongful acts using ICTs;
d. States should consider how best to cooperate [with each other] . . . ;
e. States . . . should respect . . . the right to privacy in the digital age, to guarantee full respect for human rights, including the right to freedom of expression;
f. States should not conduct or knowingly support ICT activity contrary to its obligations under international law that intentionally damages critical infrastructure or otherwise impairs the use and operation of critical infrastructure to provide services to the public;
g. States should take appropriate measures to protect their critical infrastructure from ICT threats . . . ;
h. States should respond to appropriate requests for assistance by another State whose critical infrastructure is subject to malicious ICT acts. States should also respond to appropriate requests to mitigate malicious ICT activity aimed at the critical infrastructure of another State emanating from their territory, taking into account due regard for sovereignty.
i. States should take reasonable steps to ensure the integrity of the supply chain so that end users can have confidence in the security of ICT products. States should seek to prevent the proliferation of malicious ICT tools and techniques and the use of harmful hidden functions.
j. States should encourage responsible reporting of ICT vulnerability and share associated information on available remedies to such vulnerability to limit and possibly eliminate potential threats to ICT and ICT-dependent infrastructure. . . .

15. Given the unique attributes of ICTs, additional norms could be developed over time.

Questions

1. The report strongly suggests that the UN GGE believes cyberspace is becoming a more dangerous place, yet its recommendations are arguably weak in character. Is there a disjunction between the report's assessment of cyber threats and its recommendation? If so, why?
2. The UN GGE endorses "voluntary, non-binding norms" to control the malicious use of ICTs. Does this mean the UN is likely to follow the approach of the Shanghai Cooperation Organisation? What is the value of a voluntary "code of conduct" for cyberspace?
3. If the GGE's set of "voluntary norms" do not seek "to limit or prohibit action that is otherwise consistent with international law," then why not simply enforce international law in cyberspace, including the law of armed conflict? Does the GGE think that "voluntary norms" can elevate the "expectations of the international community" beyond those required by international law, even if the norms do not "limit or prohibit" any action consistent with international law?
4. According to the GGE, states should respect human rights, including the right to privacy and freedom of expression, but acknowledges that states have sovereignty over the internet infrastructure located within its border. Is there a potential inconsistency here?
5. According to paragraph (f), states should not use ICTs to intentionally damage critical infrastructure in vio-

lation of its obligation under international law. Does this "voluntary norm" imply that the use of ICTs for espionage purposes is lawful so long as the critical infrastructure is not damaged?

6. The GGE argues that states should report ICT "vulnerabilities" of critical infrastructure, but intelligence agencies might wish to exploit such vulnerabilities to gather "foreign intelligence information." Which of these legitimate goals is likely to trump the other? Why?

Cyber operations involving espionage, theft of personal or proprietary information, and political retaliation continued to expand and intensify. In July 2015, the federal government's Office of Personnel Management announced that hackers had stolen "sensitive information" about 21.5 million government employees who had undergone background checks over the last fifteen years, including addresses, health and financial histories, social security numbers, and some fingerprints.[22] In February 2016, both the IRS and the Department of Justice announced breaches of their systems, which compromised more than seven hundred thousand U.S. taxpayers and thirty thousand Department of Homeland Security and FBI employees. In August 2016, a group calling itself "Shadow Brokers" published a collection of intelligence cyber tools that it had hacked from the National Security Agency (NSA). In October of the same year, top U.S. intelligence officials confirmed that Russia had hacked the emails of the Democratic National Committee and dumped them on the internet through WikiLeaks. In November, the Iranian "Shamoon" virus reappeared and wiped out the data on thousands of government computers in Saudi Arabia.[23] In this context, Brian J. Egan, the State Department's legal advisor, delivered a major speech at the Berkeley Center for Law and Technology titled "International Law and Stability in Cyberspace" on November 10, 2016. The speech amplified the general principles regarding international law's relationship to cyberspace discussed by Koh in his 2012 address (see **reading 10.3**).

10.5 Brian J. Egan, "International Law and Stability in Cyberspace," November 10, 2016

We have made significant progress since . . . [Koh's 2012 speech].[24] One prominent forum in which these issues are discussed is the United Nations (UN) Group of Governmental Experts (GGE) that deals with cyber issues in the context of international security. . . . Just last year, the . . . UN GGE . . . built on the 2013 report and took an additional step of recognizing the applicability in cyberspace of the inherent right of self-defense as recognized in Article 51 of the UN Charter. The 2015 GGE report also recognized the applicability of the law of armed conflict's fundamental principles of humanity, necessity, proportionality, and distinction to the conduct of hostilities in and through cyberspace. . . . [W]e have [therefore] seen an emerging consensus that existing international law applies to States' cyber activities. Recognizing the applicability of existing international law as a general matter, however, is the easy part, at least for most like-minded nations. Identifying how that law applies to specific cyber activities is more challenging, and States rarely articulate their views on this subject publicly. . . .

States must also address these challenging issues. Interpretations or applications of international law proposed by non-governmental groups may not reflect the practice or legal views of many or most States. States' relative silence could lead to unpredictability in the cyber realm, where States may be left guessing about each other's views on the applicable legal framework. In the context of a specific cyber incident, this uncertainty could give rise to misperceptions and miscalculations by States, potentially leading to escalation and, in the worst case, conflict. . . .

In this spirit, . . . I would like to offer some additional U.S. views on how certain rules of international law apply to States' behavior in cyberspace, beginning first with cyber operations during armed conflict, and then turning to the identification of voluntary, non-binding norms applicable to State behavior during peacetime. . . .

Turning to cyber operations in armed conflict, I would like to start with the U.S. military's cyber operations in the context of the ongoing armed conflict with the Islamic State of Iraq and the Levant (ISIL). As U.S. Defense Secretary Ashton Carter informed Congress in April 2016, U.S. Cyber Command has been asked "to take on the war against ISIL as essentially [its] first major combat operation [. . .] The objectives there are to interrupt ISIL command-and-control, interrupt its ability to move money around, interrupt its ability to tyrannize and control population[s], [and] interrupt its ability to recruit externally."

The U.S. military must comply with the United States' obligations under the law of armed conflict and other applicable international law when conducting cyber operations against ISIL, just as it does when conducting other types of military operations during armed conflict. To the extent that such cyber operations constitute "attacks" under the law of armed conflict, the rules on conducting attacks must be applied to those cyber operations. For example, such operations must only be directed against military objectives, such as computers, other networked devices, or possibly specific data that, by their nature, location, purpose, or use, make an effective contribution to military action and whose total or partial destruction, capture, or neutralization, in the circumstances ruling at the time, offers a definite military advantage. Such operations also must comport with the requirements of the principles of distinction and proportionality. Feasible precautions must be taken to reduce the risk of incidental harm to civilian infrastructure and users. In the cyber context, this requires parties to a conflict to assess the potential effects of cyber activities on both military and civilian infrastructure and users.

Not all cyber operations, however, rise to the level of an "attack" as a legal matter under the law of armed conflict. When determining whether a cyber activity constitutes an "attack" for purposes of the law of armed conflict, States should consider, among other things, whether a cyber activity results in kinetic or non-kinetic effects, and the nature and scope of those effects, as well as the nature of the connection, if any, between the cyber activity and the particular armed conflict in question.

Even if they do not rise to the level of an "attack" under the law of armed conflict, cyber operations during armed conflict must nonetheless be consistent with the principles of military necessity. For example, a cyber operation that would not constitute an "attack," but would nonetheless seize or destroy enemy property, would have to be imperatively demanded by the necessities of war. Additionally, even if a cyber operation does not rise to the level of an "attack" or does not cause injury or damage that would need to be considered under the principle of proportionality in conducting attacks, that cyber operation still should comport with the general principles of the law of war. . . .

. . . I would [now] like to offer a few thoughts about the relevance of sovereignty principles to States' cyber activities.

As an initial matter, remote cyber operations involving computers or other networked devices located on another State's territory do not constitute a *per se* violation of international law. In other words, there is no absolute prohibition on such operations as a matter of international law. This is perhaps most clear where such activities in another State's territory have no effects or *de minimis* effects.

Most States, including the United States, engage in intelligence collection abroad. . . .

Such widespread and perhaps nearly universal practice by States of intelligence collection abroad indicates that there is no *per se* prohibition on such activities under customary international law. I would caution, however, that because "intelligence collection" is not a defined term, the absence of a *per se* prohibition on these activities does not settle the question of whether a specific intelligence collection activity might nonetheless violate a provision of international law.

Although certain activities—including cyber operations—may violate another State's domestic law, that is a separate question from whether such activities violate international law. . . . [A violation of a State's domestic law does] not resolve the independent question of whether the activity violates international law.

In certain circumstances, one State's non-consensual cyber operation in another State's territory *could* violate international law, even if it falls below the threshold of a use of force. This is a challenging area of the law that raises difficult questions. The very design of the Internet may lead to some encroachment on other sovereign jurisdictions. Precisely when a non-consensual cyber operation violates the sovereignty of another State is a question lawyers within the U.S. government continue to study carefully, and it is one that ultimately will be resolved through the practice and *opinio juris* of States.

Relatedly, consider the challenges we face in clarifying the international law prohibition on unlawful intervention. As articulated by the International Court of Justice (ICJ) in its judgment on the merits in the *Nicaragua Case*, this rule of customary international law forbids States from engaging in coercive action that bears on a matter that each State is entitled, by the principle of State sovereignty, to decide freely, such as the choice of a political, economic, social, and cultural system. This is generally viewed as a relatively narrow rule of customary international law, but States' cyber activities could run afoul of this prohibition. For example, a cyber operation by a State that interferes with another country's ability to hold an election or that manipulates another country's election results would be a clear violation of the rule of non-intervention. For increased transparency, States need to do more work to clarify how the international law on non-intervention applies to States' activities in cyberspace. . . .

Before leaving the topic of sovereignty, . . . I want to underscore an important point. Some States invoke the concept of State sovereignty as a justification for excessive regulation of online content, including censorship and access restrictions, often undertaken in the name of counterterrorism or "countering violent extremism." And sometimes, States also deploy the concept of State sovereignty in an attempt to shield themselves from outside criticism.

So let me repeat what Koh made clear: Any regulation by a State of matters within its territory, including use of and access to the Internet, must comply with that State's applicable obligations under international human rights law.

There is no doubt that terrorist groups have become dangerously adept at using the Internet and other communications technologies to propagate their hateful messages, recruit adherents, and urge followers to commit violent acts. This is why all governments must work together to target online criminal activities—such as illicit money transfers, terrorist attack planning and coordination, criminal solicitation, and the provision of material support to terrorist groups. U.S. efforts to prevent the Internet from being used for terrorist purposes also focus on criminal activities that facilitate terrorism, such as financing and recruitment, not on restricting expressive content, even if that content is repugnant or inimical to our core values.

Such efforts must not be conflated with broader calls to restrict public access to or censor the Internet, or even—as some have suggested—to effectively shut down entire portions of the Web. Such measures would not advance our security, and they would be inconsistent with our values. The Internet must remain open to the free flow of information and ideas. Restricting the flow of ideas also inhibits spreading the values of understanding and mutual respect that offer one of the most powerful antidotes to the hateful and violent narratives propagated by terrorist groups.

That is why the United States holds the view that use of the Internet, including social media, in furtherance of terrorism and other criminal activity must be addressed through lawful means that respect each State's international obligations and commitments regarding human rights, including the freedom of expression, and that serve the objectives of the free flow of information and a free and open Internet. To be sure, the incitement of imminent terrorist violence may be restricted. However, certain censorship and content control, including blocking websites simply because they contain content that criticizes a leader, a government policy, or an ideology, or because the content espouses particular religious beliefs, violates international human rights law and must not be engaged in by States. . . .

[Last,] . . . I will focus on the issue of attribution in the legal sense.

From a legal perspective, the customary international law of state responsibility supplies the standards for attributing acts, including cyber acts, to States. For example, cyber operations conducted by organs of a State or by persons or entities empowered by domestic law to exercise governmental authority are attributable to that State, if such organs, persons, or entities are acting in that capacity.

Additionally, cyber operations conducted by non-State actors are attributable to a State under the law of state responsibility when such actors engage in operations pursuant to the State's instructions or under the State's direction or control, or when the State later acknowledges and adopts the operations as its own.

Thus, as a legal matter, States cannot escape responsibility for internationally wrongful cyber acts by perpetrating them through proxies. [If] a cyber act engaged in by a non-State actor . . . [can] be attributed legally to a State under one of the standards set forth in the law of state responsibility, the victim State has all of the rights and remedies against the responsible State allowed under international law.

The law of state responsibility does *not* set forth explicit burdens or standards of proof for making a determination about legal attribution. In this context, a State acts as its own judge of the facts and may make a unilateral determination with respect to attribution of a cyber operation to another State. Absolute certainty is not—and cannot be—required. Instead, international law generally requires that States act reasonably under the circumstances when they gather information and draw conclusions based on that information.

I also want to note that, despite the suggestion by some States to the contrary, there is *no* international legal obligation to reveal evidence on which attribution is based prior to taking appropriate action. . . .

I want to turn now to the question of what options a victim State might have to respond to malicious cyber activity that falls below the threshold of an armed attack. As an initial matter, a State can always undertake unfriendly acts that are not inconsistent with any of its international obligations in order to influence the behavior of other States. Such acts—which are known as acts of retorsion—may include, for example, the imposition of sanctions or the declaration that a diplomat is *persona non grata*.

In certain circumstances, a State may take action that would otherwise violate international law in response to malicious cyber activity. One example is the use of force in self-defense in response to an actual or imminent armed attack. Another example is that, in exceptional circumstances, a State may be able to avail itself of the plea of necessity, which, subject to certain conditions, might preclude the wrongfulness of an act if the act is the only way for the State to safeguard an essential interest against a grave and imminent peril.

In the time remaining, however, I would like to talk about a type of State response that has received a lot of attention in discussions about cyberspace: countermeasures. The customary international law doctrine of countermeasures permits a State that is the victim of an internationally wrongful act of another State to take otherwise unlawful measures against the responsible State in order to cause that State to comply with its international obligations, for example, the obligation to cease its internationally wrongful act. Therefore, as a threshold matter, the availability of countermeasures to address malicious cyber activity requires a prior internationally wrongful act that is attributable to another State. As with all countermeasures, this puts the responding State in the position of potentially being held responsible for violating international law if it turns out that there wasn't actually an internationally wrongful act that triggered the right to take countermeasures, or if the responding State made an inaccurate attribution determination. That is one reason why countermeasures should not be engaged in lightly. . . .

Questions

1. Egan argues that "significant progress" has been made, in part because the UN GGE recognized the inherent right of self-defense in cyberspace and the applicability of the "fundamental principles" of the law of armed conflict. Do you agree with him? Does this amount to "significant progress"?
2. How has "significant progress" been achieved if, as Egan notes, states do not publicly identify how international law applies to specific cyber activities?
3. Egan seems to be claiming that effects on civilians from a cyber operation that are less than those associated with an "armed attack," such as civilian injury or property damage, need not be subject to proportionality analysis, yet at the same time "feasible precautions must be taken to reduce the risk of incidental harm to civilian infrastructure and users." What is "incidental harm"? Disruption of software? Theft of information? Loss of data?
4. Is Egan suggesting that certain "non-kinetic" effects of a cyber operation can still qualify as an attack if the "scope of those effects" is large and if the cyber activity in question is "connected" in some way to the armed conflict? Can you suggest a type of cyber activity that would satisfy these criteria?
5. Even if the principle of proportionality is not applicable to a cyber operation that does not qualify as an "attack," Egan argues that the operation must comport with the principle of military necessity and other general principles of the law of war. What does "military necessity" actually require? Does it permit only, as Egan seems to imply, what is "imperatively demanded by the necessities of war," or is the standard lower?
6. Is Egan's claim that certain cyber operations in armed conflict do not constitute attacks consistent with Koh's position that any "illegal use of force" would trigger the United States' inherent right of self-defense?
7. Egan argues that electronic surveillance and espionage do not infringe upon other states' sovereignty and therefore do not violate international law. Do you agree?
8. Even if electronic surveillance and espionage are consistent with international law, Egan concedes that a "non-consensual cyber operation in another State's territory *could* violate international law, even if it falls below the threshold of a use of force," presumably because it encroaches in some way on "other sovereign jurisdictions." Why doesn't espionage "encroach" upon the jurisdiction of a sovereign? In your view, what other types of "non-consensual cyber operations" might infringe upon sovereignty and therefore constitute a violation of international law? What about Egan's example of a cyber operation that "interferes with another country's ability to hold an election or that manipulates another country's election results"?
9. With the exception of "incitement of imminent terrorist violence," Egan argues that sovereignty does not justify a state regulating or "shutting down" the internet in any way that violates international human rights law. Do you expect Russia, China, North Korea, and Iran ever to accept such a

norm of international law? What is the basis for the United States to insist upon this rule? Is it simply a means for the United States to propagate its values through the internet?

10. According to Egan, cyber operations of "proxies" can legally be attributable to a state if they act "under the State's direction or control, or when the State later acknowledges and adopts the operations as its own," but the victim state is not obliged by international law to apply any "burden" or "standard" of proof to the issue of attribution other than the duty to act "reasonably." In your view, is this a valid norm of international law? Does it implicitly encourage hostile responses to adverse cyber operations? And what about the supposed rule that there is no international-law requirement that a victim state reveal the evidence underlying the finding of attribution? How can nations evaluate whether a state is in compliance with international law if there is no uniform standard of proof and if crucial evidence is kept secret?
11. According to Egan, the "law of countermeasures" permits a state that is the victim of an internationally wrongful act of another state "to take otherwise unlawful measures against the responsible State in order to cause that State to comply with its international obligations." Does this mean a state can respond to a cyber operation that does not qualify as an "attack" in a way that violates international law, but only for the purpose of forcing the other state "to cease its internationally wrongful act"? What kind of responses that violate international law would be appropriate in such a context? Why does Egan claim that such "countermeasures" should not be taken "lightly"?
12. Egan has endorsed three layers of international law relevant to cyber operations: the law of armed conflict; the law of "countermeasures" in response to cyber operations that are less than "attacks"; and finally, a nonbinding voluntary code of conduct relevant to peacetime. Is it arguable that such a trilevel approach to international law is far too complex, producing situations of legal uncertainty that will encourage misunderstandings, confusion, and perhaps conflict?

In January 2017, the Office of the Director of National Intelligence published its declassified version of an official report titled "Accessing Russian Activities and Intentions in Recent US Elections." The report concluded that Russian president Vladimir Putin had "ordered an influence campaign in 2016 aimed at the US presidential election." The goals of the campaign were "to undermine public faith in the U.S. democratic process, denigrate Secretary [Hillary] Clinton, and harm her electability and potential presidency." The upshot was that "Putin and the Russian government developed a clear preference for President-elect [Donald] Trump." All of the agencies of the U.S. intelligence community "had high confidence in these judgments." The Russian electoral influence campaign "followed a longstanding Russian messaging strategy that blends covert intelligence operations—such as cyber activity—with overt efforts by Russian Government agencies, state-funded media, third-party intermediaries, and paid social media users or 'trolls.'" Regarding the covert cyber operations, the Russian intelligence agencies collected information from "US primary campaigns, think tanks, and lobbying groups they viewed as likely to shape future US policies." Russian intelligence entities in July 2015 "gained access to Democratic National Committee (DNC) networks and maintained that access until at least June 2016," and in March 2016 they compromised the "e-mail accounts of Democratic Party officials and political figures." Soon thereafter, the Russians strategically released the hacked information publicly on the internet through Guccifer 2.0, DCLeaks, WikiLeaks, and other exclusive media outlets. According to the report, the 2016 influence campaign was the "boldest" effort ever undertaken by the Russian government to influence a U.S. election.[25]

A number of commentators, from a variety of political perspectives, including Senator John McCain, DNC chairwoman Donna Brazile, former vice president Dick Cheney, and Nikki Haley, the Trump administration's U.S. ambassador to the UN, called the Russian interference in the U.S. election an "act of war," presumably triggering the United States' inherent right of self-defense and justifying the use of military force.[26] In contrast, the Obama administration reacted more moderately. Instead of going to war, it placed sanctions on four Russian intelligence officers, two Russian intelligence agencies, and three Russian companies; ordered thirty-five Russian diplomats out of the country; and closed two Russian compounds in the United States. Although Obama characterized Russian interference with the presidential election as a violation of international norms, none of his responses qualified as a "countermeasure" or an "armed attack." They were all "acts of retorsion," which are "unfriendly" acts that are designed to influence the behavior of a state but are not inconsistent with any international legal obligation. Republican senators John McCain and Lindsey Graham called Obama's retaliatory measures a "small price for Russia to pay" and demanded stronger sanctions.[27]

In evaluating whether Russian interference in the 2016 presidential election was consistent with international law, a violation of international law because it infringed upon U.S. sovereignty, or an "act of war" justifying a military response, it should be noted that the Russian cyber operation did not harm U.S. lives or property, whether military or civilian, but merely gathered information from the private computers of the DNC, think tanks, and individuals and released this information through public outlets. In addition, they tried to sway public opinion in battleground states by posting polarizing rhetoric and "fake news" on social media sites, but there was no attempt to manipulate election results by altering the data on the public computers that registered and recorded electoral votes.[28] However, the Russian cyber operation was clearly intended to influence a U.S. presidential election—a central political institution within the core sovereign framework of the United States.

Fortunately, to aid in the assessment of the Russian cyber operation, NATO's CCDCOE published in February 2017 its timely *Tallinn Manual 2.0 on the International Law Applicable to Cyber Operations*, an expanded version of the 2013 manual, including within its scope not just cyber warfare but also the international norms regulating cyber operations during peacetime. The manual argued that a cyber operation only violated sovereignty if it violated the "non-intervention principle"—that is, if it is "related to matters that involve the internal or external affairs of the target State" and is "coercive in nature."[29] Regarding this test, Michael Schmitt, general editor of *Tallinn Manual 2.0*, observed that "active debate surrounds whether the Russian operations satisfy the 'coercion' element that is necessary to establish an act of prohibited intervention under international law. The implication was that it was unclear whether the United States would be justified by reacting to the Russian interference with "countermeasures," measures that are themselves violations of international law but lawful since they are responses to previous violations, or only with "acts of retorsion," acts that do not violate international law, such as sanctions, but are intended to influence behavior[30]—an implication that highlights the imprecision of international norms regulating cyber conflict versus cyber disruption or rivalry.

Disclosure of the Russian interference campaign triggered investigations by the FBI, the Senate Intelligence Committee, the House Intelligence Committee, and, following Trump's dismissal of FBI director James B. Comey, by Special Counsel Robert Mueller. All of these investigations focused in part on whether there was active "collusion" between candidate Trump's campaign organization and the Russian government. President Trump repeatedly denied any contact between his campaign and the Russian government, calling the story of Russian interference in the 2016 presidential election a "big democratic HOAX," a subterfuge to explain why they lost the election.[31] Given this assessment, it is not surprising that Trump did nothing to impose any additional sanctions on Russia for months after he took office in January 2017.

In June 2017, the fifth UN GGE failed to reach consensus on a new report on developments in the field of information and telecommunications in the context of international security—an unexpected and huge roadblock for the emergence of international norms regulating cyberspace. In a declaration, Miguel Rodríguez, Cuba's representative to the fifth GGE, explained that consensus was not feasible because information and telecommunications "should be instruments to promote peace, not to promote war." In response, Michele G. Markoff, deputy coordinator for cyber issues for the U.S. State Department, explained that consensus could not be achieved because the final draft of the report "insufficiently" addressed "international humanitarian law" and the "inherent right of self-defense." The following reading draws upon these two conflicting accounts, drawing attention to the obstacles for any future consensus on international norms regulating cyberspace.

10.6 Why the Fifth United Nations GGE Failed in 2017

Information and telecommunications should be tools to promote well-being, knowledge and human development, based on strict respect for the UN Charter and International Law.[32] They should be instruments to promote peace, not to promote war, the use of force, interventionism, destabilization, unilateralism or terrorist actions.

Urgent action is required within the framework of the United Nations to prevent the covert and illegal use by individuals, organizations and States of the computer systems of other nations to attack third countries for their potential to provoke international conflicts. . . .

I must register our serious concern over the pretension of some . . . to convert cyberspace into a theater of military operations and to legitimize, in that context, unilateral punitive force actions, including the application of sanctions and even military action by States claiming to be victims of illicit uses of ICTs.

We consider unacceptable the formulations contained in the draft, aimed to establish equivalence between the malicious use of ICTs and the concept of "armed attack," as provided for in Article 51 of the Charter, which attempts to justify the alleged applicability in this context of the right to self-defense.

To establish as a precedent this dangerous reinterpretation of the norms of international law and the Charter of the United Nations would be a fatal blow to the collective security and peacekeeping architecture established in the Charter of the United Nations. The "Law of the Jungle" cannot be imposed, in which the interests of the most powerful States would always prevail to the detriment of the most vulnerable.

The final draft also made reference to the supposed applicability in the context of ICT of the principles of International Humanitarian Law. We cannot accept such affirmation, since it would legitimize a scenario of war and military actions in the context of ICT.

We have consistently emphasized in this Group the priority of initiating, without further delay, a negotiating process within the framework of the United Nations, to adopt an internationally legally binding instrument to respond effectively, on the basis of cooperation, to the significant existing legal gaps in the context of cybersecurity and the growing challenges and threats we face in this area. This very important element was absent in the draft.

. . . We reiterate our position that . . . the issue of information and telecommunication in the context of international security should be considered in a Working Group of the General Assembly open to all States, to ensure full transparency and inclusiveness and participation in equal rights in discussions and decision-making. We hope that this year the UNGA First Committee will take the decision to convene this Open-ended Working Group.

EXPLANATION BY MICHELE G. MARKOFF

Throughout the 2016–2017 GGE, I have sought clear and direct statements on how certain international law applies to States' use of ICTs, including international humanitarian law, international law governing States' exercise of their inherent right of self-defense, and the law of State responsibility, including countermeasures.[33] I sought such statements in the interests of international peace and security, based on my strong conviction that the framework of international law provides States with binding standards of behavior that can help reduce the risk of conflict by creating stable expectations of how States may and may not respond to cyber incidents they face. The final draft of the report insufficiently addresses these issues. . . .

. . . I am coming to the unfortunate conclusion that those who are unwilling to affirm the applicability of these international legal rules and principles believe their States are free to act in or through cyberspace to achieve their political ends with no limits or constraints on their actions. That is a dangerous and unsupportable view, and it is one that I unequivocally reject.

During the GGE, I heard repeated assertions on the part of some participants that a discussion of . . . *jus ad bellum* . . . would be incompatible with the messages the Group should be sending regarding the peaceful settlement of disputes and conflict prevention. This is a false dichotomy that does not withstand scrutiny. A report that . . . omits a discussion of the lawful options States have to respond to malicious cyber activity they face would not only fail to deter States from potentially destabilizing activity, but also fail to send a stabilizing message to the broader community of States that their responses to such malicious cyber activity are constrained by international law.

. . . It is unfortunate that the reluctance of a few participants to seriously engage on the mandate on international legal issues has prevented the Group from reaching consensus on a report that would further the goal of common understandings among UN Member States on these important issues. . . . But our work has been in vain. . . .

Questions

1. Is Rodríguez suggesting that some members of the GGE were in favor of using ICTs "to promote war, the use of force, interventionism," and such, and

converting "cyberspace into a theater of military operations"? To whom is he referring?
2. Is Rodríguez claiming that it is not "legitimate" for state-victims of "illicit uses of ICTs" to respond with either sanctions or military force? Is he right? What if economic sanctions are not typically considered violations of international law?
3. Is Rodríguez implying that no "malicious use of ICTs" can ever constitute an "armed attack" that would justify an armed response?
4. If, as Rodríguez maintains, the "Law of the Jungle" cannot be imposed on cyberspace since powerful states would always prevail, would not weaker states be able to make "malicious use" of ICTs against strong states with impunity? Is that his goal?
5. Rodríguez advocates "an internationally legally binding instrument," such as a treaty, but the instrument would be based on "cooperation." Is this a legally binding treaty that would only require voluntary cooperation at the discretion of the member states? Is this similar to the voluntary "Code of Conduct" that China, Russia, and other countries have endorsed (see **reading 10.2**)?
6. Do you agree with Rodríguez's suggestion that the UN General Assembly should establish a Working Group "open to all States," rather than another Group of Governmental Experts? Is it likely that the United States would oppose such a proposal? Why?
7. Markoff argues that not including law-of-war principles into norms governing cyberspace would encourage, rather than discourage, conflict, which seems to be in direct contradiction to Rodríguez's position. Which position is more convincing?
8. Why does Markoff claim that those opposed to incorporating law-of-war principles into the GGE draft in fact want cyberspace to be a law-free zone? How can she be correct if Rodríguez is arguing that ICTs should be used "to promote peace"?
9. What does Markoff call a "false dichotomy that does not withstand scrutiny"?
10. If only a "few" participants refused to address "seriously" issues of international law, why didn't the GGE issue a nonunanimous report? Would that have been better than no report at all? Or would such a nonunanimous report have polarized the international community even more than it already is?

The June 2017 stalemate at the UN regarding how international law applies to cyber war, conflict, and competition between states is substantial proof that there is currently a lack of consensus at the international level regarding how the internet should be regulated. Each country seems to want to follow its own rules. In that vein, it is worth noting that Congress, unhappy with Trump's reluctance to take any action against Russia, in July 2017 enacted Countering America's Adversaries through Sanctions Act (CAATSA), which imposed sanctions on Iran, North Korea, and Russia, the latter for its interference in the 2016 presidential election.[34] Citing constitutional concerns, Trump reluctantly signed it, but he did not implement the law against Russia until weeks after the law's October 1 deadline, at which point he imposed sanctions on thirty-nine Russian entities, from aircraft manufacturers to engineering firms.[35] In contrast to Congress's point of view, other countries appear to believe that cyber weapons are a legitimate "asymmetric and low-cost means" to achieve their international political goals, often in opposition to U.S. interests and policies. A recent example is Russia's 2017 "NotPetya" attack, which wiped data from the computers of banks, energy companies, and public officials in Ukraine (a former republic of the Soviet Union that Russia wants to keep in its sphere of influence) as well as in Western Europe, Asia, and the Americas, causing billions of dollars in damage.[36] Of course, it cannot be argued that the United States has "clean hands." Stuxnet, the Snowden revelations, and the disclosure that Shadow Brokers, a hacking group possibly linked to Russia, has uncovered a large cache of classified NSA offensive cyber weapons suggest that the United States has only a wavering commitment to a peaceful, conflict-free internet.[37] Therefore, the emergence of international law as the basic legal framework of cyberspace has a long way to go. It is likely that future developments will be bilateral or regional in focus. For example, the United States and China have recently agreed to stop engaging in economic cyber espionage, along with the United Kingdom, Germany, and Canada,[38] but it is not clear whether China will keep its word. In any case, many such "small steps" must be implemented to establish the international trust that is a prerequisite for taking on broader issues of international cyber war, conflict, rivalry, and competition. It is a work in progress, and there is no guarantee of success.

NOTES

1. Department of Justice, *Prosecuting Computer Crimes*, OLE Litigation Series (Washington, DC: Office of Legal Education, 2015), https://www.justice.gov.
2. UN General Assembly A/RES/53/70, "Resolution Adopted by the General Assembly," United Nations, http://www.un.org.
3. See, generally, Tim Maurer, "Cyber Norm Emergence at the United Nations—An Analysis of the UN's Activities regarding Cyber-Security?" Discussion Paper 2011-2011, Belfer Center for Science and International Affairs, Harvard Kennedy School, Cambridge, MA, September 2011, esp. 21–22.
4. Maurer, "Cyber Norm Emergence," 18, 22.
5. UN General Assembly, "Resolution Adopted by the General Assembly on 6 December 2006," A/RES/61/54, NATO Cooperative Cyber Defence Centre of Excellence (CCDCOE), https://ccdcoe.org.
6. See Kim Zetter, *Countdown to Zero Day: Stuxnet and the Launch of the World's First Digital Weapon* (New York: Broadway Books, 2014), 401n57; and Ian Traynor, "Russia Accused of Unleashing Cyberwar to Disable Estonia," *Guardian*, May 16, 2007, https://www.theguardian.com.
7. See John Markoff, "Before the Gunfire, Cyberattacks," *New York Times*, August 12, 2008, http://www.nytimes.com.
8. See "U.S. Cyber Command (USCYBERCOM)," U.S. Strategic Command, September 30, 2016, http://www.stratcom.mil.
9. UN General Assembly, report of the "Group of Governmental Experts on Developments in the Field of Information and Telecommunications in the Context of International Security," July 30, 2010, A/65/201, NATO Cooperative Cyber Defence Centre of Excellence (CCDCOE), https://ccdcoe.org.
10. The SCO's code of conduct is available at United Nations General Assembly, A/66/359, September 14, 2011, NATO Cooperative Cyber Defence Centre of Excellence (CCDCOE), http://ccdcoe.org.
11. See, generally, Kim Zetter, *Countdown to Zero Day*, esp. chaps. 16–18.
12. William J. Broad, John Markoff, and David E. Sanger, "Israeli Test on Worm Called Crucial in Iran Nuclear Delay," *New York Times*, January 15, 2011.

13. Harold Hongju Koh, "International Law in Cyberspace," USCYBERCOM Inter-Agency Legal Conference, September 18, 2012, U.S. Navy Judge Advocate General's Corps, http://www.jag.navy.mil.
14. Michael N. Schmitt, ed., *Tallinn Manual on the International Law Applicable to Cyber Warfare* (Cambridge: Cambridge University Press, 2013), rule 11, 45–52.
15. See Michael N. Schmitt, "International Law in Cyberspace: The Koh Speech and Tallinn Manual Juxtaposed," *Harvard International Law Journal* 54 (December 2012): 27.
16. Schmitt, *Tallinn Manual*, rule 39, 134–37.
17. Fred Kaplan, *Dark Territory: The Secret History of Cyber War* (New York: Simon & Shuster Paperbacks, 2016), 221–22.
18. Kaplan, *Dark Territory*, 268–71.
19. See UN General Assembly, *International Code of Conduct for Information Security*, A/69/723, January 13, 2015, NATO Cooperative Cyber Defence Centre of Excellence (CCD-COE), https://ccdcoe.org.
20. Office of General Counsel, *Department of Defense Law of War Manual* (Washington, DC: Author, 2015), iii, 994, U.S. Department of Defense Archives, http://archive.defense.gov.
21. UN General Assembly, "Group of Governmental Experts on Developments in the Field of Information and Telecommunications in the Context of International Security," A/70/174, July 25, 2015, United Nations, http://www.un.org.
22. Julie Hirschfeld Davis, "Hacking of Government Computers Exposed 21.5 Million People," *New York Times*, July 9, 2015, https://www.nytimes.com.
23. See "Significant Cyber Incidents since 2006," Center for Strategic and International Studies, https://www.csis.org.
24. Brian J. Egan, "International Law and Stability in Cyberspace," *Just Security*, November 10, 2016, https://www.justsecurity.org.
25. Office of the Director of National Intelligence, "Accessing Russian Activities and Intentions in Recent US Elections," January 6, 2017, https://www.dni.gov.
26. See Theodore Schleifer and Deidre Walsh, "McCain: Russian Cyberintrusions an 'Act of War,'" CNN, December 30, 2016, http://www.cnn.com; Morgan Chalfant, "Former DNC Chair: Russian Election Hacking an 'Act of War,'" *The Hill*, March 29, 2017, http://thehill.com; Kyle Feldscher, "Cheney: Russian Interference in Election Could Be 'an Act of War,'" *Washington Examiner*, March 27, 2017, http://www.washingtonexaminer.com; Jordan Smith, "Nicki Haley Says Russian Interference Is Act of War," Opposing Views, October 20, 2017, http://www.opposingviews.com.
27. See Evan Perez and Daniella Diaz, "White House Announces Retaliation against Russia: Sanctions, Ejecting Diplomats," CNN, January 2, 2017, http://www.cnn.com.
28. See Office of the Director of National Intelligence, "Accessing Russian Activities," 3.
29. Michael N. Schmitt, ed., *Tallinn Manual 2.0 on the International Law Applicable to Cyber Operations* (Cambridge: Cambridge University Press, 2017), rule 66, para. 6, 314.
30. See Michael Schmitt, "*Tallinn Manual 2.0* on the International Law of Cyber Operations: What It Is and Isn't," *Just Security,* February 9, 2017, https://www.justsecurity.org.
31. Phillip Rucker, "Trump: Russian Interference Is 'All a Big Dem HOAX!'" *Washington Post*, June 22, 2017, https://www.washingtonpost.com.
32. "Declaration by Miguel Rodríguez, Representative of Cuba, at the Final Session of Group of Governmental Experts on Developments in the Field of Information and Telecommunications in the Context of International Security," June 23, 2017, *Just Security*, https://www.justsecurity.org.
33. Michele G. Markoff, "Explanation of Position at the Conclusion of the 2016–2017 UN Group of Governmental Experts (GGE) on Developments in the Field of Information and Telecommunications in the Context of International Security," June 23, 2017, U.S. Department of State, https://www.state.gov.
34. Pub. Law No. 115-44.

35. Conor Finnegan, "Timeline of Trump's Delays on Russia Sanctions," ABC News, October 27, 2017, http://abcnews.go.com/Politics/timeline-trumps-delays-russia-sanctions/story?id=50733408.
36. "UK and US blame Russia for 'malicious' NotPetya cyber-attack," BBC News, February 15, 2018, http://www.bbc.com/news/uk-politics-43062113.
37. For a discussion of the seriousness of the Shadow Brokers' hack of the NSA, see Scott Shane, Nicole Perlroth, and David E. Sanger, "Security Breach and Spilled Secrets Have Shaken the N.S.A. to Its Core," *New York Times*, November 13, 2017, https://www.nytimes.com.
38. See Rogier Creemers, "Can the World Agree upon Cyberspace Norms?" China and US Focus, August 14, 2017, https://www.chinausfocus.com.

Subject Index

Legal Cases Index

★ ★ ★

About the Author

★ ★ ★

H. L. Pohlman is the A. Lee Fritschler Professor of Public Policy at Dickinson College in Carlisle, Pennsylvania. His teaching interests include political and legal philosophy, American constitutional law, national security law, and other law-related topics. Pohlman has written or edited a number of books, including *Terrorism and the Constitution: The Post-9/11 Cases* (2008), a three-volume series of constitutional law textbooks titled *Constitutional Debate in Action* (2005), *The Whole Truth: A Case of Murder on the Appalachian Trail* (1999), *Justice Oliver Wendell Holmes: Free Speech and the Living Constitution* (1991), and *Justice Oliver Wendell Holmes and Utilitarian Jurisprudence* (1984). He was the judicial fellow at the Supreme Court of the United States from 1996 until 1998 and the executive director of the Clarke Forum for Contemporary Issues at Dickinson College from 2008 until 2015. Pohlman received his BA from the University of Dayton in 1974 and his PhD from Columbia University in 1982.

www.ingramcontent.com/pod-product-compliance
Ingram Content Group UK Ltd.
Pitfield, Milton Keynes, MK11 3LW, UK
UKHW051932150926
475560UK00005B/355

9 781538 104026